NORTH AMERICAN BIRDS EGGS

by

Chester A. Reed

Revised, and with a new Preface by
Paul A. Buckley

DOVER PUBLICATIONS, INC.
NEW YORK

A NOTE ON EGG COLLECTING

At one time collecting the eggs of wild birds was a very popular hobby in the United States. In general this did little harm, but the high price tag placed on the eggs of such rare birds as the California Condor posed a definite threat to their existence. Soon egg collecting went out of style, partly because of wise legislation and partly perhaps because one naturally looks askance at a hobby that involves robbing the nests of our favorite songbirds.

It would certainly be unfortunate if the present reprint of Reed's book on the nests and eggs of North American birds were to revive interest in egg collecting, but there is no reason to believe that it will be the case. Nowadays we are more interested in watching birds and in studying their habits. It is a definite asset to the field man to be able to identify nests and eggs even when the parents are not in evidence. For the more casual observer, a glimpse at the delicately constructed nest of one of our native songbirds, with its complement of tiny, colorful eggs is one of the treasures of nature.

DEAN AMADON
AMERICAN MUSEUM OF NATURAL HISTORY
NEW YORK CITY

PREFACE TO THE DOVER EDITION

When in 1904 Chester A. Reed published his book on the eggs of North American birds, the hobby of egg-collecting (occasionally elevated to a science, oölogy) was very popular. Reed himself was no collector, however, and so he included nothing in his book on the esoteric art of "blowing" eggs. Private collections of wild birds' eggs are now outlawed by the Federal Migratory Bird Act.

Today, with the growing interest in bird-watching, both for pleasure and for science, there are many times when one wishes to identify nests or eggs found in the absence of the parents or to learn more about their structure, etc. It has therefore seemed worthwhile to reprint Reed's book.

The almost sixty years that have elapsed since the first publication of this book have witnessed some of the most spectacular and important changes in the biological sciences, especially the staggering amount of evolutionary research which has clarified the interrelationships of living birds. Such research is normally codified in the form of nomenclature, and the current concepts of avian relationships are expressed in the *Check-list of North American Birds*, the 5th Edition of which was published in 1957 by the American Ornithologists' Union. It is against this standard that almost all names and ranges have been judged. A few others have been taken from Eisenmann's *Species of Middle American Birds* (1955), and in a dozen or so cases neither source was followed where serious reasons suggested such action. It should be noted that North America as used by Reed and the A.O.U. *Check-list* includes only North America north of the Mexican border, plus the peninsula of Lower (Baja) California.

Perhaps one of the more obvious changes in this reprinting is that many birds formerly considered valid species are now known to be merely geographical representatives of a widespread species; their names have been changed accordingly. A corollary to this procedure has been the restriction of common or vernacular names to the species as a whole, with the various races or varieties or subspecies receiving only technical designation in their scientific names. Thus, an American Robin is an American Robin, whether in New York (formerly American Robin), California (formerly Western Robin), or Georgia (formerly Southern Robin), and so forth.

It should be noted that Reed used the terms "species," "race," "subspecies," "variety," and "form" interchangeably. This is at variance with the modern species concept in which a species is defined as a population intrinsically reproductively isolated from other populations. Under such a concept the terms race, form, and variety would be equivalent to subspecies. The species, then, remains the natural biological unit in evolution and is the only one given a common or vernacular name. Moreover, eggs do not vary geographically as extensively as birds' plumage, so this restriction benefits the student of birds' eggs.

A number of subspecies formerly regarded as distinct have since been shown to be merely part of the normal variation in the parent species and have accordingly been synonymized; these are listed in the present edition as "No longer recognized as a valid form." Similarly, there are several hypothetical species and subspecies that have been erroneously recorded from North America. These are listed as "Not recorded from North America." Lastly, there are a few birds that are new to North America since this book first appeared. Since these do not for the most part appreciably alter the picture of our breeding birds, they have not been included.

Major changes resulting in the shifting of families of birds from one order to another as relationships become apparent have been incorporated into the 5th Edition of the *Check-list*, but not here. Readers are referred to the more technical works for this information.

The numbers in front of each species formerly were used as an aid in cataloging eggs, and were used in the 1st Edition of the *Check-list*, published in 1886. This *Check-list* has been brought up to date and all forms still on the list appear in brackets after the name of each form. Each subspecies retains the species number but is followed by a lower case letter to designate the race. As new subspecies are described, new letters are added, *e.g.*, 325a, 325b, etc. As new species are added to the North American list they are given numbers that will place them in their proper relationship to other North American forms. This is done by giving them the number of the nearest relative and adding a decimal point followed by a numeral, *e.g.*, 215.1, 215.2, etc. In a few cases there are gaps in the notation. These gaps indicate that the intervening forms have been dropped from the North American list.

The *Index* in the back of the book indicates citations for the names of the genera (in italics) and for the vernacular names of all forms treated. This will provide easy access to any account in the book.

The writer wishes to acknowledge the help and advice of Eugene Eisenmann and Dr. Dean Amadon of the American Museum of Natural History and of his fellow students at Cornell University, notably Roger B. Clapp, Neal R. Foster, and Douglas J. Futuyma.

PAUL A. BUCKLEY
LABORATORY OF ORNITHOLOGY
CORNELL UNIVERSITY
ITHACA, NEW YORK

PREFACE TO FIRST EDITION

The greatest interest in the study of birds centers in their home life. Soon after their arrival from their winter quarters, all birds take upon themselves the duties of reproduction, the first step of which is the securing of a satisfactory location; some species, such as Auklets, Petrels, Burrowing Owls, Kingfishers, Bank Swallows, etc., nest at the end of burrows or holes in the ground; a great many nest upon the ground, some laying their eggs upon the bare sand, leaves, or rock, while others build nests, either bulky or slight as suits their respective tastes; hundreds construct their homes among the branches of trees or bushes, some close to the ground, others among the highest branches, and still others swaying from the ends of the outermost limbs; other species lay their eggs at the bottom of holes in trees, either in natural cavities or in holes dug by their own efforts, the most noticeable in the latter class being the Woodpeckers, which often chisel their way into limbs of living trees.

The study of nests alone is most interesting; the rude and slight platforms of the Herons, Cuckoos, Grosbeaks, etc.; the rough but substantial structures of the Robin; and the exquisite, architectural creations of the Hummingbirds, Flycatchers, Orioles, Bushtits, etc. Surely the work of some of these little feathered creatures, these "homes without hands," show as great a degree of skill and artistic temperament as is seen in the human race.

The eggs of the different species vary through all the tints from white to blue, green and brown, some unmarked, others handsomely specked, spotted, blotched or wreathed with different shades of brown, lilac and lavender, and their sizes vary from that of the diminutive Hummingbird to the Albatross, Swan and California Vulture as the largest North American eggs, and the Ostrich of Africa whose egg will contain several quarts.

The nesting season ranges from January with some of the Owls to August in the case of the American Goldfinch, but by far the majority of species lay their eggs during May or June. It is at this period during their lives, that birds are at their best; their plumage is the brightest, their voices are the sweetest, and their actions the most brilliant.

The purpose of this volume is to furnish a reference and guide to all bird students who may desire to study the home life of our feathered creatures, by a description of how, when and where they build their nests, and the appearance of their eggs. At some time during youth,

[1] Now California Condor.

the desire to collect something is paramount; it has very frequently culminated in the indiscriminate collecting of birds' eggs, merely to gratify a passing whim or to see how large a number could be gotten together, without regard to classification. It is this in conjunction with the many natural enemies that birds have had to contend with, that has caused the great decrease in numbers of certain birds. It is neither the author's wish nor intention that this volume shall tend in the least to stimulate this desire in our youths. Knowledge does not imply possession and it is far more enjoyable to intimately know the birds in life than to possess empty eggshells or stuffed skins. With the exception of a very few species, we now have all the information that can be derived from specimens of either eggs or birds, and it is especially desirable to study their habits and peculiarities in life, as this has been sadly neglected in the desire to possess. In regard to the few rare birds whose breeding habits are practically unknown, it will probably be for the best if we remain in ignorance. While the discovery of nests of Kirtland's Warbler establishes the breeding range of that bird and the probable route of migration, I fear that it will swiftly lead to the total extermination of that very rare species. Those who are the possessors of cameras can get a great deal of pleasure by photographing nests with eggs or young birds in natural situations, just as they were found. The examples of this class of work found on the following pages are the best efforts of some of the leading workers in this field.

In the preparation of this volume, the author has had the cooperation of many active field oölogists and his thanks are especially due Col. John E. Thayer, Lancaster, Mass., Mr. Chauncey W. Crandall, Woodside, N. Y., and Mr. John Lewis Childs of Floral Park, N. Y., each of whom kindly placed their very extensive collections at his disposal for study and photographing, and to the Academy of Sciences, Philadelphia, for permission to photograph the egg of the Great Auk in their collection, their specimen being the best of the only two in this country, both of which were formerly in this institution.

CHESTER A. REED.

Worcester, Massachusetts, 1904.

TABLE OF CONTENTS

ILLUSTRATIONS OF
NESTS AND EGGS

NEST AND EGGS OF GREEN HERON.

Photo from life by Dr. J. B. Pardoe.

YOUNG BLUE JAYS.

LOONS, GREBES and ALCIDS. Orders GAVIIFORMES, PODICIPEDIFORMES and CHARADRIIFORMES (part).

GREBES. Family PODICIPEDIDAE.

Grebes are birds having a ducklike body, but with pointed bills. Their feet, too, are unlike those of the Ducks, each toe having its separate web, and having a broad flat nail. Their wings are very small for the size of the body, making it impossible for them to rise in flight from the land. They rise from the water by running a few yards along the surface until they have secured sufficient headway to allow them to launch themselves into the air. After having risen from the water their flight is very swift and strong. On land they are very awkward and can only progress by a series of awkward hops; they generally lie flat on their breasts, but occasionally stand up, supporting themselves upon their whole tarsus. Grebes, together with the Loons, are the most expert aquatic birds that we have, diving like a flash and swimming for an incredible distance under water.

1. Western Grebe. *Aechmorphorus occidentalis.*

Range.—Western parts of North America, from southern Alaska southward; east to Minnesota and south in winter to the southern parts of the United States and Mexico. Breeds from the Dakotas and northern California northward.

[Chalky bluish white, stained buff.]

These are the largest of the American Grebes; owing to their unusually long necks, they are frequently called "Swan Grebes". They are very timid birds and conceal themselves in the rushes on the least suspicion of danger. At times, to escape observation, they will entirely submerge their body, leaving only their head and part of the long neck visible above the water This Grebe cannot be mistaken for any other because of the long slender neck and the long pointed bill, which has a slight upward turn. They nest abundantly in the marshes of North Dakota and central Canada. Their nests are made of decayed rushes, and are built over the water, being fastened to the rushes so that the bottom of the nest rests in the water. The nesting season is at its height during the latter part of May. They lay from three to five eggs, the ground color of which is a pale blue; this color is, however, always concealed by a thin chalky deposit, and this latter is frequently stained to a dirty white. Size 2.40 x 1.55. Data.—Sweetwater Lake, N. D., May 28, 1899. 4 eggs. Nest of decayed blades of rushes in cane and rushes about ten rods from shore. Water three feet deep under the nest. Collector, Wm. A. Bowman.

2. Red-necked Grebe. *Podiceps grisegena.*

[White, stained buff.]

Range.—Throughout North America, breeding from northern United States northward and wintering from the middle to the southern portions of the United States.

In regard to size this Grebe comes next to the Western, being 19 in. in length. This bird can be distinguished by the white cheeks and throat and the reddish brown foreneck. They breed abundantly in the far north placing their floating islands of decayed vegetation in the water in the midst of the marsh grass. They lay from three to six eggs of a dingy white color which have the stained surface common to Grebes eggs. Size 2.35 x 1.25. Data.—Northern Manitoba, Can., June 15, 1898. 5 eggs laid on a rank mass of decayed rushes floating in two feet of water in a slough. Collector, E. A. Hartshorn.

3. Horned Grebe. *Podiceps auritus.*

Range.—The whole of North America, breeding in the interior from North Dakota northward; winters along the Gulf Coast. This species is one of the most beautiful of the Grebes, having in the breeding season buffy ear tufts, black cheeks and throat, and chestnut neck, breast and sides. They breed abundantly in the marshy flats of North Dakota and the interior of Canada. They build a typical Grebe's nest, a floating mass of decayed matter which stains the naturally white eggs to a dirty brown.

[Buffy white, nest stained.]

The number of eggs varies from three to seven. Size 1.70 x 1.15. Data.—Devils Lake, N. Dakota, June 20,1900. 6 eggs much stained. Nest floating in 4 ft. of water, a large mass of rotten rushes and weeds. Collector, James Smalley.

[Bluish white, stained.]

4. Eared Grebe. *Podiceps caspicus.*

Range.—North America west of the Mississippi, breeding from Texas to Manitoba and wintering along the Pacific Coast of the United States and from Texas southward.

Eared Grebes differ from the preceding in having the entire neck blackish. They nest very abundantly throughout the west, in favorable localities, from Texas to Minnesota and Dakota. Their nests are constructed in the same manner as the preceding varieties and are located in similar localities. As do all the Grebes when leaving the nest, they cover the eggs with the damp rushes from around the base of the nest. This is probably for the purpose of assisting incubation during their absence, by the action of the sun's rays on the wet mass. As they are nearly always thus covered upon the approach of anyone, this may be done also as a protection from discovery. They lay from three to eight bluish white eggs with the usual chalky and discolored appearance. The breeding season is at its height early in June, or earlier, in the southern portions of its range.   Size 1.75x1.20.   Data.—Artesian, S. Dakota, June 21, 1899. Nest of rushes, floating in three feet of water.   Large colony in a small lake. Collector, F. A. Patton.

5. Least Grebe.   *Podiceps dominicus.*

Range.—Southern Texas and Lower California southward to South America, breeding throughout its range.

[Deep buff or rich brown.]

The Least Grebe is by far the smallest of the Grebes in this country, being but 10 in. in length; it can not be mistaken for any other, the Eared Grebe being the only other species of this family found in the same localities during the summer.   These little Grebes nest very abundantly along the Rio Grande Valley in Texas, the nesting season lasting from the latter part of May until well into December.

Their nests are floating piles of grass and weeds upon which they lay from three to five chalky white eggs, which are always discolored, sometimes to a deep chocolate hue. These eggs average a great deal darker in color than do any of the other Grebes.   In a series of fifty sets fully half were a rich brown tint.   Size 1.40x.95. Data.—Brownsville, Texas, May 26, 1900.   5 eggs.   Nest of weeds and trash floating on a small fresh pond.   Collector, Frank B. Armstrong.

NEST AND EGGS OF PIED-BILLED GREBE.

Photo by Walter Raine.

NEST AND EGGS OF RED-NECKED GREBE.
[Lake Winnipegosis, Manitoba.]

6. Pied-billed Grebe. *Podilymbus podiceps.*

Range.— From the British provinces southward to Argentine Republic, breeding locally throughout the northern portions of its range.

[Deep buff.]

The Dabchick, as this bird is called, is the most evenly distributed bird of this family. It is nowhere especially abundant, nor is it, except in a very few localities, regarded as rare. Consequently it is the best known bird of the species. They do not congregate in such large numbers as the other Grebes during the nesting season, but one or more pairs may be found in almost any favorable locality. These birds render their floating nest a little more substantial than those of the preceding varieties by the addition of mud which they bring up from the bottom of the pond; this addition also tends to soil the eggs more, consequently the eggs of this bird are, as a general rule, browner than the other Grebes with the exception of the Least. The bird may always be known by the shape of its bill which is higher than it is broad, and in the summer is white with a black band across the middle. The throat is also black at this season. They lay from five to nine eggs commencing about the middle of May. Size 1.70 x 1.18. Data.—Rice Lake, Minn., May 15. 1899. 5 eggs on a mass of moss and decayed rushes, floating on the water. Collector, A. Hewitt.

LOONS. Family GAVIIDAE.

Loons may be likened to gigantic Grebes from which they differ externally, chiefly in the full webbed foot instead of the individually webbed toes of the Grebe, and in the sharper, more pointed and spear-like bill. These birds are similar in their habits to the Grebes, except that their homes are generally more substantially built and are placed upon a solid foundation, generally upon an island is some inland lake.

Both Loons and Grebes are literally "water witches", being practically, and in the case of Grebes, actually, born in the water and living in it ever afterwards. Loons are strong fliers, but like the Grebes, because of their small wings they must get their first impetus from the water in order to rise; in case there is any wind blowing they also make use of this by starting their flight against it. They are very peculiar birds and the expression "crazy as a loon" is not a fanciful one, being formed from their early morning and evening antics when two or more of them will race over the top of the water, up and down the lake, all the while uttering their demoniacal laughter. They vie with the Grebes in diving and disappear at the flash of a gun.

Photo by Walter Raine.

NEST AND EGGS OF HORNED GREBE.
[Saltcoats Marshes, Assiniboia, June, 6, 1901.]

7.　Common Loon.　*Gavia immer.*

Range.—North America north of the Mexican boundary, breeding from the northern parts of the United States northward.

[Dark greenish brown.]

Unlike the Grebes, Loons do not build in colonies, generally not more than one, or at the most two pairs nesting on the same lake or pond ; neither do they seek the marshy sloughs in which Grebes dwell, preferring the more open, clear bodies of water.　The common Loon may be known in summer by the entirely black head and neck with the complete ribbon of black and white stripes encircling the lower neck and the narrower one which crosses the throat.　The back is spotted with white.　In some sections Loons build no nest, simply scooping a hollow out in the sand, while in other places they construct quite a large nest of sticks, moss and grasses.　It is usually placed but a few feet from the water's edge, so that at the least suspicion the bird can slide off its eggs into the water, where it can cope with any enemy.　The nests are nearly always concealed under the overhanging bushes that line the shore ; the one shown in the full page illustration, however, was located upon the top of an old muskrat house.　The two eggs which they lay are a very dark greenish brown in color, with black spots.　Size 3.50 x 2.25.　Data.—Lake Sunapee, N. H., June 28,1895.　Nest placed under the bushes at the water's edge.　Made of rushes, weeds and grasses ; a large structure nearly three feet in diameter.　Collector, H. A. Collins.

8.　Yellow-billed Loon.　*Gavia adamsii.*

Range.—Northwestern North America, along the Arctic and northern Alaskan coasts.

Photo by J. A. Munro, Toronto.

NEST AND EGGS OF COMMON LOON.

[This nest is built on top of a Muskrat house.]

[Dark greenish brown.]

The Yellow-billed Loon with the exception of its whitish or yellowish bill in place of the black, is practically otherwise indistinguishable from the common Loon. It averages somewhat larger in size. This is one of the most northerly breeding birds and it is only within a very few years that anything has been learned about the breeding habits. Their nesting habits and eggs are precisely like the preceding except that the latter average a little larger. Size 3.60x2.25. Data.—Mackenzie River, Arctic America, June 21, 1898. Two eggs laid on island in the river. Nest of twigs and grasses, six feet from the water. Collector, Capt. J. Smythe.

10. Arctic Loon. *Gavia arctica.*

Range.—From northern United States northward, breeding along the Arctic Coast.

This species can be easily separated from the Loon by the gray crown and white streaks down the back of the neck. Its size, too, is about five inches shorter. The nesting habits are the same as the Loons and the eggs have rather more of an olive tint besides having the majority of spots at the larger end. Size 3.10x2.00.

[Olive brown.]

10. Pacific Loon (should be Arctic Loon). *Gavia arctica.*

Range.—Western North America along the coast chiefly, breeding from Alaska south to British Columbia. In winter, south along the coast to Mexico.

This species differs from the Black-throated[1] only in the tint of the head reflections. The habits are the same as those of the other members of the family. They lay two eggs of a greenish brown or greenish gray hue with black spots. Size 3.10 x 1.90. Data.—Yukon River, Alaska, June 28, 1902. Nest of rubbish on an island ; found by a miner.

[Greenish brown or gray.]

11. Red-throated Loon. *Gavia stellata.*

Range.—Northern parts of North America, breeding from southern Canada northward in the interior and on both coasts. South to the middle portions of the United States in winter.

This is the smallest of the Loon family being twenty-five inches in length. In plumage it is wholly unlike any of the other members at all seasons of the year. In summer the back, head and neck are gray, the latter being striped with white. A large chestnut patch adorns the front of the lower part of the neck. In winter the back is spotted with white, whereas all the others are unspotted at this period. The nesting habits are identical with the other species ; the ground color of the two eggs is also the same. Size 2.90x1.75. Data.—North Iceland, May 20, 1900. Nest on the ground on bank of river.

[Deep olive brown.]

[1] Now Arctic Loon.

ALCIDS. Family ALCIDAE.

Puffins, Auks and Murres are all sea birds and are only found inland when blown there by some severe storm of winter. At this season numbers of them are apt to lose their bearings and may sometimes be found with their feet frozen in some of our inland ponds. Puffins are heavily built birds in appearance, but are very active both on the wing and in the water. Their wings are much larger comparatively than those of the other members of this family, so they are enabled to perform evolutions in the air, which are withheld from the others. They stand upright on the sole of the foot and are able to walk quite easily on land. Puffins have very heavy and deep but thin bills, which are entirely unlike those of any other bird and often give them the name of Parrot Auks. Puffins, Auks and Murres are otherwise recognized by the presence of but three toes which are webbed.

12. Tufted Puffin. *Lunda cirrhata.*

Range.—Pacific Coast from Alaska southward to southern California, breeding locally throughout their range.

Tufted Puffins are the largest of the Puffins. In the breeding plumage, they are a sooty brownish or black color; the cheeks are white, and a long tuft of straw colored feathers extends back from each eye; the bill is bright red and greenish yellow. They breed commonly on the Farallones, where two or three broods are raised by a bird in a single season, but much more abun-

[White.]

dantly on the islands in the north. Their single eggs are laid in burrows in the ground or else in natural crevices formed by the rocks. The eggs are pure white or pale buff and are without gloss. They very often have barely perceptible shell markings of dull purplish color. The eggs are laid about the middle of June. Size 2.80 x 1.90. Data.—Farallone Is., May 22, 1887. Single egg laid in crevice of rocks. Collector, W. O. Emerson.

13. Common Puffin. *Fratercula arctica.*

Range.—North Atlantic Coast, breeding from the Bay of Fundy northward. Winters from breeding range along the New England Coast.[1]

The common Puffin has the cheeks, chin and underparts white; upper parts and a band across the throat, blackish. Bill deep and thin, and colored with red, orange and yellow. They breed in large numbers on Bird Rock in the Gulf of St. Lawrence. The nest is either among the natural crevices of the

---

[1] Breeds south to northern Maine, on offshore islands.

[White.]

rocks, or in burrows excavated in the ground by the birds. These burrows' vary in length from two and a half to four or five feet. Except upon the positive knowledge of the absence of the bird, it is a hazardous thing to put the hand in one of these burrows for the bird can, and will nip the fingers, sometimes to the bone. They lay but a single egg, usually dull white and unmarked, but in some cases obscurely marked with reddish brown. Size 2.50 x 1.75. Data.—So. Labrador, June 23, 1884. Single egg laid at end of burrow in the ground. Collector, J. H. JAMESON.

13a. Large-billed Puffin (should be Common Puffin). *Fratercula arctica.*

A more northerly subspecies of the last, inhabiting the Arctic region on the Atlantic side. The bird is somewhat larger but otherwise indistinguishable from the common species. The eggs are exactly the same or average a trifle larger. Size 2.55 x 1.80. Data.—Iceland, July 6, 1900. Single egg in hole under a rock. Collector, Chas. Jefferys.

14. Horned Puffin. *Fratercula corniculata.*

Range.—Pacific Coast from Alaska to British Columbia. The Horned Puffin differs from the common in that the blackish band across the throat extends upwards in a point to the bill. Their nesting habits are precisely the same as those of the preceding species. A single pure white egg is laid; the shell is slightly rougher than those of the others. Size 2.65 x 1.80. Data.—Round Is., Alaska, June 24, 1884. Single egg laid at end of burrow in ground; no nest. Collector, G. L. Kennedy.[1]

15. Rhinoceros Auklet. *Cerorhinca monocerata.*

Range.—Pacific Coast, breeding from British Columbia northward and wintering southward to Lower California.

The Rhinoceros Auklet or Horned Auk has a much smaller bill than the Puffins ; in the summer this is adorned at the base by a horn from which it takes its name. There are also slender plumes from above and below the eyes. Unlike the Puffins, these birds sit upon their whole tarsus.

They nest on islands of the North Pacific Coast from Vancouver northward. A single egg is laid in crevices among the rocks or in burrows in the ground. It is similar both in size and shape to that of the Puffins, but is often quite heavily blotched with brown. Size 2.70 x 1.80. Data.—Unak Is., Alaska, June 30, 1900. Egg laid in a fissure of the rocks; no nest. Collector, F. Weston.

---

[1] Breeds only in Alaska.

RHINOCEROS AUKLET.
[Color white, sometimes heavily blotched, as above, and again unspotted.]

Photo by Walter Raine.

CHARACTERISTIC NEST OF COMMON LOON.
[Lake Winnipegosis, June 13, 1903.]

16. Cassin's Auklet. *Ptychoramphus aleutica.*

Range.—Pacific Coast from Alaska to Lower California, breeding nearly throughout its range.

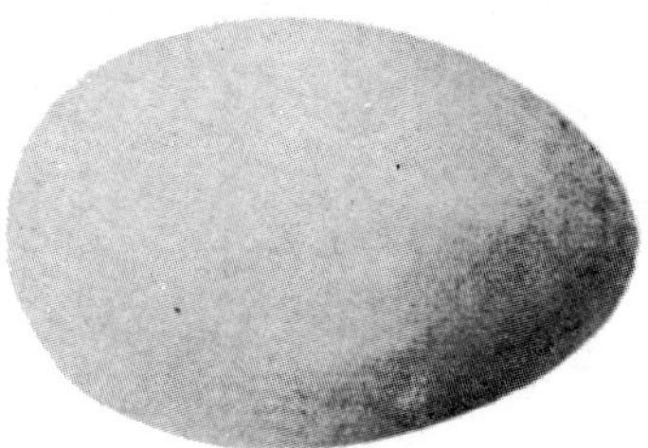

[White.]

A plain appearing bird about 9 in. in length, with blackish upperparts relieved only by a white spot over the eye; breast and throat gray and belly white. This Auklet is fairly abundant on the Farallones, breeding on the lower portions of the island. The late Mr. C. Barlow says that it is found in deserted rabbit burrows and in all probability often excavates its own burrows. It also nests among the cliffs placing its eggs among the rocks in any crevice or tunnel which may offer a dark retreat during the day for they are nocturnal in their habits. The single egg which they lay is dull white in color, the inside of the shell being a pale green, which color can only be seen by holding the egg to the light. They are generally slightly nest stained. Size 1.80 x 1.30. Data.—Coronado Islands, Cal., March 23, 1897. Single egg laid on the bare ground at end of a burrow three and one half feet long. Collector, E. A. Shives.

17. Parakeet Auklet. *Cyclorrhynchus psittacula.*

Range.—The Alaskan Coast, casually farther south in winter.
This bird is about the same size as the preceding, and the plumage is similar, except that it has no white spot over the eye, and the breast is white. It also has a slender plume extending from back of the eye. The bill is very peculiar, being quite deep and rounded and having an upward tendency. It is orange red in color. They breed very commonly on the islands of Bering Strait. Their eggs are laid in the crevices of the cliff, often several feet in and by a crooked path so that it is impossible to reach them. The single chalky white egg is laid in May. Size 2.30 x 1.45. Data.—Rocky Islet in the Aleutians, June 22, 1890. Single egg laid on bare rock in a deep crevice. Collector, Capt. S. Wilson.

18. Crested Auklet. *Aethia cristatella.*

[White.]

Range.—Alaskan Coast. Similar in form and plumage to the latter, except that the whole under parts are gray and it has a crest of recurved feathers. The nesting season begins in May, the birds nesting upon the same islands and in the same kinds of sites as the last species. The single egg is chalky white. Size 2.10x1.50. Data.— Unak Is., Alaska, July 1, 1900. Egg laid in a crevice among the rocks. Collector, F. Weston.

19. Whiskered Auklet. *Aethia pygmaea.*

Range.—The Alaskan Coast.

Much smaller than the preceding; but 7.5 in. in length.   Breast gray, **belly white; a small tuft of recurved feathers on the forehead and slender white plumes from base of bill over the eye and from under the eye, backwards.   The bill in summer is a bright vermilion color.   On some of the islands of the Aleutian chain they breed quite abundantly.   The nests are placed back in the crevices of the rocks, where the single white eggs are laid.   Size 2.00 x 1.25.**

20. Least Auklet. *Aethia pusilla.*

[White.]

Range. — North Pacific on the islands and coast of Alaska. This is the smallest of the Auklets; length 6.5 in.   This species has no crest, but has the slender white plumes extending back from the eye. The entire under parts are white sparsely spotted with dusky. This species is by far the most abundant of the water birds of the extreme Northwest, and thousands of them, accompanied by the two preceding species, nest on the rocky cliffs of the islands of Bering Sea. Their nesting habits are the same as those of the other Auklets, they placing their single white egg on the bare rocks, in **crevices** on the cliffs. Size 1.55 x 1.10. Data.—Pribilof Is., Alaska, June 8, 1897. **Single egg laid in crevice. Thousands breeding on the island. Collector, W. Macoun.**

21.   Ancient Murrelet. *Synthliboramphus antiquum.*

Range.—Pacific Coast, breeding from the border of the United States, northward, and wintering south to southern California.

[Buff.]

The Murrelets have no crests or plumes and the bills are more slender than the Auklets and are not highly colored. The ancient Murrelet or Black-throated Murrelet, as it is also called, has a gray back, white under parts and a black head and throat, with a broad white stripe back of the eye and another formed by the white on the breast extending up on the side of the neck. They breed abundantly on the islands in Bering Sea, laying one or two eggs at the end of burrows in the banks or on the ground, and in some localities in crevices on the cliffs. The eggs are a buffy white color and are faintly marked with light brown, some of these being in the shape of spots and others lengthened. Size 2.40x1.40. Data.—Sanak Islands, July 1, 1894. Two eggs on the ground under a tuft of grass and in a slight excavation lined with fine grass. Collector, C. L. Littlejohn.

23.   Marbled Murrelet.   *Brachyramphus marmoratum.*

Range.—North Pacific Coast, breeding from Vancouver Island. South in winter to southern California.

In the breeding plumage, this bird is brownish black above, barred with rusty and below is marbled with brownish gray and white. Its nesting habits and eggs are very similar to those of the Ancient Murrelet, they placing their single eggs in holes in the ground or crevices among the cliffs.   Size   2.20 x 1.40.

[Buff.]

Data.—Chichagof Is., Alaska, June 18, 1898. Single egg in crevice on face of cliff. Large colony breeding in company with Ancient Murrelets.

24.   Kittlitz's Murrelet.   *Brachyramphus brevirostre.*

[White.]

Range.—North Pacific Coast in the Aleutian Islands and north to Unalaska, breeding on isolated islands throughout its range. This species is very similar to the Marbled Murrelet, the chief difference being in the bill which is shorter. They have been found breeding on the same islands with the preceding species. Their single white egg is laid in crevices in the cliffs. Size 2.40 x 1.30.   Data.—Sanak Is., Alaska, June 25, 1899. Nest in a hollow under a bunch of rank matted grass. Many ancient Murrelets breeding on same island. Collector, Capt. Tilson.

25.   Xantus' Murrelet.   *Endomychura hypoleuca.*

Range.—Resident along the coasts of southern and Lower California.

This bird is blackish above and entirely white below, including the sides of the head below the eye. The whole of the under surface of the wing is also white. They breed on the coast islands from Santa Barbara southward. The single egg is laid at the end of a burrow or in crevices among the rocks. It is a pale buffy white in color and thickly, but finely dotted over the whole surface with purplish brown, and with some larger spots at the larger end. Size 2.05 x 1.40. Data.—Galapagos Islands, March 2, 1901. No nest. Single egg laid in a crevice in the rocks. Collector, Rollo H. Beck.

[Pale buff.]

26. Craveri's Murrelet. *Endomychura craveri.*

Range.—Both coasts of Lower California, breeding chiefly on the Gulf side. Craveri's Murrelet is very similar to the last but the under surfaces of the wings are dusky. Breeds on the islands near Cape St. Lucas, burrowing in the ground as do most of the others of this species. They lay a single egg, the ground color of which is buff; they are quite heavily blotched with brownish. Size 2.00 x 1.40.

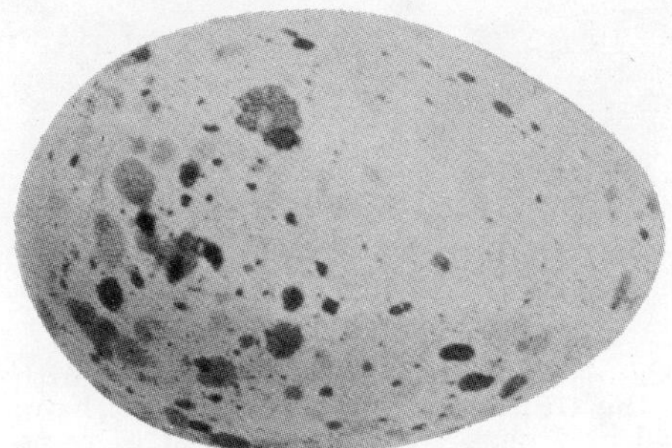

[Bluish white.]

27. Black Guillemot. *Cepphus grylle.*

Range.—Coasts and islands of the North Atlantic, breeding from Maine northward to southern Greenland. Guillemots are larger birds than the Murrelets (length 13 inches) and their plumage is entirely different. This species in summer is entirely black except the wing coverts which are white. The bases of the greater coverts, however, are black, this generally breaking the white mirror as it is called. The under surfaces of the wings are white. Legs red. These birds breed abundantly on the rocky islands and high cliffs along the coast. Soon after the first of June the eggs are laid in the crevices of the rocks and sometimes upon the bare ledges. Two or three eggs make the set. The ground color is a pale bluish or greenish white and the markings are various shades of brown and black. Size 2.40 x 1.60. Data.—Grand Manan, June 15, 1896. Two eggs laid in a cavity back of large boulder. No nest. Collector, D. H. Eaton.

28. Mandt's Guillemot (should be Black Guillemot). *Cepphus grylle.*

Range.—North Atlantic coast, more northerly than the preceding, breeding from Labrador to northern Greenland.

The bird differs from the Black Guillemot only in having the bases of the coverts white also. The nesting habits and eggs are identical. They nest in colonies of thousands and place the eggs upon the bare rock with no attempt at nest building. Generally the eggs are in the crevices so as to be difficult to get at. Size 2.30 x 1.55. Data.—Depot Island, Hudson Bay, June 6, 1894. Two eggs laid on bare rocky ground. Collector John Comer.

[Grayish white.]

29. Pigeon Guillemot. *Cepphus columba.*

Range.—The Pacific Coast of North America, breeding from southern California northward. This bird is very similar to the Black Guillemot except that the under surfaces of the wings are dark. They breed abundantly on some of the islands of Bering Sea and a few of them nest on the Farallones. They lay their two eggs on the bare rock in dark crevices. The color is grayish or pale greenish blue and the markings are brown and black with paler shell markings of lilac. Size, 2.40 x 1.60. Data.—S. Farallone Islands, Cal. Two eggs laid on gravel at the end of a burrow, about two feet from the entrance and 285 feet above the sea level. Collector, Claude Fyfe.

30. Common Murre. *Uria aalge.*   [Pale bluish gray.]

Range.—North Atlantic coasts and islands, breeding from Bird Rock northward. Murres are similar in form to the Guillemots, but are larger, being about 16 inches in length. Entire head and neck sooty brown; rest of upper parts grayish black except the tips of the secondaries which are white. Under parts white. These birds nest by thousands on Bird Rock and on the cliffs of Labrador. They build no nests but simply lay their single egg on the narrow ledges of cliffs, where the only guarantee against its rolling off is its peculiar shape which causes it, when moved, to revolve about its smaller end instead of rolling off the ledge. The eggs are laid as closely as possible on the ledges where the incubating birds sit upright, in long rows like an army on guard. As long as each bird succeeds in finding an egg to cover, on its return home, it is doubtful if they either know or care whether it is their own or not. The ground color's of eggs vary from white to a deep greenish blue and the markings of blackish brown vary in endless patterns, some eggs being almost wholly unspotted.   Size 3.40 x 2. Data.—South Labrador, June 19, 1884. Single egg laid on the bare cliff. Large colony breeding. Collector, M. A. Frazar.

[White, buff, or deep greenish blue.]

30a. California Murre (should be Common Murre). *Uria aalge.*

Range.—Pacific Coast, breeding from the Farallones north to Alaska.

This Pacific form of the common Murre is the most abundant breeding bird on the Farallones. Their eggs are used in enormous numbers for commercial purposes and these islands being located, as they are, within easy distance from San Francisco, thousands of dozens of the eggs are sold yearly, chiefly to bakeries. Although continually robbed, their numbers have not diminished to any great extent. They lay but a single egg on the bare ledge. Individual eggs are indistinguishable from the last species but in a large series the ground color averages brighter. They show the same great difference in color and markings. The first set is laid in May, but owing to their being so often molested, fresh eggs can be found during August. Data.—Farallones, July 4, 1895. Single egg laid on bare cliff. Collector, Thos. E. Slevin.

31. Thick-billed Murre. *Uria lomvia.*

Range.—North Atlantic Coast, breeding range the same as the common Murre.

[Varies from white to greenish blue.]

This species differs from the common Murre in having a shorter and thicker bill, the base of the cutting edge of which is less feathered. They breed on the same islands in company with the common Murres and their eggs are indistinguishable. Data.—Coast of South Labrador. Single egg laid on ledge of cliff. About three hundred birds in the colony.

31a. Pallas' Murre (should be Thick-billed Murre). *Uria lomvia.*

Range.—The North Pacific coasts and islands.

This is the Pacific form of Brunnich Murre.[1] Its breeding range is more northerly than that of the California variety. Countless thousands of them breed on the islands off the coast of Alaska, their breeding habits and eggs being the same as the more southern form.

[1] Now Thick-billed Murre.

EGG OF THE GREAT AUK.

[Photographed from the specimen in the Academy of Natural Sciences, Philadelphia; but
two of these eggs are in this country; the one figured which is the best marked specimen,
and one in the Smithsonian Institution at Washington.]

JAEGERS, GULLS, TERNS and SKIMMERS. Order CHARADRIIFORMES (part).

JAEGERS and SKUAS. Family STERCORARIIDAE.

Skuas and Jægers are birds having a Gull or Tern-like form and with a hooked bill, the base of which is covered with a scaly shield. They have webbed feet and are able to swim and dive, but they commonly get their living by preying upon the Gulls and Terns, overtaking them by their superior speed and by their strength and ferocity forcing them to relinquish their food. The Jægers especially are one of the swiftest and most graceful birds that fly.

35. Skua. *Catharacta skua.*

Range.—Coasts and islands of the North Atlantic, chiefly on the European side ; rare on the Atlantic coast of North America.

Skuas are large (22 inches in length) and very powerfully built birds, having the general form of a Gull. Their whole plumage is a dingy brownish black color, palest below. Breeds in Iceland and possibly on some of the islands in Hudson Strait. The nest is a hollow on the ground in the marsh grass and is lined with grass. The two eggs which they lay have an olive greenish ground, spotted with dark brown. Size 2.75 x 1.90. Data.—Iceland, June 9, 1900. Two eggs. Nest a pile of grass and moss on an island.

[Olive brown.]

36. Pomarine Jaeger. *Stercorarius pomarinus.*

[Deep olive brown.]

Range. — Northern Hemisphere, breeding within the Arctic Circle, more commonly in the Old World.

In the breeding plumage, this Jæger has the crown and face blackish ; back and sides of head, throat and under parts pure white, except the pointed stiffened feathers of the neck which are yellow. Back, wings and tail blackish, the latter with the two middle feathers lengthened about four inches beyond the rest of the tail, and broad to their tips, which are twisted so that the feathers are vertical. They breed throughout the Arctic regions, but not as commonly in America as the following species. The nest is on the ground in the marsh grass and is made of grass and moss. They lay two and rarely three eggs of an olive brown or greenish color. These are spotted with brown and black. Size 2.20 x 1.70.

37. Parasitic Jaeger. *Stercorarius parasiticus.*

Range.—Northern Hemisphere, wintering south to South America.

[Brownish.]

The Parasitic Jaeger is very similar to the Pomarine except that the central tail feathers are pointed and are straight instead of twisted. It is an abundant bird in Alaska, breeding from the Aleutian Chain northward.

They locate their nests in the highest parts of marshy places, the nest itself being only a depression in the ground lined with grass and moss. The two eggs have an olive greenish or brownish ground and are marked with various shades of brown and black. Size 2.15 x 1.65. Data.—So. Greenland, June 28, 1900.

Two eggs. Nest made of moss and seaweed and placed on the ground. Collector, Wilhelm Schulter.

38. Long-tailed Jaeger. *Stercorarius longicaudus.*

Range.—Arctic America; south in winter to South America.

The long-tailed Jaeger is according to length, the largest of the Jaegers, being 21 in. long; this is, however, due to the long sharp pointed central pair of tail feathers, which extend about eight inches beyond the others, and form the most noticeable distinguishing point from the former species. The plumages that have been described are the light phases; all the Jaegers have a dark phase in which the plumage is a nearly uniform sooty brown, lightest below.

[Olive brown.]

The Long-tailed Jaegers are the most numerous in Alaska and are even more graceful in flight than are the Gulls and Terns, floating, skimming, sailing, plunging, and darting about with incredible swiftness and ease. Like the others of this family, they pilfer their food from the Gulls, and are also very destructive to young birds and eggs. Their eggs are either laid on the bare ground or in a slight depression, scantily lined with grasses. The eggs are indistinguishable from those of the preceding species except that they average a trifle smaller. Size 2.10 x 1.50. Data.—Baillie Is., North West Territory, July 12, 1901. Two eggs. Nest on the ground, lined with willow leaves. Collector, Capt. H. H. Bodfish.

GULLS and TERNS.   Family LARIDAE.

Gulls are webbed footed birds having a slight hook to the end of the upper mandible. Their plumage is generally a silvery gray above and white below. They nest in large colonies, some on the bodies of fresh water inland, but mostly on the sea coast. They procure their food from the surface of the water, it consisting mostly of dead fish and refuse matter, and crustacea which they gather from the water's edge. When tired they rest upon the surface of the water, where they ride the largest waves in perfect safety.

Terns are birds of similar plumage to the Gulls, but their forms are less robust and the bills are generally longer and sharply pointed. Their food consists chiefly of small fish which they secure by hovering above the water, and then plunging upon them. They are less often seen on the surface of the water than are the Gulls.

39. Ivory Gull. *Pagophila eburnea.*

Range.—Arctic regions ; south in winter to the northern border of the United States.

The little Snow Gull, as it is often called, is eighteen inches in length. In the breeding season the plumage is entirely white ; the bill is tipped with yellow and there is a red ring around the eye. These Gulls nest in large colonies in the Arctic Regions, placing their nests on the high rocky cliffs. The nest is made of grass, moss and rubbish, and the three eggs are laid during June. The eggs are olive color and the markings are dark brown.

40. Black-legged Kittiwake. *Rissa tridactyla.*

Range.—North Atlantic and Arctic regions, breeding from the Gulf of the St. Lawrence northward and wintering south to the Great Lakes and Long Island.

The Kittiwake is sixteen inches in length, has a pearly gray mantle, black tips to the primaries, and remainder of plumage white. Its hind toe is very small being apparently wanting in the eastern form, while in the Pacific it is more developed. These are very noisy Gulls, their notes resembling a repetition of their name. They are very common in the far north, placing nests on the ledges of high rocky cliffs, often in company with Murres and Auks.

[Buff.]

They gather together a pile of sticks, grass and moss, making the interior cup-shaped so as to hold their two or three eggs. Large numbers of them breed on Bird Rock, they occupying certain ledges while the Gannets and Murres which also breed there, also have distinct ledges on which to make their homes. The breeding season is at its height during June. The eggs are buffy or brownish gray and are spotted with different shades of brown. Size 2.25x1.60. Data.—So. Labrador, June 15, 1884. Three eggs. Nest made of seaweed and moss, placed on ledge of cliff. Many Murres nesting on other ledges. Collector, H. Jameson.

40a.   Pacific Kittiwake (should be Black-legged Kittiwake).   *Rissa tridactyla.*

Range.—Coast of the North Pacific, wintering south to California.

The Pacific Kittiwake breeds in immense rookeries on some of the islands in Bering Sea. They are well distributed over Copper Island where they nest in June and July, choosing the high ledges which overhang the sea. The nesting habits and eggs are precisely the same as those of the common Kittiwake. Data.—Island in Norton Sound, Alaska, June 10, 1900. Three eggs on a cliff; nest a heap of seaweed. Collector, Capt. H. H. Bodfish.

41.   Red-legged Kittiwake.   *Rissa brevirostris.*

Range.—Northwestern coasts, breeding in high latitudes.

This Kittiwake is similar to the preceding, with the exception that the legs are bright red, the mantle is darker, and the bill is shorter. This species was found by Dr. Leonard Stejneger to be a very abundant nesting bird on islands in Bering Sea, selecting steep and inaccessible rocks and ledges on which to build its nest. Their nesting habits are precisely the same as the Pacific Kittiwake, but they most often nest in separate colonies, but can be distinguished readily when nesting together by the darker mantles when on the nest and the red legs when flying. Grass, moss and mud are used in the nest. The ground color of the eggs is buffy or brownish, and the spots are dark brown and lilac. Size 2.15 x 1.50. Data.—Island in Norton Sound, Alaska, May 10, 1900. Nest made of seaweed and located on ledge of high cliff. Collector, H. H. Bodfish.

[Brownish buff.]

42. Glaucous Gull. *Larus hyperboreus.*

Range.—Arctic regions, south in winter to Long Island, the Great Lakes, and San Francisco Bay.

This Gull shares with the Great Black-backed Gull the honor of being the largest of the Gulls, being 28 inches in length. Mantle light gray; it is distinguished by its size and the primaries, which are white to the tips. A powerful bird that preys upon the smaller Gulls and also devours the young and eggs of smaller birds.

They nest on the ground on the islands and shores of Hudson Bay, Greenland etc. The nest is made of seaweed, grass and moss and is generally quite bulky. The two or three eggs are laid in

[Buffy brown.]

June. They are of various shades of color from a light drab to a brownish, and are spotted with brownish and black. Size about 3 x 2.20. Data.—Iceland, June 8, 1888. Nest of seaweed on ledge of sea cliff. Three eggs.

42.1. Point Barrow Gull (should be Glaucous Gull). *Larus hyperboreus.*

Range —Northwest coast from Bering Sea to Point Barrow.

[Buff.]

This species is almost identical with the Glaucous Gull, but perhaps a trifle smaller. Its standing as a distinct species is still questioned and has not yet been decided satisfactorily. Early in June their nests are built on remote islands in Bering Sea. These nests are the same as the last species, large piles of vegetation, hollowed on top for the reception of the eggs. The eggs have the same variations in color and markings as the Glaucous Gull. Size 3 x 2.10. Data.—Herschel Is. Alaska. July 1, 1900. Nest made of seaweed and grass; placed on the ground. Three eggs. Collector, Rev. I. O. Stringer.

43. Iceland Gull. *Larus glaucoides.*

Range.—Arctic regions, south in winter to the Middle States.

This Gull in appearance is precisely like the two preceding ones but is considerably smaller; 24 inches in length. A very common bird in the north, breeding in colonies of thousands on many of the islands. It is regarded as one of the most common of the larger Gulls in Bering Sea and also nests commonly in Hudson Bay and Greenland, as well as in the Eastern Hemisphere. They nest indifferently on high rocky cliffs or on low sandy islands. Except when the eggs are laid in a sandy depression in the soil, quite bulky nests are made of seaweed and moss. The eggs are laid about the first of June; they number two to three and have a ground color of brownish or greenish

[Greenish brown.]

brown and are blotched with umber. Size 2.80 x 1.83. Data.—Mackenzie Bay, Arctic America. June 18, 1899. Nest made of seaweed and grass on an island in the bay.

44. Glaucous-winged Gull. *Larus glaucescens.*

Range.—North Pacific coast, breeding from British Columbia northwards and wintering from the same country to southern California.

This Gull is very like the preceding except that the primaries are the same color as the mantle, and are tipped with white. Length about 27 inches. Not so northerly distributed a bird as the previous ones, and consequently better known. They breed in large numbers both on the high rocky cliffs of the islands along the coast and on the low sandy islands of the Aleutian Chain. On Copper Island they breed on the inaccessible cliffs overhanging the water. As in the case of the Iceland Gull, when the nests are on the cliffs, a large nest of seaweed is made, whereas if they are on the ground, especially in sandy

[Pale greenish brown].

places no attempt is made at nest-building. The eggs have a greenish brown ground color and dark brown spots. Size 2.75 x 2.05. Data.—West Coast of Vancouver Island. June 20, 1896. Three eggs; nest made of seaweed. Located on a low ledge. Collector, Dr. Newcombe.

45. Kumlien's Gull (should be Iceland Gull). *Larus glaucoides*.

Range.—North Atlantic coast, breeding in Cumberland Sound and wintering as far south as Long Island. [1]

This bird differs from the Glaucous-winged only in the pattern of the gray markings of the primaries and in having a little lighter mantle. It is quite common in its breeding haunts where it places its nest high up on the ledges of the cliffs. The eggs are not different apparently from *glaucescens*.

46. Nelson's Gull. *Larus nelsoni*. [2]

Range.—Coast of Alaska.

Plumage exactly like that of Kumlien's Gull and questionably a new species. The nests and eggs are not to be distinguished from the preceding.

47. Great Black-backed Gull. *Larus marinus*.

Range.—North Atlantic on both the American and European sides ; breeds from Nova Scotia northward and winters south to the Great Lakes and the Middle States. [3]

The largest of the Gulls (thirty inches long) and unlike any other. The mantle is dark slaty black, and the primaries are black with white tips. The bill is very large and powerful and quite strongly hooked. They are quite abundant birds in their range, and are very quarrelsome, both among themselves and other species. They do not breed in as large colonies as do the other Gulls, half a dozen pairs appropriating a small island to the exclusion of all other birds. They are very rapacious birds and live to a great extent, especially during the breeding season, upon the eggs and young of other birds such as

[Grayish buff.]

Ducks, Murres and smaller Gulls. They place their nests upon the higher portions of sandy islands. They are made of grasses and seaweed. The three eggs are laid early in June ; they are grayish or brownish, spotted with brown and lilac. Size 3 x 2.15. Data.—South Labrador, June 21, 1884. Three eggs. Nest on a small island off the coast ; of grasses and moss.

[1] Breeds on coast of Baffin Island.
[2] No longer recognized as a valid form.
[3] Breeds south to L.I., N.Y.

48. Slaty-backed Gull. *Larus schistisagus.*

Range.—North Pacific and Arctic Oceans. [1]

This Gull, which is similar to the Great Black-backed, but is smaller and has a lighter mantle, does not breed in any considerable numbers on the American side of the Pacific. It nests in June on some of the islands in Bering Sea and probably more commonly farther north. They often nest in company with other species, placing their small mounds of seaweed on the ground on the higher parts of the islands. The full set contains three eggs of grayish or brownish color, spotted with dark brown or black. Size 2.90 x 2. Data.—Harrowby Bay, N. W. T. Canada, June 11, 1901. Nest of grass, roots and mud and lined with dry grass; on point

[Gray.]

making into the bay. Collector, Capt. H. H. Bodfish.

49. Western Gull. *Larus occidentalis.*

Range.—Pacific Coast, breeding from southern California to British Columbia.

This bird, which is the most southerly distributed of the larger Gulls is twenty-four inches in length. Mantle slate colored; primaries black, both these and the secondaries being broadly tipped with white.

These Gulls nest abundantly on the Farallones, the majority of them showing a preference for the lower portions of the island, although they nest on the ledges also. Besides man, these Gulls are the greatest enemies that the Murres have to contend against. They are always on the watch and if a Murre leaves its nest, one of the Gulls is nearly always ready to pounce upon the egg and carry it away bodily in his bill. They also devour a great many young birds. The Gulls too suffer when the eggers come, for their eggs are

[Pale greenish buff.]

gathered up with the Murres for the markets. They make their nests of weeds and grass, and during May and June lay three eggs showing the usual variations of color common to the Gulls eggs. Size 2.75 x 1.90. Data.—Farallone Is., Cal., June 20, 1897. Nest a mass of Farallone weed on a ledge.

[1] Does not breed in North America; casual in Alaska.

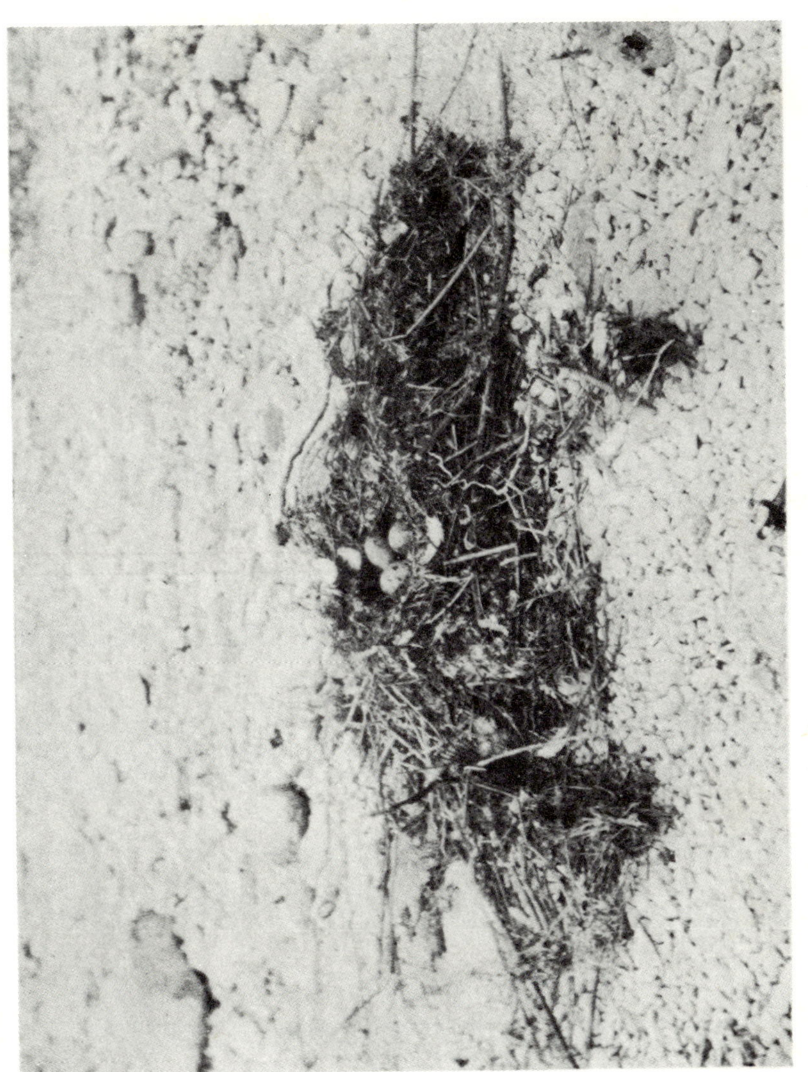

Photo by Walter Raine.

NEST AND EGGS OF HERRING GULL.
[Lake Winnipegosis, June 20, 1903.]

50. Siberian Herring Gull. *Larus fuscus affinis.*

This bird does not nest in North America, and has a place on our list, by its accidental occurrence in Greenland. It is an Old World species and its nesting habits and eggs are like those of the Herring Gull.[1]

51. Herring Gull. *Larus argentatus.*

Range.—Whole of the Northern Hemisphere, breeding from Maine and British Columbia northward and wintering south to the Gulf. [2]

[Buff.]

This Gull, which formerly was No. 51a, a sub-species of the European variety, is now regarded as identical with it, and is no longer a sub-species. It is twenty-four inches in length, has a light gray mantle and black primaries which are tipped with white. The Herring Gulls nest in colonies in favorable localities throughout their range, chiefly on the coasts and islands. A few pairs also nest on islands in some of the inland bodies of fresh water. Except in places where they are continually molested, when they will build in trees, they place their nests on the ground, either making no nest on the bare sand, or building a bulky nest of seaweed in the grass on higher parts of the island.   They lay three eggs of a grayish color marked with brown. In rare cases unspotted bluish white eggs are found. Size 2.8 x 1.7. Data.—Deer Is. Maine, June 11, 1891. Three eggs ; nest of weeds and grass on high portion of the island. Collector, R. N. Knight.

52. Vega Gull (should be Herring Gull).
Larus argentatus.

Range.—Coast of Alaska, south in winter to California. [3]

Similar to the Herring Gull, but with the mantle darker, but not so dark as in the Western Gull. The nesting habits and eggs are the same as those of the Herring Gull, except that in a series, the eggs of the Vega will average a little darker in ground color. It nests during May on the coasts and islands of Bering Sea, placing its eggs in a hollow on the ground. Size 2.75 x 1.65.   Data.— Yukon River, June 20, 1899. Nest a large mass of weeds on an island in the river. Collector, J. Weston.

[Brownish buff.]

[1] No longer recognized as a valid form.
[2] Breeds from coastal Virginia north.
[3] Breeds only in Asia, purely casual in North America.

53. California Gull. *Larus californicus.*

Range.—Western North America, breeding in the interior.

A smaller Gull than the Herring with the primaries grayish instead of black ; length twenty-five inches.   This Gull is found in winter on the coast from British Columbia southward to Lower California, but nests in the interior from Utah northward.   They nest very abundantly around the Great Salt Lake, placing

[Grayish brown.]

their nests generally upon the bare ground.   Sometimes there is a scant lining of grasses or weeds and again the nests will be situated in the midst of a tussock of grass.   Three or four eggs generally constitute a set, but occasionally five are laid.   The usual nesting time is during May.   They show the same great variations in color and markings common to most of the Gulls. Size 2.60 x 1.80. Data. —Pyramid Lake, Nevada, May 26, 1898.   Slight nest of grasses on the rocks on an island.   Collector, R. D. Wheeler.

54. Ring-billed Gull. *Larus delawarensis.*

Range.—Whole of North America, breeding from the United States northward and wintering south to the Gulf States.

A small Gull, eighteen inches in length, with a light gray mantle, black primaries with white tips, and always to be distinguished in the breeding season by the black band around the middle of the greenish yellow bill.   They nest in enormous colonies on islands in the interior of the country and in smaller colonies on the coasts.   Thousands of them breed on the lakes of the Dakotas and   northward. The majority of them nest on the ground, although on the coast they are often found on the cliffs.   They commonly lay three eggs placing them in a slight hollow in the ground, generally

[Gray.]

on the grassy portions of the islands.   The color varies from grayish to brownish, marked with brown and lilac.   The height of the nesting season is in June. Size of eggs, 2.80 x 1.75. Data.—Larimore, N. Dakota, May 31, 1898. Three eggs. Nest a hollow in the sand on an island, lined with a few grasses.   Collector, T. F. Eastgate.

55. Short-billed Gull (should be Mew Gull). *Larus canus.*

Range.—Breeds from the interior of British Columbia northward to Alaska; south in winter to Lower California.

The Short-billed or American Mew Gull is seventeen inches in length, has a short, stout bill and is otherwise similar to the preceding species. Nests on islands in the lakes and along the river banks of Alaska. The nest is made of grass, weeds and moss and is placed on the ground. Early in June the birds lay their set of three eggs, the ground color of which is greenish brown marked with dark brown. Size 2.25 x 1.60. Data.—Mackenzie River, N. W. T., June 18, 1900. Three eggs. Nest made of seaweed and grass and placed on the ground on an island in the river.

[Pale greenish brown.]

[Pale greenish brown.]

56. Mew Gull. *Larus canus.*

This is the European variety of the above species, breeding commonly both in the British Isles and northern Europe. This species is given a place in our avifauna because of its accidental appearance in Labrador. [1]

57. Heermann's Gull. *Larus heermanni.*

Range.—Pacific Coast of North America from British Columbia south to Panama, breeding chiefly south of the United States border.

A very handsome species, often called the White-headed Gull, and wholly unlike any other; length seventeen inches. Adults, in summer, have the entire head, neck and throat white, this shading quite abruptly into the slaty upper and under parts; the primaries and tail are black, the latter and the secondaries being tipped with white. The legs and bill are vermilion. They are found off the coast of California, but are not believed to breed there. They are known to breed on some of the islands off the Mexican coast nesting on the ground the same as the other species. The three eggs are greenish drab in color and are marked with different shades of brown and lilac. Size 2.45 x 1.50.

[1] Labrador and elsewhere.

58. Laughing Gull. *Larus atricilla.*

Range.—Eastern North America, breeding from the Gulf to Nova Scotia, chiefly on the coast.   A beautiful Gull, 16 inches long, with a dark slate colored head, gray mantle, black primaries, and white neck, underparts and tail. Bill and feet red. This bird has its name from its peculiar laughing cry when alarmed or angry; it is also called the Black-headed Gull. They nest by thousands on the islands off the Gulf Coast and along the South Atlantic States. The nest is placed on the ground and is made of seaweed. Three, four and sometimes five eggs are laid, of a grayish to greenish brown color, marked with brown and lilac. Size 2.25 x 1.60. Data.—Timbalin Is., La., June 3, 1896. Three eggs. Nest of drift grass thrown in a pile about 8 inches high, slightly hollowed on top, in low marsh back of beach. Collector, E. A. McIlhenny.

Pale grayish brown.]

59. Franklin's Gull. *Larus pipixcan.*

Range.—Interior North America, breeding from middle United States northward.

Like the last but smaller and with the primaries light. Underparts rosy in breeding season. Nests very abundantly in the marshes of Minnesota and northward. Nest made of grasses and placed in the marsh grass barely above the surface of the water. Eggs same color as the last but the markings more inclined to zigzag lines.   Size   2.10 x 1.40.   Data.— Heron Lake, Minn., May 26, 1885. Nest of wet sedge stalks and rubbish placed in a bunch of standing sedge in shallow water; at least five thousand birds in rookery. Collector, J. W. Preston.

[Grayish brown.]

60. Bonaparte's Gull. *Larus philadelphia.*

Range.—Breeds in the northern parts of North America; winters from Maine and British Columbia to the southern border of the United States.

Smaller than the last; 14 inches long. Plumage similar, but bill slender and black. They nest in great numbers on the marshes of Manitoba and to the northward. The nests of sticks and grass are placed on the higher parts of the marsh and the usual complement of three eggs is laid during the latter part of June. The eggs are grayish to greenish brown, marked with dark brown and lilac. Size 1.90 x 1.30.

[Pale grayish brown.]

60.1. Little Gull. *Larus minutus.*

[Greenish gray.]

This Gull is the smallest of the family; it is a European bird, and has accidentally strayed to our shores but a few times. Its plumage is similar to that of the Bonaparte Gull but the bill is red. It breeds in the marshes around the Baltic Sea, placing its nest of dead vegetation on the highest parts of the marsh. They lay three eggs of a greenish gray color marked with dark brown and lilac. Size 1.75 x 1.25.

61. Ross' Gull. *Rhodostethia rosea.*

Range.—The Arctic regions, south in winter to Alaska, Greenland, northern Europe and Asia.

This beautiful bird is the most rare of all the Gulls, being very difficult to obtain because of its extreme northerly distribution. It is in form and plumage like Bonaparte's Gull, with the exceptions that the head is white, there being a narrow black collar around the neck, the tail is wedge shaped, and the whole under parts from the chin to the tail are rosy in the breeding plumage. The nests and eggs remain still undiscovered, although Nansen, in August 1896, found a supposed breeding ground in Franz Josef Land, because of the numbers of the birds, but found no nests.

62. Sabine's Gull. *Xema sabini.*

[Greenish brown.]

Range.—Arctic regions, breeding from Alaska and Greenland northward, and wintering south to New England. [1]

A handsome bird, having the slaty hood bordered behind with a black ring, the primaries black, white tipped, and the tail slightly forked. They breed abundantly on the marshes of northern Alaska and Greenland, nesting the same as others of the species. The two or three eggs are laid in June. They are greenish brown in color and are marked with dark brown. Size 1.75 x 1.25. Data.—Hudson Bay, August 1, 1894. Eggs laid on the ground in the moss; no nest except the hollow in the moss. Collector, G. Comer.

[1] Winters only in Pacific Ocean off Peru; only suspected in south Atlantic.

63. Gull-billed Tern. *Gelochelidon nilotica.*

Range.—Found in North America along the Gulf Coast and on the Atlantic Coast north to Virginia and casually farther.[1]

[Pale greenish buff.]

This is one of the largest of the Terns, is 14 inches long, has a short, thick, black bill and a short slightly forked tail; the crown is black, mantle pearly gray, white below. This species is very widely distributed, being found in Europe, Australia, Asia and Africa. They are known locally as "Marsh Terns" where they breed in immense numbers on some of the marshes about the Gulf, particularly in Texas. They also breed on many of the islands along the Coast, rarely making any nest, but laying the eggs in a hollow in the sand. They nest most abundantly in the latter part of May, generally laying three eggs. They are of a yellowish, grayish or greenish buff color and are spotted with brown and lilac. Size 1.80 x 1.30. Data.— Northhampton Co., Va., May 28, 1882. Three eggs laid on a mass of seaweed on marsh above tide water. Collector, T. S. Hayward.

64. Caspian Tern. *Hydroprogne caspia.*

Range.—Like the preceding species, this bird is nearly cosmopolitan in its range, in North America breeding from the Gulf Coast and Texas northward to the Arctic Regions.

This beautiful bird is the largest of the Tern family, being about 22 inches in length, with the tail forked about 1.5 inches. The bill is large, heavy and bright red; the crest, with which this and the next three species are adorned,

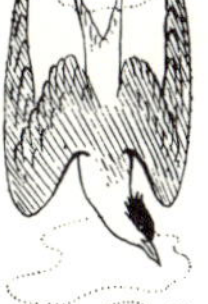

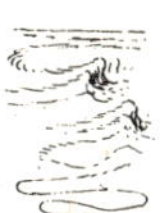

is black. The mantle is pale pearl and the under parts white. These Terns sometimes nest in large colonies and then again only a few pairs will be found on an island. In Texas, the breeding season commences in May, it being later in the more northern breeding grounds. They may be regarded as largely eastern birds, as while they are common in the interior of the country, they are rarely found on the Pacific Coast. Two or three eggs constitute a complete set; these are laid on the

[Grayish buff.]

sand in a slight hollow scooped out by the birds. They vary from gray to greenish buff, marked with brown and lilac. Size 2.60 x 1.75. Data.—Hat Island, Lake Michigan, July 1, 1896. No nest. Two eggs laid in a hollow in the gravel. Fully a thousand terns nesting on about one acre. Collector, Charles L. Cass.

---

[1] Breeds north to New Jersey.

65. Royal Tern. *Thalasseus maximus.*

Range.—Temperate North and South America, breeding in the United States locally from Texas and the Gulf States northward to the northern boundary of the United States. [1]

The Royal Terns nest in great numbers on the coasts and islands on the South Atlantic and Gulf States and in the marshes of southern Texas. Like the former species they lay two or three eggs in a hollow on the bare sand. The eggs are the same size but differ in being more pointed and having a lighter ground and with the markings more bold and distinct. Size 2.60 x 1.70. Data. —Ragged Is., Bahamas. No nest. Eggs laid on sand bank. Never have seen in the Tropics more than a single egg in a nest. Collector, D. P. Ingraham.

[Grayish buff.]

66. Elegant Tern. *Thalasseus elegans.*

Range.—Pacific Coast of South and Central America ; north to California in summer.

A similar bird to the Royal Tern, but easily distinguished by its smaller size, slenderer bill, and more graceful form. In the breeding plumage the under parts of these Terns are tinged with rosy, which probably first gave the birds their name. They breed on the coasts and islands of Mexico and Central America, placing their eggs on the sand. They are believed to lay but a single egg, like that of the Royal Tern, but smaller. Size 2.40 x 1.40. Data.— Honduras, Central America, June 5, 1899. Single egg laid on the sandy beach.

[Cream color.]

[Cream color.]

67. Sandwich Tern. *Thalasseus sandvicensis.*

Range.—A tropical species breeding regularly north to the Bahamas and Florida ; casually farther north. A beautiful bird distinguished from the three preceding ones by its smaller size (sixteen inches) and by the bill which is black with a yellow tip. They nest in colonies on the shores of islands in the West Indies and Bahamas, but not to a great extent on the United States Coast. Their two or three eggs have a creamy ground and are boldly marked with brown and black. Size 2.10 x 1.40. [2]

[1] Breeds only north to Maryland.
[2] Breeds along the Gulf coast, and as far north as North Carolina on the Atlantic side.

Photo by P. B. Peabody.

NEST AND EGGS OF COMMON TERN.

68. Trudeau's Tern.   *Sterna trudeaui.*

Range.—South America ; accidental along the coast of the United States.

A rare and unique species with a form similar to the following, but with the coloration entirely different.   About fifteen inches in length ; tail long and deeply forked ; bill yellow with a band of black about the middle.   Whole head pure white, shading into the pearly color of the upper and under parts.   A narrow band of black through the eye and over the ear coverts.   A very rare species that is supposed to breed in southern South America.   Given a place among North American birds on the strength of a specimen seen by Audubon off Long Island.

69. Forster's Tern.   *Sterna forsteri.*

Range.—Temperate North America, breeding from Manitoba, Mass. and California, south to the Gulf Coast and Texas.[1]

Length about fifteen inches ; tail long and deeply forked ; crown black, back and wings pearl and under parts white.   Bill orange red.   This species and the

[Brownish buff.]

three following are the most graceful of birds in appearance and flight.   Their movements can only be likened to those of the Swallows, from which they get the name of "Sea Swallows."   Their food consists of fish, which they get by diving, and marine insects.   They breed by thousands in the marshes from Manitoba to Texas and along the South Atlantic coast.   The eggs are laid in a hollow on the dry grassy portions of the islands or marshes.   They generally lay three eggs and rarely four.   They are buffy or brownish spotted with dark brown and lilac.

Size 1.80 x 1.30.   Data.—Cobb's Island, Va., June 8, 1887.   Eggs in a hollow on grassy bank.   Collector, F. H. Judson.

70. Common Tern.   *Sterna hirundo.*

Range.—Eastern North America, breeding both on the coast and in the interior from the Gulf States northward.

This bird differs from the preceding chiefly in having a bright red bill tipped with black, and the under parts washed with pearl. These are the most common Terns on the New England coast, nesting abundantly from Virginia to Newfoundland. These beautiful Terns, together with others of the family, were formerly killed by thousands for millinery purposes, but the practice is now being rapidly stopped. In May and June they lay their three, or sometimes four eggs on the ground as do the other Terns. They are similar to the preceding species but average shorter.   Data.—Duck Is.,

[Buff.]

Maine, June 30, 1896.   Three eggs in marsh grass about fifty feet from beach. No nest.   Collector, C. A. Reed.

[1] Breeds from New Jersey south.

71. Arctic Tern.   *Sterna paradisaea.*

Range.— Northern Hemisphere, breeding from New England northward to the Arctic Regions and wintering south to California and the South Atlantic States.[1] A similar bird to the last, differing in having the bill wholly red and the feet being smaller and weak for the size of the bird. A more northern bird than the last, breeding abundantly in Alaska, both on the coast and in the interior. In the southern limits of its breeding range, it nests in company with the Common Tern, its nests and eggs being indistinguishable from the latter. When their nesting grounds are approached, all the birds arise like a great white cloud, uttering their harsh, discordant "tearrr, tearrr," while now and then an individual, bolder than the rest, will swoop close by with an angry "cack." On the whole they are timid birds, keeping well out of reach. The nesting season is early in June. Eggs like the preceding. Data.—Little Duck Is., Me., June 29, 1896. Three eggs in a slight hollow on the beach, three feet above high water mark.

[Grayish or brownish.]

72. Roseate Tern.   *Sterna dougallii.*

Range.—Temperate North America on the east coast, breeding from New England to the Gulf.

[Grayish or brownish.]

These are the most beautiful birds, having a delicate pink blush on the under parts during the breeding season; the tail is very long and deeply forked, the outer feathers being over five inches longer than the middle ones; the bill is red with a black tip. They nest in large colonies on the islands from Southern New England southward, placing the nests in the short grass, generally without any lining. They lay two or three eggs which are indistinguishable from the two preceding species. Data.—Egg Is., Buzzards Bay, Mass., June 6, 1899. Three eggs in scant nest of grasses hidden under wild pea vines and grass on higher part of the island. Collector, Charles E. Doe.

73. Aleutian Tern.   *Sterna aleutica.*

Range.—Found in summer in Alaska and the Aleutian Islands.

South in winter to Japan. This handsome Tern is of the form and size of the Common Tern, but has a darker mantle, and the forehead is white, leaving a black line from the bill to the eye. They nest on islands off the coast of Alaska, sometimes together with the Arctic Tern. The eggs are laid upon the bare ground or moss, and are similar to the Arctic Terns, but average narrower. They are two or three in number and are laid in June and July. Size 1.70 x 1.15. Data.— Stuart Is., Alaska. Three eggs in a slight hollow in the moss.

[Grayish or brownish.]

---

[1] Winters in southern hemisphere only, in Pacific, Atlantic and Indian Oceans.

74. Least Tern. *Sterna albifrons.*

[Light Buff.]

Range.—From northern South America to southern New England, Dakota and California, breeding locally throughout its range.

These little Sea Swallows are the smallest of the Terns, being but 9 inches in length. They have a yellow bill with a black tip, a black crown and nape, and white forehead. Although small, these little Terns lose none of the grace and beauty of action of their larger relatives. They nest in colonies on the South Atlantic and Gulf Coasts, placing their eggs upon the bare sand, where they are sometimes very difficult to see among the shells and pebbles. They are of a grayish or buffy color spotted with umber and lilac. They number two, three and rarely four, and are laid in May and June. Size 1.25 x .95. Data.—DeSota Beach, Fla., May 20, 1884. Three eggs laid on the sandy beach. Collector, Chas. Graham.

75. Sooty Tern. *Sterna fuscata.*

[Creamy white.]

Range.—Tropical America, north to the South Atlantic States. This species measures 17 inches in length; it has a brownish black mantle, wings and tail, except the outer feathers of the latter which are white; the forehead and under parts are white, the crown and a line from the eye to the bill, black. This tropical species is very numerous at its breeding grounds on the small islands of the Florida Keys and the West Indies.[1] They lay but a single egg, generally placing it on the bare ground, or occasionally building a frail nest of grasses. The egg has a pinkish white or creamy ground and is beautifully sprinkled with spots of reddish brown and lilac. They are laid during May. Size 2.05 x 1.45. Data.—Clutheria Key, Bahamas, May 28, 1891. Single egg laid on bare ground near water. Collector, D. P. Ingraham.

76. Bridled Tern. *Sterna anaethetus.*

[Creamy White.]

Range.—Found in tropical regions of both hemispheres; casual or accidental in Florida. This Tern is similar to the last except that the nape is white and the white of the forehead extends in a line over the eye. The Bridled Tern is common on some of the islands of the West Indies and the Bahamas, nesting in company with the Sooty Terns and Noddies. The single egg is laid on the seashore or among the rocks. It is creamy white, beautifully marked with brown and lilac. Size 1.85 x 1.25. Data. Bahamas, May 9, 1892. Single egg laid in a cavity among the rocks. Collector, D. P. Ingraham.

[1] i.e. the Dry Tortugas.

Photo by William H. Fisher.

LEAST TERN'S NEST.

77.   Black Tern.   *Chlidonias niger.*

Range.—Temperate America, breeding from the middle portions of the United States northward to Alaska; south in winter beyond the United States border.

The identity of these Terns cannot be mistaken.   They are but ten inches in length; the whole head, neck and under parts are black; the back, wings and tail are slaty and the under tail coverts are white.   Their dainty figure with their long slender wings gives them a grace and airiness, if possible, superior to other species of the family. They are very active and besides feeding upon all manner of marine crustacea, they capture many insects in the air.   They nest in large colonies in marshes, both along the coast and in the interior, making a nest of decayed reeds and grasses, or often laying their eggs upon rafts of decayed vegetation which are floating on the water. The nesting season commences in May, they laying three eggs of a brownish or greenish color, very heavily blotched with blackish brown.   Size 1.35 x .95.   Data.—Winnebago City, Minn., May

[Deep greenish brown]

31, 1901.   Three eggs.   Nest made of a mass of weeds and rushes floating on water in a swamp.   Collector, R. H. Bullis.

78.   White-winged Black Tern.   *Chlidonias leucopterus.*

[Greenish buff.]

Range.—Eastern Hemisphere, its addition to American birds being made because of the accidental appearance of one bird in Wisconsin in 1873.   They nest very abundantly among the lakes and marshes of southern Europe, placing their eggs the same as the American species upon masses of decayed reeds and stalks.   They lay three eggs which have a somewhat brighter appearance than the common Black Terns because of a somewhat lighter ground color.

79.   Brown Noddy.   *Anoüs stolidus.*

Range.—Tropical America, north to the Gulf and South Atlantic States.   A peculiar but handsome bird (about fifteen inches long,) with a silvery white head and the rest of the plumage brownish, and the tail rounded.   They breed in abundance on some of the Florida Keys, the West Indies and the Bahamas.   Their nests are made of sticks and grass, and are placed either in trees or on the ground. They lay but a single egg with a buffy or cream colored ground spotted with chestnut and lilac.   Size 2.00 x 1.30. Atwood's Key, Bahamas, June 1, 1891.   Nest made of sticks and grasses, three feet up a mangrove.[1] Collector, D. P. Ingraham.

[Buff.]

[1] Breeds only on Dry Tortugas off Key West, Fla.

SKIMMERS. Family RYNCHOPIDAE.

Skimmers are Tern-like birds having a very strangely developed bill. The lower mandible is much longer than the upper and very thin, the upper edge being as sharp as the lower. The lower mandible is rounded at the end while the upper is more pointed. Young Skimmers are said to have both mandibles of the same length, the abnormal development not appearing until after flight. Skimmers are very graceful birds, and, as implied by their name, they skim over the surface of the water, rising and falling with the waves, and are said to pick up their food by dropping the lower mandible below the surface, its thin edge cutting the water like a knife. There are four species of Skimmers, only one of which is found in North America.

80. Black Skimmer. *Rynchops nigra.*

Range.—The South Atlantic and Gulf Coasts, breeding from New Jersey southward. The Black Skimmer is about eighteen inches in length, and besides the remarkable bill is a bird of striking plumage ; the forehead, ends of the secondaries, tail feathers and under parts are white ; the rest of the plumage is black and the basal half of the bill is crimson. Skimmers nest in large communities, the same as do the Terns, laying their eggs in hollows in the sand. They are partially nocturnal in their habits and their hoarse barking cries may be heard after the shadows of night have enveloped the earth. Fishermen call them by the names of "Cut-water" and "Sea Dog." The nesting season commences in May and continues through June and July. They lay from three to five eggs, having a creamy or yellowish buff ground, blotched with black, chestnut and lilac. Size 1.75 x 1.30. Data.— Cobb's Is., Va., June 8, 1894. Three eggs laid in a hollow on the beach. No nest.

[Buffy yellow.]

ALBATROSSES,   SHEARWATERS   and   allies.   Order PROCELLARIIFORMES.

ALBATROSSES. Family DIOMEDEIDAE.

Albatrosses are the largest of the sea birds and have an enormous expanse of wing, the Wandering Albatross, the largest of the family, sometimes attaining an expanse of fourteen feet. Their nostrils consist of two slightly projecting tubes, one on each side near the base of the bill. They are unsurpassed in powers of flight, but are only fair swimmers and rarely, if ever, dive, getting their food, which consists of dead animal matter, from the surface of the water.

81. Black-footed Albatross. *Diomedea nigripes.*

Range.—North Pacific from California northward. This Albatross is thirty-two inches in length ; it is of a uniform sooty brown color shading into whitish at the base of the bill, which is rounded. Like the other members of the family, this species is noted for its extended flights, following vessels day after day without any apparent period of rest, for the purpose of feeding on the refuse that is thrown overboard. They breed during our winter on some of the small isolated islands in the extreme southern portions of the globe. They lay a single white egg on the bare ground.

82. Short-tailed Albatross. *Diomedea albatrus.*

Range.—North Pacific Ocean in summer, from Lower California to Alaska.[1] With the exception of the Wandering Albatross, which is now regarded as doubtful as occurring off our coasts, the Short-tailed Albatross is one of the largest of the group, measuring thirty-six inches in length, and has an extent of seven feet or more. With the exception of the black primaries, shoulders and tail, the entire plumage is white, tinged with straw color on the back of the head. They breed on the guano islands in the North Pacific off the coasts of Alaska and Japan. They lay a single white egg on the bare ground or rocks. As with the other members of the family, the eggs are extremely variable in size, but average about 4.25 x 2.50.

82.1. Laysan Albatross. *Diomedea immutabilis.*

Range.—Laysan Island of the Hawaiian Group, appearing casually off the coast of California. This species breeds in large numbers on the island from which it takes its name. The birds are white with the exception of the back, wings and tail, which are black. The birds, having been little molested in their remote island, are exceedingly tame, and it is possible to go among the sitting birds without disturbing them. Mr. Walter K. Fisher has contributed an admirable report on this species in the 1903 Bulletin of the Fish Commission, the report being illustrated with numerous illustrations of the birds from photos by the author. Their single white eggs are laid on the bare ground.

83. Yellow-nosed Albatross. *Diomedea chlororhynchos.*

This is a species which inhabits the South Pacific and Indian Oceans, and is said to rarely occur on the California coast. They breed during our winter on some of the small islands and during our summer are ocean wanderers. An egg

---

[1] Nests only off Japan; practically extinct.

in the collection of Col. John E. Thayer was taken on Gough Island, South Atlantic Ocean; Sept. 1st., 1888. The nest was a mound of mud and grass about two feet in height. The single white egg measured 3.75 x 2.25. It was collected by Geo. Comer.

84. Sooty Albatross. *Phoebetria fusca.*

Range.—Southern seas, north in our summer along the Pacific coast of the United States.[1]

This species is entirely sooty brown except the white eyelids. It is similar to the Black-footed Albatross from which species it can be distinguished in all plumages by the narrow base of the bill, while the bill of the former species is broad and rounded. They breed commonly on isolated islands in many quarters of the southern hemisphere. Sometimes this species constructs a mound of mud on which to deposit its single white egg, and also often lays it on the bare ground or rock. A specimen in Mr. Thayer's collection, taken by Geo. Comer on So. Georgia Is. in the South Atlantic Ocean was laid in a hollow among loose stones on the ledge of an overhanging cliff. Size 4.10 x 2.75.

[White.]

FULMARS, SHEARWATERS and PETRELS. Families PROCEL-LARIIDAE and HYDROBATIDAE.

Fulmars and Shearwaters are Gull-like birds with two nostril tubes located side by side, in a single tube, on the top of the bill at it's base.

The Fulmars are mostly northern birds while the majority of the Shearwaters nest in the extreme south during our winter, and appear off our coasts during the summer. Their food consists of fish or offal which they get from the surface of the water; large flocks of them hover about fishermen, watching their chance to get any food which falls, or is thrown, overboard.

[1] Not recorded from North America.

85. Giant Fulmar. *Macronectes giganteus.*

Range.—This Petrel is a native of the southern seas and is only casually met with off the Pacific coast. [1]

It is the largest of the family being about three feet in length, and is normally a uniform sooty color, although it has light phases of plumage. They nest in December on many of the islands south of Africa and South America, laying their single white egg on the bare rocks.

86. Northern Fulmar. *Fulmarus glacialis.*

Range.—North Atlantic coasts from New England northward, breeding from Hudson Bay and southern Greenland northward.

This bird which is 19 inches in length, in the light phase has a plumage very similar to that of the larger Gulls. They nest by thousands on the rocky islands of the north, often in company with Murres and Gulls. Owing to the filthy habits of the Fulmars, these breeding grounds always have a nauseating odor, which is also imparted to, and retained by the egg shell. Their single white eggs are laid on the bare rocks, in crevices of the cliffs, often hundreds of feet above the water. Size 2.90 x 2. Data.—St. Kilda, off Scotland. June 5, 1897. Single egg laid on rock on side of sea cliff. Collector, Angus Gillies.

[White.]

86b. Pacific Fulmar (should be Northern Fulmar). *Fulmarus glacialis.*

This sub-species of the preceding, has a darker mantle than the common Fulmar;[2] it is found on the northern Pacific coasts where it breeds on the high rocky cliffs, the same as its eastern relative. They nest in large colonies, every crevice in the rocks having its tenant. Their flight is graceful like that of the Gulls, which they closely resemble. They lay but a single white egg, the average dimensions of which are slightly smaller than those of the common Fulmar.[2] Data.—Copper Is. Alaska. May 14, 1889. Egg laid in a crevice among the cliffs.

[1] Not recorded from North America.

[2] Now Northern Fulmar.

86.1.   Rodgers' Fulmar (should be Northern Fulmar).   *Fulmarus glacialis.*

Range.—North Pacific, breeding in large numbers on some of the islands in Bering Sea; south to California in winter. Very similar to the two preceding species except that the back is mixed with whitish, it is not believed to have a dark phase. Their breeding habits and eggs do not differ from the common Fulmar.[1] The eggs are laid on the rocky cliffs during June.

87.   Slender-billed Fulmar.   *Priocella antarctica.*

Range.—Southern seas, appearing on the Pacific coast of the United States in the summer. This species has a paler mantle than the others of the family, and the primaries are black. The make-up and plumage of the whole bird is more like that of the Gulls than any of the others. They probably breed in the far south during our winter, although we have no definite data relative to their nesting habits.[2]

88.   Cory's Shearwater.   *Puffinus diomedea.*

This species probably breeds in the far south. It has been found only off the coast of Massachusetts and Long Island. This is the largest of our Shearwaters, and can be distinguished from the next species by its wholly white underparts, its light mantle and yellowish bill. We have no data relative to its nesting habits.[3]

89.   Greater Shearwater.   *Puffinus gravis.*

Range.—The whole of the Atlantic Ocean.[4]
Thousands of them spend the latter part of the summer off the New England coast, where they are known to the fishermen as Haglets. Their upper parts are brownish gray, darker on the wings; bill and feet dark; under parts white, with the middle of the belly and the under tail covers dusky. Length about 20 inches. Little is known concerning their nesting quarters, although they are said to breed in Greenland. From the fact of their early appearance off the New England coast it is probable that the greater part of them nest in the far south.

90.   Manx Shearwater.   *Puffinus puffinus.*

This species inhabits the North Atlantic ocean chiefly on the European side, being abundant in the Mediterranean and in the British Isles. These birds deposit their single pure white eggs in crevices among the cliffs, on the ground or in burrows dug by themselves. Size of egg 2.35 x 1.60. Data.—Isle of Hay, North Scotland. June 1, 1893. Single egg laid at the end of a three foot burrow.

91.   Pink-footed Shearwater.   *Puffinus creatopus.*

Range.—Pacific Ocean, north on American side to California in summer.
This species, whose breeding habits are little known, is similar in size and color to the Greater Shearwater, differing chiefly in the yellowish bill and pinkish colored feet.

[1] Now Northern Fulmar.
[2] Not recorded from North America.
[3] Occurs along entire Atlantic coast from Nova Scotia to Carolinas; breeds in south Atlantic.
[4] Breeds in central south Atlantic only.

92. Audubon's Shearwater. *Puffinus lherminieri.*

Range.—Middle Atlantic, ranging north in late summer to Long Island.[1]
This bird, having a length of but twelve inches, is the smallest of the Shearwaters found along our coasts. Large colonies of them breed on some of

[White.]
the small islands and keys of the West Indies and Bahamas, and not so commonly in the Bermudas. Their eggs, which are pure white, are deposited at the end of burrows dug by the birds. Size of egg 2. x 1.35. Their nesting season commences about the latter part of March and continues through April and May. After the young are able to fly, like other members of the family, the birds become ocean wanderers and stray north to southern New England. Data.—Bahamas, April 13, 1891. Single egg laid at the end of a burrow about two feet in length. Collector, D. P. Ingraham.

92.1. Little Shearwater. *Puffinus assimilis.*

This is an Australian and New Zealand species that has accidentally strayed
to the shores of Nova Scotia.[2]

93. Black-vented Shearwater (should be Manx Shearwater). *Puffinus puffinus.*

Range.—Middle Pacific coast of the Americas, north in late summer along the
coast of California. This species breeds commonly on the islands off the coasts
of Lower California, especially on the Gulf side. Their single egg is white, size
2. x 1.30, and is located at the end of a burrow. Data.—Natividad Is., Lower
California, April 10, 1897. Single egg laid on the sand at the end of a burrow
six feet in length. Collector, A. W. Anthony.

93.1. Townsend's Shearwater. *Puffinus auricularis.*

This bird ranges from Cape St. Lucas, south along the Pacific coast of Mexico,
breeding on the Revillagigedo Islands off the Mexican coast.

95. Sooty Shearwater. *Puffinus griseus.*

Range.—A common species off the Atlantic coast in summer; breeds along
our northern coasts, and it is also supposed that many of them nest in southern
seas and reach our coasts early in the summer. These Shearwaters are entirely
sooty gray, being somewhat lighter below. They are called "black haglets" by
the fishermen, whose vessels they follow in the hope of procuring bits of refuse.
They commonly nest in burrows in the ground, but are also said to build in
fissures among the ledges. Their single white egg measures 2.55 x 1.75.[3]

---

[1] Breeds in Bermuda, Bahamas and West Indies; casual on coast of the U.S.

[2] This is an Australian and eastern Atlantic species that has accidentally strayed to
the shores of Nova Scotia.

[3] Breeds only in south Atlantic and Pacific Oceans.

95.1. Pale-footed Shearwater. *Puffinus carneipes.*

This is a southern species which, after having nested on islands in the far south during our winter, comes north and appears off the Pacific coast of the United States during the summer. It is a similar bird to the Sooty Shearwater, but is considerably darker and the under coverts are whitish. Their nesting habits are the same as those of other members of the family. Size of egg, 2.40 x 1.65. Data.—Stewart's Island, New Zealand, February 15, 1896. Single egg at the end of a long burrow.

96. Slender-billed Shearwater. *Puffinus tenuirostris.*

Range.—Northern Pacific Ocean in the summer, extending from Japan and Alaska southward. Supposed to breed in the southern hemisphere, as well as probably on some of the Aleutians in Alaska.[1]

96.1. Wedge-tailed Shearwater. *Puffinus pacificus.*

Range.—North Pacific, breeding on the Revillagigedo Islands off the coast of Mexico, and probably on some of the small islands in the Gulf of California.

97. Black-tailed Shearwater. *Adamastor cinereus.*

This is a Shearwater which inhabits the southern hemisphere, but which has accidentally wandered to the Pacific coast of the United States. It is dark above and whitish below, with black under tail coverts. It breeds in the far south.

98. Black-capped Petrel. *Pterodroma hasitata.*

This is not a common species; it is an inhabitant of tropical seas and has only been casually found on our coasts or inland. It is a handsome species with white forehead, underparts and nape with a small isolated black cap on the crown; the rest of the upper parts are blackish. It is a native of the West Indies.

99. Scaled Petrel. *Pterodroma inexpectata.*

This is another rare species which is an inhabitant of southern seas. A single specimen taken in New York State gives it a claim as a doubtful North American species. It is a handsome bird, the feathers of the grayish upperparts being edged with white, thus giving it the appearance of being barred. Its eggs have only been known to science within the past few years. Data.—Preservation Inlet, New Zealand, June 7, 1900. Single white egg. Size 2.40 x 1.75. Collector, P. Seymour. Parent bird taken with the egg.

99. Fisher's Petrel (should be Scaled Petrel). *Pterodroma inexpectata.*

This is a handsome bird known only from the type specimen taken off Kadiak Is., Alaska, by Mr. Fisher.

---

[1] Breeds only on islands near Australia.

108. Ashy Petrel. *Oceanodroma homochroa.*

Range.—California coast, breeding on the Farallones and Santa Barbara Islands.

This species, while not common, nests in all manner of locations on the Farallones, concealing their eggs under any rock or in any crevice that may attract their fancy.   Their single white egg is only faintly if at all wreathed with fine dust-like specks of reddish brown.   Size 1. 15 x .86.   Data.—Farallone Is., California, June 12, 1895.   Egg laid on sand in crevice at the base of a stone wall; well concealed.   Collector, Chester Barlow.

108.1. Socorro Petrel (should be Leach's Petrel). *Oceanodroma leucorhoa.*

Breeds on Socorro, San Benito and Coronado Islands, placing its eggs at the end of a burrow.   Data.—San Benito Is., Lower California., July 12, 1897. Single egg at the end of a burrow 3 feet in length.   Egg pure white very finely wreathed with pale reddish brown.   Size 1.15 x .87.   Collector, A. W. Anthony.

109. Wilson's Petrel. *Oceanites oceanicus.*

Breeds in the southern hemisphere in February and March and spends the summer off the Atlantic coast as far north as Newfoundland.   This species can be distinguished from Leach's Petrel by its square tail and from the Storm Petrel by its large size and yellow webs to its feet.   These birds are the greatest wanderers of the genus, being found at different seasons in nearly all quarters of the globe.   Their single egg is white.   Size 1.25 x .90.

110. Black-bellied Petrel. *Fregetta tropica.*

A small species (length about 7.5 inches) inhabiting southern seas. Recorded once at Florida.   General plumage blackish.   Upper tail coverts, bases of tail feathers, under wing coverts, and abdomen, white.

111. White-faced Petrel. *Pelagodroma marina.*

[White.]

Range.—Southern seas, accidentally north to the coast of Massachusetts.   This beautiful species is of about the same size as the Leach's Petrel.   It has bluish gray upper parts; the whole under parts, as well as the forehead and sides of head, are white.

These birds have the same characteristics as do others of the species, pattering over the water with their feet as they skim over the crests and troughs of the waves.   They are not uncommon in the waters about New Zealand where they breed.   Their single eggs are about the same size as Leach's Petrel, are brilliant white and very strongly, for a Petrel egg, wreathed about the large end with dots of reddish brown.   Size 1.32 x .90.   Data—Chatham Is., New Zealand, Jan. 7, 1901. Egg laid at end of a burrow.   Collector, J. Lobb.   This egg is in Mr. Thayer's collection.

TROPICBIRDS and allies.   Order PELECANIFORMES.

TROPICBIRDS.   Family PHAËTHONTIDAE.

Tropicbirds are Tern-like birds, having all the toes connected by a web, and having the two central tail feathers very much lengthened.

112.   White-tailed Tropicbird.   *Phaëthon lepturus.*

Range.—Tropical regions, breeding in the Bahamas, West Indies and the Bermudas, casual in Florida and along the South Atlantic coast.

The Tropicbirds are the most strikingly beautiful of all the sea birds; they are about 30 inches in length, of which their long slender tail takes about 20 inches. They fly with the ease and grace of a Tern, but with quicker wing beats. They feed on small fish, which they capture by darting down upon, and upon snails which they get from the beach and ledges. They build their nests in the crevices and along the ledges of the rocky cliffs. While gregarious to a certain extent they are not nearly as much so as the Terns. The nest is made of a mass of seaweed and weeds; but one egg is laid, this being of a creamy or pale purplish ground color, dotted and sprinkled with chestnut, so thickly as to often obscure the ground color. Size 2.10 x 1.45. Data.—Coney Is., Bermudas, May 1, 1901. Nest made of moss and seaweed in a crevice on ledge of cliff. Collector, A. H. Verrill.

[Dull purplish.]

113.   Red-billed Tropicbird.   *Phaëthon aethereus.*

Range.—Tropical seas, chiefly in the Pacific Ocean; north to southern California.

They breed on several islands in the Gulf of California. This species differs from the preceding in having a red bill, and the back being barred with black. Their plumage has a peculiar satiny appearance and is quite dazzling when viewed in the sunlight. They are strong fliers and are met with hundreds of miles from land. They often rest upon the water, elevating their long tails to keep them from getting wet. They nest, as do the preceding species, on rocky islands and are said to also build their nests in trees or upon the ground. The single egg that they lay has a creamy ground and is minutely dotted with chestnut. Size 2.40 x 1.55.

[Pale purplish.]

Data.—Daphone Is., Galapagos Is., South Pacific, March 6, 1901. Egg laid in hole of a sea cliff. The eggs are easily told from those of the white-tailed by their much larger size. Collector, R. H. Beck.

113.1.   Red-tailed Tropicbird.   *Phaëthon rubricaudus.*

Range.—Tropical regions of the Pacific and Indian Oceans, accidental off the coast of Lower California.

[Pale purplish ground color.]

This is a singularly beautiful species resembling the latter except that the central tail feathers are bright red, with the extreme tips white. During August and September they breed in large colonies on small islands in the South Seas. On Mauritius Island they build their nests either in the trees or place them on the ground; the nest is made of seaweed, sticks and weeds; numbers of them nest on Laysan Is., of the Hawaiian group, concealing their nests on the ground under overhanging brush.

The single egg has a pale purplish ground speckled with brown.

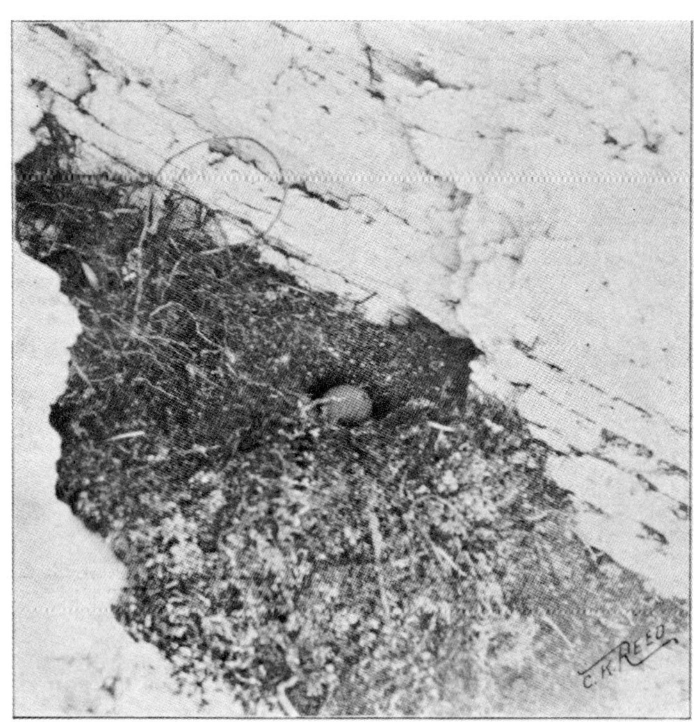

Photo by A. H. Verrill.

WHITE-TAILED TROPICBIRD'S NEST.

GANNETS and BOOBIES. Family SULIDAE.

Gannets are large stoutly built birds, having the four toes joined by a web; they have a small naked pouch beneath the bill; the bill is a little longer than the head, and the tail is quite short. The plumage of the adults is generally white, that of the young grayish.

114. Blue-faced Booby. *Sula datylatra.*

Range.—Widely distributed in the tropical seas, north casually to Florida and breeding in the Bahamas.

Like the rest of the Gannets, this one is stupid and will often remain on the nest until removed with the hand, merely hissing at the intruder. Often they lay their eggs on the bare ground, but sometimes the nest is lined with seaweed or grass. They lay either one or two eggs early in April. These eggs are of a dull white color and are heavily covered with a chalky deposit. Size 2.50 x 1.70. Data.—Clarion Is., Mexico, May 24, 1897. Nest a mere hollow in the sand near the beach. Collector, A. W. Anthony.

114.1. Blue-footed Booby. *Sula nebouxii.*

Range.—Pacific coasts and islands from the Gulf of California southward to Chile.

These birds nest in numbers on the island of San Pedro Martir in the Gulf of California. They lay but a single egg, placing it upon the bare rock. Their breeding season extends from the latter part of March into May. The egg is a dull white, generally nest stained and is covered with the usual chalky deposit. Size 2.35 x 1.60. Data.—Clarion Island, Mexico, May 21, 1897 Two eggs in a hollow in the sand near the beach. Collector, A. W. Anthony.

115. Brown Booby. *Sula leucogaster.*

Range.—Tropical coasts and islands of the Atlantic; north casually to Georgia.

The Brown Booby is an abundant bird on some of the islands of the Bahamas and Bermudas; it is commonly called the Brown Booby because the upper parts are of a brownish gray. These birds, as do the other Gannets, have great powers of flight and without apparent effort dart about with the speed of an arrow. They are quite awkward upon their feet and are not very proficient swimmers. They rarely rest upon the water except when tired hundreds and sometimes thousands of them breed in company, laying their eggs upon the bare rocks. Sometimes a few sticks or grasses will be placed about the bird to prevent the eggs from rolling away. They generally lay two eggs, chalky white and nest stained. Size 2.40 x 1.60. Data.— Key Verd, Bahamas, April 14, 1891. No nest; two eggs laid on the bare rocks.

[Chalky bluish white, nest stained.]

Photo by Herbert K. Job.

From "Among the Waterfowl."

NESTING GANNETS ON BIRD ROCKS.

115.1. Brewster's Booby (should be Brown Booby). *Sula leucogaster.*

Range.—Pacific coast from Lower California southward. This Gannet replaces the Brown Booby on the Pacific coast. It nests abundantly on many islands in the Gulf of California, and in company with the blue-footed variety, on San Pedro Martir Island. They generally lay two eggs, placing them upon the bare rocks and surrounding them with a ring of sticks and seaweed to keep them in place. The eggs are chalky white and cannot be distinguished from those of the other Boobies. Data.—San Benedicto Is., Lower California, May 18, 1897. Single egg laid on the sand amid a few blades of grass.

116. Red-footed Booby. *Sula sula.*

This is another species that is only occasionally taken on the Florida coast. The habits of the birds and their nesting habits are the same as those of the others of the family. Two chalky white eggs are laid. Data.—San Benedicto Is., Lower California, May 18, 1897. Single egg. Nest a few twigs of rank grass. Collector, A. W. Anthony.

117. Northern Gannet. *Morus bassanus.*

Range.—North Atlantic, breeding, in America, only on Bird Rocks in the St. Lawrence.[1]

These are the largest of the family, being 35 inches in length. They feed on fish which they catch by diving upon, from the air. When flying their neck is carried fully extended. They rest on the water when tired, the numerous air

[Chalky bluish white.]

cells beneath the skin causing them to sit high up in the water and enabling them to weather the severest storm in perfect safety. The only known breeding place in America is Bird Rocks where they nest by thousands, placing their nests in rows on the narrow ledges ; the nests are made of piles of seaweed, mud and stones. They lay but one egg of a dingy white color and covered with a chalky deposit. On St. Kilda Island, off the coast of Scotland, they breed by millions. They are very tame and will frequently allow themselves to be touched with the hand. It is said that thousands of the young are killed by fishermen every year and marketed in Edinburgh and other places. Data.—St. Kilda Island, Scotland, June 18, 1896. Single egg laid on a large mass of seaweed on a sea cliff. Collector, H. McDonald.

[1] A number of colonies in Maritime Provinces.

DARTERS. Family ANHINGIDAE.

118. Anhinga. *Anhinga anhinga.*

Range.—Tropical America, north to the South Atlantic States and up the Mississippi Valley to Illinois.

Anhingas or Snake Birds are curiously formed creatures with a Heron-like head and neck, and the body of a Cormorant. They live in colonies in

[Chalky bluish white.]

inaccessible swamps. Owing to their thin and light bodies, they are remarkable swimmers, and pursue and catch fish under water with ease. When alarmed they have a habit of sinking their body below water, leaving only their head and neck visible, thereby having the appearance of a water snake. They also fly well and dive from their perch into the water with the greatest celerity.

They nest in colonies in the swamps, placing their nests of sticks, leaves and moss in the bushes over the water. They breed in April laying from three to five bluish eggs, covered with a chalky deposit. Size 2.25 x 1.35. Data.— Gainesville, Florida, May 18, 1894. Nest in the top of a button-wood tree, made of leaves and branches, overhanging the water. Collector, Geo. Graham.

CORMORANTS. Family PHALACROCORACIDAE.

Cormorants have a more bulky body than do the Anhingas; their tail is shorter and the bill strongly hooked at the tip. Cormorants are found in nearly all quarters of the globe. They are very gregarious and most species are maritime. They feed upon fish which they catch by pursuing under water. Most of the Cormorants have green eyes.

119. Great Cormorant. *Phalacrocorax carbo.*

Range.—The Atlantic coast breeding from Maine to Greenland.[1]

The Great Cormorant or Shag is one of the largest of the race, having a length of 36 inches.

In the breeding plumage, the black head and neck are so thickly covered with slender white plumes as to almost wholly obscure the black. There is also a large white patch on the flanks. They nest in colonies on the rocky shores of Newfoundland and Labrador, placing their nests of sticks and seaweed

---

[1] Does not breed south of northern Nova Scotia. The Shag is a totally distinct species occurring only in Europe.

Photo by Walter Raine.

NESTS OF DOUBLE-CRESTED CORMORANTS.
[Lake Winnipegosis. June 14, 1903.]

[Chalky greenish or bluish white.]

in rows along the high ledges, where they sit, as one writer aptly expresses it, like so many black bottles. A few pairs also nest on some of the isolated rocky islets off the Maine coast. During the latter part of May and during June they lay generally four or five greenish white, chalky looking eggs. Size 2.50 x 1.40. Data.—Black Horse Rock, Maine coast, June 6, 1893. Four eggs in a nest of seaweed and a few sticks; on a high ledge of rock. Collector, C. A. Reed.

120. Double-crested Cormorant. *Phalacrocorax auritus*.

Range.—The Atlantic coast and also in the interior, breeding from Nova Scotia and North Dakota northward.

This is a slightly smaller bird than *carbo*, and in the nesting season the white plumes of the latter are replaced by tufts of black and white feathers from above each eye. On the coast they nest the same as *carbo* and in company with them on rocky islands. In the interior they place their nests on the ground or occasionally in low trees on islands in the lakes. They breed in large colonies, making the nests of sticks and weeds and lay three or four eggs like those of the common Cormorant but averaging shorter. Size 2.30 x 1.40. Data.—Stump Lake, North Dakota, May 31, 1897. Nest of dead weeds on an island. Six eggs. Collector, T. F. Eastgate.

120a. Florida Cormorant (should be Double-crested Cormorant). *Phalacrocorax auritus*.

This sub-species is a common breeding bird in the swamps and islands of the Gulf coast and north to South Carolina and southern Illinois. The nests are placed in the mangroves in some of the most impenetrable swamps and are composed of twigs and lined with leaves or moss. They lay three or four chalky bluish white eggs. Size 2.30 x 1.40. Data.—Bird Is., Lake Kissimee, Florida. April 5, 1898. Three eggs. Nest made of weeds and grass, in a willow bush.

120b. White-crested Cormorant (should be Double-crested Cormorant). *Phalacrocorax   auritus*.

Range.—Northwestern coast of North America, breeding in Alaska, and south to the northern boundary of the United States, breeding both in the interior and on the coast, in the former case generally on the ground or in low trees on swampy islands and in the latter, on the rocky cliffs of the coasts and islands. The nests are built in the same fashion as the other Cormorants, and the three to five eggs are similar. Size 2.45 x 1.40.

120c. Farallone Cormorant (should be Double-crested Cormorant).
Phalacrocorax auritus.

Range.—This sub-species breeds on the coasts and islands of California and southward.

In company with other species of Cormorants, these birds breed in large numbers on the Farallones, placing their nests well up on the higher ridges and rocks. They breed most abundantly during May. When nesting on the inland islands, they place their nests in low bushes. Their nests and eggs are similar to those of the other Cormorants. Size 2.40 x 1.50. Data.—Farallones, California. Nest of weeds and seaweed on the rocks. Collector, W. O. Emerson.

121. Olivaceous Cormorant. *Phalacrocorax olivaceus.*

Range.—Breeds abundantly from southern Texas, south through Mexico; north rarely to Kansas; has recently been found breeding in limited number on some of the Bahamas. In the interior they nest in trees, chiefly those overhanging or growing in the water. On the coasts they nest on the rocky ledges, as do the other Cormorants. They nest in colonies building their abode of twigs and weeds, and during May laying three or four eggs, greenish white in color and chalky, as are all the Cormorants. Size 2.25 x 1.35.

[Greenish White.]

122. Brandt's Cormorant. *Phalacrocorax penicillatus.*

Range.—Pacific coast breeding along the whole coast of the United States. This species is found more abundantly on the Farallones than is the Farallone Cormorant. Like the other Cormorants breeding on these islands, these cling closely to their nests, for fear of being robbed by the Gulls, that are ever on the watch to steal either eggs or young. Their nesting habits and eggs are identical with those of the other species. Size 2.50 x 1.50. Data.—Bird Is., California, May 24, 1885. A very bulky nest of seaweed on the rocks. Collector, A. M. Ingersoll.

123. Pelagic Cormorant. *Phalacrocorax pelagicus.*

Range.—Coast of Alaska.[1]
These are perhaps the most beautiful species of Cormorants, having brilliant violet green metallic reflections and, in the breeding plumage, crests on the forehead and nape, as well as large white flank patches. They breed in large colonies on the Aleutian Islands, placing their nests of sticks and sea mosses on the rocky ledges, often hundreds of feet above the sea level. Three or four eggs are laid during May and June. The young birds when hatched are naked and black, and are repulsive looking objects, as are those of all the other Cormorants. The eggs are greenish white with the usual calcareous deposit. Size 2.30 x 1.40. Data.—Copper Is., Bering Sea, July 2, 1899. Nest made of seaweed on the rocks. Collector, Capt. Tilson.

[1] Breeds south to Lower California.

Courtesy of "The Condor".

NESTS OF OLIVACEOUS CORMORANTS.

123a. Violet-green Cormorant. *Phalacrocorax pelagicus.* [1]

This sub-species is found on the Pacific coast from Washington to the Aleutian Islands. Their habits and nests and eggs are the same as those of the Pelagic Cormorant, nesting on the high cliffs of the rocky islands. The eggs are the same size as those of the preceding. Data.—Sitka Sound, July 28, 1896. Nest on shelf of rock, 50 feet above surf; saucer-shaped, of seaweed and decomposed grass. Collector, Joseph Grinnell.

123b. Baird's Cormorant (should be Pelagic Cormorant). *Phalacrocorax pelagicus.*

This variety breeds on the Pacific coast from Washington south to Mexico. They nest on the Farallones, but in smaller numbers than the other varieties found there. Both the birds and their eggs are smaller than the preceding. Size of eggs 2.20 x 1.40.

124. Red-faced Cormorant. *Phalacrocorax urile.*

Range.—Southwest coast of Alaska, migrating to Japan in the winter.

This species differs from the Pelagic chiefly in having the forehead bare. They do not differ in their breeding habits from others of the family. That the Cormorants are expert fishermen may be seen from the fact that the Chinese tame and have them catch fish for them, placing a ring around their neck to prevent their swallowing the fish. Their nesting places are very filthy, being covered with excrement and remains of fish that are strewn around the nests. They breed in June laying three or four eggs. Size 2.50 x 1.50.

PELICANS. Family PELECANIDAE.

Pelicans are large, short legged, web footed (all four toes joined by a web) birds, the most noticeable feature of which is the long bill with its enormous pouch suspended from lower mandible. This pouch, while normally contracted, is capable of being distended to hold several quarts. It is used as a scoop in which to catch small fish. Their skin is filled with numerous air cells, making them very light and buoyant.

125. White Pelican. *Pelecanus erythrorhynchos.*

Range.—Temperate North America, breeding in the interior, from Utah and the Dakotas northward. These large birds, reaching a length of five feet, are entirely white except for the black primaries. They get their food by approaching a school of small fish and, suddenly dipping their head beneath the surface, sometimes scoop up a large number of fish at a time; after allowing the water to run out of the sides of the mouth, they proceed to swallow their catch. They nest in large communities on islands in some of the inland lakes.

Great Salt Lake, Utah, and Shoal Lake, Manitoba, furnish breeding ground for many thousands of Pelicans. They build their simple nests on the ground, making them of sticks and weeds. They generally lay two eggs, but often three or four. Size 3.45 x 2.30. Data.—Egg Island, Great Salt Lake, June 19, 1884. Two eggs. Nest a slight hollow in the ground, surrounded by a few sticks. Collector, F. E. Leonard.

---

[1] No longer recognized as a valid form.

[Chalky White.]

126. Brown Pelican. *Pelecanus occidentalis.*

Range.—Found on the South Atlantic and Gulf coasts of the United States. Brown Pelicans are about 50 inches in length; they have a blackish and grayish body and a white head and neck with a brown stripe down the back of the latter. The pouch is a dark greenish brown. This species is maritime and is not found inland. They breed in large colonies on many of the islands in the Gulf of Mexico and on Pelican Island on the east coast of Florida, in which latter place they are now protected from further depredations at the hand of eggers and gunners. Their fishing tactics differ from those of the White Pelican.

[Chalky White.]

They dive down upon the school of fish from the air and rarely miss making a good catch. Their nests are quite bulky structures made of sticks and weeds and grasses. These are generally located on the ground but occasionally in low mangroves, these latter nests being more bulky than the ground ones. They lay from two to five chalky white eggs during May and June. Size 3. x 1.90. Data.—Tampa Bay, Fla., May 29, 1894.   Three eggs. Nest in the top of a stout mangrove; made of sticks, branches and leaves. Collector, Geo. Graham.

127. California Brown Pelican (should be Brown Pelican). *Pelecanus occidentalis.*

Range.—Pacific coast from British Columbia south to the Galapagos Islands. This bird is similar to the preceding, but larger and the pouch is reddish. They breed abundantly on the Coronado Islands and southward. Their habits, nesting habits and eggs are the same as those of the Brown Pelican. Size of the three or four chalky white eggs is 3.10 x 1.95. Data.—Coronado Islands, Calif., Mar. 23, 1897. Three eggs. Nest of sticks, lined with green leaves, located on the ground. Collector, H. McConville.

FRIGATEBIRDS. Family FREGATIDAE.

128. Magnificent Frigatebird. *Fregata magnificens.*

Range.—Tropical seas, north regularly in America to the South Atlantic and Gulf coasts, casually farther.

[White.]

Man-o'-War Birds or "Frigates," as they are often called, are remarkable birds in many respects. In comparison with their weight they have the largest expanse of wing of any known bird. Weighing only about four pounds they have an extent of from seven to eight feet, their wings being extremely long and pointed. The length of the bird is about 40 inches, of which the tail comprises about 18 in., 10 inches of this being forked. They have a large bright orange gular sac, a long, hooked bill, and small slightly webbed feet. Their powers of flight combine the strength of the Albatrosses and the grace of the Terns. They are very poor swimmers and do not dive, so are forced to procure their food by preying upon the Gulls and Cormorants, forcing them to drop their fish, which the pirates catch before it reaches the water. They also feed upon flying fish, catching them in the air, whither they have been driven by their enemies in their natural element. They nest in large colonies on some of the Bahama Islands and on some of the small Florida Keys. Their nests are small frail platforms of sticks and twigs and the single egg is laid in March and April. It is white and has a smooth surface. Size 2.80 x 1.90. Data.—Key Verde, Bahamas, Mar. 6, 1889. Single egg. Nest a frail affair of sticks on a cactus. Collector, D. P. Ingraham.

DUCKS, GEESE and SWANS. Order ANSERIFORMES.
DUCKS, GEESE and SWANS. Family ANATIDAE.

The birds comprising this family are of greatly varying sizes, but all have webbed feet, and generally the bill is broader than high, and is serrated on the edges or provided with gutters to act as a strainer in assisting the birds to gather their food.

129. Common Merganser. *Mergus merganser.*

Range.—North America, breeding from the northern border of the United States northward.

The three species of Mergansers are almost exclusively fish eating birds. Therefore their flesh is unpalatable and they are known as "Fish Ducks." They are also sometimes called "Saw-bills" because of the teeth-like serration on both the upper and the under mandibles. Unlike the other species of ducks, their bills are long, slender and rounded instead of being broad and flat; it is also hooked at the tip. Like the Cormorants, they often pursue and catch fish under the water, their teeth-like bills enabling them to firmly hold their prey.

The American Mergansers,[1] Goosanders, or Sheldrakes, as they are often called, are found both on the coast and in the interior. Except in certain mountainous regions, they breed chiefly north of the United States. The male bird has no crest and the head is a beautiful green, while the female has a reddish brown crest and head, shading to white on the chin. They build their nest in hollow trees near the water. It is made of grasses, leaves and moss and is lined with feathers from the breast of the

[Creamy buff.]

female. During May, they lay from six to ten eggs of a creamy or buff color. Size 2.70 x 1.75. Data.—Gun Is., Lake Winnipeg, June 16, 1903. Eleven eggs in a nest of white down, located between two large boulders. Collector, Walter Raine.

130. Red-breasted Merganser. *Mergus serrator.*

Range.—North America, breeding from northern United States northward.

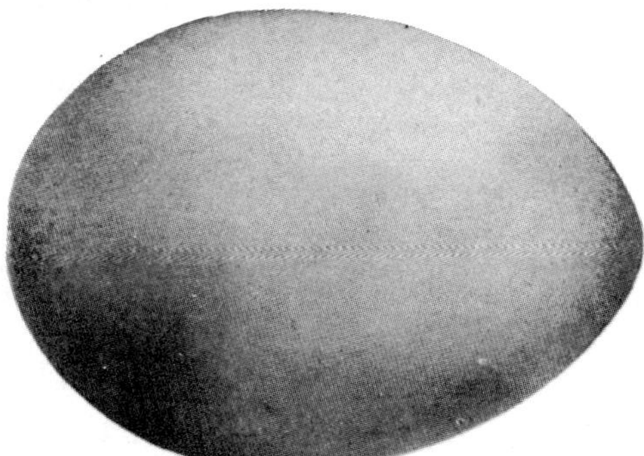

[Clear buff.]

This species is more abundant than the preceding. It is slightly smaller, being 22 inches in length, and the male is crested. Found abundantly in the United States in winter. Breeds commonly in the interior of British America and in Labrador and Newfoundland. They make their nests on the ground, near the water, concealing them under rocks or tufts of grass. The nest is made of grasses, leaves and moss and lined with feathers. They lay, generally, about ten eggs of a buffy or greenish buff color. Size 2.50 x 1.70.

Data.—Lake Manitoba, N. W. Canada. under a patch of rose bushes near shore. Two eggs in a hollow lined with down, Collector, Jos. Hamaugh.

131. Hooded Merganser. *Lophodytes cucullatus.*

Range.—North America, breeding locally throughout its range, in the interior. These are beautiful little Ducks distinguished from all others by the semi-circular, compressed crest which is black with an enclosed white area. They make their nests in hollow trees, in wooded districts near the water, lining the cavity with grasses and down. They lay ten or twelve grayish white eggs. Size 2.15 x 1.70.

[1] Now Common Merganser.

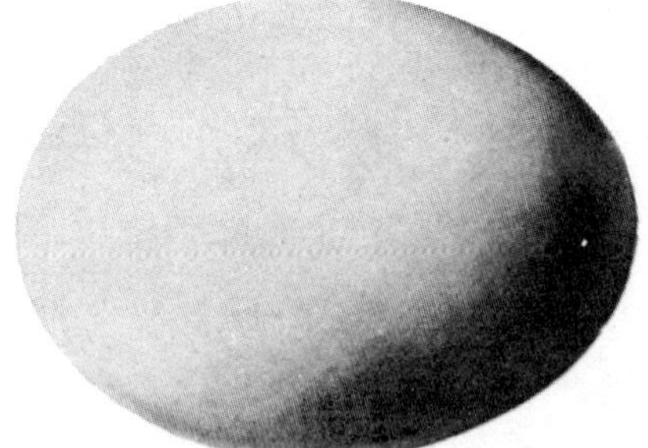

[Grayish white.]

[Lake Winnipegosis, June 16, 1902.]   Photo by Walter Raine.

NEST AND EGGS OF COMMON MERGANSER.

This species usually nest in holes in trees, but on this island they were nesting in holes under boulders.

132. Mallard. *Anas platyrhynchos.*

Range.—Northern Hemisphere, breeding in America from northern United States northward, and wintering south to Panama and the West Indies.

[Pale olive buff.]

Contrasting with the preceding Fish Ducks, the Mallards are regarded as one of the most esteemed table birds. They feed on mollusks and marine insects which they generally reach by tipping in shallow water. They nest in many localities in the United States but more abundantly north of our borders. They nest in fields in close proximity to ponds or lakes, placing their nests of grasses and feathers in the tall grass. In May and June they lay from six to ten eggs of a buffy or olive green color. Size 2.25 x 1.25. Data.—San Diego, California, May 19, 1897. Nest made of grass, lined with down, placed on the edge of a field near a pond.

133a. Black Duck. *Anas rubripes.*

Range.—Eastern North America, breeding from the middle portions north to the Hudson Bay territory and Labrador.

Throughout their breeding region, one or more pairs of these ducks nest in nearly every favorable locality. Their nests are placed on the ground in marshes, swamps or fields bordering a pond or lake, the nest being concealed in the long grass or reeds. They breed in equal abundance, either in the interior or along the sea coast; in the latter case their nests are often placed to the side of, or under an overhanging rock. It is made of weeds, grass and moss and is lined with feathers and down. They lay from six to twelve eggs during May and June; these are buff or greenish buff in color. June 3, 1893. Nest of grasses, Collector, C. K. Reed.

[Pale greenish buff.]

Size 2.30 x 1.70. Data.—Duck Is., Maine, concealed in a large tuft on water's edge.

133a. Red-legged Black Duck (should be Black Duck). *Anas rubripes.*

This new sub-species has but recently been separated from the preceding. Their range is more northerly than the common Black Duck. The birds are larger and are especially distinguished by the red legs whereas the common species has legs of a greenish brown color.

The habits, nesting habits and eggs will not vary from those of the common species. The plumage of the male bird, like that of the preceding, does not differ from that of the female, both being similar but darker than the female Mallard.

134. Florida Duck (should be Mottled Duck). *Anas fulvigula.*

Range.—Florida and the Gulf coast of the Mississippi.
This is a similar, lighter colored, locally distributed race of the foregoing.
The most noticeable difference in plumage between this and the Black Duck is
the absence of marking on the chin. The habits are the same, and the eggs,
which are deposited in April, are similar to those of the Black Duck, but
smaller. Size 2.15 x 1.60.

134a. Mottled Duck. *Anas fulvigula.*

Range.—Gulf coast of Texas and up the Mississippi Valley to Kansas.
The habits of this bird differ in no way from the preceding ones. The six to
ten eggs are greenish buff in color. Size 2.15 x 1.55.

135. Gadwall. *Anas strepera.*

[Creamy buff.]

Range.—Northern Hemisphere,
breeding in America, chiefly in the
United States and north to Manitoba,
chiefly in the interior.
South in winter to the Gulf. The
males of these birds may be identified
by the white speculum and the chestnut wing coverts. Gadwalls nest on
the ground among the reeds of marshes
or in the long grass of bordering fields;
they make little or no nest but line
the cavity with down from their
breasts. They lay from seven to
twelve eggs of a creamy buff color.
Size 2.10 x 1.60. Data.—Benson Co.,
North Dakota, June 19, 1898. Eight
eggs. Nest on the ground among rank grass on a low island in Devils Lake.
Made of weeds lined with down. Collector, E. S. Rolfe.

136. Eurasian Widgeon. *Mareca penelope.*

Range.—Northern Hemisphere,
breeding in America, only in the
Aleutian Islands; rare or accidental
in other parts of the country.
The Eurasian Widgeon is similar
in build and plumage to the following species, except that the whole
head, with the exception of the white
crown, is chestnut. They build
their nests in the rushes, making
them of reeds and grass and lining
them with feathers. They lay from
six to ten light buff colored eggs.
Size 2.20 x 1.50.

[Pale buff.]

137. American Widgeon.   *Mareca americana.*

Range.—North America, breeding in the interior from Texas north to Hudson Bay.

[Creamy white.]

The Baldpate (so-called because of the white crown) or American Widgeon is a handsomely marked bird and is regarded as a great table delicacy. The male birds cannot be mistaken for any other species because of the white crown, wing coverts and underparts and the broad green stripe, back of the eye. They breed locally in many parts of the country, building their nests of grass and weeds, neatly lined with feathers, on the ground in marshes. They lay from six to twelve creamy eggs. Size 2.15 x 1.50. Data.—Lac Aux Morts, North Dakota. Eight eggs. Nest of grass and down on ground in a grassy meadow. Collector, E. S. Bryant.

138. Eurasian Teal.   *Anas crecca.*

An Old World species that is casually found on both coasts of America.[1]

139. Green-winged Teal.   *Anas carolinensis.*

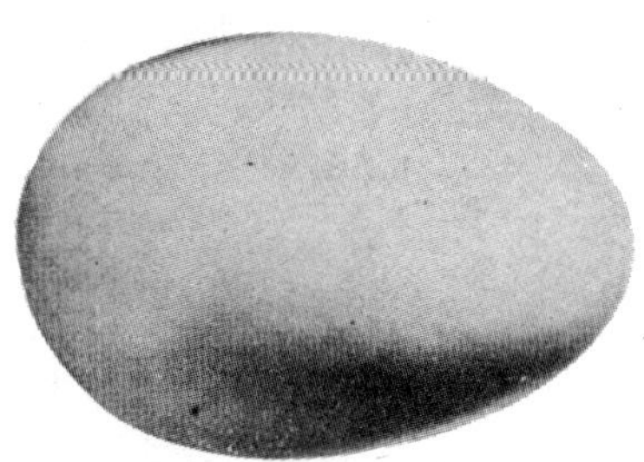

[Buff.]

Range.—Whole of North America, breeding chiefly north of the United States.

A small, handsome species, the male of which can readily be identified by the reddish brown head and neck, with the large green patch behind each ear ; length fourteen inches. Green-winged Teals are our smallest representative of the Duck family. They are eagerly sought by sportsmen, both because of their beauty and the excellence of their flesh. They are among the most common of Ducks in the interior, where they nest generally in tufts of grass along ponds, lakes or brooks. Nest of grass and weeds, lined with down from the bird. Eggs buffy, four to ten in number. Size 1.85 x 1.25.

140. Blue-winged Teal.   *Anas discors.*

Range.—North America, breeding from northern United States northward ; rare on the Pacific coast.[2]

Another small species, known by the blue wing coverts and the white crescent in front of eye. They nest in the same localities with the preceding species, placing their nest of grass and weeds on the ground in meadows near water. Eggs buffy white. Six to twelve in number. Size 1.90 x 1.30.

[1] Resident in Aleutians.

[2] Breeds over most of U.S.

141. Cinnamon Teal. *Anas cyanoptera.*

Range.—Western United States, chiefly west of the Rocky Mountains. Casually east to Texas, Illinois and British Columbia.

The Cinnamon Teal is another small Duck, marked by the uniform rich chestnut plumage and light blue wing coverts. The speculum is green. The nesting habits are the same as those of the other Teals, the nests being placed on the ground in marshes or fields near water. Their nests are closely woven of grass and weeds and lined with down and feathers from the breast of the bird. The eggs are pale buff and number from six to fourteen. Size 1.85 x 1.35.

141.1. Ruddy Sheld-Duck. *Cascara ferruginea.*

This is an Old World species that has accidentally occurred in Greenland.

142. Northern Shoveler. *Spatula clypeata.*

Range.—Whole of North America, breeding in the interior from Texas northward.

This strikingly marked Duck is twenty inches in length, has a green head and speculum, blue wing coverts and chestnut belly. The bill is long and broad at the tip. It makes its nest on the ground in marshy places, of grass, weeds and feathers. Six to ten eggs constitute a complete set. They are greenish or leaden gray color. Size 2.10 x 1.50. Data.—Graham's Is., N. Dakota, May 28, 1899. Nest of dead weed stems and grass, lined with down. Ten eggs. Collector, E. S. Bryant.

[Lead gray.]

143. Pintail. *Anas acuta.*

Range.—Northern Hemisphere, breeding in North America from northern United States northward, wintering south to Panama. This species, which is also known as the Sprig-tail, is very common in the United States in the spring and fall migrations. It is about thirty inches long, its length depending upon the development of the tail feathers, the central ones of which are long and pointed. They breed casually in many sections of the United States, but in abundance from Manitoba to the Arctic Ocean. They nest near the water, laying from six to twelve eggs of dull olive color. Size 2.20 x 1.50. Data.—Graham's Is., Devil's Lake, N. Dakota, June 15, 1900. Ten eggs. Nest on the ground, of weeds, lined with down. Colony breeding. Collector, E. S. Bryant.

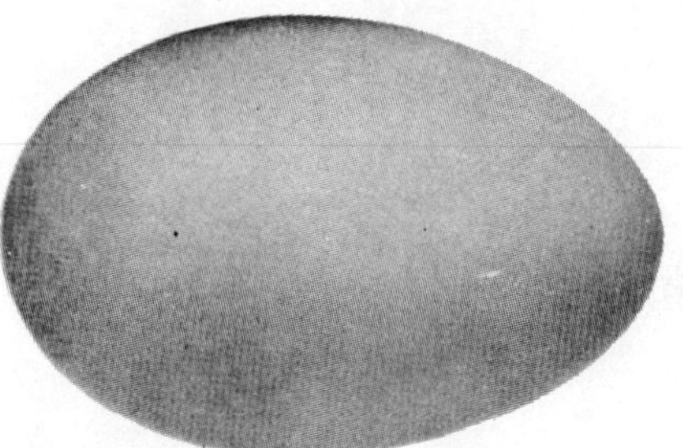

[Dull olive gray.]

Photo by P. B. Peabody.

NEST AND EGGS OF GADWALL.

Photo by P. B. Peabody.

NEST AND EGGS OF PINTAIL.

144. Wood Duck. *Aix sponsa.*

Range.—Temperate North America breeding from Labrador and British Columbia south to Florida.

[Rich buff.]

Bridal Duck is a name often given to this, the most beautiful of all Ducks. They are beautifully marked, have a large crest, and are iridescent with all colors of the rainbow. They frequent wooded country near ponds and lakes, feeding on water insects and mollusks in the coves. They build their nests in hollow trees and stumps, often at quite a distance from the water. When the young are a few days old, they slide, scramble, or flutter down the tree trunk to the ground below, and are led to the water. The nest is made of twigs, weeds and grass, and warmly lined with down. The eggs are a buff color and number eight to fifteen. Size 2. x 1.5.

145. Rufous-crested Duck. *Netta rufina.* [1]

A European species; a single specimen taken on Long Island in 1872.

146. Redhead. *Aythya americana.*

Range.—North America at large, breeding from northern United States northward, chiefly in the interior.

A bird commonly seen in the markets where it is often sold as the following species because of their similarity. The nests are placed on the ground in marshes or sloughs, and are made of grasses, lined with feathers. Eggs from six to fourteen in number, of a buffy white color. Size 2.40 x 1.70.

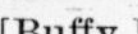

[Buffy.]

147. Canvasback. *Aythya valisineria.*

Range.—Whole of North America, breeding chiefly in the interior from the United States to the Arctic Ocean.

A noted table bird, especially in the south where it feeds on wild celery. Can be distinguished from the Redhead by its darker head, lighter back, and gradually sloping bill. They nest abundantly in Manitoba, their habits being the same as the preceding. They lay from six to ten eggs of a darker shade than the Redheads. Size 2.40 x 1.70. Data.—Haunted Lake, N. Alberta, June 12, 1897. Ten eggs. Nest of reeds in a heavy reed bed out in the lake. Collector, Walter Raine.

[1] Not recorded from North America.

148. Greater Scaup. *Aythya marila.*

Range.—North America, breeding from North Dakota northward, chiefly in the interior; south in winter to Central America.

[Pale greenish gray.]

This and the following species are widely known as "Blue-bills" owing to the slaty blue color of that member. Their plumage is black and white, somewhat similar in pattern to that of the Redhead, but darker, and the whole head is black. They nest in marshes about many of the ponds and lakes in the interior of British America. The nest is made of marsh grasses and lined with feathers. The six to ten eggs are pale grayish or greenish gray. Size 2.50 x 1.70. Data.— Saltcoats Marshes, N. W. Canada, June 15, 1901. Ten eggs. Nest in the grass; a depression lined with down and dried grasses. Collector, Walter Raine.

149. Lesser Scaup. *Aythya affinis.*

Range.—North America, breeding from North Dakota and British Columbia northward; winters south to Central America.

This Duck is distinguished from the preceding, chiefly by its size which is about two inches less, or 17 inches in length. The nesting habits are the same as those of the Greater Scaup and the eggs are similar but smaller. Size 2.25 x 1.55. Data.—Northern Assiniboia, June 10, 1901. Ten eggs on grass and down at the edge of a lagoon. Collector, Walter Raine.

150. Ring-necked Duck. *Aythya collaris.*

Range.—North America, breeding in the interior, from North Dakota and Washington northward. Winters from Maryland on the east and British Columbia on the west to Central America.

Similar to the Lesser Scaup in size and plumage, except that it has a narrow chestnut collar around the neck, the back is black instead of barred with white, and the speculum is gray instead of white. The habits and nesting habits of the Ring-neck do not differ from those of the other Scaups. They lay from six to twelve eggs. Size 2.25 x 1.60. Data.—Cape Bathurst, N. W. T., June 18, 1901. Ten eggs in a slight hollow in the moss, lined with down. Collector, Captain Bodfish.

151. Common Goldeneye. *Bucephala clangula.*

Range.—North America, breeding both on the coast and in the interior, from the northern border of the United States northward to the Arctic Ocean.

These are handsome Ducks known as "Whistlers" from the noise of their wings when flying, and "Great-heads" because of the puffy crest. The head is greenish with a large round white spot in front of, and a little below, the eye. The rest of the plumage is black and white. This species nests in hollow trees near the water, lining the cavity with grass, moss and leaves, and lining the nest with down from their breasts. In May and June they lay from six to ten eggs of a grayish green color. Size 2.30 x 1.70.

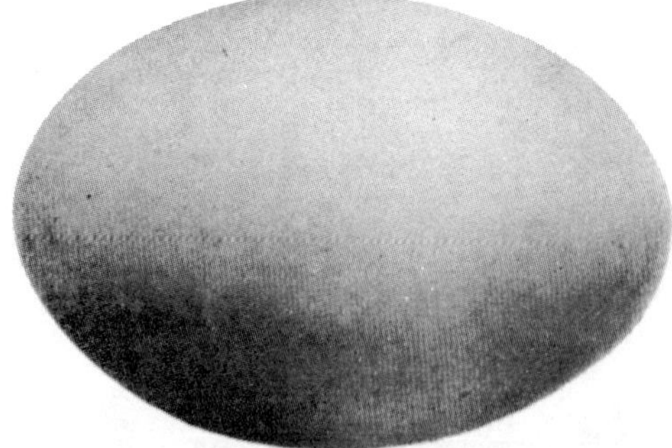

[Grayish green.]

152. Barrow's Goldeneye. *Bucephala islandica.*

Range.—Northern North America, breeding north of the United States except from the mountainous portions of Colorado northward.

This Goldeneye differs from the preceding chiefly in the shape of the white spot before the eye, which in this species is in the form of a crescent. The size is the same, about 20 inches in length. The reflections on the head are purplish rather than greenish as in the preceding. The nesting habits are the same, they building in hollow trees near water. The six to ten eggs are not different from the preceding. Size 2.30 x 1.65. Data.—Alfusa, Iceland, June 30, 1900. Seven eggs. Nest of grass and down in a box attached to a tree by an islander.

153. Bufflehead. *Bucephala albeola.*

Range. — North America, breeding from United States northward. Winters south to Mexico.

Gunners know this handsome little duck by the names of "Butter-ball," and "Dipper," a name also given to Grebes. It is quite similar, but smaller (15 in. long), to the Common Goldeneye but has a large white patch on the back of the head, from eye to eye. It is an active bird and, like the two preceding, is capable of diving to a great depth to get its food. Its nesting habits are like the preceding. Eggs eight to fourteen. Size 2. x 1.40. Data.— Alberta, Canada, June 6, 1899. Seven eggs. Nest in hole in tree stump, lined with down. Collector, Dr. George.

[Dull buff.]

154. Oldsquaw. *Clangula hyemalis.*

Range.—Northern Hemisphere, breeding in the Arctic regions; south in winter to New Jersey and Illinois.

[Buff.]

The Long-tailed Duck, as it is called, is especially noticeable because the breeding plumage of the male differs markedly from that in the winter. In summer their general plumage is blackish brown, with a white patch around the eye, and white belly. In winter they are largely white. The central tail feathers are much lengthened. They breed abundantly in Greenland, Alaska and the Hudson Bay Territory, placing their nests of grasses and weeds on the ground near the water. It is generally concealed in the long grass. The eggs number from six to twelve. Size 2. x 1.50. Data.—N. Iceland, June 10, 1900. Nest on ground, lined with down. Collector, S. H. Wallis.

From "Among the Waterfowl."

Photo by Herbert K. Job.

A MARSH SCENE.

"A splendid slough over a mile long, with clumps of reeds growing out of the water." The large clump at the left sheltered a Canvasback's nest; that near the center a Coot's and that on the right a Pied-billed Grebe's,

155. Harlequin Duck. *Histrionicus histrionicus.*

Range.—Northern Hemisphere in America, breeding from Newfoundland and the Rocky Mountains in Colorado, northward. South in winter to California and New England.

[Greenish buff.]

A beautiful and most gorgeous bird, not in colors, but in the oddity of the markings, the colors only including black, white, gray and chestnut. Either sex can be recognized by the small short bill. They breed mostly in single pairs along swiftly running streams, placing their nest, which is woven of weeds and grasses, in the ground near the water. It is also claimed that they sometimes nest in hollow trees. They lay from five to eight eggs, yellowish or greenish buff in color. Size 2.30 x 1.60. Data.—Peel River, Alaska, June 13, 1898. Seven eggs in a hollow in river bank, lined with down. Collector, C. E. Whittaker.

156. Labrador Duck. *Camptorhynchus labradorium.*

This fine bird, whose range was from Labrador to New Jersey in the winter, has probably been extinct since 1875 when the last authentic capture was made. It is a strange fact that a bird of this character should have been completely exterminated, even though they were often sold in the markets. Only forty-one specimens are known to be preserved at present and nothing is known in regard to their nesting habits or eggs.

157. Steller's Eider. *Polysticta stelleri.*

Range.—Arctic regions in America, chiefly on the Aleutian Islands and northwest coast of Alaska.

A very beautiful species eighteen inches long ; head white, washed with greenish on the forehead and nape; chin, throat, neck, back, tail and crissum, black; underparts chestnut ; wing coverts white, the long scapulars black and white. It breeds on the rocky coasts and islands of Bering Sea. The six to nine eggs are pale olive green in color. Size 2.25 x 1.60. Data.—Admiralty Bay, Alaska, June 22, 1898. Nest on a hummock of the tundra, near a small pool, lined with grass and down. Collector, E. A. McIlhenny.

[Pale olive green.]

158. Spectacled Eider. *Lampronetta fischeri.*

Range.—Coast of Alaska from the Aleutians to Point Barrow.

Like the rest of the true Eiders, this species is black beneath and mostly white above. The head is largely washed with sea green, leaving a large patch of white, narrowly bordered by black around each eye, thus resembling a pair of spectacles. The nests are made of grass and seaweed and lined with down ; they are placed on the ground in clumps of grass or beneath overhanging stones. The five to nine eggs are an olive drab or greenish color. Size 2.70 x 1.85. Data. —Point Barrow, Alaska, June 15, 1898. Six eggs. Nest of moss and down in a hollow in dry tundra. Collector, E. A. McIlhenny.

159.   Northern Eider (should be Common Eider).   *Somateria mollissima.*

Range.—North Atlantic coast, breeding from Labrador to Greenland and wintering south to New England.

A large Duck similar to the next species, but with the base of the bill differing, as noted in the description of the following species, and with a more northerly distribution. The nesting habits are the same as those of the other Eiders. Six to ten eggs generally of a greenish drab color. Size 3. x 2.

160.   American Eider (should be Common Eider).   *Somateria mollissima.*

Range.—Atlantic coast, breeding from Maine to Labrador and wintering south to Delaware.

This species differs from the preceding only in the fleshy part of the base of the bill, which extends back on each side of the forehead, it being broad and rounded in this species and narrow and pointed in the Northern or Greenland Eider. This species, but m o r e especially the Northern Eider, are the ones chiefly used for the eider-down of commerce. The preceding species is often semi-domesticated in Greenland, the people protecting them a n d encouraging them to nest in the neighborhood. They make their nests of seaweed and grass and warmly line it with down from their breast; this down is continually added to the nest during incubation until there is a considerable amount in each nest, averaging about an ounce in weight. The birds are among the strongest of the sea ducks and get their food in very deep water. Their flesh is not good eating. Their eggs number from five to ten and are greenish drab. Size 3. x 2.

[Greenish drab.]

161.   Pacific Eider (should be Common Eider).   *Somateria mollissima.*

Range.—North Pacific from the Aleutian Islands northward, and east to Great Slave Lake.

This bird is, in plumage, like the Northern Eider, except that it has a black V-shaped mark on the throat. They nest sparingly on the Aleutian Islands, but in great numbers farther north on the coast about Point Barrow. Their habits, nests and eggs are precisely the same as those of the eastern forms. Their eggs number from five to ten and are of olive greenish color. Size 3. x 2. Data.—Cape Smythe, Alaska, June 8, 1900. Eight eggs. Nest a hollow in the moss, lined with grass and down.

162. King Eider. *Somateria spectabilis.*

Range.—Northern Hemisphere, breeding in America from Labrador to Greenland and the Arctic Ocean; south in winter to the New England States and rarely farther on the eastern side, and to the Aleutians on the Pacific; also casually to the Great Lakes in the interior.

A handsome and very different species from any of the foregoing, having the crown ashy blue, and the long scapulars black instead of white. It also has a broad V-shaped mark on the throat. Like all the other Eiders, the female is mottled brown and black, the different species being very difficult to separate. The nests are sunk in the ground and lined with down. Eggs number from six to ten. Size 2.80 x 1.80. Data.—Point Barrow, Alaska, July 5, 1898. Five eggs. Nest a hollow in the moss on tundra lined with moss and down. Collector, E. A. McIlhenny.

163. Black Scoter. *Oidemia nigra.*

Range.—Northern North America, breeding from Labrador, the Hudson Bay region and the Aleutian Islands northward; winters south to Virginia, the Great Lakes and California.

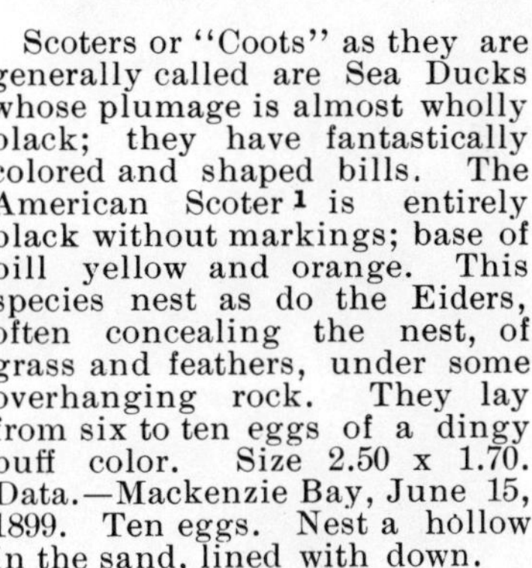

[Buff.]

Scoters or "Coots" as they are generally called are Sea Ducks whose plumage is almost wholly black; they have fantastically colored and shaped bills. The American Scoter [1] is entirely black without markings; base of bill yellow and orange. This species nest as do the Eiders, often concealing the nest, of grass and feathers, under some overhanging rock. They lay from six to ten eggs of a dingy buff color. Size 2.50 x 1.70. Data.—Mackenzie Bay, June 15, 1899. Ten eggs. Nest a hollow in the sand, lined with down.

164. Velvet Scoter. *Melanitta fusca.*

An Old World species that has accidentally occurred in Greenland.

165. White-winged Scoter. *Melanitta deglandi.*

Range.—Abundant in North America, breeding from Labrador, North Dakota and British Columbia, northward. Wintering south to the Middle States, southern Illinois and southern California.

The largest of the Scoters, length 22 inches, distinguished by a large white speculum on the wing, also a white comet extending from under the eye backwards. It also has a yellow eye. Like the other Scoters, this species often feeds in very deep water. They are strong, active diving birds, and are also strong on the wing, generally flying close to the surface of the water. Their flesh is not regarded as good eating, although they are often sold for that purpose. They nest on the ground, generally in long grass or under low bushes making a coarse nest of grasses, and sometimes twigs, lined with feathers. They lay from five to eight eggs of a pale buff color. Size 2.75 x 1.85.

[1] Now Black Scoter.

166. Surf Scoter. *Melanitta perspicillata.*

Range.—Northern North America, breeding north of the United States boundary, and wintering south to Virginia and southern California.

The male of this species is entirely black, except for the white patches on the forehead and nape, and the vari-colored bill of black, white, pink and yellow. They nest either along the coast or in the interior, building a nest lined with down, in the marsh grass bordering small ponds. They lay from five to eight buffy cream colored eggs. Size 2.40 x 1.70. The females of all the Scoters are a dingy brownish color, but show the characteristic marking of the species, although the white is generally dull or sometimes mottled. Data.—Mackenzie River, June 25, 1894. Six eggs in a nest of down on an island in the river.

167. Ruddy Duck. *Oxyura jamaicensis.*

Range.—Whole of North America, breeding chiefly north of the United States border, except locally on the Pacific coast. Winters along the Gulf and through Mexico and Central America.[1]

[Grayish white.]

This peculiar species may always be recognized by the brownish or chestnut upper parts, blackish crown, white cheeks and silvery white underparts. The bill is very stout and broad at the end, and the tail feathers are stiff and pointed, like those of a Cormorant. They build their nests in low marshy places, either placing them on the ground near the water or in the rushes over it. Their nests are made of rushes and grasses, sometimes lined and sometimes not, with down from the parents' breast. The eggs number from six to twelve and are grayish in color. Size 2.40 x 1.75. Data.— Northern Assiniboia, Canada, June 6, 1901. Eight eggs. Nest made of aquatic grasses, lined with down. Built in a tuft of rushes in a marsh. Collector, Walter Raine.

168. Masked Duck. *Oxyura dominica.*

This is a tropical species which is resident in Mexico, Central America and in the West Indies. It occurs in Mexico north to the lower Rio Grande Valley and has in three known instances strayed to northeastern United States. The general plumage is a rusty chestnut, mottled with blackish, it has a black face and throat, and white wing bars.

[1] Breeds in northeast and north-central states.

169. Lesser Snow Goose (should be Blue Goose). *Chen caerulescens.*

[Grayish white.]

Range.—North America west of the Mississippi Valley, breeding in northern Alaska and the Mackenzie River district.

This smaller species of the Snow Goose nests on islands in rivers along the Arctic coast. The nest is a depression in the ground, lined with grasses and occasionally down. They lay from four to eight eggs of a buffy or yellowish white color. Size 2.75 x 1.75.[1]

169a. Greater Snow Goose (should be Blue Goose). *Chen caerulescens.*

Range.—Eastern North America, breeding in the Arctic regions and wintering chiefly on the Atlantic coast, south to Cuba.

This bird is like the preceding; except in size; about thirty-six inches, instead of twenty-six inches in length as is the lesser variety. The entire plumage is white except for the black primaries. They construct their nests of grasses on the ground the same as the preceding variety. The eggs number from five to eight and are cream colored. Size 3.40 x 2.40.

169.1. Blue Goose. *Chen caerulescens.*

Range.—North America, principally in the interior, breeding from Hudson Bay northward and wintering along the Gulf coast.

This species may always be recognized by the entirely white head and neck, the body being grayish or bluish gray. They nest on the ground as do the other geese laying from four to eight eggs of a brownish buff color. Size 2.50 x 1.75. Data.—Cape Bathurst, Arctic coast, June 29, 1899. Four eggs laid in a depression lined with grass, on an island. Collected with the parent birds by the Esquimaux.

170. Ross' Goose. *Chen rossii.*

Range.—This beautiful species,which is similar in plumage to the large Snow Goose, is but twenty-one inches in length. It breeds in the extreme north, and in winter is found in the western part of the United States as far south as the Gulf of Mexico. Their nesting habits and eggs probably do not differ from others in the family except in the matter of size.[2]

171. White-fronted Goose. *Anser albifrons.*

This European species is exactly like the American except that it is said to average a trifle smaller. It is occasionally found in Greenland.

[1] The "Lesser Snow Goose" has been conclusively shown to be a color phase of the Blue Goose, both types occurring in mixed populations in the Arctic. The "Greater Snow Goose" is a monomorphic, allopatric subspecies.

[2] Winters only in California.

171a. American White-fronted Goose (should be White-fronted Goose).
Anser albifrons.

Range.—Whole of North America, breeding in the Arctic regions and wintering south to the Gulf coast; not common on the Atlantic coast during migrations.

These birds may be recognized by their mottled plumage, dark head and white forehead. This species is more abundant than any of the preceding and nests in large colonies along the Arctic coast and in Alaska. Their nests are made of dried grasses, feathers and down and are placed on the ground in a slight depression. From four to nine eggs are laid; these have a dull buff ground. Size 3.00 x 2.05. Data.—Island in delta of Mackenzie River, June 10, 1899. Four eggs. Nest of grass and feathers on the ground on a small island. Collector, Rev. I. O. Stringer.

171.1. Bean Goose. *Anser fabalis.*

This European species is casually found in Greenland.[1] It is one of the most common of the Old World species.

172. Canada Goose. *Branta canadensis.*

Range.—The whole of North America, breeding from northern United States northward, and wintering in the southern parts of the United States.

This species is the most widely known of American Geese and is the most abundant. Its familiar "honk" has long been regarded as the signal of the coming of spring, and the familiar V-shaped formation in which the flocks migrate is always an object of interest to everyone. With the exception of in northern Dakota and Minnesota, they breed chiefly north of the United States. They construct quite a large nest of weeds and grass, and warmly line it with down and feathers. They lay from four to nine eggs of a buff or drab color. Size about 3.50 x 2.50. Data.—Ellingsars Lake, North Dakota, May 18, 1896. Five eggs. Nest on an island in the lake, constructed of weeds and trash, and lined with a few feathers. Collector, Edwin S. Bryant.

[Buffy drab.]

[1] Breeds in eastern Greenland.

Photo by P. B. Peabody.

NEST AND EGGS OF CANADA GOOSE.

172a.   Hutchins' Goose (should be Canada Goose).   *Branta canadensis.*

This sub-species is like the preceding except that it is smaller, thirty inches in length. It is a western variety, breeding in Alaska and along the Arctic coast and wintering to southern California. Its breeding habits, nests and eggs are the same as the common goose except that the eggs are smaller. Size 3.00 x 2.05.

172b.   White-cheeked Goose (should be Canada Goose).   *Branta canadensis.*

This bird is about the same size as the Canada Goose and the plumage is very similar except that the black sometimes extends on the throat, thereby isolating the white cheek patches, and there is a white collar below the black of the neck. It is a western species. breeding in Alaska and wintering along the Pacific coast of the United States. Its nesting habits and eggs are the same as those of the Canada Goose except that the latter are a trifle smaller.

172c.   Cackling Goose (should be Canada Goose).   *Branta canadensis.*

This bird is really a miniature of the Canada Goose, being but twenty-four inches in length. It breeds in Alaska and along the Arctic coast and migrates into the western parts of the United States. They are abundant birds in their breeding range, where they place their nests upon the shores of ponds, or on islands in inland rivers or lakes. The nests are made of weeds and grasses, lined with down. The eggs, which are buff colored, number from four to nine and are laid during June and July. Size 2.90 x 1.95.

173a. Brant.   *Branta bernicla.*

Range.—Eastern North America, breeding in the Arctic regions and wintering in the United States east of the Mississippi.

The Brant resembles a small Canada Goose, except that the black of the neck extends on the breast, and only the throat is white. They are one of the favorite game birds and thousands are shot every fall and spring. Their nests and eggs are the same as the next species.

174.   Black Brant.   *Branta nigricans.*

Range. — Western North America, breeding in Alaska and wintering on the Pacific coast of the United States. Rare east of the Mississippi.

This species is like the last except that the black extends on the under parts. This species nests very abundantly in northern Alaska, laying their eggs in a depression in the ground, lined with down. Favorite locations are the many small islets in ponds and small lakes. They lay from four to eight grayish colored eggs. Size 2.80 x 1.75. Data.—Cape Bathurst, North

[Grayish.]

West Territory, June 22, 1901. Seven eggs in a small hollow in the ground, lined with down. Collector, Capt. H. H. Bodfish.

175. Barnacle Goose. *Branta leucopsis.*

This Old World species occurs frequently in Greenland and very rarely is found on the mainland of this continent.

176. Emperor Goose. *Philacte canagica.*

Range.—Alaska, south in winter casually to California.

This handsome species is twenty-six inches in length; it may be known from the mottled or "scaly" appearance of the body, and the white head with a black chin and throat. While not uncommon in restricted localities, this may be considered as one of the most rare of North American Geese. Their nests are built upon the ground and do not differ from those of other geese. They lay from three to seven eggs of a dull buff color. Size 3.10 x 2.15. Data.—Stuart Island, Alaska, June 16, 1900. Six eggs laid in a slight hollow in the ground, lined with a few feathers and some down. Collector, Capt. H. H. Bodfish.

177. Black-bellied Tree Duck. *Dendrocygna autumnalis.*

Range.—Tropical America, north in the Rio Grande Valley to southern Texas.

These peculiar long-legged Ducks are very abundant in southern Texas during the summer months. They build their nests in hollow trees, often quite a distance from the water. They lay their eggs upon the bottom of the cavity with only a scant lining, if any, of feathers and down. They are very prolific breeders, raising two broods in a season, each set of eggs containing from ten to twenty. These eggs are creamy or pure white. Size 2.05 x 1.50. The first set is laid during the latter part of April or early in May, and fresh eggs may be found as late as July. They are especially abundant about Brownsville and Corpus Christi, Texas. Data.—Hidalgo, Mexico, May 29, 1900. Ten eggs in a hole in an old elm tree on side of lake in big woods near town. Eight feet from the ground. Collector, F. B. Armstrong.

[White.]

178. Fulvous Tree Duck. *Dendrocygna bicolor.*

Range.—This species is tropical like the last, but the summer range is extended to cover, casually, the whole southwestern border of the United States.

This bird is long-legged like the last, but the plumage is entirely different, being of a general rusty color, including the entire under parts. The nesting habits and eggs are the same as those of the Black-bellied Duck, the white eggs being laid at the bottom of a cavity in a tree. They number from eight to (in one instance) thirty-two eggs in one nest. This species is nearly as abundant as the preceding in southern Texas.

179.   Whooper Swan.   *Olor cygnus.*

This European variety frequently is found in Greenland and, formerly, regularly bred there.   It nests in secluded swampy places in northern Europe.

180.   Whistling Swan.   *Olor columbianus.*

Range.—North America, breeding in the Arctic Circle, and wintering south to the Gulf of Mexico.

These birds, which are nearly five feet in length, are snow white with the exception of the black bill and feet.   The Whistling Swan is distinguished from the next species by the presence of a small yellow spot on either side of the bill near its base.   Their nests are made of a large mass of rubbish, weeds, grass, moss, feathers and occasionally a few sticks.   It is generally placed in a somewhat marshy place in the neighborhood of some isolated pond.   The eggs are of a greenish or brownish buff color, and number from three to six.   Size 4.00 x 2.75.   Data.—Mackenzie River.   Nest a mass of weeds, sods and grass, lined with feathers; on an island near the mouth of the river. Collector, I. O. Stringer.

[Brownish buff.]

181.   Trumpeter Swan.   *Olor buccinator.*

Range.—Interior of North America from the Gulf of Mexico northward, breeding from northern United States northward.

This is a magnificent bird, about five and one-half feet in length.   Its plumage is exactly like that of the preceding except that the bill is entirely black, and the nostril is located nearer the eye.   Their nesting habits and eggs are the same as those of the Whistling Swan.   While a few pairs may breed within the United States by far the greater number are found in the extreme north, from Hudson Bay to Alaska.   The eggs may average a trifle larger than those of the preceding species.

FLAMINGOES.   Order CICONIIFORMES (part).

FLAMINGOES.   Family PHOENICOPTERIDAE.

182.   American Flamingo. *Phoenicopterus ruber.*

Range.—Tropical and subtropical America on the Atlantic coasts, breeding in the Bahamas and West Indies; north to Florida and casually to the South Atlantic States.

These remarkable and grotesque appearing birds attain a length of about 48 inches.   The plumage varies from white to a deep rosy red.   It requires several years for them to attain the perfect adult plumage, and unlike most birds, they are in the best of plumage during the winter, the colors becoming faded as the nesting season approaches.   The birds are especially noticeable because of the crooked, hollow, scoop-shaped bill, and the extremely long legs and neck.   The feet are webbed, but more for the purpose of supporting them upon the mud flats than for use in swimming.   They nest in large colonies, one examined by Mr. Frank M. Chapman, containing upwards of two thousand nests.   The nests are usually built on a sandy point of an island; they are mounds of earth, grass and rubbish from one to two feet in height, the top being hollowed to receive the eggs.   One or two eggs are a complete set.   The shell is pale blue, but this is covered with a heavy white chalky deposit.   The eggs are laid in June and July.   Size 3.40 x 2.15.

[Chalky bluish white.]

HERONS and allies.   Order CICONIIFORMES (part).

The members of this order are wading birds, consequently they all have long legs and necks.   They have four toes, not webbed.

SPOONBILLS.   Family THRESKIORNITHIDAE (part).

183.   Roseate Spoonbill. *Ajaia ajaja.*

Range.—Tropical America, north in summer to the Gulf States.   They formerly nested in remote swamps along the whole Gulf coast, but are now confined chiefly to the Everglades in Florida.[1]

---

[1] Now breeds along entire Gulf Coast, but locally.

This bird, with its broad, flat bill, bare head, and rosy plumage with carmine epaulets and tail coverts, seems more like the fanciful creation of some artist than a real bird of flesh and blood. Its plumage and colors are strikingly clear

[Pale greenish blue.]

and beautiful. Full plumaged adult birds have very brilliant carmine shoulders and tail coverts, a saffron colored tail, and a lengthened tuft of bright rosy feathers on the foreneck. This species breed in small colonies in marshy places, often in company with herons and ibises. Their nests are rather frail platforms of sticks, located in bushes or trees, from four to fifteen feet from the ground. The eggs are laid during the latter part of May and June. They are three or four in number and have a ground color of dull white, or pale greenish blue and are quite heavily blotched with several shades of brown. Size 2.50 x 1.70.

IBISES. Family THRESKIORNITHIDAE (part).

Ibises are gracefully formed birds having a long curved bill and a bare face.

184. White Ibis. *Eudocimus albus.*

Range.—This is a tropical and sub-tropical species which is found along the Gulf coast, and north to South Carolina, west to Lower California.

These handsome birds are wholly white, with the exception of black primaries. The legs and the bare skin of the face are orange red. These birds are very abundant in most marshy localities along the Gulf coast, especially in Florida, where they nest in rookeries of thousands of individuals. Owing to their not having plumes, they have not been persecuted as have the white herons. They build their nests of sticks and grasses, in the mangroves a few feet above the water. In other localities they build their nests entirely of dead rushes, attaching them to the standing ones a foot

[Grayish.]

or more above the surface of the water. They are quite substantially made and deeply cupped, very different from the nests of the Herons. Their eggs are from three to five in number, vary from grayish ash to pale greenish or bluish in color, blotched with light brown. Size 2.25 x 1.60. The nesting season is during May and June. Data.—Tampa Bay, Fla., June 4, 1895. 3 eggs. Nest of sticks and a few weeds in small bushes on an island. Collector, Fred Doane.

185. Scarlet Ibis. *Eudocimus ruber.*

Range.—Occasionally, but not recently met with in the southern states. Their habitat is in tropical America, they being especially abundant along the Orinoco River in northern South America.

Full plumaged adults of this species are wholly bright scarlet, except for the primaries, which are black. Their nests are built in impenetrable thickets, rushes or mangroves, the nests being constructed like those of the White Ibis. The eggs, too, are very similar to those of the preceding species, but both the ground color and the markings average brighter. While still common in some localities, the species is gradually becoming less abundant, chiefly because of the demand for their feathers for use in fly-tying.

[Pale greenish blue.]

186. Glossy Ibis. *Plegadis falcinellus.*

Range.—This tropical and sub-tropical species is chiefly found in the Old World. It is occasionally found in southeastern United States where it sometimes breeds. Its habits, nesting habits and eggs are just the same as the next species.[1]

187. White-faced Ibis. *Plegadis chihi.*

Range.—A sub-tropical species found in the southwestern parts of the United States, rarely found east of the Mississippi.

[Greenish blue.]

This species differs from the Glossy Ibis in having the feathers on the front of the head white, the rest of the plumage is a dull brownish chestnut, with greenish reflections on the back. As these birds are not in demand commercially, their numbers have not decreased, and thousands of them breed in colonies in southern Texas. They build a substantial nest of reeds and rushes woven about the upright canes, close to the surface of the water. Their eggs are laid during May, and number from three to four. They are easily distinguished from those of the Herons, being of a deeper greenish blue color and averaging more elongate. Size 1.95 x 1.35.

Data.—Corpus Christi, Texas, May 26, 1899. Four eggs. Nest of twigs and rushes in growing rushes on side of river. Collector, F. B. Armstrong.

[1] Breeds north to L.I., N.Y. along the coast.

STORKS. Family CICONIIDAE.

188. Wood Stork. *Mycteria americana.*

[White.]

Range. — A sub-tropical species which is resident along the Gulf coast and which strays casually north to New England and Colorado.

This peculiar member of the Stork family has the whole head and part of the neck bare and covered with numerous scales ; the bill is large, long and heavy; the plumage is white, except for the black primaries and tail. It is a large bird about four feet in length. They are quite abundant in swamps along the Gulf coast, where they place their nests, which are platforms of sticks, in trees and bushes over the water. They lay three eggs which are white, and have a rough surface. Size 2.75 x 1.75.

189. Jabiru. *Jabiru mycteria.*

This large bird, which is the only true Stork that claims a place in our avifauna, is a native of South and Central America, wandering north, casually to Texas. Their nests are large platforms of sticks in very high trees.[1]

HERONS and allies. Family ARDEIDAE.

Herons and Bitterns are long legged waders, having straight, pointed bills, and with the head feathered, except for the lores.

190. American Bittern. *Botaurus lentiginosus.*

Range.—United States and southern British provinces, breeding in the northern half of the United States and wintering in the southern portion.

This species, with its mottled rusty brownish plumage, is one of the best known of the Heron family. It is known locally by a great many names, nearly all of which have reference to the "booming" or "pumping" sound made during the mating season. They build their nests in swampy or marshy places, placing them on the ground, frequently on a tussock, entirely surrounded by water. The nest proper is only a few grasses twisted about to form a lining to the hollow. They lay from three to five eggs of brownish drab. Size 1.95 x 1.50.

[Brownish drab.]

---

[1] Not recorded from North America.

Photo by P. B. Peabody.

NEST AND EGGS OF AMERICAN BITTERN.

They do not breed in colonies, generally but one or two pairs nesting in one marsh. Data.—Worcester, Mass., June 3, 1897. Four eggs laid in a grass lined hollow in middle of a hummock of earth and grass, in middle of marsh. Collector, James Jackson.

191. Least Bittern. *Ixobrychus exilis.*

Range.—Common throughout the United States, especially in the eastern parts, and in the southern British provinces.

[Pale bluish white.]

This small variety of Bittern is very common in the southern portions of the United States, but less so and locally distributed in the northern portions of its range. They are very quiet and sly birds, and their presence is often unsuspected when they are really quite abundant. When approached, they will remain perfectly quiet, with the body erect and the head and neck pointed skyward, in which position their yellowish brown plumage strongly resembles the rushes among which they are found. Their nests are made of strips of rushes woven about upright stalks, generally over water. They lay from three to five eggs of a pale bluish white color. Size 1.20 x .90. Data.—Avery's Island, La., May 1, 1896. Four eggs. Nest of strips of rushes woven together to form a platform and fastened to saw grass growing on the bank of a stream. Collector, E. A. McIlhenny.

191.1. Cory's Least Bittern (should be Least Bittern). *Ixobrychus exilis.*

This rare species, of which about twenty specimens are known, is probably resident in Florida, wandering north in the summer, specimens having been taken in Ontario, Canada, and in several localities in eastern United States. It is very different from the Least Bittern, having a more uniform chestnut coloration, especially on the under parts. It is twelve inches in length. Mr. C. W. Crandall has a set of five eggs of this species, taken on the Caloosahatchee River, Fla., April 15, 1891, by S. B. Ladd. Nest was made of grasses and rushes placed in the cane two feet above the water.[1]

192. Great White Heron (should be Great Blue Heron). *Ardea herodias.*

Range.—This species occurs in the United States regularly, only in the southern parts of Florida. It is a resident of the West Indies.[2]

This large white Heron is about the same size as the Great Blue Heron; it has none of the slender plumes found on the smaller White Herons. These birds are not uncommon in southern Florida, especially on the Keys, where they build their nests in company with Great Blue Herons. Their nesting habits and eggs

[1] Simply a now-extinct color phase.

[2] The "Great White Heron" has been shown to be only a color phase of the local Great Blue, restricted to southern Florida.

are very similar to those of the Blue Heron. Size of eggs 2.25 x 1.80. **Data.—** Outside of Torch Key, Florida, June 16, 1899. Nest a platform of sticks about five feet from the ground, in a mangrove tree. Three eggs. Collector, O. Tollin.

194. Great Blue Heron. *Ardea herodias.*

Range.—Nearly the whole of North America, except the extreme north; resident south of the middle portions of the United States and migratory north of there.

This handsome Heron is about four feet in length. Its general color is a bluish gray, relieved by a black crest, primaries and patches on the sides, and a white crown. In the south they breed in large colonies, often in company with many other species. In the northern portions of their range they breed singly or in companies of under a hundred individuals. They generally place their rude platforms of sticks well up in trees, near ponds, swamps or rivers, but in the most northerly parts of their range, where trees are scarce, they often build on the ground. Unless they are disturbed, they return to the same breeding grounds, year after year. They lay from three to five eggs of a greenish blue color. Size 2.50 x 1.50. Data.—Duck Island, Maine, May 20, 1883. Three eggs. Nest of sticks and twigs, about fifteen feet from the ground. Collector, R. B. Gray.

[Pale greenish blue.]

194a. Northwest Coast Heron (should be Great Blue Heron). *Ardea herodias.*

This darker sub-species of the preceding is found along the Pacific coast, north to Sitka, Alaska. Its nests and eggs do not differ from the former species.

194b. Ward's Heron (should be Great Blue Heron). *Ardea herodias.*

This sub-species is a resident in Florida. It is a lighter variety than the common. It nests together with the Great Blue Heron and its habits are the same.

195. Gray Heron. *Ardea cinerea.*

This species is only an accidental straggler in Greenland. It is very similar to our Blue Heron and is the one which was formerly used to furnish sport for the royalty when falconry was at its height.

196. Common Egret. *Casmerodius albus.*

Range.—Resident in the southern portions of the United States, straggling northward casually to the northern parts.[1]

This is one of the beautiful Herons which have been sought by plume hunters till they are upon the verge of extermination. They are entirely white, with a long train of beautiful straight "aigrettes" flowing from the middle of the back.

---

[1] Breeds commonly north to L.I., N.Y. along the coast.

In remote localities, quite large colonies of them may still be found, but where they numbered thousands, years ago, they can be counted by dozens now. They breed in impenetrable swamps, very often in company with the following species, and also with Louisiana and Little Blue Herons, and White Ibises. Their nests are but frail platforms, generally in bushes over the water. Their usual complement of eggs numbers from three to five, four as the most common number. They are generally laid during the latter part of May, but often on account of their being disturbed, nests with eggs may be found in July. The eggs are a light bluish green in color. Size 2.25 x 1.45. Data.—Gainesville, Florida, April 14, 1894. Four eggs on a platform of sticks and grass, in a button-wood bush over six feet of water. Collector, George Graham.

[Light bluish green.]

197. Snowy Egret. *Leucophoyx thula.*

Range.—Common now only in restricted localities in the Gulf States and Mexico. [1]

This species, which is smaller than the last, being but twenty-four inches in length, is also adorned with "aigrettes," but they are beautifully recurved at the tips. Owing to the merciless slaughter to which they have been subjected, their ranks have been woefully decimated, and it is to be hoped that the remaining ones may be safely protected. Their nesting habits are the same as the last, although, of course, the eggs are smaller. Size 1.80 x 1.25.

[Light bluish green.]

198. Reddish Egret. *Dichromanassa rufescens.*

[Light greenish blue.]

Range.—In the United States, this species is confined chiefly to the Gulf States.

It is somewhat larger than the last species, the head and neck are rufous, the body is bluish gray, and the back is adorned with slender gray plumes. It also has a white phase. This Egret is very abundant along the whole Gulf coast, but especially so in Texas. Their nesting habits are identical with those of the other small Herons and Egrets. The three or four eggs are rather of a more greenish blue than the preceding. Size 1.90 x 1.45. Data.—Gainesville, Florida, April 14, 1894. Three eggs. Nest of sticks and straw in a button-wood tree, two feet above the water. Collector, George Graham.

[1] Breeds abundantly north to Cape Cod, Mass. along the coast.

199. Louisiana Heron. *Hydranassa tricolor.*

Range.—Subtropical America, north regularly to the Gulf States and casually farther.[1]

This Heron is of about the size of the Reddish Egret, but the neck is longer, more slender and dark, while the chin, throat and underparts are white. The plumes from the back are short, reaching barely to the end of the tail. They nest in large colonies in company with Egrets and Little Blue Herons, placing their nests in the mangroves, only a few feet above the water. Their nests are the same as those of the other species, a slight platform of sticks, and the three to five eggs are practically not distinguishable from those of the Snowy or Little Blue Herons. Size 1.75 x 1.35.

[Pale bluish green.]

200. Little Blue Heron. *Florida coerulea.*

Range.—South Atlantic and Gulf coasts, north casually to New England and Manitoba; west to Kansas and Nebraska.[2]

[Pale bluish green.]

A smaller species than the preceding, length 22 inches, plumage a uniform slaty blue changing to purplish red on the head and neck. They also have a white phase, but always show traces of the slaty blue, especially on the primaries. Young birds are always white. They breed in immense rookeries during April and May. Their nesting habits and eggs are very similar to the last species, although the eggs average a trifle smaller. Size 1.75 x 1.25. Data.—Avery's Island, Louisiana, April 21, 1896. 5 eggs. Nest a flat and frail platform of twigs in a Mimosa tree growing in floating turf, over deep water in a large swamp. Collector, E. A. McIlhenny.

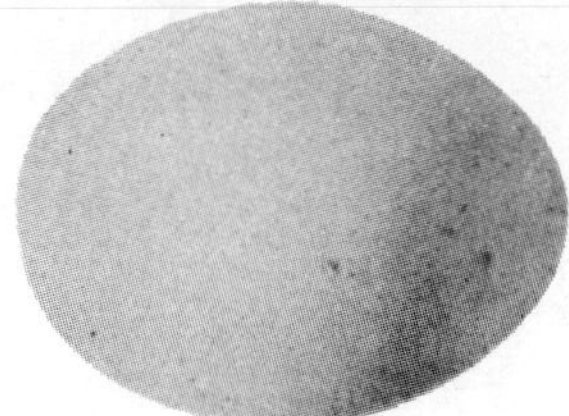

201. Green Heron. *Butorides virescens.*

Range.—Temperate and subtropical America, breeding north to the British Provinces.

This is the smallest of our Herons, and is well known all over the country. Sometimes they breed in numbers in rookeries, in company with the larger Herons, but in most sections of the country they will be found nesting, one or two pairs together, along the border of some swamp or stream. They have a greater diversity of building sites than do any of the other Herons, and frequently nest a long ways from water. Their nests may be found in alders, birches or even apple trees. It is the usual Heron type of platform,

[Light bluish green.]

---

[1] Breeds regularly north to New Jersey along the coast.

[2] Breeds regularly north to L.I., N.Y. along the coast.

upon which the three to six eggs are laid. They are a pale greenish blue in color, and measure 1.45 x 1.10. Data.—Avery's Island, Louisiana, April 10, 1894. 5 eggs on a platform of twigs placed in a willow tree growing on the edge of a pond. Collected by E. A. McIlhenny.

201a.   Frazar's Green Heron (should be Green Heron).   *Butorides virescens.*

A darker variety found in Lower California; nesting the same as the common species.

201b.   Anthony's Green Heron (should be Green Heron).   *Butorides virescens.*

A lighter, desert form found in the arid portions of the interior of southwestern United States and Mexico.

NEST AND EGGS OF GREEN HERON.

202.   Black-crowned Night Heron.   *Nycticorax nycticorax.*

Range.—North America from southern British Provinces, southward; winters along the Gulf coast and beyond.

A well-known bird, often called "quawk" from the sound of its note frequently heard in the evening. While, in some localities, only a few pairs of these birds are found nesting together, most of them gather together into large colonies during the breeding season. In New England they generally select a remote pine grove as their breeding grounds. If not disturbed they will return to this same place each year. Their nests are built of sticks and lined with small twigs, and are placed well up towards the tops of the trees.

Frequently several nests will be found in the same tree, and I have counted as many as fifty nests in view at the same time. In large swamps in the south they generally nest at a low elevation, while in the marshes of Wisconsin and Minnesota, large colonies of them nest on the ground, making their nest of rushes. Like all Heronries, those of this species have a nauseating odor, from the remains of decayed fish, etc., which are strewn around the bases of the trees. Their eggs number from three to five and are of a pale bluish green color. Size 2.00 x 1.40. Data.—Uxbridge, Mass., May 30, 1898.

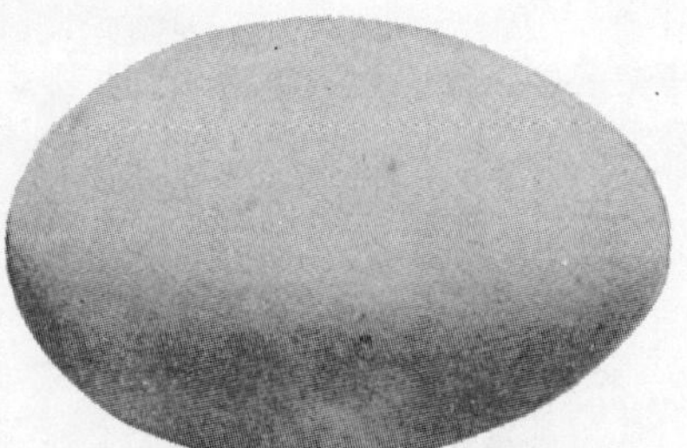
[Pale bluish green.]

4 eggs. Nest of sticks, about thirty feet up in a pine tree. Many other nests. Collector, H. A. Smith.

203. Yellow-crowned Night Heron. *Nyctanassa violacea.*

Range.—Subtropical America, breeding along the Gulf coast and to Lower California; casually farther north, to Illinois and South Carolina.[1]

A handsome grayish colored species, with long lanceolate plumes on the back, and two or three fine white plumes from the back of the head, like those of the Black-crowned species. Its black head, with tawny white crown and ear coverts, renders it unmistakable. This species nests in colonies or by pairs, like the preceding, and very often in company with other Herons. They lay from three to six eggs, very similar in size, shape and color to those of the Black-crowned Heron.

CRANES, RAILS and allies. Order GRUIFORMES.

CRANES. Family GRUIDAE.

Cranes are large, long-legged, long-necked birds, somewhat resembling Herons. Their structure and mode of living partake more of the nature of the Rails, however. They are found upon the prairies, where, besides shell fish from the ponds, they feed largely upon grasshoppers, worms, etc.

204. Whooping Crane. *Grus americana.*

Range.—Interior of North America, breeding from about the latitude of Iowa northward to the Arctic regions; winters in the Gulf states and southward.[2]

The Whooping Crane is the largest of the family in America, measuring 50 inches or more in length. The plumage of the adults is pure white, with black primaries. The bare parts of the head and face are carmine. It is a very locally distributed species, in some sections being practically unknown, while in a neighboring locality it may be rated as common. They are very shy birds and are not easily obtained. They nest either upon the solid earth or in marshy places over the water. In either case the nest is a very bulky mass of grass and weeds from two to three feet in diameter and raised perhaps a foot above the ground. They lay two eggs of a brownish buff color, irregularly blotched with brown, and with fainter marking of gray. Size 3.75 x 2.50. Data.—Torkton, northern Assiniboia, northwest Canada. Nest a mass of marsh hay, three feet in diameter, on the prairie. The birds seen, but very wary. Collector, Cowbry Brown.

[1] Breeds regularly north to Cape Cod, Mass. along the coast.

[2] Only about 36 individuals still in existence.

[Brownish buff.]

205.   Little Brown Crane (should be Sandhill Crane).   *Grus canadensis.*

Range.—North America in the interior, breeding from Hudson Bay and southern Alaska north to the Arctic coast; south in winter to Mexico.

This uniform gray colored Crane differs from the next species only in size, being about three feet in length, while the Sandhill averages three and one-half feet. The eggs cannot be distinguished with any certainty.

[Buff.]

Photo by Walter Raine.

NEST AND EGGS OF SANDHILL CRANE.
[Saltcoats Marshes, Assiniboia, June 6, 1901.]

206. Sandhill Crane. *Grus canadensis.*

Range.—Temperate North America, breeding from the Gulf States, locally north to the southern parts of the British Provinces.[1]

This is the most common and the most southerly distributed member of the family. In some sections of Florida and Texas it is regarded as abundant. They nest in marshy places near secluded ponds. The nests are masses of grass, weeds and roots, generally placed in marshes and entirely surrounded by water. The two eggs are similar to those of the Whooping Crane, but the ground color is lighter. The eggs of the two species cannot always, with certainty, be distinguished. Size 3.75 x 2.40. Data.—Carman, Manitoba, May 31, 1903. 2 eggs. Nest on a knoll in a marsh, hidden by dead rushes and weeds; a flat loose structure of broken rushes and reeds. Collector, Chris Forge.

[Buff.]

LIMPKINS. Family ARAMIDAE.

207. Limpkin. *Aramus guarauna.*

[Buffy white.]

Range.—This bird is a native of the West Indies and Central America, but occurs regularly north to the southern portions of Florida.

This strange bird is the only member of its family found in the United States. It may be likened to a large Rail or a small Crane, being, apparently, a connecting link between the two. It is about two feet in length, and the plumage is mottled brownish and white. It lives in the marshes, from whence, until late at night, emanate its strange cries, which are likened to those of a child in distress. They nest in the most impenetrable parts of swamps, building their nests of

[1] Breeds locally along Gulf; then a gap until extreme north-central U.S. and Canada.

rushes, grass and weeds, in tangled masses of vines a few feet above the ground or water. They lay from three to eight eggs having a ground color of buff or grayish white and blotched with light brown. Their coloration is very similar to those of the Cranes. Size 2.30 x 1.70. They nest in April and May.

RAILS and allies. Family RALLIDAE.

Members of this family are almost exclusively frequenters of marshes, where they lead a shy, retiring life and are more often heard than seen.

208. King Rail. *Rallus elegans.*

Range.—Fresh water marshes of eastern United States from New England and the Dakotas, southward. Very abundant on the South Atlantic coast, in the inland marshes.

This is one of the largest of the Rails (17 inches in length) and may be known by the richness of its plumage, the breast and wing coverts being a rich cinnamon color. It is almost exclusively a fresh water species and is very rarely found around a salt water marsh. Its nest is built on the ground, in a tuft of grass or a clump of rushes; it is made of grass and weeds woven about the upright stalks. They lay from five to twelve eggs having a cream colored ground, sparingly speckled with brown and lilac. Size 1.60 x 1.20. Data.— Clark County, Missouri, June 6, 1893. 10 eggs.

[Cream color.]

Nest composed of reed stalks; a slightly concave mass 8 inches across, and only two inches above the water, in a clump of reeds. Collector, Ed. S. Currier.

209. Belding's Rail (should be Clapper Rail). *Rallus longirostris.*

Range.—Lower California and the islands in the Gulf.

This is a locally confined species, very similar to the preceding but darker and with the flank bars narrower. Its nesting or eggs will not differ from those of the King Rail.

210. California Clapper Rail (should be Clapper Rail). *Rallus longirostris.*

Range.—Salt marshes of the Pacific coast of the United States.

[Light buff.]

This species is like a dull colored King Rail, with reference to the markings of the back, or a bright colored Clapper Rail, as it has a cinnamon colored breast. It is an abundant species in nearly all the salt marshes along the coast. They make their nests on the higher parts of the marsh, where it is comparatively dry, building them of grass and strips of rushes. They lay from four to nine eggs of a light buff color, boldly spotted with brown, and with fainter markings of lilac. Size 1.75 x 1.25. Data.— Palo Alto, Cal., May 1, 1899. Nest of marsh grass under a small bush on bank of slough. Collector, Ernest Adams.

211. Clapper Rail. *Rallus longirostris.*

Range.—Salt marshes of the Atlantic coast from southern New England southward.

[Buff.]

A grayish colored Rail, about the size of, and with the markings similar to those of the King Rail. It is as exclusively a salt water species as the King Rail is a fresh water one. With the possible exception of the Carolina or Sora Rail, this is the most abundant of all the Rails, hundreds nesting in a single marsh on the South Atlantic coast. Their nests are built of rushes and weeds, and are placed on the ground either in the tall grass bordering the marshes or attached to the rushes in the midst of the marsh. The nesting season commences during April and continues through May. They lay from six to fourteen eggs, of a buff color spotted irregularly with brown and gray. Size 1.70 x 1.20.

211a. Louisiana Clapper Rail (should be Clapper Rail). *Rallus longirostris.*

The habitation of this subspecies is limited to the coast of Louisiana. It is very similar to the preceding but is said to be brighter in plumage.

211b. Scott's Clapper Rail (should be Clapper Rail). *Rallus longirostris.*

Range.—Western coast of Florida.
This bird is also similar to 211 but is much darker and brighter.

211c. Wayne's Clapper Rail (should be Clapper Rail). *Rallus longirostris.*

Range.—South Atlantic coast from North Carolina to Florida.
This subspecies is a little darker than 211, being about midway between that species and 211b. The nests and eggs of any of these subspecies cannot be distinguished from those of the common Clapper Rail.

211.2. Caribbean Clapper Rail (should be Clapper Rail). *Rallus longirostris.*

Range.—West Indies and east coast of Mexico, north to southern Texas.
This species is similar to the Clapper, but has a shorter and relatively stouter bill.

212. Virginia Rail. *Rallus limicola.*

Range.—Temperate North America, breeding from the Middle States and California, northward to British Columbia and Labrador, and wintering along the Gulf coast; most abundant in the east.

A small Rail, 9 inches long, very similar in markings and coloration to the King Rail. It is found chiefly in fresh water swamps, where it builds its nests in tufts of rushes. The eggs number from six to fourteen, and are creamy white, or white, specked with reddish brown. Size 1.25 x .90. Data.—Fighting Island, Detroit River, Michigan, May 30, 1894. Nest made of marsh grass, in rushes, 6 inches above the water. Collector, E. Leroy King.

[Creamy white.]

213. Spotted Crake. *Porzana porzana.*

This common European species is casually found in Greenland. It breeds in large numbers throughout temperate Europe, nesting as do the American Rails.

214. Sora. *Porzana carolina.*

Range.—Temperate North America, breeding from the southern parts of the British possessions, south to the Gulf coast.

[Bright buff.]

This abundant species of Rail may be readily known by its small, size, about 8 inches long, and the black face and throat of the adult. These are the "Railbirds" or "Ortolans" which are annually slaughtered by thousands, for sport and marketing, during their fall migration. It is only because of the large families that they rear, that they are able to withstand this yearly decimation in their ranks. They nest either in salt or fresh water marshes, making a rude structure of grass, weeds and strips of rushes, on the ground, generally concealed in a tuft of grass in a tangled swamp or marsh. During May, they lay from six to sixteen eggs of a bright, buffy gray color, spotted with reddish brown and lavender. Size 1.25 x .90.

215. Yellow Rail. *Coturnicops noveboracensis.*

Range.—Locally distributed in temperate North America, from New England and Nova Scotia, to California and British Columbia; south to the Gulf States in winter.

[Rich buff.]

This is a very handsome species, with plumage of glossy brown, yellowish buff, black and white; length 7 inches. They are very shy and secretive, and are probably more common than generally supposed. Their nesting habits are the same as those of the preceding. Their eggs are of a rich buff color, speckled in the form of a wreath about the large end, with reddish brown. They are relatively narrower than those of other Rails. Size 1.10 x .80. Data.—Benson Co., North Dakota, June 4, 1901. Set of ten eggs collected by Rev. P. B. Peabody. This fine set is in the collection of Mr. John Lewis Childs.

216. Black Rail. *Laterallus jamaicensis.*

Range.—Temperate North America, breeding from northern United States southward.

Smallest of the Rails; 5 inches in length. A dark slaty colored bird with white specks, and a patch of dark chestnut on the fore back. This diminutive species is very hard to find because of its retiring habits, but according to Mr. Brewster it may be located by the clicking sound of its song.

Their nests are woven of strips of rushes or grasses, and are well "cupped" to receive the eggs. They are on the ground on the border of, or in, marshy places. Mr. Childs has a fine set of eight eggs, taken by Arthur T. Wayne, at Mt. Pleasant, S. C., June 10, 1903. The nest was located in an oat field. The eggs have a creamy white ground, and are specked all over with reddish brown. Size 1.03 x .75.

216.1. Farallone Black Rail (should be Black Rail). *Laterallus jamaicensis.*

Known only from a single specimen, which is slightly smaller than 216 and without the white specks on the back.

217. Corn Crake. *Crex crex.*

This European Rail is casually found in Greenland and along the Atlantic coast of North America. It is the most abundant of European Rails and is found breeding in marshes, meadows and along streams.

218. Purple Gallinule. *Porphyrula martinica.*

Range.—South Atlantic and Gulf States; casually north in eastern United States to Massachusetts and Ohio.

[Pale Buff.]

A very handsome bird with purplish head, neck and under parts, and a greenish back. Like all the Gallinules and Coots, this species has a scaly crown plate. An abundant breeding species in the southern parts of its range. Its nests are made of rushes or grasses woven together and either attached to living rushes or placed in tufts of grass. They lay from six to ten eggs of a creamy or pale buff color sparingly blotched with chestnut. Size 1.60 x 1.15. Data.—Avery's Island, Louisiana, May 7, 1896. 10 eggs. Nest of dry rushes, woven to standing ones growing around an "alligator hole" in a marsh. Collector, E. A. McIlhenny.

219. Common Gallinule. *Gallinula chloropus.*

Range.—Temperate North America, from New England, Manitoba and California, southward.

A grayish colored bird of similar size to the last (13 inches long), with flanks streaked with white, and with the bill and crown plate reddish. They nest in colonies in marshes and swamps, building their nests like those of the Purple Gallinule. The eggs, too, are similar, but larger and slightly duller. Size 1.75 x 1.20. Data.—Montezuma marshes, Florida, June 6, 1894. 11 eggs. Nest of dead flags, floating in two feet of water. Collector, Robert Warwick.

[Pale buff.]

220. European Coot. *Fulica atra.*

A European species very similar to the next, and only casually found in Greenland. Nesting the same as our species.

221. American Coot. *Fulica americana.*

Range.—Whole of temperate North America, from the southern parts of the British Provinces, southward; very common in suitable localities throughout its range.

[Grayish.]

The Coot bears some resemblance to the Florida Gallinule,[1] but is somewhat larger, its bill is white with a blackish band about the middle, and each toe has a scalloped web. They inhabit the same marshes and sloughs that are used by the Rails and Gallinules as nesting places, and they have the same retiring habits, skulking through the grass to avoid observation, rather than flying. Their nests are either floating piles of decayed vegetation, or are built of dead rushes in clumps of rushes on the banks. They generally build in large colonies. The eggs number from six to sixteen and have a grayish ground color, finely specked all over the surface with blackish. Size 1.80 x 1.30.

SHOREBIRDS and allies.   Order CHARADRIIFORMES (part).

PHALAROPES.   Family PHALAROPODIDAE.

Phalaropes are small Plover-like birds, but with lobate webbed feet, similar to those of the Grebes and Coots.

222. Red Phalarope. *Phalaropus fulicarius.*

Range.—Northern Hemisphere, breeding in the far north, and migrating to the middle portions of the United States, chiefly on the coasts.

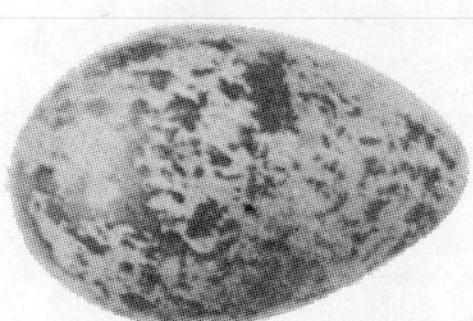

[Greenish buff].

The Red Phalarope during the breeding season has the underparts wholly reddish brown; they are very rarely seen in the United States in this dress, however, for it is early changed for a suit of plain gray and white. This species has a much stouter bill than the two following; it is about nine inches in length. All the Phalaropes are good swimmers, and this species, especially, is often found in large flocks off the coast, floating on the surface of the water; they feed largely upon small marine insects. Nests in hollows on the ground, lined with a few grasses. The eggs are three or four in number, generally of a greenish buff color, spotted and blotched with brown and blackish. Data.—Myvates, Iceland, June 19, 1897. Collector, C. Jefferys.

[1] Now Common Gallinule.

Photo by P. B. Peabody.

NEST AND EGGS OF WILSON'S PHALAROPE.

NEST AND EGGS OF AMERICAN WOODCOCK.

223.   Northern Phalarope.   *Lobipes lobatus.*

Range.—Northern Hemisphere, breeding in the northern parts of the British Provinces.

This is the smallest of the Phalaropes, being about 8 inches long; in summer it has a chestnut band across the breast and on the side of the neck.   Its habits and nesting habits vary but little from those of the Red Phalarope, although its distribution is a little more southerly, and it is not as exclusively maritime as the preceding species.   It is found on both coasts of the United States, but more common on the Pacific side, during the fall and spring, when going to or returning from its winter quarters in the tropics.   Their eggs cannot, with certainty, be distinguished from the preceding species.

[Greenish buff.]

224.   Wilson's Phalarope.   *Steganopus tricolor.*

Range.—Interior of temperate North America, breeding from the latitude of Iowa, northward, and wintering south of the United States.

This is the most handsome species of the family, being of a very graceful form, of a grayish and white color, with a broad black stripe through the eye and down the neck, where it fades insensibly into a rich chestnut color.   It is an exclusively American species and is rarely found near the coast.   It builds its nest generally in a tuft of grass, the nests also being of grass.   The eggs are of a brownish or greenish buff color, spotted and blotched with black and brown.   Size 1.30 x .90.

[Brownish buff.]

Data.—Larimore, N. D., May 30, 1897.   Nest a shallow depression, scratched in the sand, under a tuft of grass on an island.   Collector, T. F. Eastgate.

AVOCETS and STILTS.   Family RECURVIROSTRIDAE.

225.   American Avocet.   *Recurvirostra americana.*

Range.—Western North America, breeding north to Northwest Territory.

The Avocet can be known from any other bird by its up-curved bill, light plumage, webbed feet and large size (length about 17 inches).   These waders are quite numerous in suitable localities throughout the west, constructing their nests in the grass, bordering marshy places.   The nest is simply a lining of grass in a hollow in the ground.   They lay three or four eggs of a dark greenish or brownish buff color, boldly marked with brown and black.   Size 1.90 x 1.30.   Data.— Rush Lake, Assiniboia.   4 eggs laid in a depression in the sand, lined with dry weeds.   Many birds nesting in the colony.

[Greenish buff.]

226. Black-necked Stilt. *Himantopus mexicanus.*

Range.—Like the last, this species is rarely found east of the Mississippi, but is very abundant in the United States west of that river.

[Greenish buff.]

A black and white wader, with extremely long red legs; otherwise a gracefully formed bird. It breeds in large colonies anywhere in its range, making its nests of weeds and sometimes a few twigs, on the ground beside of, or in the marshes. Their eggs number three or four and are brownish or greenish buff with numerous markings of brownish black, these markings being somewhat lengthened and mostly running lengthwise of the shell. They nest during April in the southern parts of their range and through May and June in the northern. Size of eggs 1.80 x 1.25. Data.—Freshwater Lake, southern California, June 5, 1891. 4 eggs laid on a mud flat near the water's edge; no nest. Collector, Evan Davis.

SANDPIPERS and allies. Family SCOLOPACIDAE.

Members of this family are long-legged waders, of either large or small size, and found either about streams or ponds in the interior or along the coasts. They feed upon small shell fish, or insects which they get usually by probing in the soft mud.

227. Eurasian Woodcock. *Scolopax rusticola.*

This European bird is similar to the American Woodcock, but is larger and is barred beneath. Their habits are the same as those of our species.

228. American Woodcock. *Philohela minor.*

Range.—Eastern North America, north to the British Provinces, breeding throughout its range.

This is one of the most eagerly sought game birds of the east. Their flight is very rapid and erratic, and accompanied by a peculiar whistling sound made by the rapid motion of the wings; it requires a skillful marksman to bring them down. They frequent boggy places, especially "runs" lined with alders, where they bore in the soft ground for worms and grubs. Their eggs are laid upon the bare ground among the leaves and sticks; they are of about the color of dead leaves, as is also the bird, making it quite difficult to discover their nests. They lay three or four eggs of a buffy color, with yellowish brown spots. Size 1.50 x 1.15.

[Buffy gray.]

Photo from life by C. A. Reed.

AMERICAN WOODCOCK ON HER NEST.

229. English Snipe (should be Common Snipe). *Capella gallinago.*

A common species in Europe; of casual or accidental appearance in Greenland. The bird does not differ essentially from our Snipe and its habits are the same.

230. Wilson's Snipe (should be Common Snipe). *Capella gallinago.*

Range.—North America, breeding from northern United States northward; winters along the Gulf States and to California, and southward.

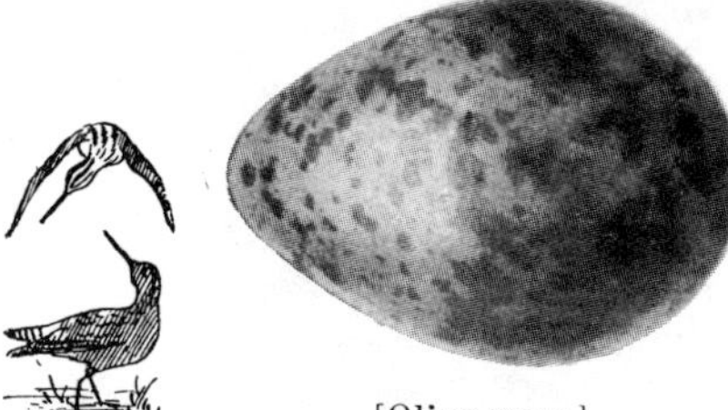

[Olive gray.]

Another favorite game bird, but one which requires skill to hunt successfully. Of about the same size as the Woodcock (11 inches long.) This species, to a great extent,frequents the same haunts used by Woodcock, but is especially fond of open marshy meadows, with winding brooks. Their nests are depressions in grassy banks, generally unlined; the three or four eggs have an olive gray color and are strongly marked with blackish brown. Size 1.50 x 1.10. Data.—Lake Winnipegosis, Manitoba. June 10, 1903. Nest in a hollow on a tuft of marsh grass, the four eggs having their points together. Collector, Walter Raine.

230.1. Great Snipe. *Capella media.*

A European species, only American as having accidentally occurred at Hudson Bay; similar in appearance to the preceding species.[1]

231. Short-billed Dowitcher. *Limnodromus griseus.*

Range.—North America, most abundant in the eastern parts; breeds in the extreme north, and winters from the Gulf States to northern South America.

This species is commonly known as "Red-breasted Snipe" in late spring and summer because of the rich rusty red coloration of the underparts, and as "Gray-back" in winter because of its general grayish color at that season. They are very common along the Atlantic coast during the Spring migration; they can be easily identified by their very long bills, which are over two inches in length and nearly one quarter the length of the whole bird. They nest during June, placing their three or four eggs in a slight hollow, which may or may not be lined with dried grass or leaves. The eggs have a greenish or brownish buff color

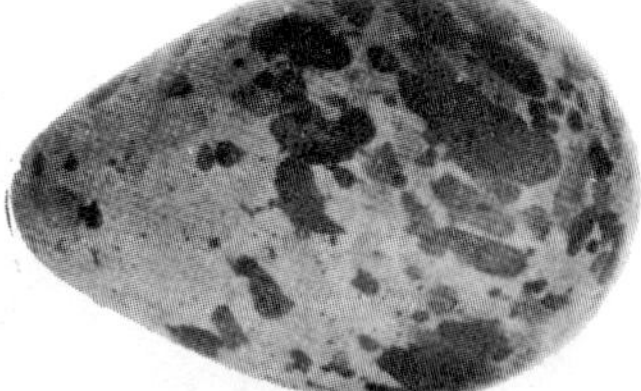

[Greenish buff.]

and are boldly marked with dark brown. They do not differ greatly from those of the Snipe. Data.—McKenzie River, June 27, 1900. 4 eggs in a hollow in the grass, lined with dead grass. Collector, Walter Raine.

[1] Not recorded from North America.

232. Long-billed Dowitcher. *Limnodromus scolopaceus.*

Range.—Whole of North America, but not common on the Atlantic coast; breeds in the Arctic regions and migrates chiefly through the central and western parts of the United States to Mexico.

This bird is practically the same as the last, but is a trifle larger and the bill averages about a half inch longer. They are very numerous in their breeding haunts, and, during their migrations, fly in large compact flocks. They are not very timid, and consequently fall an easy prey to the gunners. Their nesting habits and eggs are the same as the last species, except that the eggs may average a trifle larger. Size 1.75 x 1.15. Data.—Norton Is., Alaska, June, 1900. Nest a small hollow in the dry ground. 4 eggs. Collector, Capt. H. H. Bodfish.

[Greenish buff.]

233. Stilt Sandpiper. *Micropalama himantopus.*

Range.—North America, east of the Rocky Mountains; breeds in the Arctic regions and winters from the Gulf States southward.

In the summer, these birds may be known by the reddish coloration of the underparts, which are numerously barred; they are smaller than the preceding, length about 8 inches. Their nesting habits are the same as those of the majority of the members of the family. The three or four eggs are buffy or grayish, and are blotched and spotted with shades of brown. Size 1.40 x 1.00.

234. Red Knot. *Calidris canutus.*

Range.—Arctic regions in summer; south through the United States, chiefly on the Atlantic coast, to South America.

Of about the same size as the Dowitchers, length 10.5 inches, but with a much shorter bill. In summer the entire under parts are a uniform reddish chestnut color. They are known to breed in Arctic America, from Point Barrow and Hudson Bay, northward, but no authentic eggs are known, at present, to exist in collections. One taken from a bird by Lieut. Greely, was a pea green color, specked with brown; size 1.10 x 1.00. As it was not fully developed, it was probably correct neither as to size nor color.

235. Purple Sandpiper. *Erolia maritima.*

Range.—Arctic regions, wintering south to the Middle States and the Great Lakes, but chiefly on the coast.

[Grayish buff.]

A grayish and blackish colored species, about 9 inches long. It nests in northern Labrador, about Hudson Bay and in Iceland. Its eggs are a grayish buff color, handsomely splashed with rich shades of brown and obscure markings of darker gray. Data.—Northern Iceland, June 7, 1897. 4 eggs. Nest a hollow in the ground among grass and weeds and lined with a few grasses. Collector, C. Jefferys.

235a. Aleutian Sandpiper (should be Rock Sandpiper).   *Erolia ptilocnemis.*

Range.—Supposed to be a resident on the coast and islands of Alaska, from the Aleutians northward.

[Grayish buff.]

A very similar species to the preceding; scarcely distinguishable. These Sandpipers, which are found in Alaska at all seasons of the year, breed during May and June. Their nesting habits are the same as those of the preceding bird and the eggs are indistinguishable. Size 1.40 x 1.00. Data.—Unalaska, Bering Sea, June 3, 1898. Nest containing four eggs, a depression in the moss, lined with grasses and bits of moss. The eggs were laid with their small ends together.

235b. Pribilof Sandpiper (should be Rock Sandpiper).   *Erolia ptilocnemis.*

Range.—Coast and islands of Bering Sea, south in winter to southern Alaska.

This bird, which is 10 inches in length, has the feathers of the upper parts edged with rusty, and the underparts light, with a distinguishing patch of black on the breast. Similar in appearance to the Red-backed Sandpiper, but not so reddish above, and the latter has the black patch on the belly. They breed commonly on the Pribilof and other islands in Bering Sea, nesting the same as other Sandpipers. Their four eggs are similar to those of the preceding but average darker. Size 1.50 x 1.05.

238.   Sharp-tailed Sandpiper.   *Erolia acuminata.*

Range.—An Asiatic species, quite abundant in Alaska in the summer; supposed to migrate south in winter, wholly on the Asiatic side of the Pacific.

A similar bird, in appearance, to the following, but slightly smaller and with the breast more ruddy. Its nesting habits probably do not differ from those of the following Sandpiper.[1]

239.   Pectoral Sandpiper.   *Erolia melanotos.*

Range.—Whole of North America, breeding in the Arctic regions, and wintering south of the United States, most abundant in the eastern parts of the United States during migrations.

This species is blackish brown above, with light brown edgings to the feathers, and white below, except the chest, which is brownish, streaked with black. A very peculiar species, having the power, during the mating season, of inflating the throat to a great extent, making a balloon-like appendage, nearly the size of the bird. They have more the habits of Snipe, than do most of the Sandpipers, frequenting grassy meadows or marshes, in preference to the seashore. Their nests are grass lined depressions, and the eggs are grayish or greenish buff, blotched with brown. Size 1.45 x 1.00. Data.—Cape Smythe, Alaska, June, 1900. 4 eggs in a hollow in the ground, lined with grass and a few leaves. Collector, H. H. Bodfish.

[1] Rare migrant in Alaska.

240. White-rumped Sandpiper. *Erolia fuscicollis.*

Range.—North America, breeding from Labrador and southern Greenland, northward and wintering from Central to southern South America; most common on the Atlantic coast.

This species is 7.5 inches in length, and has white upper tail coverts; otherwise it is marked similarly to the preceding Sandpiper. Its nesting habits are the same as those of the majority of the family, and the three or four eggs that they lay cannot be distinguished from those of the following species. Size 1.30 x .90. These are one of the most common of the beach birds along the Atlantic coast during migrations; they are very often known as Bonaparte Sandpiper.

241. Baird's Sandpiper. *Erolia bairdii.*

Range.—North America, chiefly in the interior, breeding along the Arctic coast and about Hudson Bay, and wintering south of the United States.

A very similar species to the preceding, but without the white rump. These birds are not uncommon at their breeding ground, as a rule being found nesting in the grass bordering small fresh ponds, rather than near the seashore. Their nests are hollows in the ground, generally concealed in a tuft of grass, and lined with grasses and a few leaves. They lay three or four eggs having a grayish colored ground, and marked with different shades of brown, and also with some faint markings of lilac. Size 1.30 x .90. Data.—

[Grayish.]

Peel River, Arctic America, June 18, 1898. 4 eggs, taken with the bird by an Indian. Eggs in a slight hollow on the river bank.

242. Least Sandpiper. *Erolia minutilla.*

Range.—North America, breeding from the southern parts of the British Provinces northward; winters from southern United States southward. Common in the interior and on both coasts.

[Grayish.]

This is the smallest of our Sandpipers, being under 6 inches in length. Except for size, they are similar in appearance to Baird's Sandpiper, but the back is browner. A very abundant species during migrations, being found on the seashore or in marshes, nearly always in company with other species of the family. Their nests are the same as other Sandpipers, and the eggs are grayish, thickly specked with brown. Size 1.15 x .80. Data.—Peel River, Arctic America, June 20, 1899. Nest simply a depression in the river bank, lined with grass.

242.1. Long-toed Stint. *Erolia subminuta.*

An Asiatic species accidentally found on the Alaskan shores. It is a very similar bird to the Least Sandpiper, and about the same size. As implied by its name, it has unusually long toes.

243. Dunlin. *Erolia alpina.*

A very common Sandpiper in the British Isles and in Europe, but only casually occurring as a straggler along the Atlantic coast. Very similar to the next species, but a trifle smaller. The nest and eggs do not differ from the following.

243a. Red-backed Sandpiper; American Dunlin (should be Dunlin). *Erolia alpina.*

Range.—Whole of North America, breeding from southern Greenland, Labrador, Hudson Bay and the Yukon, northward, wintering from the Gulf States southward. This handsome species is similar to the Pribilof Sandpiper, but is smaller (length eight inches), the upper parts are more reddish, the breast more heavily streaked, and it has a black patch on the belly instead of on the breast as in *ptilocnemis*. Their nesting habits are similar to others of the family; they lay three or four eggs with a brownish or greenish buff color, heavily blotched and spotted with shades of brown and chestnut. Size 1.40 x 1.00. Data.—Peel River, Arctic America, June 30, 1899. Nest a simple cavity in the ground, lined with a few grasses and three or four leaves. Collector, J. O. Stringer.

[Greenish buff.]

244. Curlew Sandpiper. *Erolia ferruginea.*

Range.—A common Old World species, but regarded as rare in eastern North America and northern Alaska.[1]

A bird of slighter build, but similar coloration to Red Knot; smaller (length eight inches) and with a slightly decurved bill. Until within recent years, eggs of these birds were rarely seen in collections, and I believe they have not yet been taken in this country, although a few pairs nest along our Arctic coast. Their eggs are very similar to those of the Red-backed Sandpiper, but average somewhat larger. Size 1.50 x 1.05. Data.—Kola, northern Lapland, June 15, 1898. 4 eggs laid in a grass lined hollow in the ground. Collector, J. Ramberg.

[Greenish buff].

245. Spoon-bill Sandpiper. *Eurynorhynchus pygmeum.*

A very rare Asiatic species, which has been taken in Kotzebue Sound, Alaska. A very peculiar bird having the end of the bill broadened and flattened into a sort of spatula. Otherwise very similar to the Least Sandpiper, but with the breast and sides of neck ruddy in summer. About 75 specimens of this rare bird are known to exist.

[1] Not known to breed in North America.

246. Semipalmated Sandpiper. *Ereunetes pusillus.*

Range.—Whole of North America, but chiefly in the eastern and central parts, breeding about the ponds and streams of Labrador and Hudson Bay, and northward. These little Sandpipers are abundant during the migrations either in marshes or on beaches. They are most often found in company with other species, such as the Spotted and Least Sandpipers. Their appearance is very similar to that of the Least Sandpipers, but they are slightly larger and the feet are partially webbed. Their eggs have a greenish buff or grayish ground color and are spotted with brownish or blackish, sometimes so heavily as to completely obscure the shell color.

[Grayish].

Size 1.20 x .80. Data.—Small island near Okak, Labrador, July 3, 1895. 2 eggs. Nest a hollow at the foot of a tuft of grass, lined with a few bits of grass and small leaves. Eggs unmistakable in this dark type. Collected for J. D. Sornberger.

247. Western Sandpiper. *Ereunetes mauri.*

[Grayish buff]

Range.—Western North America, breeding in the Arctic regions and migrating through the United States, chiefly west of the Mississippi to the Gulf States and southward.

Scarcely to be distinguished from the preceding species, but the upper parts are said to be brighter, and the bill to average a trifle longer. The nesting habits and eggs are precisely the same as those of the Semipalmated variety. Data.—Cape Prince of Wales, Alaska, June 28, 1898. Four eggs. Nest a neatly rounded hollow, sunk into a mossy hummock in marshy ground. Collector, Joseph Grinnell.

248. Sanderling. *Crocethia alba.*

Range.—Found in all parts of the Northern Hemisphere, breeding within the Arctic Circle and wintering, in North America, from California and South Carolina southward.[1]

A handsome and abundant species, found during migrations by thousands on beaches and about large bodies of water in the interior. They are one of the lightest colored of the Sandpipers, either in winter or summer plumage. In summer the upper parts are a light rusty color and black, and the whole underparts are white. Owing to their extreme northerly distribution in summer, but few of their eggs have been taken. Their nesting habits are like those of the other Sandpipers. The three or four eggs are greenish buff in color, spotted and blotched with brown. Size 1.45 x .95. Data.— Peel River, Alaska, June 18, 1897. Three eggs in a depression on the ground.

[Greenish buff].

[1] Winters from New England south.

Photo by Walter Raine.

NEST AND EGGS OF MARBLED GODWIT.

[Crescent Lake, Assiniboia, June 6, 1901.]

249. Marbled Godwit. *Limosa fedoa.*

Range.—North America, breeding, chiefly in the interior, from northern United States northward.

[Greenish buff.]

Godwits are large Plovers with long slightly upcurved bills. This species is 18 inches in length, is of a nearly uniform ruddy color and is handsomely marbled above, and barred below with black. Their eggs are laid upon the ground in the vicinity of ponds or rivers; sometimes there is no lining and again a few straws or grasses may be twisted around the depression. Their eggs number three or four and have a ground color of grayish or greenish buff, sometimes quite dark, and are blotched with dark brown. Size 2.25 x 1.60. Data.— Devil's Lake, N. D., June 10, 1895. Four eggs laid on the ground in the middle of an un-used road. Lined with a few grasses. Collector, W. F. Hill.

250. Bar-tailed Godwit. *Limosa lapponica.*

Range.—Coasts and islands of the Pacific Ocean on the Asiatic side, north in summer to Alaska.

This species is more uniform and brighter ruddy beneath than the preceding, and the back is not marbled as strongly. Even in Alaska where it breeds, it is not a common species, and it only occurs elsewhere on the Pacific coast of America casually. The nesting habits are the same, but the eggs are somewhat darker than those of the preceding, but not as dark as those of the following species. Size 2.20 x 1.45.

251. Hudsonian Godwit. *Limosa haemastica.*

Range.—North America, east of the Rocky Mountains, breeding in the Arctic regions and wintering south of the United States.

This species is apparently not as common or is more locally distributed during migrations than is the Marbled Godwit. They are more abundant in their breeding grounds and are occasionally seen in large flocks. They are smaller than the Marbled Godwit (length 18 inches) and are deep reddish brown below. They lay four eggs on the ground, in marshes or near ponds or streams, lining the hollow with weeds and dried leaves. The eggs have a dark brownish buff ground color and are blotched with brownish black. Size 2.20 x 1.40. Data.—Mackenzie River, Arctic America. Four eggs laid in a hollow in the ground. Collector, J. O. Stringer.

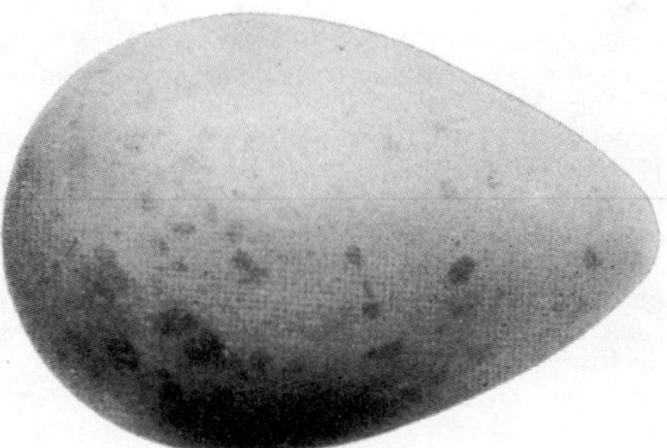

[Brownish.]

252. Black-tailed Godwit. *Limosa limosa.*

A European and Asiatic species only casually occurring in Greenland. Very similar in appearance to our Hudsonian Godwit, which is frequently called by the name of this species. The nesting habits and the eggs are precisely like those of the American bird.

253. Greenshank. *Totanus nebularia.*

A common bird in Europe and the British Isles, but only American as having been taken once in Florida. A very similar species to the following.[1]

254. Greater Yellowlegs. *Totanus melanoleucus.*

Whole of North America, nesting in the British Provinces and rarely in the northern part of the Mississippi Valley.[2]

[Grayish white.]

This and the next species are much sought by sportsmen during their migrations; they are commonly known as "Tell-tale," the present species being the "Greater Tell-tale." They are blackish above, specked with white, and below are white and, in summer, marked with arrowhead spots of black. The legs, as implied by the name of the bird, are yellow and long; length of bird, 14 inches. They nest most abundantly in localities, remote from habitations, in the interior of Canada. The eggs are generally laid on the ground, near a marsh or on the bank of a stream, with little or no lining to the nest. They are grayish white, boldly splashed with several shades of brown, and with lilac. Size 1.65 x 1.25. Data.—Whale River, Labrador, June 10, 1902. Eggs laid on the ground in an open marsh. Collector, E. H. Montgomery.

255. Lesser Yellowlegs. *Totanus flavipes.*

Range.—North America, breeding chiefly in the interior and eastern parts of Canada, and rarely in the upper Mississippi Valley.[3] This species is very similar to the preceding, but is smaller; length 10.5 inches. It is also called the "Lesser Tell-tale," a name applied because of their wariness, and because, when they fly, they warn all other species within hearing of danger. Their eggs are laid on the ground, and in similar localities to the preceding. They are three or four in number, grayish or buffy in color, and are quite heavily blotched and spotted with rich brown and grayish or lilac. Size 1.60 x 1.20. Data.—Whale River, Labrador, June 14, 1902. Four eggs laid on the ground in a large marsh. Collector, E. H. Montgomery.

[Buffy.]

[1] Not recorded from North America.

[2] Breeds only in northern Canada.

[3] Breeds only in northern Canada.

256.   Solitary Sandpiper.   *Tringa solitaria.*

Range.—Eastern North America, breeding chiefly north of the United States boundary, but apt to be found nesting in any part of its range; winters south of the United States. [1]

[Clay-colored.]

A bird with a greenish gray back, barred with white, and white below; length 8.5 inches. This species is one of the oddities among the waders. They are most always met with singly or in pairs, and are very rarely seen even in very small flocks. Their preference is for small ponds or streams in wet woods or open meadows, rather than marshes which are frequented by other species. They are occasionally seen during the nesting season, even in the southern parts of their range, and they probably breed there although their eggs are very rarely found. The eggs are clay-colored, spotted with brownish black. Data.—Simco Island, Kingston, Ontario, June 10, 1898. 5 eggs in a shallow depression on the ground, lined with a few grasses. Collector, Dr. C. K. Clarke. This set is in the collection of Mr. Childs.

256a.   Western Solitary Sandpiper (should be Solitary Sandpiper).   *Tringa solitaria.*

Range.—North America, west of the Plains; breeds in British Columbia and probably south of there, also. [2]

This bird is like the last, except that the spots on the back are buffy instead of white. Its nest and eggs will not differ in any respect from those of the eastern form.

257.   Green Sandpiper.   *Tringa ochropus.*

This species, which very closely resembles our Solitary Sandpiper, is common in the northern parts of the Old World. It has only accidentally strayed to our shores. [3]

258.   Willet.   *Catoptrophorus semipalmatus.*

Range.—Eastern United States, breeding north to the Middle States and occasionally straying to the Canadian border, especially in the Mississippi Valley. [4]

These large waders are among the most abundant of the marsh or beach birds. They breed in small companies in marshes, frequently in those which are covered with water at high tide, building a frail nest of grasses and weeds, where it will be barely out of reach of the highest water. The three or four eggs have a brownish, or sometimes greenish, buff ground color and are blotched with umber, and have fainter markings of lilac. Size 2.00 x 1.50. Data.—Sandy Bank, South Carolina, May 3, 1901. Nest on the ground, secreted in the high grass. Made of dead marsh grass, lined with finer grasses. Collector, M. T. Cleckley.

[Buff.]

---

[1] Breeds only in northern Canada.   [2] Does not breed south of British Columbia.

[3] Not recorded from North America.

[4] Breeds along Atlantic Coast to New Jersey; also in Nova Scotia.

Photo by Walter Raine.

NEST AND EGGS OF UPLAND SANDPIPER.
[Crescent Lake, Assiniboia, June 9, 1901.]

258a. Western Willet (should be Willet). *Catoptrophorus semipalmatus.*

Range.—Western North America, breeding north to Manitoba and British Columbia. Casually found on the South Atlantic coast during migrations.

A larger and paler form of the preceding species; length, 15.5 in. The nesting habits are the same, and the eggs cannot be distinguished from those of the common Willet. Data.—Refugio, Texas, May 18, 1900. 4 eggs in a grass lined depression on the bay shore flat. Collector, J. W. Preston.

259. Wandering Tattler. *Heteroscelus incanum.*

Range.—Pacific coast of North America, breeding from British Columbia northward.[1]

This is a handsome species, uniform grayish above and white below, closely barred (in summer) with blackish. During the breeding season it is found on the rugged coasts and islands of Alaska, and casually south. It breeds in the marsh grass near the shores and along the banks of streams.

260. Ruff. *Philomachus pugnax.*

A common European species, occasionally found on the Atlantic coast of North America. It is a species remarkable for its pugnacity during the mating season; in size and appearance it is about like the Bartramian Sandpiper,[2] with the exception of the "ruff" which adorns the neck and breast of the male bird.

261. Upland Sandpiper. *Bartramia longicauda.*

Range.—North America, chiefly east of the Rocky Mountains, breeding from middle United States, northward.[3]

A handsome bird, 12 inches in length, generally known as the "Upland Plover," from its habit of frequenting dry side hills, where it feeds upon grasshoppers and worms. It is a favorite bird with many sportsmen. It builds a nest of grasses, on the ground in a tuft of grass in the middle of fields. The three or four eggs have a buff ground and are blotched with yellowish brown. Size 1.75 x 1.25. Data.—Stump Lake, N. D., June 10, 1897. Nest of grass, lined with wool, under a tuft of grass left by the mower. Collector, Alf. Eastgate.

[Buff.]

262. Buff-breasted Sandpiper. *Tryngites subruficollis.*

Range.—Interior of North America, breeding from the Hudson Bay region to the Arctic coast.

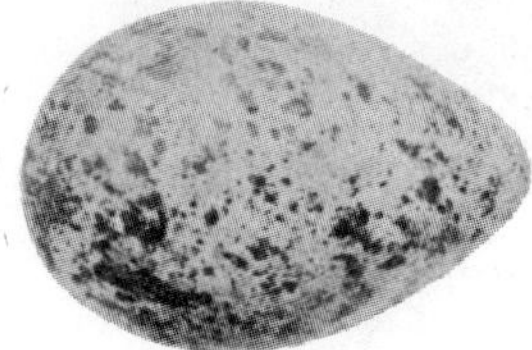

[Grayish white.]

A buffy colored species, with a peculiarly marbled back. Size 8.5 inches long. It is an upland species like the last. The nests are scantily lined depressions in the ground. The eggs have a grayish white ground and are boldly blotched with rich brown and chestnut with fainter markings of lilac. Size 1.45 x 1.05. Data.—Cape Smythe, Alaska, June 1900. 4 eggs in a hollow in dry spot on a marsh. Collector, H. H. Bodfish.

[1] Breeds only in high, inland mountains.
[2] Now Upland Sandpiper.
[3] Breeds from middle U.S. north to southern Canada.

263.   Spotted Sandpiper.   *Actitis macularia.*

Range.—Whole of North America from Hudson Bay southward, breeding throughout its range.

A small wader about 7.5 inches in length, with brownish gray upper parts, and white underparts thickly spotted with blackish, especially on the breast and flanks. This is the most abundant of all the shore birds, and its "peet-weet" is a familiar sound to every country boy. It has a peculiar habit of continually moving its tail up and down, when at rest on a stone or when running along the shore; from these characteristic actions it has received the very common names of "Teeter-tail" and "Tip-up." They build their nests on the ground near ponds, brooks or marshes, generally concealing it in a tuft of grass or weeds on the shore or in the high grass at the edge of the meadow. The eggs number

NEST AND EGGS OF SPOTTED SANDPIPER.

from three to five and are of a grayish buff color, spotted and blotched with blackish brown. The young, like those of all the shore birds, are hatched covered with down, and run about as soon as born. They are anxiously attended by the parents and at the least sign of danger, conceal themselves beneath a tuft of grass or behind a small stone, where they remain perfectly motionless until called by the old birds. The adults frequently attempt to lead an enemy away from the young by feigning a broken wing, or lameness. Size of eggs 1.35 x. 90. Data.—Parker Co., Ind., May 22, 1901. Nest about six yards from bank of creek, among weeds on a sand bar; a hollow in the sand lined with weeds. Collector, Winfield S. Catlin.

[Buff.]

264. Long-billed Curlew. *Numenius americanus.*

Range.—Breeds in the South Atlantic states and northward in the interior to Manitoba and British Columbia. [1]

[Greenish buff.]

This is the largest of the family of shore birds, having a length of about 24 inches. Its plumage is of a buffy color, much variegated above with black and brown; the bill is strongly curved downward and is from four to eight inches in length. Their nests are located on the ground in meadows or on the prairies, and three or four eggs are laid, of a buff or greenish buff color, covered with numerous spots of brownish black. Eggs of the common Curlew of Europe, have been very frequently used as belonging to this species, but the eggs of our species have a lighter and more greenish ground, and the spots are smaller and more numerous. Size, 2.50 x 1.80.

265. Hudsonian Curlew (should be Whimbrel). *Numenius phaeopus.*

Range.—Whole of North America, breeding in the Arctic regions and wintering south of the United States.

This species is smaller (length 17 inches), darker, more grayish and has a shorter bill than the preceding species. It also has white median and lateral stripes on the top of the head. The nesting habits are the same as those of the Long-billed species; the three or four eggs have a brownish buff ground color and are blotched with blackish brown. Size 2.25 x 1.60. Data. — McKenzie River, Arctic America. Nest a pile of grass, moss and weeds on an island in the river. Collector, J. O. Stringer.

[Brownish buff.]

[1] Breeds only in west-central U.S. and Canada, from Texas to British Columbia.

266.   Eskimo Curlew.   *Numenius borealis.*

Range.—Eastern North America, breeding in the Arctic regions and wintering in South America; migrating through the eastern half of the United States, more abundantly in the interior than on the coast. [1]

A still smaller species than the last (length 14 inches) and very similar to it. These birds are more abundant than the last, and nearly as numerous as the Long-billed Curlews; they are very often found, during migration, in company with other waders such as the Golden or Black-bellied Plovers. Their nests are simply hollows in the plains, lined with a few grasses, dried leaves, or moss. The three or four eggs are the same as the last for color but are smaller; size 2.00 x 1.45.

267.   Whimbrel.   *Numenius phaeopus.*

A European species casually appearing in Greenland; very similar to the Hudsonian Curlew, but with the rump white.

[Olive brown.]

This species is known as the Jack Curlew in England and Scotland, where it is very abundant, and is a favorite game bird. It breeds in the northern parts of Europe and Asia, and in the extreme north of Scotland and on the Shetland Islands. The eggs are laid in hollows in the ground on higher parts of the marshes. The three or four eggs have an olive or greenish brown color and are blotched with dark brown.   Size 2.30 x 1.60. Data—Native, Iceland, May 29, 1900. Six eggs. Nest a depression in the ground, lined with dried grass.

268.   Bristle-thighed Curlew.   *Numenius tahitiensis.*

Range.—Islands and coast on the Asiatic side of the Pacific; casually found in Alaska. A very peculiar species with many of the feathers on the flanks terminating in long bristles. [2]

PLOVERS.   Family CHARADRIIDAE (part).

Plovers are stouter built birds than those of the previous family, have larger heads, shorter necks and but three toes.

269.   Lapwing.   *Vanellus vanellus.*

An abundant European species accidentally occurring on the Atlantic coast. It may readily be recognized by its long black crest, black chin and throat, and white under parts. It breeds throughout temperate Europe laying its eggs in hollows on the ground. The eggs have a dark grayish buff ground and are spotted with black.   Size 1.85 x 1.30.

[Grayish.]

[1] Now practically extinct.

[2] Only known breeding ground is in Alaska, not Asia.

269.1.   Dotterel.   *Eudromias morinellus.*

A European bird supposed to have been accidentally taken on the Atlantic coast.

270.   Black-bellied Plover.   *Squatarola squatarola.*

Range.—Northern Hemisphere, breeding in the Arctic regions and wintering from the Gulf States to northern South America. [1]

This is a remarkably handsome species when in the summer dress. The upper parts are largely white with black spots and bars on the back, wings and tail; the throat, sides of head, breast and fore under parts, black. This species has a very small hind toe. It is a very familiar bird to sportsmen and gunners, to whom it is generally known by the names of "Bull-head," or "Beetle-head Plover." They are very numerous in the fall, during which season the underparts are entirely white. The eggs are either laid upon the bare ground or upon a slight lining of grasses or dead leaves. They are three or four in number, brownish or greenish buff in color and boldly marked with black.   Size 2.00 x 1.40.   Data.— Point Barrow, Alaska, June, 1900.   Nest a small hollow on side of a hillock, lined with dry grass.   Collector, H. H. Bodfish.

[Greenish buff.]

271.   Eurasian Golden Plover.   *Pluvialis apricaria.*

A European bird, similar to the next, casually found in Greenland.
It is a very abundant bird throughout Europe, breeding in the northern **parts.** Its habits, nests and eggs are the same as those of the American bird.

272.   American Golden Plover.   *Pluvialis dominica.*

Range.—Whole of North America, breeding in the Arctic regions and wintering south to Patagonia.

[Greenish buff.]

This handsome bird is about the same size as the Black-bellied Plover (10.5 inches long); the black of the underparts extends to the lower tail coverts, and the upperparts are variegated with black, golden yellow and white. Their habits are the same as those of the Black-bellied Plover and the two are frequently met with together during migrations. They nest abundantly along the coast and islands of the Arctic Ocean. The four eggs are very similar to those of the preceding, but smaller.   Size 1.90 x 1.30. Data.—Peel River, Arctic America, June 1, 1898.   Nest of grasses and leaves on the ground in the moss. Col., C. E. Whittaker.

[1] Winters from Massachusetts south.

272a.   Pacific Golden Plover (should be American Golden Plover).   *Pluvialis dominica.*

Range.—An Asiatic species, breeding in northern Asia and on the islands and coast of Alaska.   Very like the preceding, but more yellow.   Nesting and eggs the same. [1]

273.   Killdeer.   *Charadrius vociferus.*

Range.—Temperate North America from the southern parts of Canada southward.   Next to the Spotted Sandpiper, this bird is the most common of the shore

birds in the United States.   It is rarely seen in New England, but is common south of there and in the interior of the country to Canada.

They are very noisy birds, continually uttering their "kil-deer, kil-deer" from which they take their name.   They nest anywhere on the ground, generally near water, placing their nests in fields, cornfields or meadows.   The eggs are drab or greenish buff and profusely spotted with black.   Size 1.50 x 1.10.   Data.—Refugio county, Texas, May 11, 1899.   4 eggs in a depression in the ground, lined with a few grasses.   Collector, J. J. Carroll.

[Grayish buff.]

274.   Semipalmated Plover.   *Charadrius semipalmatus.*

Range.—North America, breeding in the interior of Canada and wintering south from the Gulf States.

This "ringed" Plover is much smaller than the Killdeer, being about 7 inches long.   It has but one black band across the breast, and as indicated by its name, there is a web between the inner toes.   The birds' habits and eggs are very similar to those of the Killdeer, although of course the eggs are smaller; size 1.30 x .90.

[Buff.]

275.   Ringed Plover.   *Charadrius hiaticula.*

Range.—A European bird that breeds abundantly in Greenland.   It nests in great numbers on the banks of streams and in fields, laying its eggs in hollows on the ground, generally without any lining.   Their three or four eggs are practically not distinguishable from those of the Semipalmated Plover, but they average a trifle larger; size, 1.40 x 1.00.   The bird, too, is similar but the toes are not palmated, and the black breast band is wider. [2]

[Buffy.]

276.   Little Ringed Plover.   *Charadrius dubius.*

An Old World species, accidentally occurring on the Pacific coast.   Like the last species but smaller.   The eggs, too, are smaller; size 1.20 x .85. [3]

[1] Breeds in northwestern Alaska.

[2] Breeds on Baffin Island.

[3] Not recorded from North America.

Photo by A. R. Spaid.

NEST AND EGGS OF KILLDEER.

277. Piping Plover. *Charadrius melodus.*

Range.—Eastern North America, chiefly along the Atlantic coast, breeding from the Carolinas north to Newfoundland.

A handsome little bird, with a black crescent on each side of neck, a small black patch on top of the head, and without any black on the lores or ear coverts. It is the lightest colored of any of the eastern Plovers. Length, 7 inches. They lay their eggs upon the sandy beaches in slight, and generally unlined, hollows. The eggs have a pale clay colored ground and are sparsely specked with small black dots. Size 1.25 x 1.00.

277a. Belted Piping Plover (should be Piping Plover). *Charadrius melodus.*

Range.—Interior of North America, breeding from Illinois to Manitoba.

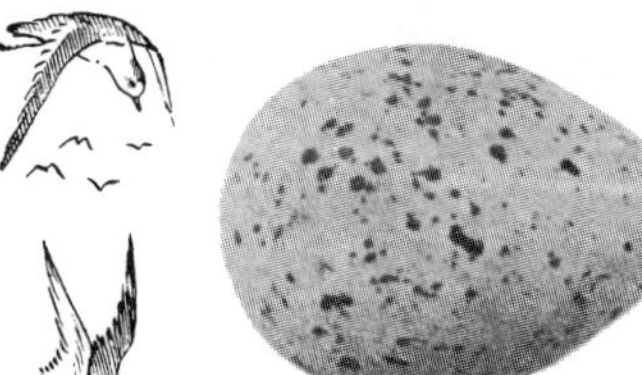

[Clay color.]

This subspecies is like the last, except that the two black crescents on the sides meet in front to form a breast band. They have the same pleasing, mellow whistle of the eastern form, and which gives them their name. Their nesting habits are the same as the last, except of course, that they nest on the beaches of inland ponds and lakes. The eggs cannot be distinguished from those of the common Piping Plover. Data.—Benson Co., N. D., May 26, 1901. Nest a pebble-lined depression in a strip of gravel shingle along the shore of Devil's Lake. The sitting bird ran away when we were fifty yards from the nest, but stealthily returned while watched from a distance. Collector, Eugene S. Rolfe.

278. Snowy Plover. *Charadrius alexandrinus.*

Range.—Breeds along the Pacific coast of the United States, and from Texas to Manitoba in the interior. Winters on the California coast and south to Chili.[1]

[Pale buff.]

Snowy Plovers are very much like the Piping, but are smaller (length 6.5 inches), have a longer and more slender bill, and have a small black patch on the side of head. It is the palest colored of the Plovers. Large numbers of them nest along the Pacific coast and in Texas; north of Texas, in the interior, they are locally distributed. The eggs are pale clay color, marked with small scratchy dots of black. Size 1.20 x .90. Data.—Newport Beach, California, May 1, 1897. Nest a hollow in the sand, a short distance above high water; lined with broken shell. Collector, Evan Davis.

279. Mongolian Plover. *Charadrius mongolus.*

An inhabitant of the Old World, awarded a place in our avifauna because of its accidental occurrence at Alaska. [2]

[1] Also breeds and winters along Gulf of Mexico.

[2] Breeds in Alaska.

280. Wilson's Plover. *Charadrius wilsonia.*

Range.—An abundant breeding species on the Gulf coast, coast of Lower California, and on the Atlantic coast north to Virginia, and casually farther. [1]

A common Plover, which may be distinguished from others of the genus by its comparatively large heavy black bill, and the single broad black band across the breast, and not extending around the back of the neck. They nest on pebbly "shingle" or in the marsh back of the beaches. Their eggs are an olive gray color and are spotted and scratched with blackish brown, with some fainter markings of gray. Size 1.40 x 1.05. Data.—Corpus Christi, Texas, May 10, 1899. 4 eggs laid on the ground among drifted grass on a salt marsh near town. Collector, Frank B. Armstrong.

[Olive gray.]

281. Mountain Plover. *Eupoda montana.*

Range.—Plains and prairies of western North America, breeding from the central portions north to Manitoba, and wintering in California and southward.

[Brownish gray.]

A very peculiar species, inhabiting even the driest portions of the western prairies. It is 9 inches in length, and has a plumage of a pale buffy tone. It seems to be less aquatic than any other American Plover and is rarely found in the vicinity of bodies of water. It nests on the ground anywhere on the prairie, laying its eggs in a slight hollow. The eggs are brownish gray in color and are spotted and blotched with blackish brown. Data.—Morgan county, Colorado, May 7, 1902. Nest a slight hollow on the ground, near a large cactus bed and close to a water hole. No lining to nest. Collector, Glenn S. White.

SURFBIRDS and TURNSTONES. Family CHARADRIIDAE (part).

282. Surfbird. *Aphriza virgata.*

This species, which is found on the Pacific coast from Alaska to Chili, seems to be the connecting link between the Plovers and the Turnstones, having the habits of the latter combined with the bill of the former. Its nest and eggs are not known to have been yet discovered. [2]

[Creamy.]

283. Turnstone (should be Ruddy Turnstone). *Arenaria interpres.*

Range.—The distribution of this species, which is grayer above than the following, is supposed to be confined, in America, to the extreme north from Greenland to Alaska. Its habits and eggs are precisely like the next. [3]

[1] Breeds north to New Jersey.

[2] Breeds in mountains of south-central Alaska.

[3] Breeds only in Europe and Asia.

283.1. Ruddy Turnstone. *Arenaria interpres.*

Range.—Breeds in the Arctic regions, and migrates through all parts of the United States, south to the southern parts of South America. This species has the upperparts variegated with reddish brown, black and white; the underparts are pure white, except for a black patch on the throat, branching upward to the eye and back to the sides of the breast. It has a peculiar, slightly up-turned bill, which is used, as their name implies, for turning over pebbles and stones in their search for food. They nest commonly in northern Labrador, about Hudson Bay and in Alaska, laying their eggs in scantily lined hollows in the ground near water. The eggs are very peculiar and beautiful, having a light grayish or cream color ground, peculiarly marbled with many shades of brown and lilac. Size 1.65 x 1.10. Data.—Mackenzie River, Arctic America, June 28, 1900. Four eggs in a grass-lined depression in the sand.

284. Black Turnstone. *Arenaria melanocephala.*

[Grayish]

Range.—Pacific coast of North America, breeding from British Columbia northward, and wintering south to Lower California.

This species, which has the form and habits of the preceding, is blackish above and on the breast; the rump and the base of the tail are white, being separated from each other by the black tail coverts. Their nesting habits are in no wise different from those of the common Turnstone. The eggs are similar but the markings are not so strikingly arranged. Size 1.60 x 1.10. Data.—Kutlik, Alaska, June 21, 1898. Nest simply a depression in the sand on the sea beach. Collector, Capt. Tilson.

OYSTERCATCHERS. Family HAEMATOPODIDAE.

285. European Oystercatcher. *Haematopus ostralegus.*

This European species is very similar to the American one which follows. It casually occurs in Greenland.

286. American Oystercatcher. *Haematopus palliatus.*

Range—Breeds on the coast of the South Atlantic States and Lower California and winters south to Patagonia.[1] Oyster-catchers are large, heavy bodied birds, with stocky red legs and long, stout red bills. The present species has the whole upper parts and entire head and neck, blackish; underparts and ends of secondaries, white; length, 19 inches. They are abundant breeding birds on the sandy beaches of the South Atlantic States, and casually wander north to Nova Scotia. They lay their two or three eggs on the ground in slight hollows scooped out of the sand. The eggs are of a buffy or brownish buff color, and are irreg-

[Buff.]

¹ Breeds north to L.I., N.Y.

ularly spotted with blackish brown, with subdued markings of lavender. Size 2.20 x 1.50. Data.—Sandy Point, S. C., May 12, 1902. Three eggs on the sand just above high water mark; nest a mere depression on a small "sand dune" lined with pieces of shells. Collector, M. T. Cleckley, M. D.

286.1. Frazar's Oystercatcher (should be American Oystercatcher). *Haematopus palliatus.*

Range.—Lower California.

This species is darker on the back than the preceding, and the breast is mottled with dusky. It is not an uncommon wader in its somewhat restricted range. Its nesting habits are the same as those of the preceding one, but the markings are generally more sharply defined. The one figured is from a set in the collection of Mr. C. W. Crandall.

[Brownish buff.]

287. Black Oystercatcher. *Haematopus bachmani.*

[Olive buff.]

Range.—Pacific coast of North America from Lower California north to Alaska.

This species is the same size as the Oyster-catcher,[1] but the plumage is entirely black both above and below. They are found upon the rocky coasts and islands, more frequently than upon sandy beaches. Their eggs are laid upon bare rocks or pebbles with no attempt at lining for the nest. The eggs are an olive buff in color, spotted and blotched with brownish black. Size 2.20 x 1.55. Data.—Valdez Is., B. C., June 1, 1895. Three eggs laid on the rocks above high water; no nest. Collector, Percie Smith.

JAÇANAS. Family JACANIDAE.

288. American Jaçana. *Jacana spinosa.*

Range.—Tropical America, north in summer to the Lower Rio Grande Valley in Texas, and casually to Florida.

This interesting species has most of its structural characters similar to the Plovers, but has more the appearance and habits of the Rails. They are about eight inches long, the head and neck are black, the body chestnut, and the wings largely greenish yellow. They have long legs, long toes and extremely long toe nails, a scaly leaf on the forehead, and a sharp spur on the shoulder of the wing. Owing to their long toes and nails, they are enabled to walk over floating weeds and rubbish that would sink beneath

[Yellowish olive.]

---

[1] Now European Oystercatcher.

their weight, otherwise. They build their nests on these little floating islands in the marsh; they are also sometimes made of weeds and trash on floating lily pads. They lay from three to five eggs of a yellowish olive color, curiously scrawled with brown and black. Size 1.22 x .95. Data.—Tampico, Mexico, June 3, 1900. Three eggs. Nest of weeds and drift on lily leaf floating in fresh water pond near town. Collector, F. B. Armstrong.

MEGAPODES, CURASSOWS and allies.   Order GALLIFORMES.

GROUSE and allies.   Families TETRAONIDAE and PHASIANIDAE (part).

The members of this family are birds of robust form, subdued (not brightly colored) plumage, comparatively short legs and necks; the tarsi and toes are feathered in the Ptarmigan, the tarsi, only, feathered in the Grouse, and the tarsi and toes bare in the Partridges and Bobwhites. They feed upon berries, buds, grain and insects.

289. Bobwhite. *Colinus virginianus.*

Range.—United States east of North Dakota and Texas and from the southern British Provinces to the Gulf coast.

A celebrated "game bird" which has been hunted so assiduously in New England that it is upon the verge of extermination, and the covers have to be continually replenished with birds trapped in the south and west. They frequent open fields, which have a luxuriant growth of weeds, or grain fields in the fall. Their nests are built along the roadsides, or beside stone walls or any place affording satisfactory shelter. The nest is made of dried grasses and is arched over with grass or overhanging leaves so as to conceal the eggs. They lay from ten to twenty pure white eggs, which are very fre-quently nest stained when found. Size 1.20 x .95. Often two or three broods are raised in a season, but frequently one or more broods are destroyed by rainy weather.

[White].

289a. Florida Bob-white (should be Bobwhite). *Colinus virginianus.*

Range.—This sub-species, which is found in the southern half of Florida, is very much darker than the northern Bobwhite, and is numerously barred below with black.   Its nesting habits and eggs are identical with those of the preceding.

289b. Texan Bob-white (should be Bobwhite). *Colinus virginianus.*

Range.—Texas; casually north to Kansas. A grayer variety of the Bobwhite. The nesting habits and eggs are the same as those of the Bobwhite, except that the eggs may average a trifle smaller. Size 1.18 x .92.

Photo by C. A. Reed.

NEST AND EGGS OF BOBWHITE.

291.   Masked Bob-white (should be Bobwhite).   *Colinus virginianus.*

Range.—Sonoran region of Mexico north to southern Arizona.
This handsome species is marked similarly to the Bobwhite on the upper parts, but has a black throat, and the rest of the underparts are reddish brown, this color being brightest on the breast.   The female of this species is like that of the Texan Bobwhite.   Their nesting habits and eggs are in all respects like those of the other Bobwhites.   Size of eggs, 1.20 x .95.

292.   Mountain Quail.   *Oreortyx pictus.*

Range.—Pacific coast of North America from California to Washington.

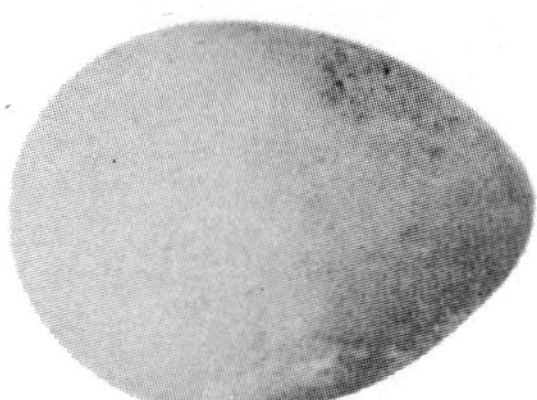

This is the largest of the Partridges, being 11 inches in length.   It is of a general grayish color, with chestnut throat patch, and chestnut flanks, barred with white.   Two long plumes extend downward from the back of the head.   This species nests abundantly in the mountainous portions of northern California and throughout Oregon, and is gradually increasing in numbers in Washington.   As a rule, they nest only on the higher mountain ranges, placing their nest of leaves under the protection of an overhanging bush or tuft of grass.   Their eggs number from six to fifteen, and are of a pale reddish buff color.   Size 1.35 x 1.05.

[Reddish buff.]

292a.   Plumed Partridge (should be Mountain Quail).   *Oreortyx pictus.*

Range.—Mountain ranges of California and Lower California, chiefly in the southern parts of the former.   This species is like the latter except that it is grayer on the back of the head and neck.   Its nesting habits and eggs are like the preceding.

292b.   San Pedro Partridge (should be Mountain Quail).   *Oreortyx pictus.*

Range.—San Pedro Mountains, Lower California.
This species, which is grayer above than the preceding two, breeds only in the highest peaks of its range.   Otherwise its nesting habits and eggs are the same as the other Plumed Partridges.

293.   Scaled Quail.   *Callipepla squamata.*

Range.—Mexico and southwestern border of the United States.

[Creamy white.]

This blue gray species is 10 inches in length; the feathers on the neck and underparts have narrow dark borders, thus giving the plumage a scaly appearance, from which the birds take their name. They have a small tuft of whitish or buffy feathers on the top of the head.   It is especially abundant in the dry arid portions of its range, being found often many miles away from water.   Their eggs are laid in a shallow hollow under some small bush or cactus, and number from eight to sixteen; they are creamy white, finely specked with buff or pale brownish. Size 1.25 x .95.

293a.   Chestnut-bellied Scaled Partridge (should be Scaled Quail).   *Callipepla squamata.*

Range.—Lower Rio Grande Valley in Texas and southward into Mexico.
This subspecies is like the last with the addition of a chestnut patch on the belly.   Their breeding habits do not vary in any particular way from those of the Scaled Partridge.[1] In comparing a large series of the eggs of each species, no differences can be found in either color or markings.

294.   California Quail.   *Lophortyx californicus.*

Range.—Coast region of California, Oregon, Washington and British Columbia.

This is one of the most beautiful of the Partridges, with its crest of feathers rising from the crown and curving forwards so that the broadened ends hang directly over the bill.   It is about the size of the preceding species, and is distinguished from the following one by its white forehead, chestnut patch on the belly and the scaly appearance of the feathers in that region, by its dark crown and the gray flanks with white streaks. Their nests are placed on the ground, under bushes, hedges, brush piles, or in almost any conceivable place 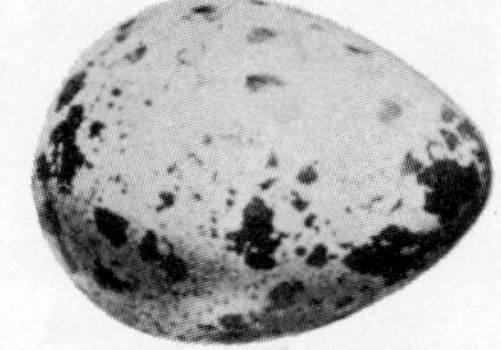

[Creamy white.]

that will offer concealment.   The birds are very tame and frequently nest in door yards.   They lay from eight to twenty eggs with a creamy white or buffy ground color, handsomely blotched with shades of brown and yellowish brown. Size 1.20 x .93.

294a.   Valley Partridge (should be California Quail).   *Lophortyx californicus.*

Range.—Interior portions of California, Oregon and Washington.
The nesting habits of this grayer subspecies do not differ in any manner from those of the above species.   The eggs are indistinguishable.

295.   Gambel's Quail.   *Lophortyx gambelii.*

Range.—Southwestern United States from Texas to California; north to Utah.

This handsome species differs from the California in the chestnut crown and flanks, and the black patch on the belly.   They are very abundant in Arizona, both on the mountains and in the valleys, and apparently without any regard to the nearness to, or remoteness from, a water supply.   They breed during May, laying their eggs on the ground under any suitable cover.   The eggs cannot be distinguished from those of the California Quail, except that they average a trifle larger.   Size 1.25 x .95.

[Buff.]

296.   Harlequin Quail.   *Cyrtonyx montezumae.*

Range.—Mexico, north to southern Arizona and New Mexico, and to western Texas.
A remarkable species about 9 inches long; often called "Fool Quail" because of its eccentric and clownish markings, streaks and spots of black, white, buff, gray and chestnut.   It is met with in small flocks on the mountains and less

---

[1] Now Scaled Quail.

frequently in the valleys.   It frequents scrubby wooded places rather than open hill sides and is very easy to approach and kill; this confidence or stupidity together with its clownish appearance are the reasons for its commonly used local name.   Their nests are hollows in the ground, lined with grasses and concealed by overhanging tufts of grass.   The eggs, which are pure white, are not distinguishable with certainty from those of the Bobwhite, but average longer. Size 1.25 x .95.

297.   Blue Grouse.   *Dendragapus obscurus.*

Range.—Rocky Mountain region from central Montana south to New Mexico.
With the exception of the Sage Grouse, this species is the largest of the family, being about 20 inches in length.   The general tone of its plumage below is gray; above, blackish gray and the tail blackish with a broad terminal band of light gray.   They frequent the wooded and especially the coniferous districts, where they build their nests under fallen trees or at the bases of standing ones.   They lay from six to ten eggs of a buffy color, sparsely spotted and blotched with brownish.   Size 2.00 x 1.40.

297a.   Sooty Grouse (should be Blue Grouse).   *Dendragapus obscurus.*

[Rich buff.]

Range.—Mountain ranges along the Pacific coast from California to British Columbia.
Like the last, this somewhat darker subspecies is met with in timbered regions, where its habits are about the same as those of the Ruffed Grouse, except, of course, that they are not nearly as shy as the Grouse in New England.   Their eggs are laid in hollows beside stumps or under logs. The eggs are buff colored, spotted with reddish brown.   Size 2.00 x 1.40.

297b.   Richardson's Grouse (should be Blue Grouse).   *Dendragapus obscurus.*

Range.—Northern Rocky Mountains from central Montana to British Columbia.
A dark variety with no terminal band of gray on the tail.   Its habits, nesting and eggs are precisely like those of the preceding species.

298.   Spruce Grouse.   *Canachites canadensis.*

Range.—Northern United States and southern British Provinces; west to Minnesota.

A dark species, smaller than the last (15 inches long), and easily recognized by its black throat and extensive black patch on the breast.   The habits of this species and the two varieties into which it has been sub-divided, are the same; as a species, they are very tame, will not fly unless actually obliged to, and frequently allow themselves to be knocked down with sticks.   Their nests are hollows in the leaves on the ground, generally under the sheltering branches of a low spreading fir tree.   The six to fifteen eggs are a bright buff color, blotched and spotted boldly with various shades of brown.   Size 1.70 x 1.25.

[Bright buff.]

298b.   Alaskan Spruce Grouse (should be Spruce Grouse).   *Canachites canadensis.*

Range.—Alaska.

This variety is practically the same as the preceding, the birds not always being distinguishable; the nest and eggs are the same as the Canada Grouse. [1]

298c.   Hudsonian Spruce Grouse (should be Spruce Grouse).   *Canachites canadensis.*

Range.—Labrador and the Hudson Bay region.

Like the last, this variety is hardly to be distinguished from the Canada.[1] Its nesting habits and eggs are the same.

299.   Franklin's Grouse (should be Spruce Grouse).   *Canachites canadensis.*

Range.—Northwestern United States and British Columbia.

[Brownish buff.]

This species is very similar to the Canada Grouse,[1] the most apparent difference being the absence of the brownish gray tip to the tail, and the upper coverts are broadly tipped with white. This species, which is very abundant in the northwest, has the same stupid habits of the eastern bird. During the mating season, the males of both this and the preceding species have the same habit of "drumming" that the Ruffed Grouse has. Their nests are placed on the ground under bushes of fir trees and from eight to fifteen eggs are laid. These are brownish buff in color, spotted and blotched with rich brown. They are very similar to the eggs of the Canada Grouse. Data.—Moberly Peak, Cascade Mts., British Columbia, June 9, 1902. 7 eggs in a slight hollow on the ground. Collector, G. F. Dippie.

300.   Ruffed Grouse.   *Bonasa umbellus.*

Range. Eastern United States from Minnesota to New England; south to Virginia.

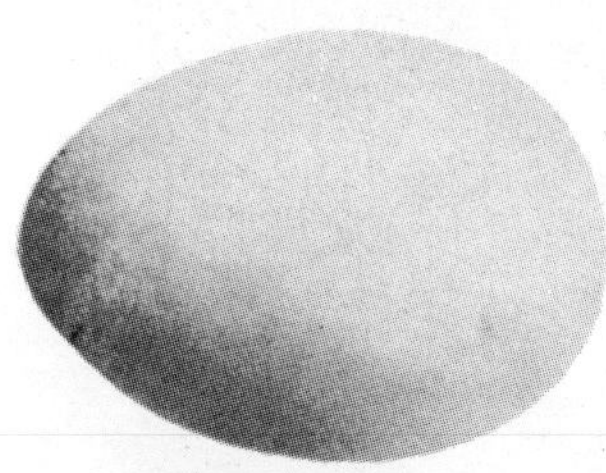

[Brownish buffy.]

The Ruffed Grouse is "King of the Game Birds" in the east, where it has been hunted so freely, that it has become very wary and requires a skillful marksman to bring it down. Because of the cutting off of all heavy timber, and the vigor with which they are pursued by hunters, they are becoming very scarce in New England, and within a few years they will probably be practically extinct in that section. Their favorite resorts are heavily timbered woods or low growth birches. Their nests are hollows in the leaves under fallen trees, beside some stump or concealed among the small shoots at the base of a large tree. The bird sits very close, but when she does fly, goes with the familiar rumble and roar, which always disconcerts the novice, the wind created by her sudden flight generally causing the leaves to settle in the nest and conceal the eggs. They lay from eight to fifteen eggs, of a brownish buff color, sometimes with a few faint markings of brown, but generally unspotted. Size 1.55 x 1.15. The young of all the Partridges and Grouse are born covered with down and follow their parents soon after leaving the shell. The adults are very skillful in leading enemies away from their young, feigning lameness, broken wings, etc. The nesting habits and eggs of the three sub-species are precisely the same in every respect as those of this bird.

[1] Now Spruce Grouse.

300a.   Canadian Ruffed Grouse (should be Ruffed Grouse).   *Bonasa umbellus.*

Range.—Northern United States and southern British Provinces from Maine and Nova Scotia west to Washington and British Columbia.

300b.   Gray Ruffed Grouse (should be Ruffed Grouse).   *Bonasa umbellus.*

Range.—Rocky Mountain region from Colorado to Alaska.
A grayer species than the common.

300c.   Oregon Ruffed Grouse; Red Ruffed Grouse (should be Ruffed Grouse).   *Bonasa umbellus.*

Range.—Pacific coast from California to British Columbia.
A dark species with the prevailing color a reddish tone.

Photo by J. B. Pardoe.

NEST AND EGGS OF RUFFED GROUSE.

301.　Willow Ptarmigan.　*Lagopus lagopus.*

Range.—Arctic regions, in America south nearly to the United States border, and casually to Maine.

Ptarmigan are Grouse-like birds, feathered to the toe nails; they have many changes of plumage, in winter being nearly pure white, and in summer largely reddish brown or grayish, barred with black.　In the breeding plumage they have red comb-like wattles over the eye.　In other seasons, their plumage varies in all degrees between winter and summer.　They nest on the ground in hollows among the leaves, lined with a few grasses, and sometimes feathers.　They lay from six to sixteen eggs which have a ground color of buff or brownish buff, heavily speckled, blotched and marbled with blackish brown.　Size 1.75 x 1.25.

[Brownish buff.]

301a.　Allen's Ptarmigan (should be Willow Ptarmigan).　*Lagopus lagopus.*

Range.—Newfoundland.　A very similar bird to the preceding; eggs indistinguishable.

[Buff].

302.　Rock Ptarmigan.　*Lagopus mutus.*

Range.—Chiefly in the interior of British America, from the southern portions to Alaska and the Arctic Ocean. [1]

A species with a smaller bill and in summer a grayer plumage, more finely barred with black.　Its nesting habits are the same as the other species, it nesting on the ground in such localities as would be frequented by the Ruffed Grouse.　Its eggs cannot be positively distinguished from those of the Willow Ptarmigan. Size 1.70 x 1.20.

302a.　Reinhardt's Ptarmigan (should be Rock Ptarmigan).　*Lagopus mutus.*

Range.—Labrador and Greenland; an eastern variety of the preceding species. Its habits, nesting habits and eggs are just the same as those of Rock Ptarmigan.

302b.　Nelson's Ptarmigan (should be Rock Ptarmigan).　*Lagopus mutus.*

Range.—Unalaska, of the Aleutian chain.　An abundant species in its restricted range, making its nest on the ground in the valleys.　Eggs like the others.

302c.　Turner's Ptarmigan (should be Rock Ptarmigan).　*Lagopus mutus.*

Range.—Atka Island of the Aleutian chain.　Nests and eggs not distinctive.

302d.　Townsend's Ptarmigan (should be Rock Ptarmigan).　*Lagopus mutus.*

Range.—Kyska Island of the Aleutian group.

On account of the constantly changing plumage of these birds, while interesting, they are very unsatisfactory to study, and it is doubtful if anyone can identify the different sub-species of the Rock Ptarmigan, granting that there is any difference, which is doubtful.

---

[1] Arctic regions; more northerly than Willow Ptarmigan.

302.1.   Evermann's Ptarmigan (should be Rock Ptarmigan).   *Lagopus mutus.*

Range.—Attu Island of the Aleutian group.

This is, in summer, the darkest of the Ptarmigans, having little or no rufous and much blackish.   The nesting habits and eggs are the same as those of the Rock Ptarmigan.

303.   Welch's Ptarmigan (should be Rock Ptarmigan).   *Lagopus mutus.*

[Buff.]

Range.—Newfoundland.

This species, in summer, is more grayish than the Rock Ptarmigan, and is very finely vermiculated with blackish.   It is a perfectly distinct species from the Allen Ptarmigan, which is the only other species found on the island.   They inhabit the higher ranges and hills in the interior of the island, where they are quite abundant.   They build their nests on the ground under protection of overhanging bushes.   The eggs are laid in a hollow in the dead leaves, sometimes with a lining of grasses. The eggs do not differ in size or appearance from those of the Rock Ptarmigan.   Data.—Newfoundland, June 3, 1901.   Nest a slight hollow in the moss, beside a fallen stump; lined with a few feathers. Collector, E. H. Montgomery.

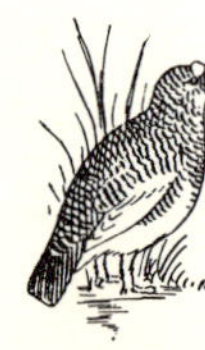

304.   White-tailed Ptarmigan.   *Lagopus leucurus.*

Range.—Higher ranges of the Rocky Mountains, from New Mexico north to Alaska.

This species differs from any of the preceding in having at all seasons of the year, a white tail; it is also somewhat smaller than the Rock Ptarmigan.   They nest abundantly near the summits of the ranges in Colorado, making their nests among the rocks, and generally lining them with a few grasses.   During June, they lay from six to twelve eggs having a creamy background, speckled and blotched with chestnut brown.   Size 1.70 x 1.15.

304a.   Kenai White-tailed Ptarmigan (should be White-tailed Ptarmigan).   *Lagopus leucurus.*

Range.—Kenai Peninsular, Alaska.   A similar but paler (in summer) variety of the preceding.   The nesting habits or eggs will not differ.

305.   Greater Prairie Chicken.   *Tympanuchus cupido.*

Range.—The prairies, chiefly west of the Mississippi; north to Manitoba, east to Ohio, and west to Colorado.

This familiar game bird of the west is about 18 inches in. length, brownish above and grayish below, with bars of brownish black both above and below. In the place of the ruffs of the Ruffed Grouse, are long tufts of rounded or square ended feathers, and beneath these a peculiar sac, bright orange in the breeding season, and capable of being inflated to the size of a small orange; this is done when the bird makes its familiar "booming" noise. They are very good "table birds" and although they are still very abundant in most of their range, so many are being killed for market, that it has become necessary to make more stringent laws relating to the killing and sale of Pinnated Grouse, as they are often called. They nest anywhere on the prairie, in hollows in the ground under overhanging bushes or tufts of grass. They lay from eight to fifteen eggs having a buffy or olive buff ground color, sparingly and finely sprinkled with brown; size 1.70 x 1.25.

[Olive buff.]

305a. Attwater's Prairie Hen (should be Greater Prairie Chicken). *Tympanuchus cupido.*

Range.—Coast region of Louisiana and Texas.

This is a slightly smaller and darker variety of the Pinnated Grouse. Its eggs cannot be distinguished from those of the more northerly distributed bird.

306. Heath Hen (should be Greater Prairie Chicken). *Tympanuchus cupido.*

Range.—Island of Martha's Vineyard, Mass.[1]

This species is similar to the preceding, but has the scapulars more broadly tipped with buff, the axillars barred, and the pinnated feathers on the neck pointed. It is slightly smaller than the western species. It is found on the wooded portions of the island, where its breeding habits are the same as those of the Ruffed Grouse. Mr. Brewster probably has the only authentic set of the eggs of this species. They are of a yellowish green color and are unspotted. Size 1.70 x 1.25. A number of Prairie Hens[2] liberated on the island several years ago are apparently thriving well, and nests found there now would be fully as apt to belong to this species.

[Pale buff.]

307. Lesser Prairie Chicken. *Tympanuchus pallidicinctus.*

Range.—Prairies from southwestern Kansas through Indian Territory to western Texas.

A smaller and paler species than the Prairie Hen.[2] Never as abundant as the common Pinnated Grouse, this species appears to be becoming scarcer each year. Its nests are concealed under overhanging brush or placed under a large tuft of prairie grass, and are generally lined with a few grasses or leaves. They lay from eight to twelve eggs of a buffy color, much lighter than those of the Prairie Hen, and unmarked. Size 1.65 x 1.25.

[1] Extirpated from Atlantic seaboard.

[2] Now Greater Prairie Chicken.

Photo by P. B. Peabody.

NEST AND EGGS OF GREATER PRAIRIE CHICKEN.

308. Sharp-tailed Grouse. *Pedioecetes phasianellus.*

Range.—Interior of British America, from the United States boundary northwest to the Yukon.

Sharp-tailed Grouse are similar in form to the Prairie Hen,[1] but are somewhat smaller and very much lighter in color, being nearly white below, with arrowhead markings on the breast and flanks. This species is very abundant in Manitoba and especially so on the plains west of Hudson Bay. Their nests are generally concealed under a thicket or a large tuft of grass, and are lined with grasses and feathers. They lay from six to fifteen eggs of a drab color, very minutely specked all over with brown. Size 1.70 x 1.25. Data.—Quill Lake, Saskatchewan, N. W. T. Nest a depression on the ground, lined with grass and feathers. Collector, Chris Forge.

[Buffy drab.]

308a. Columbian Sharp-tailed Grouse (should be Sharp-tailed Grouse). *Pedioecetes phasianellus.*

Range.—Northwestern United States and British Columbia to central Alaska. Both the nesting habits and eggs of this variety are the same as the last, with which species, the birds gradually intergrade as their ranges approach.

308b. Prairie Sharp-tailed Grouse (should be Sharp-tailed Grouse). *Pedioecetes phasianellus.*

Range.—Plains of the United States from the Mississippi to the Rockies. This sub-species shades directly into the two preceding where their ranges meet, and only birds from the extreme parts of the range of each show any marked differences. The nesting habits and eggs of all three are not to be distinguished.

309. Sage Grouse. *Centrocercus urophasianus.*

[Pale greenish drab.]

Range.—Sage plains of the Rocky Mountain region from British Columbia to New Mexico, and from California to Dakota. This handsome bird is the largest of the American Grouse, being about 30 inches long (the hen bird is about six inches shorter). It may easily be recognized by its large size, its peculiar graduated tail with extremely sharply pointed feathers, and the black belly and throat. Their nests are hollows scratched out in the sand, under the sage bushes, generally with no lining. The nesting season is during April and May. They lay from six to twelve eggs of a greenish drab color, spotted with brown. Size 2.15 x 1.50.

[1] Now Greater Prairie Chicken.

PHEASANTS; TURKEYS. Families PHASIANIDAE (part) and MELEAGRIDIDAE.

309.1. Ring-necked Pheasant. *Phasianus colchicus.*

Several species of Pheasants have been introduced into the United States, among them being the Ring-necked, English, and Green Pheasants. The ring-necked species seems to be the only one that has obtained a really strong foothold, it being now very abundant in Oregon and Washington, and adjacent states, and also found in abundance on many game preserves in the east. The males of any of the species may at once be distinguished from any of our birds by the long tail. Their nests are hollows in the leaves under tufts of grass or bushes. They lay from eight to fourteen eggs of a buff or greenish buff color, unmarked; size 1.50 x 1.30.

[Greenish buff.]

310. Wild Turkey. *Meleagris gallopavo.*

Range.—Eastern United States from southern Middle States south to central Florida and west to the Mississippi Valley and eastern Texas. These magnificent birds, which once ranged over the whole of eastern United States, are being yearly confined to a smaller range, chiefly because of the destruction of their natural covers, and from persecution by hunters. They are generally very wary birds and either escape by running through the underbrush or by flying as soon as a human being appears in sight. Their nests are made under tangled growths of underbrush or briers. Their eggs, which are laid during April and May, range from eight to sixteen in number. They are of a buff color sprinkled and spotted with brownish.   Size 2.55 x 1.90.   Data.—Hammond, La., April 17, 1897. Fifteen eggs. Nest hollow scraped in the ground under a bush on the edge of a pine woods; lined with grasses and leaves. Collector, E. A. McIlhenny.

[Buff].

310a. Merriam's Turkey (should be Wild Turkey). *Meleagris gallopavo.*

Range.—Southwestern United States from Colorado south through western Texas, New Mexico and Arizona to Mexico.
This variety is abundant throughout its range, its nesting habits and eggs being practically indistinguishable from those of the eastern form.

310b. Florida Wild Turkey (should be Wild Turkey).
Meleagris gallopavo.

Range.—Southern Florida.
A small variety of the Wild Turkey about 42 inches long. They breed in the tangled thickets in the higher portions of the southern half of Florida, laying from ten to sixteen eggs of a brighter and deeper buff color than the northern variety, and smaller; size 2.30x1.75. Their nests are generally lined with grasses and occasionally with feathers. The female sits very close when incubating and will not fly until almost trod upon, trusting to her variegated markings to conceal her from observation.

[Greenish buff.]

310c. Rio Grande Turkey (should be Wild Turkey).   *Meleagris gallopavo.*

Range.—Lowlands of the southern parts of Texas and northern Mexico. A sub-species which differs slightly in plumage and not at all in nesting habits or eggs from the common Wild Turkey.

CURASSOWS and GUANS.   Family CRACIDAE.

311. Plain Chachalaca.   *Ortalis vetula.*

[Buffy white.]

Range.—Eastern portions of Mexico, north to the Lower Rio Grande Valley in Texas.
A very peculiar grayish colored bird with a greenish gloss to the back, and a long, broad tail, quite long legs, and with the face and sides of the throat devoid of feathers. They are very abundant birds in some localities, and very noisy during the breeding season, their notes resembling a harsh trumpeting repetition of their name. They are ground inhabiting birds but nest in low bushes. Their nests are made of sticks, twigs, leaves, or moss and are generally frail, flat structures only a few feet above the ground. During April, they lay from three to five buffy white eggs, the shells of which are very rough and hard. Size 2.25 x 1.55.

PIGEONS and DOVES.   Order COLUMBIFORMES.

PIGEONS and DOVES.   Family COLUMBIDAE.

Pigeons and Doves are distributed throughout nearly every temperate and tropical country on the globe, nearly five hundred species being known, of which twelve occur within our limits. Their plumage is generally of soft and subdued colors, the head small, the wings strong and the flight rapid.

312. Band-tailed Pigeon. *Columba fasciata.*

Range.—The Rocky Mountains and westward to the Pacific, from British Columbia south to Mexico.

[White.]

This large species may be generally recognized by the white crescent on the nape; it is about 15 inches in length. They nest abundantly on the mountain ranges, sometimes in large flocks, and again, only a few pairs together. Their nests are rude platforms of sticks and twigs either in bushes or in large trees in heavily wooded districts. The two eggs which are laid during May or June are pure white in color, and like those of all the pigeons, equally rounded at each end. Size 1.55 x 1.10.

312a. Viosca's Pigeon (should be Band-tailed Pigeon). *Columba fasciata.*

Range.—Southern Lower California. This is a paler variety of the preceding species and is not noticeably different in its habits, nesting, or eggs.

313. Red–billed Pigeon. *Columba flavirostris.*

Range.—Mexico and Central America, north to southern Texas, Arizona and New Mexico. [1]

This species, characterized by its red bill, purplish colored head, neck and breast and absence of iridescent markings, is abundant in the valley of the Lower Rio Grande, where they build their frail nests in thickets and low bushes, and during May and June lay their white eggs. Size of eggs, 1.55 x 1.10.

314. White-crowned Pigeon. *Columba leucocephala.*

Range.—Resident in the West Indies; in summer, found on the Florida Keys. This species, which can be identified by its white crown, nests in trees or mangroves on certain of the Florida Keys, laying its two white eggs on its rude platform of sticks and twigs. Size of eggs, 1.40 x 1.05. Nests in April and May.

314.1. Scaly-naped Pigeon. *Columba squamosa.*

A West Indian species, a single specimen of which was taken at Key West, Florida.

A dark colored species, with purplish head, neck and breast; named from the scaly appearance of the iridescent feathers on the sides of the neck.

315. Passenger Pigeon. *Ectopistes migratorius.*

Range.—Formerly, North America east of the Rockies; now, casually seen in the upper Mississippi Valley. [2]

A handsome species with rich ruddy underparts, grayish upperparts and a long graduated tail. This species, years ago, found in flocks of thousands or millions, is now practically exterminated, chiefly by being hunted and trapped. A few pairs probably now nest in the interior, from northern United States to Hudson Bay. Their nests are very rude, frail platforms of twigs, on which two white eggs are laid, they being longer and narrower, comparatively, than those of other species. Size of eggs, 1.50 x 1.02. Data.—Southwest shore of Lake Manitoba, June 1, 1891. Nest of twigs in an aspen tree. Collector, Joe Flamay.

[White.]

[1] Ranges in U.S. to Rio Grande Valley only.

[2] Now extinct.

316. Mourning Dove.   *Zenaidura macroura.*

Range.—North America from New England, Manitoba and British Columbia, southward.

Now that the Passenger Pigeon has disappeared, this species becomes the only one found in the east, with the exception of the little Ground Dove in the South Atlantic and Gulf States.   While, sometimes, small flocks of them nest in a community, they generally nest in companies of two or three pairs.   Their nests are generally at a low elevation, in trees, bushes and often upon the ground.   Their nests are made entirely of twigs and rootlets, and eggs may be found from early in April until the latter part of September, as they often raise two or three broods a season.

[White.]

The two eggs are white. Size 1.15 x .80.   Data.—Refugio Co., Texas, May 3, 1899.   2 eggs laid on the ground in a slight cradle of twigs.   Collector, James J. Carroll.

Photo by H. B. Stough.

NEST AND EGGS OF MOURNING DOVE.

317. Zenaida Dove. *Zenaida aurita.*

Range.—West Indies; in summer, on the Florida Keys, but not in great numbers.[1]
This species is similar in size to the Mourning Dove, but it has a short and square tail, and the secondaries are tipped with white, and the underparts more ruddy. They generally nest upon the ground, but occasionally in small bushes, laying two white eggs a trifle larger than those of the preceding species. Size 1.20 x .90. The nests are made of grasses and twigs, on the ground under bushes.

318. White-fronted Dove. *Leptotila verreauxi.*

Range.—Mexico and Central America north to southern Texas.
Slightly larger than the last, much paler below, with no black ear mark as in the two preceding species, and with the forehead whitish. They build their nests of sticks, grasses and weeds, and place them in tangled vines and thickets a few feet from the ground. Their two eggs, which are laid in May and June, have a creamy white or buffy color. Size 1.15 x .85. They cannot be called a common species within our borders.

319. White-winged Dove. *Zenaida asiatica.*

Range.—Central America, Mexico and the southwestern border of the United States.

This species is 12 inches in length, has a black patch on the ear coverts, white tips to the greater and lesser coverts and some of the secondaries, and broad white tips to the outer tail feathers, which are black. This species is very abundant in some localities within our borders. Their nests are very frail platforms of twigs placed in trees or bushes or precariously suspended among tangled vines. Their two eggs are white or creamy white, and measure 1.15 x .85.

[White.]

320. Ground Dove. *Columbigallina passerina.*

Range.—South Atlantic and Gulf States to eastern Texas.
The Ground Doves are the smallest of the family, measuring but about 6.5 inches in length. Their nesting habits and eggs are exactly like those of the next to be described. They are very abundant, especially along the South Atlantic coast.

320a. Mexican Ground Dove (should be Ground Dove). *Columbigallina passerina.*

Range.—Border of the United States from Texas to southern California and southward.

This paler sub-species builds a nest of twigs and weeds, placing the flat structure either in low bushes or on the ground. Their two white eggs are laid during April to July. They sometimes rear two broods a season. Size of eggs, .85 x .65.

[White.]

320b. Bermuda Ground Dove (should be Ground Dove). *Columbigallina passerina.*

Range.—Bermuda. Smaller and paler than the last; otherwise the same in nesting habits and eggs.

---

[1] Now accidental in U.S.

321. Inca Dove. *Scardafella inca.*

Range.—Mexican border of the United States, south to Central America and Lower California.

[White.]

This handsome species is about the size of the last, but its tail is longer and graduated, consequently its length is greater, it being about 8 inches long. It is not an uncommon species along our Mexican border, but is not nearly as abundant as is the Ground Dove. It is often called "Scaled Dove" because of the blackish edges of nearly all its feathers. They build fairly compact nests of twigs, rootlets and weeds, these being placed in bushes at a low elevation. They are two in number and pure white. Size .85 x .65.

322. Key West Quail-Dove. *Geotrygon chrysia.*

Range.—West Indies, rarely found at Key West, although supposed to have been common there in Audubon's time. This species is of about the size of the Mourning Dove, has rusty colored upper parts, and is whitish below, the white below the eye being separated from that of the throat by a stripe of dusky from the base of the bill. They nest in trees, laying two buffy white eggs. Size 1.25 x .90.

322.1. Ruddy Quail-Dove. *Geotrygon montana.*

Range.—Central America, north to eastern Mexico and the West Indies; once taken at Key West. This species is similar to the last but has no white streak under the eye, and the underparts are buffy. Eggs, creamy white. Size 1.15 x .90.

323. Blue-headed Quail-Dove. *Starnoenas cyanocephala.*

Range.—Cuba, accidentally straying to Key West, but not in recent years.[1]

It is a beautiful species, with a bright blue crown, black throat and stripe through the eye, separated by a white line under the eye. The rest of the plumage is of a brownish or rusty color. Eggs buffy white. Size 1.30 x 1.05.

NESTING CAVE OF CALIFORNIA CONDOR.
[The egg was in the hole in center of picture.]

[1] Not recorded from North America.

VULTURES, HAWKS and FALCONS; OWLS. Orders FALCONIFORMES and STRIGIFORMES.

AMERICAN VULTURES. Family CATHARTIDAE.

Vultures are peculiarly formed birds of prey, having a bare head and neck, a lengthened bill strongly hooked at the end for tearing flesh, and long, strong, broad wings upon which they float in the air for hours at a time without any visible flapping. They are scavengers and do great service to mankind by devouring dead animal matter, that, if allowed to remain, would soon taint the atmosphere. Their eyesight and sense of smell is very acute. They do not, except in very unusual cases, capture their prey, but feed upon that which has been killed or died of disease.

[Ashy gray.]

324. California Condor. *Gymnogyps californianus.*

Range.—Apparently now restricted to the coast ranges of California, casually inland to Arizona, and formerly to British Columbia.[1]

This large bird, which weighs about 20 pounds, measures about 4 feet in length, and has an expanse of wings of about 10 feet. Its plumage is blackish with lengthened lanceolate feathers about the neck, and with the greater wing coverts broadly tipped with grayish white (in very old birds). The birds are very rare in their restricted range and are becoming scarcer each year, owing to their being shot and their nests robbed. While the eggs are very rarely found and only secured at a great risk, they are not as unobtainable as many suppose, as may be seen from the fact that one private collection contains no less than six perfect specimens of the eggs and as many mounted birds. These birds lay but a single egg, placing it generally in caves or recesses in the face of cliffs, hundreds of feet from the ground, and often in inaccessible locations. The eggs are of an ashy gray color and measure about 4.45 x 2.55.

[1] Only about 40 now alive.

325. Turkey Vulture. *Cathartes aura.*

Range.—America, from New Jersey on the Atlantic coast, Manitoba and British Columbia, south to southern South America, wintering in the southern half of the United States. [1]

The plumage of this small Vulture (length 30 inches,) is blackish brown, the naked head being red. It is very common in the southern and central portions of its range, where it frequents the streets and dooryards picking up any refuse that is edible. It is a very graceful bird while on the wing, and can readily be identified when at a distance from the fact that, when in flight, the tips of the wings curve upward. The two eggs which constitute a set are laid upon the ground between large rocks, in hollow stumps, under logs, or between the branching trunks of large trees, generally in large woods. They frequently nest in communities and again, only a single pair may be found in the woods. Its nesting season ranges from March until June in the different localities. The eggs are creamy or bluish white, spotted and blotched with shades of brown, and with fainter markings of lavender. Size 2.70 x 1.85.

[Creamy white.]

NEST AND EGGS OF TURKEY VULTURE.

[1] From New England south.

[Bluish white.]

326. Black Vulture. *Coragyps atratus.*

Range.—More southerly than the preceding; north regularly to North Carolina and southern Illinois, and west to the Rocky Mountains. [1]

This species is of about the same size, or slightly smaller than the Turkey Vulture; its plumage is entirely black as is also the naked head, and bill. In the South Atlantic and Gulf States, the present species is even more abundant than the preceding, and might even be said to be partially domesticated. The nesting habits are the same as those of the Turkey Vulture but their eggs average longer and the ground color is pale greenish or bluish white rather than creamy. They are spotted and blotched the same. Size 3.00 x 2.00.

FALCONS and allies. Families ACCIPITRIDAE, PANDIONIDAE and FALCONIDAE.

The members of this family are chiefly diurnal; they get their living by preying upon smaller animals or birds. They have strong, sharply hooked bills, powerful legs and feet armed with strong, curved and sharply pointed talons.

327. Swallow-tailed Kite. *Elanoïdes forficatus.*

Range.—Southern United States; casually north to New York and to Manitoba.

[White.]

This most beautiful Kite can never be mistaken for any other; its whole head, neck and underparts are snowy white, while the back, wings and tail are glossy blue black, the wings being very long and the tail long and deeply forked. The extreme length of the bird is 24 inches. As a rule nests of this bird are placed high up in the tallest trees; they are made of sticks, weeds and moss. Two eggs, or rarely three, constitute a full set. They are white or bluish white, spotted with brown. The one figured is an unusually handsome marked specimen in the collection of Mr. C. W. Crandall. Average size of eggs, 1.80 x 1.50. Data.—Yegna Creek bottoms, Texas, April 27, 1891. 2 eggs. Nest of sticks and green moss, the same moss also being used for lining; in an elm tree 80 feet up. Collector, J. A. Singley.

[1] Breeds north to Maryland and Delaware.

328. White-tailed Kite. *Elanus leucurus.*

Range.—Southern United States, north to the Carolinas, Illinois and middle California. [1]

This species can be recognized by its light bluish gray mantle, black shoulders and white tail. It is a very active species, feeding upon insects and reptiles, and small birds and mammals. The nests of this species are placed in trees at quite an elevation from the ground, being made of sticks, weeds and leaves. The eggs are creamy white, profusely blotched and spotted with reddish brown and umber. Size 1.65 x 1.25. Data.—Los Angeles, Cal., April 9, 1896. Nest in fork of willows about 25 feet up. Made of willow twigs and weed stalks, lined with pieces of bark. Collector, A. M. Shields. This handsome set, with nest, is in the collection of Col. John E. Thayer.

[Creamy white.]

329. Mississippi Kite. *Ictinia misisippiensis.*

Range.—Southeastern United States, north to South Carolina and Illinois.

[Bluish white.]

A small species (length 14 inches) with the head, neck, and underparts gray, and the back, wings and tail blackish, the tips of the secondaries being grayish. They live almost exclusively upon insects, such as grasshoppers, and small reptiles. They build their nests of sticks and weeds well up in tall trees. The eggs are two or three in number and normally bluish white, unmarked, but occasionally with very faint spots of pale brown. Size 1.65 x 1.25. Data.—Giddings, Texas, May 31, 1887. Nest of sticks and weeds, with green pecan leaves in the lining; placed in the top of a live oak sapling, 20 feet from the ground. Collector, J. A. Singley.

330. Everglade Kite. *Rostrhamus sociabilis.*

Range.—South America, north to southern Florida and Mexico.

This peculiar species has a long, slender, curved bill, blackish plumage, with white rump and bases of outer tail feather. They feed largely upon snails, both land and water varieties. They nest at a low elevation in bushes or under brush, often over the water. The nests are of sticks, weeds and leaves. The three eggs are light greenish white, spotted and splashed with chestnut brown. Size,
Data.—Everglades, Fla., Feb. 25, 1898. 3 eggs. Nest in a custard apple tree, 6 feet from the ground, built of twigs, lined with small vine stems and willow leaves. Collector, J. F. Menge. This set is in Mr. Crandall's collection.

[Pale greenish white.]

[1] Extirpated in eastern U.S.

NEST AND EGGS OF MARSH HAWK.

331. Marsh Hawk. *Circus cyaneus.*

Range.—Whole of North America, very abundant in all sections.

The adult of this species is very light colored, and young birds of the first two years have a reddish brown coloration; in both plumages the species is easily identified by the white patch on the rump. They are, almost exclusively, frequenters of fields and marshes, where they can most often be seen, towards dusk, swooping in broad curves near the ground, watching for field mice, which form the larger portion of their diet. Their nests are made in swampy ground, often in the middle of a large marsh, being placed on the ground in the centre of a hummock or clump of grass; it is generally well lined with grasses and often rushes. They lay from four to seven pale bluish white eggs, generally unmarked; size 1.80 x 1.40. Data.—Ballston, N. Y., May 20, 1894. Five eggs in a nest of twigs and grass, on the ground in a marshy pasture lot. Collector, Wm. McClair.

[Pale bluish white]

332. Sharp-shinned Hawk. *Accipiter striatus.*

Range.—Whole of North America, wintering in the United States and southward; breeds throughout its range but most abundantly in northern United States and northward. This is one of the smallest of the hawks and in the adult plumage is a beautiful species, being barred below with light brown, and having a bluish slate back. It is a very spirited and daring bird and is one of the most destructive to small birds and young chickens. Its nest is a rude and sometimes very frail platform of twigs and leaves placed against the trunk of the tree at any height but averaging, perhaps, fifteen feet. The eggs are bluish white, beautifully blotched and spotted with shades of brown. Size 1.45x1.15.

[Bluish white.]

333. Cooper's Hawk. *Accipiter cooperii.*

Range.—Whole of temperate North America, breeding throughout its range.

Although larger, (length 17 inches) the plumage of this species is almost exactly the same as that of the preceding. Like the last, this is also a destructive species. They construct their nests in the crotches of trees, generally at quite a height from the ground; the nest is made of sticks and twigs, and often lined with pieces of bark; occasionally an old Hawk's or Crow's nest is used by the birds. Their eggs are bluish white, unmarked or faintly spotted with pale brown. Size 1.90 x 1.45. Data.— Galesburg, Ill. April 16, 1891. Three eggs in an old Crow's nest, made of sticks, lined with corn husks; in large oak 50 feet from ground. Collector, F. C. Willard.

[Bluish white.]

334. Goshawk. *Accipiter gentilis.*

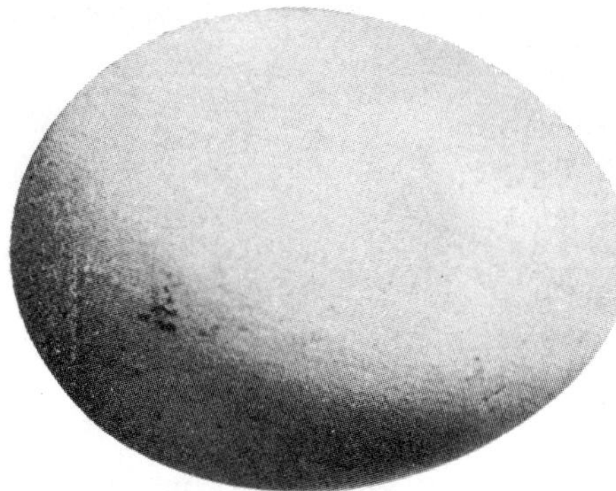

[Bluish white].

Range.—Northern North America, south in winter to the northern parts of the United States.

This species is one of the largest, strongest and most audacious of American Hawks, frequently carrying off Grouse and poultry, the latter often in the presence of the owner. It is a handsome species in the adult plumage, with bluish gray upper parts, and light under parts, finely vermiculated with grayish and with black shafts to the feathers. Length, 23 inches. Their nests are placed well up in the tallest trees, usually in dense woods, the nests being of sticks lined with weeds and bark. The three or four eggs are bluish white, generally unmarked, but occasionally with faint spots of brown. Size 2.30 x 1.70.

334a. Western Goshawk (should be Goshawk). *Accipiter gentilis.*

Range.—Western North America from Alaska to California, breeding chiefly north of the United States except in some of the higher ranges of the Pacific coast. This sub-species is darker, both above and below, than the American Goshawk.[1] Its nesting habits and eggs are precisely the same.

335. Harris' Hawk. *Parabutco unicinctus.*

Range.—Mexico and Central America, north to the Mexican border of the United States; very abundant in southern Texas.

This is a peculiar blackish species, with white rump, and chestnut shoulders and thighs. It is commonly met with in company with Caracaras, Turkey Vultures and Black Vultures, feeding upon carrion. They also feed to an extent on small mammals and birds. Their nests are made of sticks, twigs and weeds, and placed in bushes or low trees. The three or four eggs are laid in April or May. They are dull white in color and generally unmarked, although often showing traces of pale brown spots. They are quite variable in size, averaging 2.10 x 1.65.

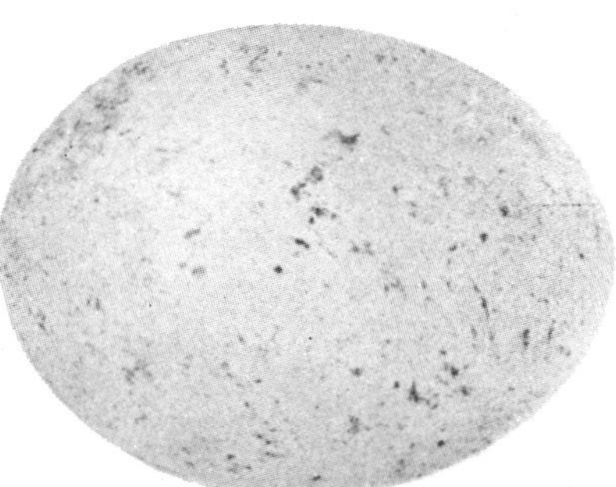

[White.]

336. European Buzzard. *Buteo buteo.*

This common Old World bird is claimed to have been taken in one instance in Michigan, thereby obtaining a doubtful standing among accidental North American birds. Their nesting habits are the same as those of the majority of the Hawks and the eggs resemble small specimens of those of the Red-tail.[2]

[1] Now Goshawk.

[2] Not recorded from North America.

Photo by Geo. L. Fordyce.

NEST AND EGGS OF COOPER'S HAWK.

337. Red-tailed Hawk. *Buteo jamaicensis.*

[Pale bluish white.]

This is one of the handsomest of the larger hawks, and is the best known in the east, where it is commonly, but wrongly, designated as "hen hawk," a name, however, which is indiscriminately applied to any bird that has talons and a hooked beak. The adult of this species is unmistakable because of its reddish brown tail; young birds are very frequently confounded with other species. Their food consists chiefly of small rodents, snakes and lizards, and only occasionally are poultry or birds taken. They nest in the tallest trees in large patches of woods, the nests being made of sticks, weeds, leaves and trash. The eggs number from two to four, and are white, sometimes heavily, and sometimes sparingly, blotched and spotted with various shades of brown. Size 2.35 x 1.80.

337a. Krider's Hawk (should be Red-tailed Hawk). *Buteo jamaicensis.*

Range.—Plains of the United States, north to Manitoba.
This subspecies is described as lighter on the underparts, which are almost immaculate. Its nesting habits and eggs are the same as those of the preceding.

337b. Western Red-tail (should be Red-tailed Hawk). *Buteo jamaicensis.*

Range.—Western North America, chiefly west of the Rocky Mountains.

This subspecies varies from the plumage of the eastern Red-tail, to a nearly uniform sooty above and below, with the dark red tail crossed by several bands; it is a generally darker variety than the Red-tail. Its nesting habits are the same and the eggs show the great variations in markings that are common to the eastern bird.

[White.]

337d. Harlan's Hawk. *Buteo harlani.*

Range.—Gulf States and southward, north to Kansas.[1]
This dark subspecies is generally nearly uniform blackish, but sometimes is lighter or even white below. Its tail is rusty, mottled with blackish and white. Its nesting habits are the same and the eggs are not distinguishable from those of the other Red-tails.

[1] Breeds north to southeastern Alaska and Alberta.

339. Red-shouldered Hawk. *Buteo lineatus.*

Range.—North America, east of the Plains and from the southern parts of the British Provinces southward; abundant and breeding throughout its range.

This species is smaller than the Red-tailed and is not as powerfully built; length 19 inches. The adults are handsomely barred beneath with reddish brown, giving the entire underparts a ruddy color. Like the last species, they rarely feed upon poultry, confining their diet chiefly to mice, rats, frogs, reptiles, etc. These Hawks nest in the larger growths of timber, usually building their nests high above the ground. The nest is of sticks, and lined with leaves, weeds and pieces of bark. They lay three or four eggs with a white ground color, variously blotched and spotted, either sparingly or heavily, with different shades of brown. Size 2.15 x 1.75. Data. — Kalamazoo, Michigan, April 25, 1898. Nest about 40 feet up in an oak tree; made of sticks and twigs and lined with bark. 4 eggs. Collector, J. C. Holmes.

[White.]

339a. Florida Red-shouldered Hawk (should be Red-shouldered Hawk). *Buteo lineatus.*

Range.—Florida and the Gulf coast; north to South Carolina. The nesting habits of this paler subspecies are precisely like those of the last species.

339b. Red-bellied Hawk (should be Red-shouldered Hawk). *Buteo lineatus.*

Range.—Pacific coast from British Columbia south to Lower California, chiefly west of the Rockies.

This variety is similar to, but darker than 339, and the under parts are a uniform reddish brown, without barring. Their nests are like those of the Red-shouldered variety, and almost always placed high up in the largest trees. The eggs are very similar, but average lighter, in markings. Size 2.15 x 1.70. Data.— San Diego, Cal., April 13, 1897. Nest in a sycamore 20 feet from ground, made of sticks, leaves and feathers. Collector, E. A. Shives.

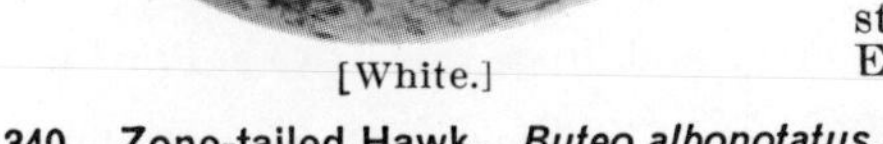
[White.]

340. Zone-tailed Hawk. *Buteo albonotatus.*

Range.—Mexico and Central America, north to the Mexican border of the United States.

This species, which is 19 inches long, is wholly black with the exception of the tail, which is banded. Their nests are built in heavy woods, and preferably in trees along the bank of a stream. The nest is of the usual Hawk construction, and the two to four eggs are white, faintly marked with pale chestnut. Data.— Marathon, Texas. Nest of sticks, lined with weeds and rabbit fur; on a horizontal branch of a cotton-wood tree, 30 feet up. Collector, E. F. Pope.

[White.]

341. White-tailed Hawk. *Buteo albicaudatus.*

[Dull white.]

Range.—Mexican border of the United States and southward.

A large, handsome Hawk which may be identified by its dark upperparts and white underparts and tail, the flanks and tail being lightly barred with grayish; the shoulders are chestnut. It is especially abundant in the southern parts of Texas, where it builds its large bulky nests of sticks and weeds, lined with grasses, leaves and moss. They nest in March and April laying two, or rarely three, eggs which are a dull white, and generally immaculate, but occasionally faintly or sparingly spotted with brown. Size of eggs, 2.25 x 1.80.

342. Swainson's Hawk. *Buteo swainsoni.*

Range.—Central and western North America, from the Mississippi Valley and Hudson Bay, to the Pacific coast, breeding throughout its range.

In the greater part of its range, this is the most abundant of the Hawk family. Its plumage is extremely variable, showing all the intergradations from a uniform sooty blackish to the typical adult plumage of a grayish above, and white below, with a large breast patch of rich chestnut. Their nesting habits are as variable as their plumage. In some localities, they nest exclusively in trees, in others, indifferently upon the ground or rocky ledges. The nest is the usual Hawk structure of sticks; the eggs are white, variously splashed and spotted with reddish brown and umber. Size 2.20 x 1.70. Data.—Stark Co., N. D., May 21, 1897. Nest of sticks, lined with weeds in an ash tree. Collector, Roy Dodd.

[White.]

343. Broad-winged Hawk. *Buteo platypterus.*

Range.—North America, east of the Plains, and from the British Provinces southward.

A medium sized species, about 16 inches in length, and with a short tail and broad rounded wings; adults have the underparts handsomely barred with brown. Their nests are usually built in large trees, but generally placed against the trunk in the crotch of some of the lower branches. It is made of sticks and almost invariably lined with bark. The two to four eggs are of a grayish white color, marked with chestnut brown and stone gray; Size 1.90 x 1.55. Data. — Worcester, Mass., May 16, 1895. Nest about 20 feet up in a large chestnut tree. The birds continually circled overhead, their weird cries sounding like the creaking of branches. Collector, A. J. White.

[Grayish white.]

Photo by Geo. L. Fordyce.

NEST AND EGGS OF RED-SHOULDERED HAWK.

344. Short-tailed Hawk. *Buteo brachyurus.*

Range.—A tropical species, which occurs north to the Mexican border and regularly to southern Florida, where it breeds in the large cypress swamps. Its eggs are pale greenish white, sparingly spotted with brown, chiefly at the large end. Size 2.15 x 1.60.

345. Black Hawk. *Buteogallus anthracinus.*

[Grayish white.]

Range.—Mexican border of the United States and southward.

A coal black species about 22 inches in length, distinguished by the white tip, and broad white band across the tail about midway. This is one of the least abundant of the Mexican species that cross our border. They are shy birds and build their nests in the tallest trees in remote woods. Their two or three eggs are grayish white, faintly spotted with pale brown; size 2.25 x 1.80. Data.—Los Angeles County, Cal., April 6, 1889. Nest of sticks, lined with bark and leaves; 45 feet up in a sycamore tree. Collector, R. B. Chapman.

346. Gray Hawk. *Buteo nitidus.*

Range.—Mexico, north to the border of the United States.

A beautiful, medium sized Hawk (17 inches long), slaty gray above, white below, numerously barred with grayish; tail black, crossed by several white bars. These are graceful and active birds, feeding largely upon small rodents, and occasionally small birds. They nest in the top of tall trees, laying two or three greenish white, unmarked eggs; size 1.95 x 1.60. Data.—Santa Cruz River, Arizona, June 3, 1902. Nest in the fork of a mesquite tree about forty feet from the ground; made of large sticks, lined with smaller ones and leaves. Three eggs. Collector, O. W. Howard.

[White.]

347. Rough-legged Hawk. *Buteo lagopus.*

An Old World species, similar to the next; regarded as doubtfully occuring in Alaska.

347a. American Rough-legged Hawk (should be Rough-legged Hawk). *Buteo lagopus.*

Range.—Northern North America, breeding chiefly north of our borders and wintering south to the middle portions of the United States.

The Rough-legs are large, heavily built birds of prey, specially characterized by the completely feathered legs. The present species is 22 inches long, and in the normal plumage has a whitish head, neck, breast and tail, the former being streaked and the latter, barred with blackish; the remainder of the upper and underparts are blackish brown. Their nests are usually placed in trees, and less often on the ground than are those of the next species. These Rough-legs are very irregularly distributed, and are nowhere as common as the next. While the greater number nest north of the United States, it is very probable that a great many nest on the higher ranges within our borders. The species is often taken in summer, even in Massachusetts. They lay three eggs of a bluish white color, boldly splashed with dark brown; size 2.25 x 1.75.

[Bluish white].

348. Ferruginous Hawk. *Buteo regalis.*

[White.]

Range.—North America, west of the Mississippi, breeding from the latitude of Colorado north to the Saskatchewan region.

This species nests very abundantly along our northern states, particularly in Dakota. It is a larger bird than the preceding and can easily be told by its reddish coloration, particularly on the shoulders and tibia. While in some localities they nest only in trees, the greater number appear to build their nests on the ground or rocky ledges, making a large heap of sticks, weeds and grass. Their three or four eggs are white, beautifully spotted and blotched, in endless variety, with various shades of brown. Size 2.60 x 2.00. Data.—Stark Co., N. D., April 29, 1900. Nest built of coarse sticks on a clay butte. Collector, Roy Dodd.

349. Golden Eagle. *Aquila chrysaëtos.*

Range.—North America, west of the Mississippi; most abundant in the Rockies and along the Pacific coast ranges.

This magnificent bird, which is even more powerful than the Bald Eagle, measures about 34 inches long, and spreads about 7 feet. Its plumage is a rich brownish black, very old birds being golden brown on the nape. They can be distinguished in all plumages from the Bald Eagle by the completely feathered tarsus. They build their nests in the tops of the tallest trees in the wild, mountainous country of the west, and more rarely upon ledges of the cliffs. The nests are made of large sticks, lined with smaller ones and leaves and weeds. Their eggs are the most handsome of the Raptores,[1] being white in color, and blotched, splashed, spotted and specked with light brown and clouded with gray or lilac, of course varying endlessly in pattern and intensity. Size 2.90x2.50. Data.—Monterey Co., Cal., May 3, 1888. Three eggs. Nest of sticks, lined with pine needles, in a pine tree, 50 feet up. Collector, A. Williams.

[Buffy white.]

350.   Harpy Eagle.   *Harpia harpyja.*

Range.—Tropical America; north casually to the Lower Rio Grande Valley in Texas. This accidental straggler to our borders is the largest and most powerful bird of prey found in America, often reaching a length of nearly four feet. They nest in the highest trees of the largest forests.[2]

351.   Gray Sea Eagle.   *Haliaeetus albicilla.*

A common species on the sea coasts of Europe; straggling to southern Greenland, where it nests upon the rocky cliffs.

352.   Bald Eagle.   *Haliaeetus leucocephalus.*

Range.—Whole of North America; most abundant on the Atlantic coast; breeds throughout its range. This large white headed and white tailed species is abundant in sufficiently wild localities along the Atlantic coast. It only attains the white head and tail when three years old, the first two years, being blackish. It is about 34 inches in length and expands about seven feet, never over eight feet, and only birds of the second year (when they are larger than the adults) ever approach this expanse. Their food consists of fish, (which they sometimes capture themselves, but more often take from the Osprey,) carrion, and Ducks which they catch in flight. Their

[White.]

nests are massive structures of sticks, in the tops of tall trees. They very rarely lay more than two eggs, which are white. Size 2.75 x 2.10. Data.—Mt. Pleasant, S. C., nest in top of a pine, 105 feet from the ground; made of large sticks and lined with Spanish moss. Two eggs. Collector, Arthur T. Wayne.

352a.   Alaska Bald Eagle (should be Bald Eagle).   *Haliaeetus leucocephalus.*

Range.—Alaska. This sub-species averages slightly larger than the Bald Eagle but never exceeds the largest dimensions of that species. Its nesting habits and eggs are the same, except that it more often builds its nests on rocky cliffs than does the Bald Eagle. The eggs are laid in February and March.

[1] Now Falconiformes.
[2] Not recorded from North America.

Photo by P. B. Peabody.

NEST AND EGGS OF FERRUGINOUS HAWK.

354b.   White Gyrfalcon (should be Gyrfalcon).   *Falco rusticolus.* [1]

[Buff.]

Range.—Arctic regions; south in winter casually to northern United States chiefly on the coast.

Gyrfalcons are large, strong, active and fearless birds, about 23 inches in length. Their food consists chiefly of hares, Ducks and Waders which abound in the far north. The present species is snowy white, more or less barred with blackish brown on the back and wings and with a few marks on the breast. They nest upon the ledges of high cliffs, laying three or four eggs of a buffy color, blotched and finely specked with reddish brown, this color often concealing the ground color. Size of eggs, 2.30 x 1.80. In America, they nest in Greenland and the Arctic regions.

354b.   Gray Gyrfalcon (should be Gyrfalcon).   *Falco rusticolus.*

Range.—Arctic regions; south in winter to northern United States.

This species is of the size of the last but the plumage is largely gray, barred with dusky. They nest more abundantly in southern Greenland than do the preceding species. The nesting habits and eggs do not differ.

[Buff.]

354b.   Gyrfalcon.   *Falco rusticolus.*

Range.—Arctic regions; south casually to Long Island.

This sub-species is hardly to be distinguished from the preceding. Its nesting habits and eggs are identical, the nests being of sticks, lined with weeds and feathers and placed upon the most inaccessible ledges of cliffs.

354b.   Black Gyrfalcon (should be Gyrfalcon).   *Falco rusticolus.*

Range.—Labrador; south casually, in winter, to Long Island.

A slightly darker variety. Eggs indistinguishable. Data.—Ungava coast, Labrador, May 25, 1900. Nest a heap of seaweed and feathers on sea cliff. 3 eggs secured by an Esquimau who was lowered to the ledge by a rope.

355.   Prairie Falcon.   *Falco mexicanus.*

[Reddish buff.]

Range.—United States west of the Mississippi, and from Dakota and Washington southward to Mexico.

This species abounds in suitable localities, generally placing its nests upon rocky ledges and cliffs, and sometimes trees, generally upon the banks of some stream. The nests are masses of sticks, lined with weeds and grasses. The three or four eggs have a reddish buff ground color, and are thickly sprinkled and blotched with reddish brown and chestnut; size 2.05 x 1.60. Data.—Obispo Co. Cal., April 6, 1901. Nest in a "pot hole" in face of limestone bluff; eggs on bare sand in a hollow. Collector, H. R. Taylor.

[1] All of the forms of the Gyrfalcon listed on this page are no more than color phases of the one species.

356. Peregrine Falcon. *Falco peregrinus.*

Range.—Whole of North America, breeding locally, chiefly in mountainous regions, throughout its range.

This beautiful species, characterized by
its black moustache, is the most graceful,
fearless, and swiftest of the Falcons, striking down birds of several times its own
weight, such as some of the larger Ducks.
It breeds quite abundantly on the Pacific
coast and in certain localities in the Dakotas, laying its eggs on the rocky ledges.
Their eggs are similar to those of the
Prairie Falcon, but are darker and brighter, in fact they are the darkest, brightest
marked, and most beautiful of Falcon
eggs; size 2.05 x 1.55. Data.—Stark Co.,
N. D., May 4, 1901.   Eggs laid on the gravel on ledge of high rocky butte.
Collector, Edw. Dodd.

[Buff or reddish buff.]

356a. Peale's Falcon (should be Peregrine Falcon). *Falco peregrinus.*

Range.—Pacific coast from northern United States north to Alaska.
A darker form of the preceding, such as occurs in this section with a great
many other birds.   The nesting habits and the eggs are precisely like those of
the Peregrine Falcon.

357. Merlin. *Falco columbarius.*

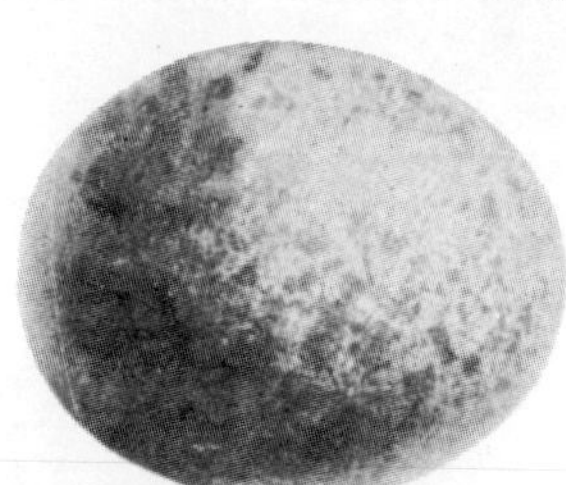

[Brownish buff.]

Range.—North America, breeding chiefly north
of the United States except in some of the higher
ranges along our northern border.   A small Falcon,
about 11 inches long, often confused with the
Sharp-shinned Hawk, but much darker and a more
stoutly built bird.   It is a daring species, often
attacking birds larger than itself; it also feeds on
mice, grasshoppers, squirrels, etc.   They generally
build a slight nest of sticks in trees, deep in the
woods; less often in natural cavities of dead trees;
and sometimes on rocky ledges.   The eggs have a
brownish buff ground color, heavily blotched with
brown and chestnut.   Size 1.50 x 1.22.   Data.—So.
Labrador, May 29, 1899.   Nest a platform of sticks, twigs and moss in a pine tree,
3 feet up.   Five eggs,   Collector, E. H. Montgomery.

357a. Black Merlin (should be Merlin). *Falco columbarius.*

Range.—Pacific coast from northern United States north to Alaska.
Very similar in appearance to the preceding, but much darker, both above and
below.   Its nesting habits and eggs will not differ in any manner from those of
the Pigeon Hawk.[1]

---

[1] Now Merlin.

357b.   Richardson's Merlin (should be Merlin).   *Falco columbarius.*

Range.—Interior of North America from the Mississippi to the Rockies and from Mexico to the Saskatchewan.

[Cream.]

This species is similar to the Pigeon Hawk,[1] but is paler both above and below, and the tail bars are more numerous and white.   Their nesting habits are the same as those of the preceding species, they either building in hollow trees, or making a rude nest of sticks and twigs in the tops of trees.   The eggs have a creamy ground and are sprinkled with dots and blotches of various shades of brown.   Size 1.60 x 1.23.   The egg figured is one of a beautiful set of four in the collection of Mr. C. W. Crandall.   Data.— Calgary, N. W. T., May 12, 1894.   Nest in a natural cavity of a black poplar, 22 feet from the ground.   Bird taken.   Collector, J. E. Houseman.

358.1.   Merlin.   *Falco columbarius.*

This common European species was once accidentally taken in southern Greenland.   Their eggs are generally laid on the ground on cliffs or banks.

359.   Aplomado Falcon.   *Falco femoralis.*

Range.—Tropical America north to the Mexican boundary of the United States.

This handsome and strikingly marked Falcon is found in limited numbers within the United States, but south is common and widely distributed.   They nest at a low elevation, in bushes or small trees, making their rude nests of twigs, lined with a few grasses.   They lay three, and sometimes four, eggs which have a creamy white ground color, finely dotted with cinnamon, and with heavy blotches of brown.   Size 1.75 x 1.30.

[Buff.]

359.1.   Eurasian Kestrel.   *Falco tinnunculus.*

[Reddish buff.]

Range.—Whole of Europe; accidental on the coast of Massachusetts.

This species is very similar in size and coloration to the American Sparrow Hawk.[2] They are much more abundant than the Sparrow Hawk is in this country and frequently nest about houses, in hollow trees, on rafters of barns, or on ledges and embankments.   Their eggs are of a reddish buff color, speckled and blotched with reddish brown, they being much darker than those of the American Sparrow Hawk.

[1] Now Merlin.

[2] Now American Kestrel.

360.   American Kestrel   *Falco sparverius.*

Range.—North America, east of the Rocky Mountains and north to Hudson Bay; winters from the middle portions of the United States, southward.

[Buffy.]

This beautiful little Falcon is the smallest of the American Hawks, being only 10 inches in length. They are very abundant in the east, nesting anywhere in cavities in trees, either in woods or open fields. The eggs are generally deposited upon the bottom of the cavity with no lining; they are creamy or yellowish buff in color, sprinkled, spotted or blotched, in endless variety, with reddish brown.   Size 1.35 x 1.10. They are very noisy, especially when the young are learning to fly, uttering a loud, tinkling, "killy, killy, killy." They have a very amiable disposition, and frequently nest harmoniously in the same tree with other birds, such as Flickers and Robins.

360a.   Desert Sparrow Hawk (should be American Kestrel).   *Falco sparverius.*

Range—Western United States from British Columbia south to Mexico.
This variety is slightly larger and paler than the eastern form.   There are no differences in the nidification of the two varieties.

360b.   St. Lucas Sparrow Hawk (should be American Kestrel).   *Falco sparverius.*

Range.—Lower California.
This variety is smaller than the eastern, and even paler than the western form.   Eggs identical with eastern specimens.

361.   Cuban Sparrow Hawk (should be American Kestrel).   *Falco sparverius.*

A darker colored West Indian form, whose habits and nesting do not vary from those of the common Sparrow Hawk;[1] casually taken in Florida.

362.   Crested Caracara.   *Caracara cheriway.*

Range—Southern border of the United States south to South America.

A strikingly marked blackish and whitish species, much barred on the fore back and the breast, with the head and throat largely white, except for a black and somewhat crested crown.   They are numerous in southern Texas and also in the interior of southern Florida, where they are resident. They build bulky, but shabby nests of sticks, weeds and grass, piled into a promiscuous heap, generally located in bushes or low trees.   Their two or three eggs have a ground color varying from buff to bright cinnamon, and are dotted and blotched with all shades of brown and umber. On the whole, these eggs show a greater diversity of markings and ground color, than those of any other species. Size 2.50 x 1.80.

[Cinnamon.]

---

[1] Now American Kestrel.

363.   Guadalupe Caracara.   *Caracara lutosa*.

Range.—Guadalupe Island and others off Lower California. [1]

This species is somewhat like the preceding but the plumage is duller, and the coloration more uniform.   Their nesting habits and eggs do not vary essentially from those of Audubon Caracara. [2] Mr. John Lewis Childs has a set of two eggs taken June 8, 1896, on Santa Anita Island, by Coolidge and Miller.   The nest was made of sticks and situated in a giant cactus.   The eggs are slightly brighter and more clearly marked than any of *cheriway* that I have ever seen.

364.   Osprey.   *Pandion haliaetus*.

Range.—Whole of Temperate America from the Arctic Circle south to the equator, most abundant along the sea coasts.

[Bright cream color.]

Probably this great fisherman is as well known from one end of the country to the other as any of our wild birds.   He is protected by law in a great many states and by custom in nearly all localities where they breed.   It is one of the pleasantest sights along the coast to watch a number of these great birds as they soar at an elevation above the water, watching for a fish to come near the surface, when, with folded wings, the bird speeds downward and plunges into the water, rarely missing his prey.   In many localities they are very tame and nest in the vicinity of houses, sometimes even in the yard.   Their nests are platforms of sticks, which, being used year after year and constantly added to, become of enormous proportions. They lay two or three eggs of a bright creamy color, handsomely blotched with bright chestnut brown.   They show a great diversity of size as well as markings, but average 2.40 x 1.80.

BARN OWLS.   Family TYTONIDAE.

365.   Barn Owl.   *Tyto alba*.

Range.—Chiefly in the southern parts of the United States; north casually to Massachusetts, Minnesota and Washington.

This is one of the lightest colored of the Owls; it has a long, peculiarly hooded face, from which it gets the name of "Monkey-faced Owl." Its plumage is yellowish buff, specked and barred lightly with blackish.

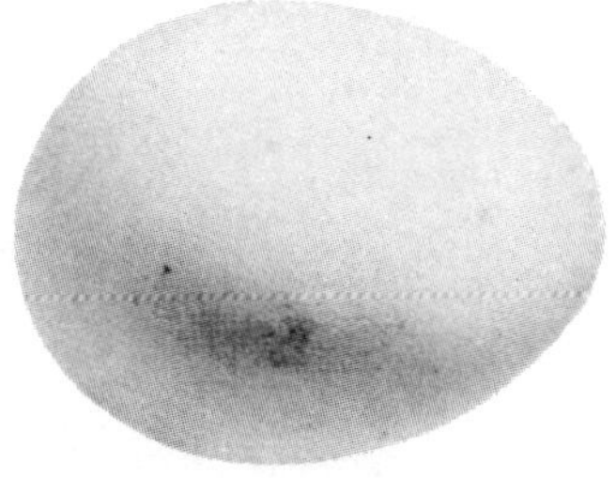

[White.]

[1] Extinct.

[2] Now Crested Caracara.

Photo from life by A. J. Myers.

OSPREY RETURNING TO ITS NEST.

It nests usually in hollow cavities of trees, but appears to have no objections to barns, holes in banks, or anywhere it can find a concealed crevice in which to deposit its four to six pure white eggs; size 1.70 x 1.30. Data.—Santa Clara Co., Cal., April 14, 1891. 4 eggs. Nest in hollow of an oak tree, 15 feet up. Collector, Rollo H. Beck.

TYPICAL OWLS. Family STRIGIDAE.

366. Long-eared Owl. *Asio otus.*

[White.]

Range.—North America, breeding from the southern parts of British America, southward.

This species is 15 inches in length; it can easily be separated from any other species by its long ear tufts, brownish face, and barred underparts. Their food consists almost entirely of small rodents, which they catch at night. Most of their nests are found in trees, they generally using old Crow's or Hawk's nests. They also, in some localities, nest in hollow trees, or in crevices among rocks. Their nesting season ranges from March in the southern parts of their range, to April and May in the northern. They lay from four to seven pure white eggs; size 1.55 x 1.35.

367. Short-eared Owl. *Asio flammeus.*

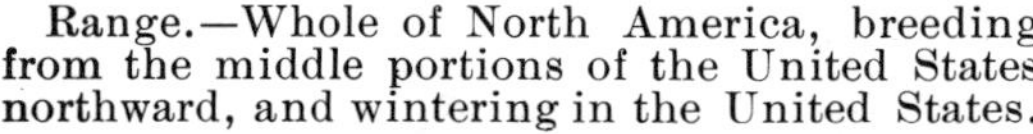

Range.—Whole of North America, breeding from the middle portions of the United States northward, and wintering in the United States.

This species is of the size of the last, but is paler, has very short ear tufts, and is streaked beneath. Its habits are the same except that it frequently hunts, over the marshes and meadows, on dark days and toward dusk.

Their four to seven, pure white eggs are laid upon the ground in marshy places, sometimes upon a lining of sticks and weeds, and are generally under a bush, or close to an old log. They nest, in different localities, from March to May. Size of eggs 1.55 x 1.25.

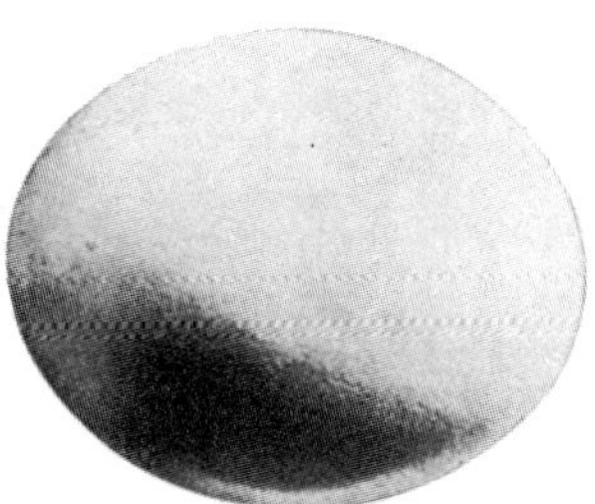

[White.]

368. Barred Owl. *Strix varia.*

Range.—Eastern North America, from the British Provinces, southward; west to the Rockies.

This species is the most common of the large owls, and can be distinguished by its mottled and barred gray and white plumage, and lack of ear tufts; length 20 inches. It is the bird commonly meant by the term "hoot owl," and being strictly nocturnal, is rarely seen flying in the day time, unless disturbed from its roosting place in the deep woods. Its food consists chiefly of rats, mice, and frogs, and sometimes, but not often, poultry. It nests in the heart of large woods, generally in hollows of large trees, and less

[White.]

often in deserted Crows' nests. The nesting season is from February in the south to April in the northern parts of their range. They lay from two to four pure white eggs, averaging considerably smaller than those of the Great Horned Owl; size 1.95 x 1.65.

368a. Florida Barred Owl (should be Barred Owl). *Strix varia.*

Range.—Florida and the Gulf States; north to South Carolina.

A slightly smaller, and darker variety of the Barred Owl. Its habits and nesting habits are the same except that it generally breeds in January and February, and lays but two eggs, which are smaller than those of the preceding; size 1.90 x 1.60.

368b. Texas Barred Owl (should be Barred Owl). *Strix varia.*

Range.—Southern Texas.

A very similar but slightly paler variety than the Barred Owl, and with the toes bare, as in 368a. Eggs indistinguishable.

369. Spotted Owl. *Strix occidentalis.*

Range.—Western United States, from southern Oregon and Colorado, southward.

Similar to the Barred Owl but spotted, instead of barred, on the back of head and neck, and much more extensively barred on the under parts. The nesting habits do not appear to differ in any respect from those of the eastern Barred Owl, and their eggs which are from two to four in number, cannot be distinguished from those of the latter species; size 2.05 x 1.80.

369a. Northern Spotted Owl (should be Spotted Owl). *Strix occidentalis.*

Radge.—Northwestern United States and British Columbia.

Similar to the preceding, but darker, both above and below; nesting the same, in hollow trees or in old Hawk's or Crow's nests. Eggs not distinguishable.

370. Great Gray Owl. *Strix nebulosa.*

Range.—Northern North America; wintering regularly south to the northern border of the United States and casually farther.

This is the largest of American Owls, being about 26 inches in length; it does not weigh nearly as much, however, as the Great Horned or Snowy Owls, its plumage being very light and fluffy, and dark gray in color, mottled with white. The facial disc is very large, and the eyes are small and yellow, while those of the Barred Owl are large and blue black. They nest in heavily wooded districts, building their nests of sticks, chiefly in pine

[White.]

trees. The two to four white eggs are laid during May and June; size 2.15x1.70.

370a. Lapp Owl (should be Great Gray Owl). *Strix nebulosa.*

A paler form of the Great Gray Owl, inhabiting the Arctic regions of the Old World; accidental on the coast of Alaska. Their nesting habits and eggs do not differ from those of the American bird.

371. Boreal Owl. *Aegolius funereus.*

[White.]

Range.—Northern North America, breeding north of the United States; winters south to our border and casually farther.

This is a dark grayish and white bird, 10 inches in length, and without ear tufts. Breeds commonly in the extensively wooded districts of British America, chiefly in the northern parts. Their three or four white eggs are usually at the bottom of a cavity in a tree, but occasionally the birds build a rude nest of sticks and twigs, lined with leaves and placed in trees at a moderate height from the ground. Size of eggs, 1.25 x 1.05.

372. Saw-whet Owl. *Aegolius acadicus.*

Range.—North America, breeding in the northern parts of the United States and in British America, and south in the Rockies to Mexico; winters south to the middle portions of the United States.

This small species (length 8 inches) is marked very similarly to the preceding, but the plumage is brown instead of gray. They normally nest in hollow trees, generally in deserted Woodpecker holes, in extensively wooded sections, and usually in mountainous country, especially in the United States. They have also been known to nest in bird boxes near farm houses and in old Crow's nests. During April or May, they lay from three to six white eggs. Size 1.20 x 1.00. They are quiet and chiefly nocturnal birds, not often seen, and may be found nesting in any of the northern states.

372a. Northwest Saw-whet Owl (should be Saw-whet Owl). *Aegolius acadicus.*

Range.—A dark variety found on the coast of British Columbia.

373. Screech Owl. *Otus asio.*

Range.—North America, east of the Plains and from the southern British Provinces to Florida.

This well-known species, which is often called "Little Horned Owl" because of its ear tufts, is found either in the type form or some of its varieties in all parts of the United States. They have two color phases, the plumage being either a yellowish brown or gray, and black and white; these color phases are not dependent upon sex or locality, as often young of both phases are found in the same nest; the gray phase is the most abundant. They nest anywhere in hollow trees, being found very frequently in decayed stubs of apple trees.

[White.]

They also often nest in barns or other old buildings which are not frequented too freely. Their food consists chiefly of mice and meadow moles, with occasionally small birds. During April or May they lay their white eggs, the full complement of which is from five to eight. Size 1.35 x 1.20. The nesting habits of all the sub-species, as far as we can learn, are exactly like those of the eastern Screech Owl; the eggs cannot be distinguished, and in most cases, even the birds cannot be distinguished.

373a. Florida Screech Owl (should be Screech Owl). *Otus asio.*

Range.—South Atlantic and Gulf coasts.
Slightly smaller and darker than 373. The eggs average slightly smaller. Size 1.30 x 1.15.

373b. Texas Screech Owl (should be Screech Owl). *Otus asio.*

Range.—Texas, and southward into Mexico. Very similar to 373a.

373c. California Screech Owl (should be Screech Owl). *Otus asio.*

Range.—Coast of California and Oregon. Size of, but darker than 373.

373d. Kennicott's Screech Owl (should be Screech Owl). *Otus asio.*

Range.—Pacific coast from Oregon to Alaska. This is the darkest of the Screech Owls and averages a trifle larger than the eastern form.

373e. Rocky Mountain Screech Owl (should be Screech Owl). *Otus asio.*

Range.—Foothills of the Rockies, from Colorado to Montana. This is the palest form of the Screech Owl. Of the same size as the last.

373f. Mexican Screech Owl (should be Screech Owl). *Otus asio.*

Range.—Western Mexico and southwestern border of the United States. A gray form with little or no buff, and more numerously barred below.

373g. Aiken's Screech Owl (should be Screech Owl). *Otus asio.*

Range.—El Paso County, Colorado. A gray form, with the dark markings coarser and more numerous than in any other.

373h. MacFarlane's Screech Owl (should be Screech Owl). *Otus asio.*

Range.—Northern border of the United States from Washington to Montana.

373i. Spotted Screech Owl (should be Screech Owl). *Otus asio.*

Range.—Mountains of southern Arizona, south into Mexico.
A grayish species, similar to 373, but paler and more finely barred beneath, and with whitish spots on the feathers of the foreback. The nesting habits and eggs are probably the same as those of the Screech Owl.

373.2.   Xantus' Screech Owl (should be Screech Owl).   *Otus asio.*
Range.—Southern Lower California.
A grayish species with the back and underparts finely vermiculated with reddish brown, and with streaks of darker.   It is not likely that the habits or eggs of this species will be found to differ from those of the Screech Owl.

374.   Flammulated Owl.   *Otus flammeolus.*
Range.—Mountain ranges of Mexico, north to Colorado and west to California.
This species is smaller than 373, has shorter ear tufts, the plumage is much streaked and edged with rusty, and the toes are unfeathered to their base.   They nest in hollow trees, generally using deserted Woodpecker holes.   Their three or four eggs are white.   Size 1.15 x .95.   This species is uncommon in all parts of its range.

374a.   Dwarf Screech Owl (should be Flammulated Owl).   *Otus flammeolus.*
Range.—Local in Idaho, eastern Washington and California.
This rare variety is smaller than the preceding and is considerably paler.   Its eggs have not been described, but should be a trifle smaller than the last.[1]

375.   Great Horned Owl.   *Bubo virginianus.*
Range.—North America, east of the Plains and north to Labrador.

[White.]

This species or its varieties are the only large Owls having conspicuous ear tufts.   They are about 22 inches in length, and have a mottled brown, black and white plumage, barred below.   This is also one of the "Hoot Owls" but is not nearly as abundant as the Barred Owl.   It is one of the strongest of the family, and captures rabbits, grouse and poultry, and is very often found to have been feeding upon, or to have been in the immediate vicinity of a skunk.   They nest very early, January, February and March.   Deserted Hawk's or Crow's nests are very frequently used by this bird, if they are located in dense woods.   They also sometimes nest in hollow cavities in large trees.   They lay from two to four pure white eggs.   Size 2.25 x 1.85.   Data.—Park County, Indiana, Feb. 15, 1900.   Nest in crevice of projecting rocks, on the pulverized sandstone.   Collector, Winfield S. Catlin.

375a.   Western Horned Owl (should be Great Horned Owl).   *Bubo virginianus.*
Range.—Western North America, except the Pacific coast.
A smaller and lighter colored form of the preceding having the same habits and the eggs being indistinguishable from those of the eastern bird.

375b.   Arctic Horned Owl (should be Great Horned Owl).   *Bubo virginianus.*
Range.—Interior of Arctic America from Hudson Bay to Alaska; south in winter to the northwestern tier of states.
A very pale colored Horned Owl with little or no buff or brownish in the plumage, some specimens (very rare) being pure white with only a few black bars on the back.   Their nesting habits are the same and the eggs do not vary appreciably from those of the eastern Horned Owl.

1 No longer recognized as a valid form.

375c.   Dusky Horned Owl (should be Great Horned Owl).   *Bubo virginianus.*

Range.—Pacific coast from California to Alaska.

This is the darkest of the Horned Owls, the extreme case being nearly black on the back and very dark below.   Nesting the same as the Great Horned Owl.

375d.   Pacific Horned Owl (should be Great Horned Owl).   *Bubo virginianus.*

Range.—California, southward and east to Arizona.

Smaller and darker than the eastern form but not as dark as the last.   Eggs the same as those of the others.

375e.   Dwarf Horned Owl (should be Great Horned Owl).   *Bubo virginianus.*

Range.—Lower California.

This is a similar but darker form of the Horned Owl and is very much smaller than the Great Horned Owl The nesting habits will be the same, but the eggs may average smaller.

376.   Snowy Owl.   *Nyctea scandiaca.*

Range.—Arctic regions, breeding within the Arctic Circle and wintering to the northern border of the United States and casually farther.

This very beautiful species varies in plumage from pure white, unmarked, to specimens heavily and broadly barred with blackish brown. It is, next to the Great Gray Owl, the largest species found in America, being 2 feet in length.   Like the Great Horned Owls, they are very strong, fearless, and rapacious birds, feeding upon hares, squirrels and smaller mammals, as well as Grouse, Ptarmigan, etc. They nest upon the ground, on banks or mossy hummocks on the dry portions of marshes, laying from two to eight eggs, white in color and with a smoother shell than those of the Great Horned Owl.   Size 2.25 x 1.75.   Data.—

[White.]

Point Barrow, Alaska, June 16, 1898.   3 eggs laid in a hollow in the moss.   Collector, Dr. J. C. Call.

377.   Hawk-Owl.   *Surnia ulula.*

Range.—Northern portion of the Old World; accidental in Alaska.

Similar to the American species but lighter and more brownish.

377a.   American Hawk Owl (should be Hawk-Owl). *Surnia ulula.*

Range.—Northern North America, breeding from the central portions of British America, northward probably also breeds in the Rocky Mountains in the northern tier of states and casually farther.

This handsome mottled and barred, gray and black owl might readily be mistaken for a Hawk, because of his Hawk-like appearance and long rounded tails.   They are very active birds, especially in the day time, for they are more diurnal than nocturnal; their food is mostly of small rodents, and also small birds.   They nest either in the tops of large fir trees, in hollows of stumps, or, in some cases, upon the ground.   When in trees their nests are made of twigs, leaves and weeds, and sometimes lined with moss and feathers; they lay from three to eight white eggs, size 1.50 x 1.20.   Data.—Labrador, May 3, 1899. 5 eggs.   Nest in the top of a dead tree, 15 feet from the ground.   Collector, E. H. Montgomery.

[White.]

378.   Burrowing Owl.   *Speotyto cunicularia.*

Range.—Western North America from the Mississippi Valley west to California; north to the southern parts of British America and south to Central America.

These peculiar birds are wholly different in plumage, form and habits from any other American Owls.   They can readily be recognized by their long, slender and scantily feathered legs.   Their plumage is brownish, spotted with white above, and white, barred with brown below; length 10 inches.   They nest, generally in large communities in burrows in the ground, usually deserted Prairie Dog holes.   While generally but a single pair occupy one burrow, as many as twenty have been found nesting together.   Sometimes the burrows are unlined, and again may have a carpet of grasses and feathers.   Their white eggs generally number from six to ten; size 1.25 x 1.00.   Data.—Sterling, Kans., May 7, 1899. 5 eggs.   Nest of bits of dry dung at the end of a deserted Prairie Dog burrow.   Collector, C. C. Cantwell.

[White.]

378a.   Florida Burrowing Owl (should be Burrowing Owl).   *Speotyto cunicularia.*

Range.—Local in the interior of Florida.

Like the last, but slightly smaller and paler, and with the tarsus less feathered. Their habits or eggs do not differ from the preceding.

Photo from life by L. S. Horton.

LONG-EARED OWL ON NEST.

379. Pygmy Owl. *Glaucidium gnoma.*

Range.—Rocky Mountain region and westward; from British Columbia southward. These interesting little Owls, which are but seven inches in length, feed in the day time upon insects, mice and, occasionally, small birds. They frequent extensively wooded districts, chiefly in the mountain ranges. They nest in tall trees, generally in deserted Woodpeckers' holes, laying three or four white eggs during May; size about 1.00 x .90.

379a. California Pygmy Owl (should be Pygmy Owl). *Glaucidium gnoma.*

Range.—Pacific coast from British Columbia, south through California. This sub-species is darker and more brownish than the last. It is not an uncommon bird in California. They nest in the tallest trees along the ranges, often being found 75 or more feet from the ground. The eggs do not differ from those of the Pygmy Owl, ranging in size from 1.00 x .85 to 1.20 x .95.

379.1. Hoskin's Pygmy Owl (should be Pygmy Owl). *Glaucidium gnoma.*

Range. Southern Lower California.

This species is smaller and more gray than the preceding. It is not probable that its manners of nesting or eggs differ in any respect from those of the others of this genus.

380. Ferruginous Owl. *Glaucidium brasilianum.*

Range.—Mexico and Central America; north to the Mexican border of the United States.

This species is of the same size as the last but is much tinged with rufous on the upper parts, and the tail is of a bright chestnut brown color, crossed by about eight bars of black. They nest in hollow cavities in trees, from ten to forty feet from the ground, laying three or four glossy white eggs; size 1.10 x .90.

381. Elf Owl. *Micrathene whitneyi.*

Range.—Mexico, north to the bordering states.

This odd little bird is the smallest member of the family found in America, attaining a length of only six inches. In plumage it may be described as similar to a very small, earless Screech Owl, only with the pattern of the markings a great deal finer. They are said to be quite abundant in the tablelands of central Mexico and in southern Arizona, where they build their nests in deserted Woodpeckers' holes, perhaps most frequently in the giant cactus. It is said to be more nocturnal than the Pygmy Owls and to feed almost exclusively upon insects. They lay from three to five eggs having a slight gloss. Size 1.02 x .90. Data.—Southern Arizona, May 22, 1902. Nest in a deserted Woodpecker hole. Two eggs. Collector, O. W. Howard.

PARROTS. Order PSITTACIFORMES.

PARROTS. Family PSITTACIDAE.

382. Carolina Parakeet. *Conuropsis carolinensis.*

Range.—Now rare in Florida and along the Gulf coast to Indian Territory.[1]
As late as 1885, the Carolina Parakeets were abun-
dant in the South Atlantic and Gulf States, but owing
to their wanton destruction by man, they have been
exterminated in the greater portion of their range,
and now are rarely seen in any locality, and then
only in the most unhabitable swamps and thickets.
A reliable account of their nesting habits is lacking,
as are also specimens of their eggs taken from wild
birds. They are said to build rude nests of sticks
upon horizontal branches of cypress trees, and to
nest in colonies; it is also claimed that they nest
in hollow trees, laying from three to five pure white
eggs. The one figured is one of three laid in confine-

[White.]

ment at Washington, D. C. by a pair of birds owned by Mr. Robert Ridgway.
It is 1.31 x 1.06 and was laid July 12, 1892. This set is in the collection of Mr.
John Lewis Childs.

382.1. Thick-billed Parrot. *Rhynchopsitta pachyrhyncha.*

Range.—Mexico, north casually to the Mexican border of the United States.
This large Parrot (16 inches long) has a heavy black bill, and the plumage is
entirely green except for the deep red forehead, stripe over the eye, shoulder, and
thighs, and the yellowish under wing coverts. Their eggs are white and are laid
in natural cavities in large trees in forests.

CUCKOOS and allies; TROGONS; KINGFISHERS and allies. Orders CUCULIFORMES, TROGONIFORMES and CORACII- FORMES (part).

CUCKOOS and allies. Family CUCULIDAE.

383. Smooth-billed Ani. *Crotophaga ani.*

Range.—Northeastern South America and the West Indies; casual in Florida,
and along the Gulf coast; accidental in Pennsylvania.
This species is similar to the next, but the bill is smoother and without
grooves. Its nesting habits are the same as those of the more common American species.

384. Groove-billed Ani. *Crotophaga sulcirostris.*

[Greenish blue.]

Range.—Mexico and the border of the United
States; common in southern Texas. This odd species has a Cuckoo-like form, but is wholly blue black
in color, and has a high thin bill with three conspicuous longitudinal grooves on each side. They build
large bulky nests of twigs, lined with leaves and
grasses, and located in low trees and bushes. They
build in small colonies but do not, as is claimed of
the common Ani,[2] build a large nest for several to
occupy. They lay from three to five eggs of a greenish blue color, covered with a chalky white deposit.
Size 1.25 x 1.00. They are laid in May or June.

[1] Extinct.

[2] Now Smooth-billed Ani.

385. Roadrunner. *Geococcyx californianus.*

Range.—Western United States from Oregon, Colorado and Kansas, southward; most abundant on the Mexican border, and wintering in central Mexico.

[White]

This curious species is known as the "Chaparral Cock," "Ground Cuckoo," "Snake-killer," etc. Its upper parts are a glossy greenish brown, each feather being edged or fringed with whitish; the tail is very long, broad and graduated, the feathers being broadly tipped with white. They are noted for their swiftness on foot, paddling over the ground at an astonishing rate, aided by their outstretched wings and spread tail, which act as aeroplanes; their legs are long and have two toes front and two back. Their food consists of lizards and small snakes, they being particularly savage in their attacks upon the latter. They build rude nests of sticks and twigs, in low trees or bushes, and during April or May lay from four to ten eggs, depositing them at intervals of several days. They are pure white and measure 1.55 x 1.20.

386. Mangrove Cuckoo. *Coccyzus minor.*

Range.—West Indies, Mexico and South America, north regularly to southern Florida.

This species is very similar to our common Yellow-billed Cuckoo, but the whole underparts are deep buff. It is a common species and nests abundantly in the West Indies, but occurs only in limited numbers in southern Florida. Their nests are shallow platforms of twigs and rootlets, placed in bushes and low trees, and upon which they lay three or four pale greenish blue eggs, similar to those of the Yellow-billed species but averaging smaller; size 1.15 x .85.

[Pale greenish blue.]

386a. Maynard's Cuckoo (should be Mangrove Cuckoo). *Coccyzus minor.*

Range.—Bahamas; accidental on Florida Keys. This is a slightly smaller and paler form than the preceding.

387. Yellow-billed Cuckoo. *Coccyzus americanus.*

[Light greenish blue.]

Range.—United States east of the Plains and from southern Canada southward.

This species is generally abundant in all localities in its range, which afford suitable nesting places of tangled underbrush or vines. It may be distinguished from the Black-billed variety by its larger size (12 inches long), blackish tail with broad white tips, and yellowish lower mandible. They are often regarded by the superstitious as forecasters of rain, and as omens of evil, probably because of their guttural croaking notes.

Their nests are made of twigs, lined with shreds of grapevine bark or catkins; the nests are generally very shabbily made and so flat on the top that the eggs frequently roll off. They are located near the ground in bushes or low trees. The three or four eggs are deposited at intervals of several days, and frequently young birds and eggs are found in the nest at the same time. Like the Flicker, this bird will frequently continue laying if one egg is removed at a time, and as many as twelve have been taken from the same nest, by this means. The eggs are light greenish blue. Size 1.20 x .90. They are usually laid during May or June.

387a. California Cuckoo (should be Yellow-billed Cuckoo). *Coccyzus americanus.*

Range.—Western North America, from British Columbia, southward.
Slightly larger and with a stouter bill than the last. Eggs not distinguishable.

388. Black-billed Cuckoo. *Coccyzus erythrophthalmus.*

Range.—United States east of the Rocky Mountains; north to Labrador and Manitoba; south in winter to Central and South America.

[Greenish blue.]

This species is rather more common in the northern parts of the United States than the Yellow-billed variety. The bird is smaller, has a black bill, and the tail is the same color as the back and only slightly tipped with white. Their nests are built in similar locations and of the same materials as used by the Yellow-bill; the three or four eggs are smaller and a darker shade of greenish blue. Size 1.15 x .85. All the Cuckoos are close sitters and will not leave the nest until nearly reached with the hand, when they will slowly flutter off through the underbrush, and continue to utter their mournful "Kuk-kuk-kuk," many times repeated.

388.1. Kamchatkan Cuckoo (should be Oriental Cuckoo). *Cuculus saturatus.*

An Asiatic subspecies of the common European Cuckoo, accidentally occurring in Alaska [1]

TROGONS. Family TROGONIDAE.

389. Coppery-tailed Trogon. *Trogon elegans.*

Range.—Southern Mexico, north to the Lower Rio Grande in Texas and in southern Arizona, in both of which localities they probably breed.

[Dull white.]

This is the only member of this family of beautiful birds which reaches our borders. This species is 12 inches in length, and is a metallic green color on the upper parts and breast, and with coppery reflections of the middle tail feathers, the outer ones being white, very finely vermiculated with black, as are the wing coverts. The underparts, except for a white band across the breast, are rosy red. This species nest in cavities in large trees, generally in large, deserted Woodpecker holes. They are also said to have been found nesting in holes in banks. Their eggs are three or four in number and are a dull white in color. Size 1.10 x .85. Data.—Tampico, Mexico, April 21, 1900. 4 eggs at the bottom of a hole in limb of a large elm. Collector, F. B. Armstrong.

---

[1] Not Common Cuckoo (*Cuculus canorus*) of Europe.

Photo by A. R. SPAID.

NEST AND EGGS OF YELLOW-BILLED CUCKOO.

KINGFISHERS. Family ALCEDINIDAE.

390. Belted Kingfisher. *Megaceryle alcyon.*

Range.—Whole of North America, breeding from southern United States, northward and wintering from the southern parts of its breeding range, southward.

This well-known bird is abundant in all localities near water, where its rattling notes are among the most familiar of sounds. Their food is almost entirely of small fish, which they catch by plunging upon from their perch on an old dead limb overhanging the water, or by hovering in the air like an Osprey. Their nests are located at the end of burrows in sand banks or the banks of creeks and rivers. These tunnels, which are dug by the birds, generally commence two or three feet from the top of the bank and extend back from six to eight feet, either in a straight line or curved; the end is enlarged to form a suitable nesting

[White.]

place, in which from five to eight eggs are laid. They are glossy and pure white in color. Size 1.35 x I.05. Data.—Lake Quinsigamond, Massachusetts, June 6, 1900. 7 eggs at the end of a six foot tunnel in a sand bank. Bird removed by hand from the nest. Collector, C. E. Howe.

390.1. Ringed Kingfisher. *Megaceryle torquata.*

Range.—Mexico, north casually to the Lower Rio Grande Valley in Texas.

This handsome species is much larger than the Belted Kingfisher and the underparts are nearly all bright chestnut, except the white throat. They nest in river banks the same as the common American species, and the eggs are white, but larger. Size 1.45 x 1.10.

391. Green Kingfisher. *Chloroceryle americana.*

Range.—Southern Texas, south through Mexico.

This variety is much smaller than the Belted, length 8 inches, and is a lustrous greenish above, variously specked with white, and is white below, spotted with greenish. It is a common and resident species in southern Texas, where it lays its eggs in holes in the banks along streams. The eggs are white and glossy, and measure .95 x .70.

WOODPECKERS and allies.   Order PICIFORMES.
WOODPECKERS.   Family PICIDAE.

Woodpeckers are well-known birds having sharp chisel-like bills, sharply pointed and stiffened tail feathers, and strongly clawed feet with two toes forward and two back, except in one genus. Their food is insects and grubs, which they get by boring in trees, and from under the bark, clinging to the sides of trunks or the under side of branches with their strong curved nails, aided by the tail, for a prop. They are largely resident where found.

392. Ivory-billed Woodpecker. *Campephilus principalis.*

Range.—Locally distributed, and rare, in Florida, along the Gulf coast and north casually to South Carolina and Arkansas. [1]

This is the largest of the Woodpeckers found within our borders, being 20 inches in length. But one other American species exceeds it in size, the Imperial Woodpecker of Mexico, which reaches a length of nearly two feet; as this species is found within a few miles of our Mexican border, it may yet be classed as a North American bird. The present species has a large, heavy, ivory-white bill. They can readily be identified, at a great distance, from the Pileated Woodpecker by the large amount of white on the secondaries. They used to be not uncommonly seen in many sections of the southeast but are now found very locally and only in the largest and remote woods. They nest in holes in large trees in the most impenetrable swamps; laying three, and probably as many as six, pure white glossy eggs measuring 1.45 x 1.00.

393. Hairy Woodpecker. *Dendrocopos villosus.*

Range.—United States east of the Plains and from North Carolina to Canada.

[White.]

The Hairy Woodpecker or its sub-species is found in all parts of North America. The nesting habits and eggs of all the sub-species are not in any way different from those of the eastern bird, consequently what is said in regard to the eastern form will apply equally to all its varieties.

Except during the winter months, this species is not as commonly seen about houses or orchards as the Downy Woodpecker. During the summer they retire to the larger woods to nest, laying their eggs in holes in the trunks or limbs of trees at any height from the ground, and generally using the same hole year after year, and often twice or three times during one season, if the first sets are taken. They lay from three to six glossy white eggs; size .95 x 70. The species can be distinguished from the Downy Woodpeckers by their larger size (9 inches long), and the white outer tail feathers, which are unspotted.

393a. Northern Hairy Woodpecker (should be Hairy Woodpecker). *Dendrocopos villosus.*

Range.—North America, north of the United States.

Slightly larger than the preceding.

393b. Southern Hairy Woodpecker (should be Hairy Woodpecker). *Dendrocopos villosus.*

Range.—Southeastern United States; north to South Carolina.

Similar to the Hairy Woodpecker, but smaller.

---

[1] Only about ten individuals still alive.

393c. Harris' Woodpecker (should be Hairy Woodpecker). *Dendrocopos villosus.*

Range.—Pacific coast from California to British Columbia.

Similar to the Hairy but with fewer or no white spots on the wing coverts, and grayish on the underparts.

393d. Cabanis' Woodpecker (should be Hairy Woodpecker). *Dendrocopos villosus.*

Range.—Southern California, east to Arizona and south into Mexico.

Like the preceding but whiter below.

393e. Rocky Mountain Hairy Woodpecker (should be Hairy Woodpecker). *Dendrocopos villosus.*

Range.—Rocky Mountains from British Columbia south to New Mexico.

Similar to 393c but slightly larger and pure white below.

393f. Queen Charlotte Woodpecker (should be Hairy Woodpecker). *Dendrocopos villosus.*

Range.—Queen Charlotte Islands, British Columbia.

Like Harris' Woodpecker, but with the flanks streaked and the middle of the back spotted with blackish.

394. Southern Downy Woodpecker (should be Downy Woodpecker). *Dendrocopos pubescens.*

Range.—Gulf and South Atlantic States; north to South Carolina.

This species, which is the smallest of the North American Woodpeckers (length 6 inches), is similar in plumage to the Hairy Woodpecker, but has the ends of the white, outer tail feathers spotted with black.   Like the last species, it is represented by sub-species in all parts of North America, the nesting habits of all the varieties being the same and the eggs not distinguishable from one another.   They nest in holes in trees, very often in orchards or trees in the neighborhood of houses.   They are not nearly as shy as the Hairy Woodpeckers, and also associate [White, glossy.] with other birds very freely.   The three to six eggs are laid upon the bottom of the cavity, with no lining.   The height of the nesting season is during May or June.   The white glossy eggs are .75 x .60.

394a. Gairdner's Woodpecker (should be Downy Woodpecker). *Dendrocopos pubescens.*

Range.—Pacific coast from northern California to British Columbia.

This sub-species is like the last, but is without spots on the wing coverts and is a dingy white below, differing the same as Harris' Woodpecker from the Hairy.

394b. Batchelder's Woodpecker (should be Downy Woodpecker). *Dendrocopos pubescens.*

Range.—Rocky Mountain region of the United States.

Like the last but whiter below.

394c. Northern Downy Woodpecker (should be Downy Woodpecker). *Dendrocopos pubescens.*

Range.—North America, east of the Plains and north of South Carolina.

Similar to the southern variety but slightly larger and whiter.

394d. Alaskan Downy Woodpecker (should be Downy Woodpecker). *Dendrocopos pubescens.*

Range.—Alaska.

Similar to the northern variety but still larger.

394e.   Willow Woodpecker (should be Downy Woodpecker).   *Dendrocopos pubescens.*

Range.—California except the northern parts and the ranges of the south.
Similar to Gairdner s Woodpecker, but smaller and whiter.

395.   Red-cockaded Woodpecker.   *Dendrocopos borealis.*

Range.—Southeastern United States, from South Carolina and Arkansas, southward. [1]
This black and white species may be known from any other because of the uniform black crown and nape, the male having a small dot of red on either side of the crown, back of the eye.   They are quite abundant in the Gulf States and Florida, where they nest during April and May, and in some localities in March.   They build in hollow trees or stumps at an elevation from the ground, laying from three to six glossy white eggs; size .95 x .70.

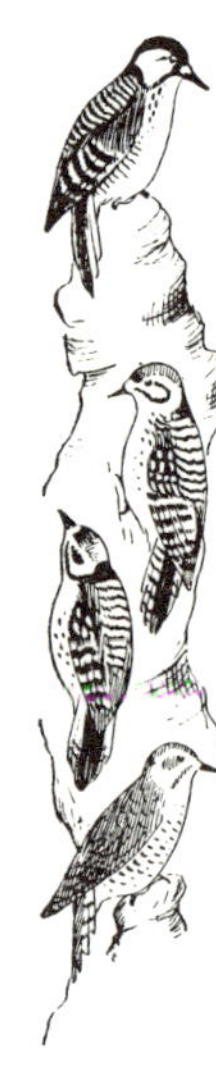

396.   Ladder-backed Woodpecker.   *Dendrocopos scalaris.*

Range.—Southwestern United States from southern Colorado south to northern Mexico.   This species is brownish white below, has the back barred with black and white, and the male has the whole crown red, shading into mixed black and whitish on the forehead.   Its habits and nesting are just the same as those of the Downy, but the three or four glossy white eggs that they lay in April are larger; size .80 x .65.

396a.   St. Lucas Woodpecker (should be Ladder-backed Woodpecker).   *Dendrocopos scalaris.*

Range.—Lower California, north to the Colorado Desert, California.
Very similar to the last; less barring on the outer tail feathers.   Eggs the same.

397.   Nuttall's Woodpecker.   *Dendrocopos nuttallii.*

Range.—Pacific coast from Oregon south to Lower California.
Similar to the Texan Woodpecker [2] but whiter below, with whitish nasal tufts, and the fore part of the crown black and white striped, the red being confined to the nape region.   They nest in holes in trees, either in dead stumps or in growing trees, and at any height above ground.   During April or May they deposit their white glossy eggs upon the bottom of the cavity.   The eggs measure .85 x .65.

398.   Arizona Woodpecker.   *Dendrocopos arizonae.*

Range.—Mexican border of the United States, chiefly in Arizona and New Mexico.
This species is entirely different from any other of our Woodpeckers, being uniform brownish above, and soiled whitish below, spotted with black.   The male bird has a red crescent on the nape.   They are said to be fairly abundant in some sections of southern Arizona.   Their nesting habits do not vary from those of the other Woodpeckers found in the same regions, and they show no especial preference for any particular kind of a tree in which to lay their eggs.   The nesting season appears to be at its height in April.   The pure white eggs average in size about 85 x .60.

[1] Breeds north sporadically to Maryland.

[2] Now Ladder-backed Woodpecker.

From "Nature and the Camera."   Photo by A. R. Dugmore.

NEST AND EGGS OF DOWNY WOODPECKER.
[Opening made to show the eggs.]

399.   White-headed Woodpecker.   *Dendrocopos albolarvatus.*

Range.—Western United States from southern California to southern British Columbia.

This odd species is wholly a dull black color, except for the white head and neck, and basal half of the primaries. They are quite abundant in some localities, particularly in California on mountain ranges. They nest at any height, but the greater number have been found under twenty feet from the ground and in old pine stubs.   They lay from four to six glossy white eggs, measuring .95 x .70.   They are said to be more silent than others of the Woodpecker family, and rarely make the familiar tapping and never drum.   It is claimed that they get at their food by scaling bark off the trees, instead of by boring.

[White.]

400.   Black-backed Three-toed Woodpecker.   *Picoïdes arcticus.*

Range.—Northern parts of the United States north to the Arctic regions.

As implied by their name, members of this genus have but three toes, two in front and one behind.   The plumage of this species is entirely black above, and whitish below, with the flanks barred with blackish.   The male has a yellow patch on the crown.   They breed abundantly in coniferous forests in mountainous regions throughout their range, laying their eggs in cavities in decayed stumps and trees, apparently at any height, from five feet up.   The eggs are laid in May or June. Size .95 x .70.

[White.]

401.   Northern Three-toed Woodpecker.   *Picoïdes tridactylus.*

Range.—From northern United States northward.

The chief difference between this species and the last is in the white on the back, either as a patch or in the form of broken bars.   The nesting habits are just the same and the eggs cannot be distinguished from those of the preceding. Both forms are found breeding in the same localities in the Adirondacks and in nearly all other portions of their range.

401a.   Alaskan Three-toed Woodpecker (should be Northern Three-toed Woodpecker). *Picoïdes tridactylus.*

Range.—Alaska, south to British Columbia and Washington.
Like the last, but with more white on the back.   Eggs like the *arcticus.*

401b.   Alpine Three-toed Woodpecker (should be Northern Three-toed Woodpecker). *Picoïdes tridactylus.*

Range.—Rocky Mountains from British Columbia south to New Mexico.
Slightly larger than the preceding and with more white on the back, almost entirely losing the barred effect of the American Three-toed[1] variety.   They nest chiefly in dead pines, laying four or five white eggs that cannot be distinguished from those of many other species. Size .95 x .70.

[1] Now Northern Three-toed.

402.   Yellow-bellied Sapsucker.   *Sphyrapicus varius.*

Range.—North America, east of the Plains; breeding from Massachusetts northward, and wintering from the Carolinas and Illinois southward. [1]

This species is one of the most handsomely marked of the family; they can easily be recognized by the red crown and throat (white on the female), each bordered by black, and the yellowish underparts. The members of this genus have been found to be the only ones that are really injurious, and these only to a slight extent, to cultivated trees. This species and the two following are the only real "sapsuckers," a crime that is often attributed to the most useful of the family. Their nesting season is during May and June. They then resort to the interior of the woods, where they deposit their four to seven glossy eggs on the bottom of holes in trees, generally at quite an elevation from the ground. Size of eggs, .85 x .60.

[White.]

402a.   Red-naped Sapsucker (should be Yellow-bellied Sapsucker).   *Sphyrapicus varius.*

Range.— Rocky Mountain region of the United States and southern Canada south to Mexico and west to California.

This variety differs from the last, chiefly in the addition of a band of scarlet on the nape in place of the white on the Yellow-bellied species. Coming as it does, midway between the ranges of the preceding species and the following, this variety, with its extension of red on the head and throat, may be regarded somewhat as a connecting link between the two species, but it is perfectly distinct and does not intergrade with either. There appears to be no difference in the nesting habits of the two varieties, except that the present one, according to Bendire, shows a preference to nesting in live aspens. The eggs measure .90 x .65.

403.   Red-breasted Sapsucker (should be Yellow-bellied Sapsucker). *Sphyrapicus varius.*

Range.—Pacific Coast from Lower California to Oregon.

Except for a whitish line from the eye to the bill, the entire head, neck and breast of this species is red, of varying shades in different individuals, from carmine to nearly a scarlet; the remainder of their plumage is very similar to that of the Yellow-bellied Sapsucker. This is an abundant species and in most parts of the range they are not timid. Like many of the Woodpeckers, they spend a great deal of their time in drumming on some dead limb. They nest commonly in aspens, preferably living ones, and are said to build a new nesting hole each year rather than use the old. The eggs are laid during May or June, being glossy white, five to seven in number, and measuring .90 x .70.

403a.   Northern Red-breasted Sapsucker (should be Yellow-bellied Sapsucker). *Sphyrapicus varius.*

Range.—Pacific coast from California to Alaska.

This is a deeper and brighter variety, and is more yellowish on the belly. Its nesting habits and eggs are the same as those of the southern form.

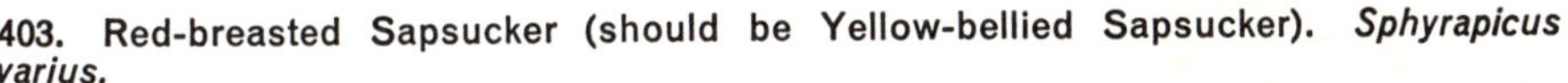

[1] Breeds in mountains south to Georgia.

404. Williamson's Sapsucker. *Sphyrapicus thyroideus.*

Range.—Mountain ranges from the Rockies to the Pacific; north to British Columbia.

This oddly marked species shows a surprising number of variations in plumage; the normal adult male is largely black on the upper parts and breast, with only a narrow patch of red on the throat, and with the belly, bright yellow. The female is entirely different in plumage and for a long time was supposed to be a distinct species; she is brownish in place of the black in the male, has no red in the plumage, and is barred with black and white on the back and wings. They nest at high altitudes in mountain ranges, either in coniferous forests or in aspens. There is no peculiarity in their nesting habits; they lay from four to seven eggs, glossy white. Size .97 x .67.

405. Pileated Woodpecker. *Dryocopus pileatus.*

Range.—Southern and South Atlantic States.

This heavily built Woodpecker is nearly as large as the Ivory-bill, being 17 inches in length. They are not nearly as beautiful as the Ivory-bills, their plumage being a sooty black instead of glossy, and the white on the wing, being confined to a very small patch at the base of the primaries; the whole crown and crest are vermilion, as is also a moustache mark in the male. They breed in the most heavily timbered districts, and generally at a high elevation; excavating a cavity sometimes 24 inches in depth and eight inches in diameter. In most localities they are very shy and difficult to approach. During April or May they lay from three to six white eggs. Size 1.30 x 1.00.

405a. Northern Pileated Woodpecker (should be Pileated Woodpecker). *Dryocopus pileatus.*

Range.—Local throughout North America, from the northern parts of the United States northward.

This variety is only very slightly larger than the preceding, it otherwise being the same. It is still abundant in many localities, but its range is rapidly being reduced, on account of cutting away the forests. Its nesting habits and eggs are the same as those of the southern variety.

406. Red-headed Woodpecker. *Melanerpes erythrocephalus.*

Range.—United States, east of the Rockies, except New England; north to southern Canada; winters in southern United States.

This beautiful species has a bright red head, neck and fore breast, glossy blue black back, wings and tail, and white underparts, rump and secondaries. It is the most abundant of the family in the greater portion of its range, where it nests in any kind of trees or in telegraph poles at any height from the ground; they also sometimes nest in holes under the eaves of buildings. They are the most pugnacious of the Woodpeckers, and are often seen chasing one another or driving away some other bird. They are also known to destroy the nests and eggs of many species,

[White.]

and also to kill and devour the young, they being the only Woodpecker, so far as known, to have acquired this disreputable habit; they also feed upon, besides ants and larvae, many kinds of fruit and berries. Their nesting season is during May and June, when they lay from four to eight white eggs, with less gloss than those of the Flicker. Size 1.00 x .75.

407. Acorn Woodpecker. *Melanerpes formicivorus.*

Range.—Mexican border of the United States, southward.

This species may be identified by the black region around the base of the bill, the white forehead, red crown and nape, yellowish throat, and blackish upper parts, extending in a band across the breast, this variety having the band streaked with white posteriorly. The habits of this variety are the same as the next which is most abundant in the United States.

407a. Californian Woodpecker (should be Acorn Woodpecker). *Melanerpes formicivorus.*

Range.—California and Oregon.

This bird differs from the last in having fewer white stripes in the black breast band. In suitable localities, this is the most abundant of Woodpeckers on the Pacific coast. They have none of the bad habits of the Red-heads, appear to be sociable among their kind, and are not afraid of mankind. It nests indifferently in all kinds of trees at any height from the ground, laying from three to seven eggs. Size 1.00 x .75. This species has the habit of storing food for future use developed to a greater extent than any other of the family. They sometimes completely honeycomb the exterior surface of decayed trees, with holes designed to hold acorns.

407b. Narrow-fronted Woodpecker (should be Acorn Woodpecker). *Melanerpes formicivorus.*

Range.—Southern Lower California.

This variety differs from the others in being slightly smaller and in having the white band on the forehead narrower. Its nesting habits are the same, but the eggs average smaller. Size .95 x .75.

408. Lewis' Woodpecker. *Asyndesmus lewis.*

Range.—Western United States from the Rockies to the Pacific coast; from British Columbia south to Mexico.

A very oddly colored species, 11 inches in length, having a dark red face, streaked red and white under parts, a gray breast band, and glossy greenish black upperparts. They are not uncommon in the greater part of their range, can not be called shy birds, and nest in all kinds of trees at heights varying from six to one hundred feet from the ground, the five to nine white eggs measuring 1.05 x .80, and being laid during May or June.

[White.]

409.   Red-bellied Woodpecker.   *Centurus carolinus.*

Range.—United States east of the Plains, breeding from the Gulf States north to Virginia and in the Mississippi Valley to Canada; casually north to southern New England.

The Red-bellied "Zebra Woodpeckers," as they are called, are very numerous in nearly all parts of their range, frequenting the more heavily timbered regions, where they nest in any place that attracts their fancy; in some localities they also commonly nest in telegraph poles. They are quite tame, and during the winter months come about yards and houses, the same as, and often in company with, Downy Woodpeckers. Their eggs, which are laid during May, are glossy white, average in size 1.00 x .75 and number from four to six.

410.   Golden-fronted Woodpecker.   *Centurus aurifrons.*

Range.—Mexico and southern Texas, resident.[1]

[White.]

This is also one of the "zebra" or "ladder-backed" Woodpeckers, having the back and wings closely barred with black and white, the same as the preceding; the forehead, nasal tufts and nape are golden yellow, and the male has a patch of red on the crown. This is a very common resident species in the Lower Rio Grande Valley in Texas, where it nests in trees or telegraph poles, sometimes so numerously in the latter situations as to become a nuisance. Their nesting habits are not in any manner peculiar, and the eggs cannot be distinguished from those of the preceding. Size 1.00 x .75. Laid during April and May.

411.   Gila Woodpecker.   *Centurus uropygialis.*

Range.—Mexican border of the United States, in southern Arizona and New Mexico.

Like the preceding but without any yellow on the head, the male having a red patch in the center of the crown. They are locally distributed in New Mexico, but appear to be abundant in all parts of southern Arizona, where they nest principally in giant cacti, but also in many other trees such as cottonwoods, mesquite, sycamores, etc. Besides their decided preference for giant cacti, there is nothing unusual in their nesting habits, and the eggs are not different from those of others of the genus. They lay from three to six eggs in April or May. Size 1.00 x .75.

[1] Breeds into Oklahoma.

412. Yellow-shafted Flicker. *Colaptes auratus.*

Range.—Southeastern United States.

[White.]

Flickers are well-known, large Woodpeckers (13 inches long), with a brownish tone to the plumage, barred on the back and spotted on the breast with black. The present species has a golden yellow lining to the wings and tail, and the shafts of the feathers are yellow; it has a red crescent on the nape, and the male has black moustache marks. This species and its sub-variety are the most widely known Woodpeckers in eastern North America, where they are known in different localities by something like a hundred local names, of which Pigeon Woodpecker and Yellow-hammer seem to be the most universal. They have the undulating flight common to all Woodpeckers and show the white rump patch conspicuously when flying. They are often found on the ground in pastures or on side hills, feeding upon ants; they are more terrestrial than any others of the family. They nest anywhere, where they can find or make a suitable cavity for the reception of their eggs; in trees in woods, or solitary trees in large pastures, in apple trees in orchards, in fence posts, in holes under the roofs of buildings, etc. They ordinarily lay from five to ten very glossy white eggs, but it has been found that they will continue laying, if one egg is removed from the nest at a time, until in one case seventy-one eggs were secured. Fresh eggs may be found at any time from May until August, as they frequently raise two broods a season. Size of eggs, 1.10 x .90 with considerable variations.

412a. Northern Flicker (should be Yellow-shafted Flicker). *Colaptes auratus.*

Range.—Whole of North America, east of the Rockies, except the southeastern portion.

Averaging larger than the preceding, but individual specimens of the northern variety are frequently found to be even smaller than the southern, and vice versa, making the distinction one of the study rather than Nature.

413. Red-shafted Flicker. *Colaptes cafer.*

Range.—United States west of the Rockies.

This species is marked similarly to the preceding, but the top of the head is brownish instead of gray, and the underparts of the wings and tail and their quills are reddish. Neither sex has the red crescent on the back of the head, except in the case of hybrids between the two species, but the male has red moustache marks. There are no differences in the nidification between this species and the preceding, but the eggs of this average a trifle larger (1.15 x .90).

[White.]

413a. Northwestern Flicker (should be Red-shafted Flicker). *Colaptes cafer.*

Range.—Pacific coast, breeding from Oregon to Alaska.

This is a much darker variety of the Red-shafted Flicker, but its nesting habits or eggs do not differ in any way.

414. Gilded Flicker. *Colaptes chrysoïdes.*

Range.—Arizona and southward through Mexico to southern Lower California.

This pale species has the yellowish lining to the wings and tail as in the Flicker, but has a pale cinnamon brown crown, no crescent on back of head, and the male has red moustache marks. It is a common species in all localities where the giant cactus abounds, and shows a preference to nesting in these strange growths, to any other trees. Their habits are, in all respects, the same as those of the other Flickers and their eggs cannot be distinguished. Size 1.10 x .90.

Photo by G. E. Moulthrope.

NEST AND EGGS OF YELLOW-SHAFTED FLICKER.

414a. Brown Flicker (should be Gilded Flicker). *Colaptes chrysoïdes.*

Range.—Northern Lower California.
This is a slightly smaller and darker variety of the Gilded Flicker.

415. Guadalupe Flicker (should be Red-shafted Flicker). *Colaptes cafer.*

Range.—Guadalupe Island. [1]
Similar to the Red-shafted Flicker, but with the crown darker and the rump a solid pinkish white. They are common in a large cypress grove in the middle of the island, but rarely found on any other portions. The eggs have been described by Mr. Walter E. Bryant, who found them breeding on the island, to be indistinguishable from those of the others of the genus.

GOATSUCKERS; SWIFTS and HUMMINGBIRDS. Orders CAPRIMULGIFORMES and APODIFORMES.

GOATSUCKERS. Family CAPRIMULGIDAE.

Goatsuckers are long-winged birds, with small bills, but with an extraordinarily large mouth, the opening of which extends beneath and beyond the eyes. They are chiefly dusk or night fliers, their food consisting of insects which they catch on the wing. Their plumage is a mottled black, brownish and white, resembling the ground upon which they lay their eggs.

416. Chuck-will's-widow. *Caprimulgus carolinensis.*

Range.—South Atlantic and Gulf States, breeding north to Virginia and Indiana, and west to Arkansas and eastern Texas. [2]

These birds are abundant summer residents in the southern portions of their range, but as they are silent and hiding in the woods during the day time, they are not as popularly known as are most birds. They rarely fly during the day time unless disturbed from their roosting place which is on the ground under underbrush or in hollow logs. Their notes, which are a rapid and repeatedly uttered whistling repetition of their name, are heard until late in the night. They nest during April, May or June, laying two eggs on the ground amid the

[Grayish white].

leaves in woods or scrubby underbrush. The eggs are grayish to creamy white in color, handsomely marked with shades of lilac, gray and brownish; size 1.40 x 1.00.

[1] Extinct on this island.

[2] Breeds north to southern New Jersey.

417. Whip-poor-will. *Caprimulgus vociferus.*

Range.—North America east of the Plains; north to the southern parts of the British possessions; winters along the Gulf coast and southward.

This species is well known, by sound, in nearly all parts of its range, but comparatively few ever observed the bird, and probably the greater number mis-

[Creamy white.]

take the Nighthawk[1] for this species. The two species can readily be distinguished at a distance by the absence of any pronounced white marking in the wings, and by the white tips to the outer tail feathers in the present species, while the Nighthawk has a prominent white band across the tail, but the tip is black, and the tail slightly forked. The Whip-poor-will rarely leaves its place of concealment before dark, and is never seen flying about cities, as are the Nighthawks. In their pursuit of insects, they glide like a shadow over fields and woods, their soft plumage giving forth no sound as their wings cleave the air. Until late at night, their whistling cry "whip-poor-will," repeated at intervals, rings out in all wooded hilly districts. Their two eggs are deposited on the ground among dead leaves, generally in dense woods. They are grayish white or cream color marbled with pale brown and gray, with fainter markings of lilac. Size 1.50 x .85. Data.—Bristol Co., R. I., May 31, 1889. Two eggs on oak leaves on the ground in low woods. Collector, H. A. Stevens.

Photo by Geo. S. Fiske.

NEST AND EGGS OF WHIP-POOR-WILL.

[1] Now Common Nighthawk.

417a. Stevens' Whip-poor-will (should be Whip-poor-will). *Caprimulgus vociferus.*

Range.—Arizona and New Mexico, south through the tableland of Mexico.

This sub-species is slightly larger and has longer mouth bristles than the eastern bird. Their nesting habits are the same and the eggs differ only in averaging lighter in color, with fainter markings, some specimens being almost immaculate.

418. Poor-will. *Phalaenoptilus nuttallii.*

Range.—United States west of the Mississippi, breeding from Kansas and northern California northward to Montana and British Columbia.

This handsome species is the smallest of the family, being under 8 inches in length. Its plumage is mottled black, white and frosty gray, harmoniously blended together. They can easily be distinguished from all other Goatsuckers by their small size and silvery appearance. They nest on the ground, either placing their two eggs upon a bed of leaves or upon a flat rock. The breeding season is from the latter part of May through July. The eggs are pure white and glossy; size 1.00 x .75.

[White.]

418a. Frosted Poor-will (should be Poor-wlll). *Phalaenoptilus nuttallii.*

Range.—Texas and Arizona, north to western Kansas.

This variety is like the last but paler, both above and below. Eggs indistinguishable from those of others of the genus.

418b. Dusky Poor-will (should be Poor-will). *Phalaenoptilus nuttallii.*

Range.—A darker race found on the coast of California, having the same nesting habits as the others.

The egg figured is of this species. Data.—Los Angeles, Cal., June 24, 1900. 2 eggs on the ground at the foot of an oak tree on the side of a hill. Collector, F. M. Palmer.

419. Pauraque. *Nyctidromus albicollis.*

Range.—Mexico, north to the Lower Rio Grande in southern Texas.

[Salmon buff.]

This species is the same length as the Chuck-will's-widow, but is not as stoutly built, and has a slightly longer tail. It can be distinguished from any other of the family by its tail, the outer feather on each side being black (or brownish barred with black in the female), and the next two having white ends for nearly half their length. Their eggs are laid on the ground in open localities, and generally under the the protection of an overhanging bush. They are two in number and differ greatly from those of any other American member of this family, being a buff or rich salmon buff in color, spotted and splashed with gray, lavender, and reddish brown; size 1.25 x .90. Data.—Brownsville, Texas, April 16, 1900. Eggs laid on the ground in a dense thicket. Collector, Frank B. Armstrong.

420. Common Nighthawk. *Chordeiles minor.*

Range.—North America, east of the Plains and from Labrador to the Gulf of Mexico; winters through Mexico to northern South America.

[Grayish white]

The Nighthawk[1] or some of its sub-species is found in nearly all parts of North America, its habits being the same in all localities. It is of the same size as the Whip-poor-will, from which species it can readily be distinguished by its lack of mouth bristles, forked tail with a white band near the end, and the white band across the primaries, the latter mark showing very plainly during flight. Besides in the country, they are very common in cities, where they will be seen any summer day towards dusk flying, skimming, sailing, and swooping over the tops of the buildings, upon the gravel roofs of which they often lay their eggs. They nest generally on rocky hillsides or in open woods, laying their two eggs upon the top of a flat rock. The eggs are a grayish white color, marbled, blotched and spotted with darker shades of gray. Size 1.20 x .85.

420a. Western Nighthawk (should be Common Nighthawk). *Chordeiles minor.*

Range.—United States west of the Plains.

A similar bird to the preceding, but with plumage somewhat more rusty. It frequents the more open portions of the country in its range, its habits and nesting habits being the same as those of the former species; the eggs average a trifle lighter in color.

[Grayish white.]

420b. Florida Nighthawk (should be Common Nighthawk). *Chordeiles minor.*

Range.—A smaller and paler form found in Florida and along the Gulf coast. No difference can be observed in the nesting habits of this as compared with the northern form, and the eggs are indistinguishable.

420c. Sennett's Nighthawk (should be Common Nighthawk). *Chordeiles minor.*

Range.—A very pale species with little or no tawny; found in the Great Plains from Texas north to the Saskatchewan; winters south of the United States.

421. Lesser Nighthawk. *Chordeiles acutipennis.*

Range.—Mexico and Central America, breeding north to southern Utah and California.

[Grayish white.]

The pattern of the marking of this species is finer and more mottled with rusty than the Nighthawk.[1] Its habits do not differ to any extent from those of the preceding species; they lay their two mottled gray eggs upon the bare ground, often on the dry sand and in arid regions where they are exposed, with no protection, to the scorching rays of the sun. The eggs vary endlessly in extent of markings, some being very pale and others very dark gray, mottled with various shades of gray, brown, and lilac. Size 1.10 x .75.

[1] Now Common Nighthawk.

Photo by J. E. Seebold.

NEST AND EGGS OF COMMON NIGHTHAWK.

SWIFTS.   Family APODIDAE.

422.   Black Swift.   *Cypseloides niger.*

Range.—Mountain ranges from Central America north to British Columbia, locally distributed throughout its range.

The plumage of this Swift is entirely sooty black, darkest above; the tail is slightly forked and is without spines; length of bird, 7 in.   Although the general habits of this species are well known, little is known of their nesting; they are seen during the breeding season about the higher ranges throughout their United States habitat, and are supposed to nest in crevices on the face of cliffs at a high altitude.

423.   Chimney Swift.   *Chaetura pelagica.*

Range.—North America east of the Plains, breeding from central Canada, south to the Gulf coast, and wintering south of our borders.

This well-known species is sooty brownish black, 5.5 in. long, and has the tail feathers terminating in sharp spines.   They are very abundant in all portions of their range, and may be seen on the wing at all hours of the day, but especially abundant in the early morning and toward dusk.   They formerly dwelt and bred only in hollow trees, and a great many still continue to do so, as

Photo by E. R. Forrest.

NEST AND EGGS OF CHIMNEY SWIFT.

large hollow stumps are known where hundreds nest every year. The majority of the eastern Chimney Swifts now nest in old chimneys that are unused, at least during the summer; some small chimneys contain but a single pair while other large ones may have from fifty to a hundred or more nests glued to the sides. The birds are on the wing during the greater part of the day, generally not frequenting the vicinity of their nesting site, but returning toward dusk, when they may be seen to dive one at a time, headforemost into the tops of chimneys. The nest is made of small twigs firmly glued to the sides of the chimney, or tree, and to each other, with the glutinous saliva of the bird making a narrow semicircular platform for the reception of their three to five white eggs which are deposited in May or June; size .75 x .50.

[White.]

424. Vaux's Swift. *Chaetura vauxi.*

Range.—Western United States, chiefly west of the Rockies; breeding north to British Columbia, and wintering south of the United States.

[White.]

Similar to the last but smaller (length 4.5 inches), and paler in color, fading to white on the throat. The habits of this species are like those of the eastern Chimney Swift, except that the majority of this species still continue to use hollow trees as nesting places. The eggs are just like those of the last bird.

425. White-throated Swift. *Aëronautes saxatalis.*

Range.—Western United States south of Canada, and chiefly in the Rocky Mountains, and in California ranges, north to Lat. 38°.

A handsome species, 6.5 inches in length, with blackish upper parts and sides, and white throat, breast and central line of under parts, flank patches and ends of secondaries; tail feathers not spined or stiffened. These birds are fairly common in some localities within their range, but appear to be found only on high ranges or in their immediate vicinity. They nest in crevices and caves in the face of cliffs, making a nest similar in construction to that of the Chimney Swift but of weed stalks instead of twigs, and lined with feathers. They lay four or five dull white eggs, during June or July; size .85 x .50.

[White.]

HUMMINGBIRDS. Family TROCHILIDAE.

Hummingbirds have been truly called "Winged Gems." They are the smallest of birds, the usual plumage being of a metallic green with throat or crown patches of the brightest of iridescent shining red, orange, blue or violet. Their nests are marvels of architecture being compactly and intricately made of plant fibres and downy feathers ornamented in some cases with lichens. Their flight is accompanied by a peculiar buzzing sound produced by their rapidly vibrating stiffened wing feathers. Their food is small insects and honey both of which they get chiefly from flowers.

426. Rivoli's Hummingbird. *Eugenes fulgens.*

Range.—Mexico, north in summer to southern Arizona where they breed at high elevations in the Huachuca Mountains.

This is one of the most gorgeous of the Hummers having the crown a violet purple color, and the throat brilliant green. This species saddles its nest upon branches often at heights of 20 or 30 feet from the ground. They are made of plant down and generally decorated with lichens on the outside, similar to nests of the Ruby-throat. The two white eggs measure .65 x .40.

427. Blue-throated Hummingbird. *Lampornis clemenciae.*

Range.—Mexico, north in summer to the border of Arizona and western New Mexico.

This species is the largest of North American Hummers being 5.25 inches long, this being slightly larger than the preceding. As the name implies, it has a patch of blue on the throat, the upper parts being a uniform greenish; the outer tail feathers are broadly tipped with white. Their nests, which are placed upon the limbs of trees, are made of mosses and plant fibres covered with cobwebs. The two eggs are laid during July and August, and measure .65 x .40.

428. Ruby-throated Hummingbird. *Archilochus colubris.*

Range.—North America east of the Plains and north to Labrador.

This is the only representative of the family found east of the Mississippi. It is a small species, 3.5 inches long, with greenish upper parts and a bright ruby throat. Its nest is as beautiful, if not more so, than that of any other species. They build their nests on horizontal limbs of trees at any height from the ground, but usually more than six feet. Branches an inch or more in diameter are usually selected, they not being particular as to the kind of tree, but oaks, pines and maples perhaps being used the most often. The nests are made of plant fibres and down, and the exterior is completely covered with green lichens so that it appears like a small bunch of moss on the limb. The two white eggs are laid in May or June; size .50 a .35.

429. Black-chinned Hummingbird. *Archilochus alexandri.*

Range.—North America west of the Rocky Mountains; north to British Columbia; winters south of the United States.

Similar in size and appearance to the Ruby-throat, but with the chin and upper throat black, the rest of the throat gorget being violet or amethyst. It is an abundant species in summer in many localities, especially in the southern half of its range. They build their nests at low elevations, rarely above ten feet, on small branches or the fork at the end of a limb. The nests are made of yellowish plant fibres and are not covered with lichens, so that they have a peculiar spongy appearance. Eggs indistinguishable from those of the Ruby-throat. Laid during April, May or June.

Exposure 3 sec.

Photo from life by J. H. Miller.

FEMALE RUBY-THROATED HUMMINGBIRD ON NEST.

430. Costa's Hummingbird. *Calypte costae.*

Range.—Southwestern United States; north to southern Utah; winters south of our border.

Smaller than the last and with both the crown and the throat gorget, violet or amethyst, the feathers on the sides of the latter being lengthened. Their nests are situated in the forks of branches generally near the ground, and seldom above six feet from it. They are made of plant down with shreds of weeds, bark and lichens worked into the outside portions, and are often lined with soft feathers. The two eggs average .48 x .32. Data.—Arroyo Seco, California, June 10, 1900. Nest in an alder bush. Collector, Charles E. Groesbeck.

431. Anna's Hummingbird. *Calypte anna.*

Range.—Pacific coast of the United States from northern California, southward, wintering in Mexico and southern California.

This handsome species has both the crown and the broadened and lengthened throat gorgets, a purplish pink; it is slightly larger than the Ruby-throat. They are very abundant in their restricted range, and nest in February and March and again in April or May, raising two broods a season. Their nests are made of plant down and covered on the outside with cobwebs and a few lichens, and are generally located at a low elevation. The white eggs average .50 x .30. Data.—Santa Monica, California, March 4, 1897. Nest in a bunch of seed pods in a gum tree, ten feet from the ground. Collector, Tom Bundy.

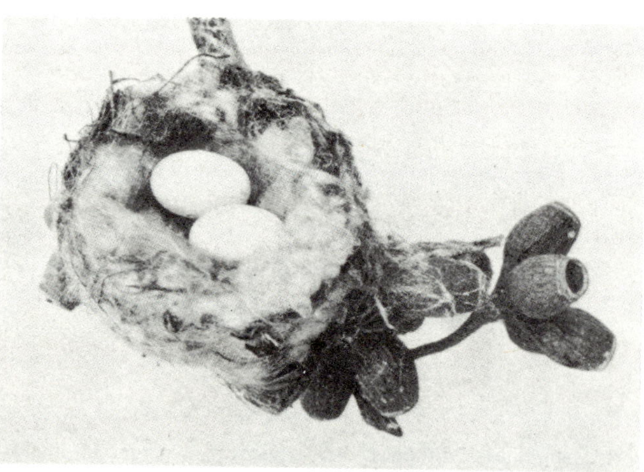

431.1. Floresi's Hummingbird. *Selasphorus floresii.*

This sub-tropical species, the nesting habits of which are not known, is supposed to have been taken in at least one instance on the Pacific coast of California. [1]

432. Broad-tailed Hummingbird. *Selasphorus platycercus.*

Range.—Rocky Mountain regions, north to Wyoming; winters south of the United States.

This species is similar to the Ruby-throat, but larger and with the back more golden green color, and the throat shining lilac. They are very abundant in Colorado and Arizona, nesting as do the Ruby-throats in the east, and their nests being similar in construction and appearance to those of that species. The eggs cannot be distinguished from those of other species.

433. Rufous Hummingbird. *Selasphorus rufus.*

Range.—Western North America, breeding from the Mexican border north to Alaska and fairly abundant in most of its range.

A handsome little species with the back and tail reddish brown, and with a throat gorget of orange red, the feathers being slightly lengthened into a ruff on the sides of the gorget. They nest in a great variety of locations and at a low elevation, such as vines, bushes and the low hanging branches of trees. The nest is made of vegetable fibres covered with cobwebs and often with lichens. The eggs do not differ from those of the other Hummers.

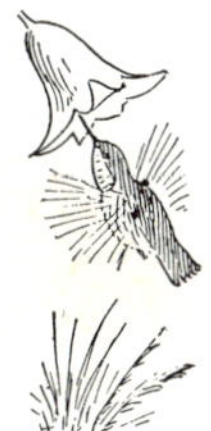

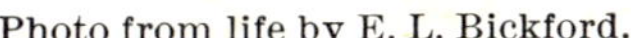

Photo from life by E. L. Bickford.

ANNA'S HUMMINGBIRD ON NEST.

[1] Not recorded from North America.

434. Allen's Hummingbird. *Selasphorus sasin.*

Range.—Pacific coast from British Columbia southward; most abundant in California.   Winters in Mexico.

This species is like the last, but the back is greenish, only the tail being reddish brown. These birds generally locate their nests at low elevations near the end of overhanging branches, on vines, weed stalks, or bushes, but have been found as high as 90 feet above ground.   The nests of this species are made of plant fibres and cobwebs, generally decorated with lichens.   The two white eggs measure .50 x .32.   Data.—Santa Monica, Cal., May 29, 1896.   Nest two feet from the ground in a sage bush.   Collector, W. Lee Chambers.

435. Heloise's Hummingbird. *Atthis heloisa.*

Range.—This species is known only from a single specimen, taken in the Huachuca Mountains, Arizona in 1896.

436. Calliope Hummingbird. *Stellula calliope.*

Range.—Western United States from British Columbia southward, and from the Rocky Mountains west to eastern Oregon and California.

This is the smallest of North American Hummers, being but 3 inches in length. It is greenish above and has a violet gorget showing the white bases of the feathers.   They build their nests in all manner of locations from high up in tall pines to within a foot of the ground in slender bushes.   The nests are made interiorly with plant down, but the outside is generally grayish colored shreds and lichens.   The eggs average but a trifle smaller than those of *colubris*, .45 x .30.

437. Lucifer Hummingbird. *Calothorax lucifer.*

Range.—Mexico, north to southwestern Texas and Arizona.

This species, which is common in parts of Central Mexico, occurs only casually north to our borders and has not yet been found nesting there.   They build small compact nests of plant down attached to the stalks or leaves of plants or weeds.

438. Reiffer's Hummingbird. *Amazilia tzacatl.*

Range.—Abundant in southern Mexico; casual in southern Texas.

This species is greenish above, with a bronzy lustre; the tail is reddish brown, and the throat and breast are metallic green.   They breed abundantly about houses and nest apparently at all seasons of the year in Central America, where they are the most common species of Hummers.

439. Buff-bellied Hummingbird. *Amazilia yucatanensis.*

Range.—Lower Rio Grande Valley in Texas and southward through Mexico.

These birds are like the last but have the underparts a pale brownish buff color. They are quite common in their summer range in the United States, nesting at a low elevation in bushes and low trees. The two eggs are white, .50 x .35. Data.—Brownsville, Texas, May 5, 1892. Nest of fine bark-like fibre on the outside, lined with lint from thistle plant; located on limb of small hackberry. Collector, Frank B. Armstrong.

440. Xantus' Hummingbird. *Hylocharis xantusii.*

Range.—Southern Lower California.

A handsome species, greenish above, with a coppery tinge and shading into reddish brown on the tail; under parts buffy, throat metallic green, and a broad white streak behind the eye. They breed on the ranges making a similar nest to those of other Hummers, placed on weeds or bushes near the ground. The eggs cannot be distinguished from those of the majority of other species.

440.1. White-eared Hummingbird. *Hylocharis leucotis.*

Range.—A Central American and Mexican species, casually found on the ranges in southern Arizona.

The plumage of this species is greenish above and below, being bright metallic green on the breast; the forehead, sides of head, and throat are iridescent blue and a white line extends back from the eye.

441. Broad-billed Hummingbird. *Cyanthus latirostris.*

Range.—Mountains of central Mexico north to southern Arizona and New Mexico.

The throat of this species is a rich metallic blue; otherwise the plumage is greenish above and below, being brighter and more iridescent on the breast. They are not uncommon on the ranges of southern Arizona, where they have been found nesting in July and August, their nest not being unlike those of the Rufous Hummer, but with the exterior largely composed of shreds of grayish bark and lichens. Their eggs are like many others of the Hummers.

PERCHING BIRDS. Order PASSERIFORMES.

COTINGAS. Family COTINGIDAE.

441.1. Rose-throated Becard. *Platypsaris aglaiae.*

Range.—Mexico; north casually to the southern border of Arizona.[1]

This peculiar species is grayish above and lighter gray below, has dark slaty crown, and a patch of rose color on the lower throat. This is the only representative of this tropical family that has been found as yet over the Mexican border, but its near ally, the Rose-throated Becard has been found within a very few miles and will doubtless be added to our fauna as an accidental visitor ere long. Their nests are large masses of grasses, weeds, strips of bark, etc., partially suspended from the forks of branches. Their eggs number four or five and are a pale buffy gray color, dotted and scratched with a pale reddish brown and dark gray. Size .95 x .70. The one figured is from a set in the collection of Mr. Crandall, taken June 1, 1897 at Presidio Sinaloa, Mexico.

[Buffy Gray.]

---

[1] Breeds sparingly in southwestern U.S.

TYRANT FLYCATCHERS.   Family TYRANNIDAE.

Flycatchers, which are found only in America and chiefly in the tropics, are insect-eating birds generally having a grayish colored plumage, sometimes adorned with a slight crest or a coronal mark of orange, red, or yellow. Only two of the species found in North America are gaudy in plumage, the Vermilion, and the Derby Flycatchers.[1] They all have the habit of sitting erect on a dead twig, and watching for passing insects, which they catch on the wing.

442. Fork-tailed Flycatcher. *Muscivora tyrannus.*

Range.—A Central and South American species accidentally having occurred in the United States on several occasions.

This is a handsome black, white and gray species of the size and form of the next.

443. Scissor-tailed Flycatcher. *Muscivora forficata.*

Range.—Mexico, north through Texas to southern Kansas; accidental in other parts of the country.

[Creamy white.]

The Scissor-tail or "Texan Bird of Paradise" is the most beautiful member of this interesting family. Including its long tail often 10 inches in length and forked for about 6 inches, this Flycatcher reaches a length of about 15 inches. It is pale grayish above, fading into whitish below, and has scarlet linings to the wings, and a scarlet crown patch. They are one of the most abundant of breeding birds in Texas, placing their large roughly built nests in all kinds of trees and at any elevation, but averaging between ten and fifteen feet above ground. The nests are built of rootlets, grasses, weeds and trash of all kinds, such as paper, rags, string, etc. The interior is generally lined with plant fibres, hair or wool. They lay from three to five, and rarely six eggs with a creamy white ground color, more or less spotted and blotched with reddish brown, lilac and gray, the markings generally being most numerous about the larger end. They average in size about .90 x .67. Data.—Corpus Christi, Texas, May 18, 1899. 6 eggs. Nest of moss, vines, etc., on small trees in open woods near town. Collector, Frank B. Armstrong.

444. Kingbird (should be Eastern Kingbird). *Tyrannus tyrannus.*

Range.—Temperate North America, breeding from the Gulf of Mexico north to New Brunswick, Manitoba and British Columbia; rare off the Pacific coast.

This common Tyrant Flycatcher is very abundant in the eastern parts of its range. They are one of the most pugnacious and courageous of birds attacking and driving away any feathered creature to which they take a dislike, regardless of size. Before and during the nesting season, their sharp, nerve-racking clatter is kept up all day long, and with redoubled vigor when anyone approaches their nesting site. They nest in any kind of a tree, in fields or open woods, and at any height from the ground, being

[Cream color.]

found on fence rails within two feet of the ground or in the tops of pines 70 or 80 feet above the earth. Nearly every orchard will be found to contain one or

[1] Now Kiskadee Flycatcher.

more pairs of these great insect destroyers; if more than one pair, there will be continual warfare as often as one encroaches on the domains of the other.   Their nests are made of strips of vegetable fibre, weeds, etc., and lined with horsehair or catkins.   They are sometimes quite bulky and generally very substantially made.   The three to five eggs are laid the latter part of May, and are of a creamy ground color splashed with reddish brown and lilac.   Size .95 x .70.   Data.— Worcester County, Massachusetts, June 3, 1895.   4 eggs.   Nest 10 feet from the ground in an apple tree; made of fibres, string, rootlets and weeds, lined with horse hair.   Collector, F. C. Clark.

Photo by G. E. Moulthrope.

NEST AND EGGS OF EASTERN KINGBIRD.

445. Gray Kingbird. *Tyrannus dominicensis.*

Range.—West Indies; north in April to Florida and the South Atlantic States to South Carolina and casually farther.

[Creamy.]

This species is slightly larger than our Kingbird, (9 inches long), grayish instead of dark drab above, white below, and without any white tip to tail. Like the Eastern Kingbird, it has a concealed orange patch on the crown. Their habits and nesting habits are the same as those of our common bird, but the nest is not generally as well built, and nearly always is made largely of twigs. The three or four eggs have a creamy or a creamy pink ground color, spotted and blotched with dark brown and lilac, most numerously about the large end. Size 1.00 x .73. Tarpon Springs, Florida, May 28, 1902. Nest of twigs and weeds in a low bush. Collector, J. A. Southley.

446. Tropical Kingbird. *Tyrannus melancholicus.*

[Buff.]

Range.—Mexico, north in summer to southern Texas. [1]
This species is very similar to the next but the throat and breast are white, and the underparts a brighter yellow. Like the other members of this genus, these build their nests in any location in trees or bushes, making them of twigs, weeds and moss. Their three or four eggs have a creamy ground with a pinkish cast and are spotted with brown and lilac. Size .97 x .12.

447. Western Kingbird. *Tyrannus verticalis.*

Range.—Western United States and southern British Provinces from Kansas and Minnesota west to the Pacific.

[Buff.]

This species has grayish upper parts, shading into darker on the wings and tail, and lighter on the throat and upper breast; the underparts are yellow, and there is a concealed patch of orange on the crown. They are very abundant throughout the west, where they have the same familiar habits of the eastern species, nesting in all sorts of locations such as would be used by the latter. Their nests are made of plant fibres, weeds, string, paper or any trash that may be handy, being sometimes quite bulky. Their eggs do not differ in any particular from those of the eastern bird, except that they may average a little smaller. Size .95 x .65.

448. Cassin's Kingbird. *Tyrannus vociferans.*

Range.—Western United States from the Rocky Mountain region to California, and from Wyoming southward.
This species is like the last except that the throat and breast are darker. Their habits, nesting habits and eggs are indistinguishable from those of the other Tyrant Flycatchers, and they are fully as courageous in the defense of their homes against either man or bird, their notes resembling those of the common Kingbird of the east.

[Buff.]

[1] Resident in southern Texas

449. Kiskadee Flycatcher. *Pitangus sulphuratus.*

Range.—Mexico and Central America, breeding north to southern Texas.

This handsome bird is the largest of the Flycatcher family found in the United States, being 11 inches in length. It has a black crown enclosing a yellow crown patch; a broad black stripe from the bill, through the eye and around the back of the head, is separated from the crown by a white forehead and line over the eye; the throat is white shading into yellow on the underparts. They are abundant in the interior of Mexico, but can hardly be classed as common over our border,

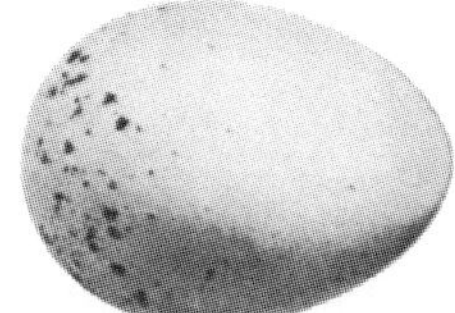
[Creamy white.]

where they nest in limited numbers. Their nests are unlike those of any of our other Flycatchers being large masses of moss, weeds and grass, arched over on top and with the entrance on the side. The three or four eggs are creamy white, sprinkled chiefly about the large end with small reddish brown or umber spots; size 1.15 x .85.

450. Giraud's Flycatcher. *Myiozetetes similis.*

Range.—Mexico and Central America, north casually to southern Texas.[1]

This species is admitted to our fauna on the authority of J. P. Giraud, although for many years it has not been found within our range. They are very common in the southern parts of Mexico, where they nest about the houses, but preferably in bushes growing on the banks of streams. Like the last species, this one builds at a low elevation, generally under twenty feet from the ground. Their nests, too, are like those of the Derby Flycatcher,[2] the entrance being on the side. The two or three eggs have a creamy white ground and are sparingly marked over the whole egg with small spots of brown, some specimens being of the shape and appearance of those of the last species, but smaller. Size .95 x .65.

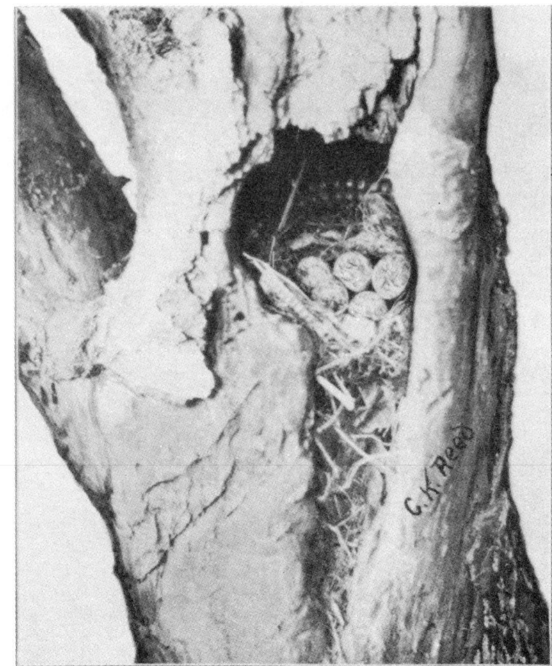

NEST AND EGGS OF GREAT CRESTED FLYCATCHER.

[1] Not recorded from North America.

[2] Now Kiskadee Flycatcher.

451. Sulphur-bellied Flycatcher. *Myiodynastes luteiventris.*

Range.—Mexico and Central America, breeding north to the Mexican border of Arizona.

[Creamy buff.]

This peculiar Flycatcher, which is unlike any other American species, can only be regarded as a rare breeding bird in the Huachuca Mts. It is 8 inches in length, has a grayish back streaked with black, the tail largely rusty brown and the underparts sulphur yellow, streaked on the breast and sides with dusky; a yellow crown patch is bordered on either side by a stripe of mottled dusky, and is separated from the blackish patch through the eye, by white superciliary lines. Their habits are similar to those of the genus *Myiarchus*, and, like them, they nest in cavities in trees, and lay from three to five eggs of a creamy buff color thickly spotted and blotched with brown and purplish, the markings not assuming the scratchy appearance of the Crested Flycatchers, but looking more like those of a Cardinal; size of egg 1.05 x .75. Data.—Huachuca Mts., Arizona, June 29, 1901. 4 eggs. Nest in the natural cavity of a live sycamore tree about fifty feet from the ground; composed of twigs. Collector, O. W. Howard.

452. Great Crested Flycatcher. *Myiarchus crinitus.*

Range.—North America, east of the Plains, and from New Brunswick and Manitoba southward; winters from the Gulf States southward.

[Buff.]

This trim and graceful, but quarrelsome, species is grayish on the head, neck, and breast, shading to greenish on the back and quite abruptly into bright yellow on the underparts; the head is slightly crested and the inner webs of all the lateral tail feathers are reddish brown. They are abundant in most of their range but are generally shy so they are not as often seen as many other more rare birds. They nest in cavities of any kind of trees and at any elevation from the ground, the nest being made of twigs, weeds and trash, and generally having incorporated into its make-up a piece of cast off snake skin. They lay from four to six eggs of a buffy color, blotched and lined with dark brown and lavender. Size .85 x .65.

453. Wied's Crested Flycatcher. *Myiarchus tyrannulus.*

Range.—Mexico, north to southern Texas.[1]

[Buff.]

This species is similar to the last but is considerably paler. They are common in some localities, nesting in holes in trees or stumps, often those deserted by Woodpeckers. Their eggs are like those of the last but average paler. Data.—Corpus Christi, Texas, May 10, 1899. Nest in hole in telegraph pole; made of red cow hair, feathers and leaves. 4 eggs. Collector, Frank B. Armstrong.

453a. Arizona Crested Flycatcher (should be Wied's Crested Flycatcher). *Myiarchus tyrannulus.*

Range.—Southern Arizona and New Mexico, south through Mexico.

This bird is very similar to, but averages slightly larger than the Mexican Flycatcher.[2] Its nesting habits are the same and the eggs cannot be distinguished from those of the latter, the nest being most frequently found in giant cacti.

[1] Breeds from Nevada south into Mexico.

[2] Now Wied's Crested Flycatcher.

454. Ash-throated Flycatcher. *Myiarchus cinerascens.*

Range.—North America, west of the Plains and south of Canada.

Similar to the others of the genus but grayish brown above and with the underparts much paler, the throat and breast being nearly white. Like the others they nest in cavities in trees, either natural or ones made by Woodpeckers. Their four to five eggs are lighter in color than those of *crinitus* but cannot be distinguished from those of the Mexican Crested Flycatcher.[1]

[Pale buff.]

454a. Nutting's Flycatcher. *Myiarchus nuttingi.*

Range.—Southern Arizona and southward.[2]

This smaller sub-species nests in the giant cacti which abound in certain parts of southern Arizona; its eggs cannot be distinguished from those of the Ash-throated Flycatcher.

454b. Lower California Flycatcher (should be Ash-throated Flycatcher). *Myiarchus cinerascens.*

Range.—Lower California.

This sub-species is similar to Nutting's Flycatcher but paler below and grayer above.

455. Lawrence's Flycatcher. *Myiarchus lawrencei.*

Range.—Eastern Mexico. Admitted to our list on the authority of Giraud as having occurred in southern Texas.[3]

This bird is similar to its sub-species which occurs in southern Arizona, but slightly darker. Its eggs are the same as those of the next to be described.

455a. Olivaceous Flycatcher. *Myiarchus tuberculifer.*

Range.—Western Mexico, north to southern Arizona.

This is the smallest of the genus found in the United States, being but 7 inches in length. Except for size it is similar to *crinitus* but with very little, if any, rusty brown on tail, except for a slight edging on the outer web. Their nesting sites are the same as those chosen by the other Crested Flycatchers, but their eggs appear to have but little of the scratchy appearance of the other members. They are pale buffy, speckled and spotted with brown and lilac; size .80 x .60. Data.—Toluca, Mexico, May 20, 1895. Nest of brown hair and feathers, in hole in tree in woods. Collector, Fred T. Francis.

[Buffy.]

456. Eastern Phoebe. *Sayornis phoebe.*

Range.—North America, east of the Rockies and north to Nova Scotia.

These very common, grayish colored birds are very often known as "Bridge Birds" because of the frequency with which they construct their nests under bridges and arches; they also build in crevices in ledges or among the hanging roots near the tops of embankments, and on the rafters or beams of old buildings. The nests are made of mud, moss and grass, lined with feathers. The four or five white eggs measure .75 x .55. Occasionally, eggs will be found that have a few minute spots of reddish brown. Freak situations in which to locate their nests are often chosen by these birds, such as the brake beam of a freight car, in the crevices of old wells, hen houses, etc. The birds are one of the most useful that we have; being very active and continually on the alert for insects and beetles that constitute their whole bill of fare.

[White.]

[1] Now Wied's Crested Flycatcher.

[2] Purely casual, occurring only in Arizona; distinct species from Ash-throated.

[3] Not recorded from North America.

457. Say's Phoebe. *Sayornis saya.*

Range.—Western United States, breeding from southern United States, north to the Arctic regions, and from Kansas and Wisconsin westward. Winters in Mexico. [1]

[White.]

This bird is slightly larger than the last (7.5 inches long), and is rusty brown color on the belly and lower breast. Like the eastern Phoebes they are one of the earliest birds to return in the spring and are abundant in the greater parts of their range. Like the latter, they often raise two broods a season, one in April and another in July. Their nests are generally placed on narrow shelves and crevices of ledges, but they also nest as commonly about houses and farms as does the eastern bird. The nests are made of weeds, mosses, fibres and wool, and are quite flat. They lay four or five white eggs. Size .78 x .58.

458. Black Phoebe. *Sayornis nigricans.*

Range.—Mexico and north in summer into the bordering States.

[White.]

This species is of the size of the last but is blackish (darkest on the head and breast), with a white belly and under tail coverts, the latter streaked with dusky. Their habits and nesting habits are the same as those of the eastern Phoebe, they building their nests of mud, moss, weeds and feathers on ledges or about buildings, and generally close to or in the vicinity of water. They breed during April or May, laying four or five white eggs which cannot be distinguished from those of the common Phoebe. Size .75 x .55.

458a. Western Black Phoebe. *Sayornis nigricans.*

Range—Pacific coast of Mexico and the United States, breeding north to Oregon.

This variety differs from the last in having the under tail coverts pure white. Its nesting habits are precisely the same and the eggs indistinguishable.

459. Olive-sided Flycatcher. *Nuttallornis borealis.*

Range.—Whole of North America, breeding from the Middle States and California northward, and in the Rockies, south to Mexico; winters south of the United States.

[Creamy white.]

These Flycatchers are nowhere abundant, and in some parts of the country, especially in the middle portion, they are very rare. They breed very locally and generally not more than one pair in any locality. In New England, I have always found them nesting in company with Parula Warblers, in dead coniferous swamps in which the branches are covered with long pendant moss. Their nests are placed high up in the trees, generally above fifty feet from the ground, and on small horizontal limbs; they are made of small twigs and rootlets, lined with finer rootlets and moss, and are very flat and shallow; as they are generally made to match the surrounding, they are one of the most difficult nests to find. They lay three or four cream colored eggs which are spotted with reddish brown and lilac, chiefly about the large end. Size .85 x .65. Data.—Lake Quinsigamond, Massachusetts, June 12, 1897. Nest of twigs and moss, about 60 feet above the ground, in a dead pine tree in center of a large wet swamp. Nest could not be seen from the ground, found by watching bird. Collector, C. K. Reed.

[1] Winters in extreme southern and western U.S.

Photo from life by G. E. Moulthrope.

EASTERN PHOEBE ON NEST.

NEST AND EGGS OF OLIVE-SIDED FLYCATCHER.

460. Coues' Flycatcher. *Contopus pertinax.*

Range.—Western Mexico, breeding north to central Arizona.

[Cream color.]

This Flycatcher builds one of the most artistic nests created by feathered creatures. It bears some resemblance on the exterior to that of the next species, but it is much more firmly made, and the walls are usually higher, making a very deeply cupped interior. The outside of the nest is made of fibres, cobwebs, catkins, etc., firmly felted together and ornamented with green lichens to match the limb upon which it is saddled. The interior is heavily lined with dried, yellowish grasses, making a very strong contrast to the exterior. They are fairly abundant birds in the ranges of southern Arizona, where they nest generally during June. They lay three eggs of a rich creamy color, spotted and blotched, chiefly about the larger end, with reddish brown and lilac gray. Size .85 x .61. Data.—Huachuca Mts., Arizona, July 8, 1897. 3 eggs. Nest in a yellow pine about 60 feet up and near the extremity of a long slender limb. Elevation 7000 feet. Collector, O. W. Howard.

461. Eastern Wood Pewee. *Contopus virens.*

Range.—North America, east of the Plains and north to the southern parts of the British Provinces. Winters south of the United States.

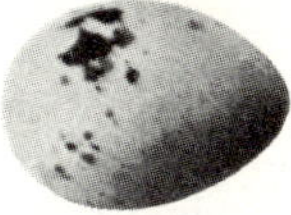

[Cream color.]

This is one of the best known and one of the most common frequenters of open woods, where all summer long its pleasing notes may be heard, resembling "pee-a-wee" or sometimes only two syllables "pee-wee." They nest on horizontal limbs at elevations of six feet or over, making handsome nests of plant fibres and fine grasses, covered on the exterior with lichens; they are quite shallow and very much resemble a small knot on the limb of the tree. They lay three or four eggs of a cream color spotted in a wreath about the large end, with reddish brown and lavender; size .80 x .55. Data.—Torrington, Conn., June 16, 1890. Nest of fibres covered with lichens, saddled on the branch of an oak tree near roadside. Collector, John Gath.

462. Western Wood Pewee. *Contopus sordidulus.*

Range.—Western United States from the Plains to the Pacific, and from Manitoba southward, wintering south of the United States.

The nesting habits of this bird are the same as those of the eastern Pewee, but their nests are more strongly built and generally deeper, and without the outside ornamentation of lichens. They are saddled upon horizontal branches, like those of the preceding, as a rule, but are also said to have been found in upright crotches like those of the Least Flycatcher. Their three or four eggs cannot be distinguished from those of the eastern Wood Pewee.

462a. Large-billed Wood Pewee (should be Western Wood Pewee). *Contopus sordidulus.*

Range.—This species which differs from the last only slightly, as is indicated by the name, inhabits the peninsula of Lower California; its nesting habits and eggs will not differ from those of the other Pewees.

463. Yellow-bellied Flycatcher. *Empidonax flaviventris.*

Range.—North America, east of the Plains and north to Labrador; winters south of the United States. [1]

[Creamy white.]

This species is slightly larger than the Least Flycatcher and is more yellowish above and below, the breast being quite bright. While common in some districts it is quite shy and frequents thickly wooded regions, where it is not very often seen. They nest near or on the ground among rocks or roots of fallen trees, chiefly in swampy places; the nests are made in bunches of moss, hollowed out and lined with very fine grasses. Their four eggs are creamy or buffy white, spotted and specked about the larger end with reddish brown and gray; size .68 x .51.

[1] Breeds only in northern U.S. and Canada.

464.   Western Flycatcher.   *Empidonax difficilis.*

Range.—Western North America, from the Rocky Mountain region to the Pacific, and north to Alaska; winters chiefly south of the United States.

This Flycatcher, which is similar to the last, nests in similar locations as well as in many others, such as crevices and fissures in rocks, holes in banks, cavities in trees, rafters in buildings, etc.   The nests are variously made, but consist chiefly of fine grasses, weeds and fibres.   The eggs are as a rule similar to those of the last species and cannot be distinguished.

[Creamy white]

464.1.   St. Lucas Flycatcher (should be Western Flycatcher).   *Empidonax difficilis.*

Range.—Lower California.

This species is similar to, but duller in plumage than the Western Flycatcher. Their nesting habits do not probably vary from those of the latter.

464.2.   Santa Barbara Flycatcher.   *Empidonax insulicola.*

Range.—Santa Barbara Islands, California. [1]

This species is very similar to 464 , but is said to be   darker and browner. Its eggs cannot be distinguished from those of the preceding.

465.   Acadian Flycatcher.   *Empidonax virescens.*

Range.—Eastern United States, breeding from the Gulf to southern New England, and in the Mississippi Valley to Manitoba.

This species is very pale below and greenish yellow on the back.   They are among the latest of the migrants to reach our borders and arrive in the Middle States about the latter part of May, when they are quite common.   They build semi-pensile nests in the forks of bushes or overhanging branches at heights of from four to twenty feet, the nests being made of rootlets, fibres, fine gras s, etc., and partially suspended from the branch; they are quite shallow and loosely constructed and often appear more like a bunch of debris deposited in the fork by the wind than like the creation of a bird.   Their three or four eggs are buffy, spotted or specked with brown; size .75 x .55.

[Buffy.]

466.   Traill's Flycatcher.   *Empidonax traillii.*

Range.—Western North America, from the Mississippi Valley to the Pacific; winters south of the United States.

This species is very similar to the next, but the back is said to be more brownish.   They are common and nest abundantly in thickets and low scrubby woods, usually placing the nest at a low elevation, preferably in a clump of willows; the nests are made of fine strips of bark, plant fibres, and very fine rootlets being woven about and firmly fastened in upright crotches. [Creamy white.]   Their eggs, which are laid in June, are buffy white, specked and spotted, chiefly at the large end, with brownish; size .70 x.54.

---

[1] No longer recognized as a valid form.

Photo by Guy H. Briggs.

NEST AND EGGS OF EASTERN WOOD PEWEE.

466a.   Alder Flycatcher (should be Traill's Flycatcher).   *Empidonax traillii.*

Range.—United States, east of the Mississippi and north to New Brunswick.

The only difference between this and the preceding variety is in the more greenish upper parts. They are quite abundant in the breeding season from New England and northern New York northward, frequenting, to a great extent, alder thickets bordering streams. Their nests and eggs do not differ appreciably from those of the western variety of Traill's Flycatcher.

467.   Least Flycatcher.   *Empidonax minimus.*

Range.—North America, east of the Rockies and north to the interior of Canada, wintering south of the United States.

[White.]

These little birds (5.5 incheslong) are common about houses and orchards on the outskirts of cities, and on the edges of forests or open woods. They are very frequently known by the name of Chebec from their continually uttered note. In nearly all instances, the nests are placed in upright forks at elevations varying from four to twenty-four feet from the ground. The nests are made chiefly of plant fibres, fine grasses, string, cobwebs, etc., and the three to five eggs are pale creamy white; size .65 x .50.

468.   Hammond's Flycatcher.   *Empidonax hammondii.*

Range.—North America, west of the Rockies and from British Columbia southward, wintering south of the United States.

This western representative of the Least Flycatcher is less abundant and more shy, but has the same nesting habits as the eastern birds, placing its nests either in upright crotches or, more rarely, upon horizontal branches at a low elevation. The eggs cannot be distinguished from those of the last species.

[White.]

469.   Dusky Flycatcher.   *Empidonax oberholseri.*

Range.—Western United States, breeding from the Mexican border to Oregon, and wintering south of the United States.

[White.]

A very similar bird to the last but whiter below. It is a much more abundant species than the last and is found breeding in open woods and thickets on all the ranges. The nests are built like those of the Least Flycatcher and nearly always are found in the crotch of trees or bushes at a low elevation; their nests, like those of the two preceding species, bear a strong resemblance to those of the Yellow Warblers which are found in the same localities and locations. The eggs are pale creamy white, four in number and measure .68 x .52.

469.1. Gray Flycatcher. *Empidonax wrightii.*

Range.—Lower California, north to southern California. [1]

This is a slightly larger species than the preceding and is grayish above and paler below, with little or no tinge of brownish or yellow. As far as I can learn its eggs have not yet been taken.

470. Fulvous Flycatcher (should be Buff-breasted Flycatcher). *Empidonax fulvifrons.*

Range.—Eastern Mexico; admitted to our fauna on the authority of Giraud as having occurred in southern Texas. [2]

This bird is similar to its sub-species but larger. Its nesting habits will not differ.

470a. Buff-breasted Flycatcher. *Empidonax fulvifrons.*

Range.—Western Mexico, north to southern New Mexico and Arizona.

This small bird, which is but 4.75 inches in length, is brownish gray above and brownish buff below. It is not a common species anywhere, but is known to nest during June or July, on high mountain ranges, saddling its nest of fibres, covered with lichens, on horizontal boughs at quite an elevation from the ground. The eggs are pale buffy white, unspotted, and measure .60 x .50.

471. Vermilion Flycatcher. *Pyrocephalus rubinus.*

Range.—Mexico, north regularly to southern Texas, Arizona and New Mexico.

This is one of the most gaudily attired of all North American birds, being brownish gray on the back, wings and tail, and having a bright vermilion crown, crest and underparts. They are quite common in southern Texas, but far more abundant in the southern parts of Arizona. Their habits do not differ from those of other Flycatchers, they living almost exclusively upon insects.   [Buff.]
The majority of nests cannot be distinguished from those of the Eastern Wood Pewee, being covered with lichens and saddled upon limbs in a similar manner, but some lack the mossy ornamentation. Their three or four eggs are buffy, boldly blotched with dark brown and lavender, chiefly in a wreath about the middle of the egg; size .70 x .50. Data.—San Pedro River, Arizona, June 10, 1899. Nest in the fork of a willow about 20 feet above the stream. Collector, O. W. Howard.

472. Beardless Flycatcher. *Camptostoma imberbe.*

Range.—Central America; north casually to the Lower Rio Grande in Texas.[3]

This strange little Flycatcher, several specimens of which have been taken in the vicinity of Lomita, Texas, is but 4.5 inches in length, grayish in color and has a short bill, the upper mandible of which is curved. It has all the habits peculiar to Flycatchers. Their eggs have not as yet been found as far as I can learn.

472a. Ridgway's Flycatcher (should be Beardless Flycatcher). *Camptostoma imberbe.*

Range.—Southwestern Mexico, north to southern Arizona.

This species is slightly larger and grayer than the last. They are rare birds, either in the United States or in Mexico and their nests and eggs have not yet been reported.

[1] Breeds in west-southwest U.S.

[2] Not recorded from North America.

[3] Breeds from southern Texas south.

LARKS.   Family ALAUDIDAE.

473.   Skylark.   *Alauda arvensis.*

Range.—Old World, straggling casually to Greenland and Bermuda. [1]

[Grayish.]

This noted foreigner has been imported and liberated a number of times in this country, but apparently is not able to thrive here, a fact which will not cause much regret when we remember the experiment with the English Sparrow.[2] They are abundant in Europe and Great Britain where they nest on the ground in cultivated fields or meadows, laying from three to five grayish eggs, marked with brown, drab and lavender.

474.   Horned Lark.   *Eremophila alpestris.*

Range.—Eastern North America, breeding in Labrador and about Hudson Bay; winters in eastern United States south to Carolina.

This variety of this much sub-divided species is 7.5 inches in length, has brownish gray upper parts and is white below with black patches on the breast and below the eye, yellowish throat and small black ear tufts.   The various sub-species are all marked alike, their distinction being based upon slight differences in size, variations in the shade of the back, or greater or lesser intensity of the yellowish throat and superciliary stripe.   The nesting habits of all the varieties are the same and the eggs differ only in the shade of the ground color, this variation among the eggs of the same variety being so great that an egg cannot be identified without knowing the locality in which it was taken.   The present variety build their nests on the ground generally under tufts of grass or in hollows in the moss which is found in their breeding range, making them of dried grasses and generally lining them with feathers.   The eggs are grayish with a slight greenish tinge, and are specked and spotted over the whole surface with drab, brownish and dark lavender.   The eggs of this and the next variety average considerably larger than those of the more southerly distributed varieties; size .92 x .65.

474a.   Pallid Horned Lark (should be Horned Lark).   *Eremophila alpestris.*

Range.—Breeds in Alaska and winters south to Oregon and Montana.

This is the largest of the Horned Larks and has the throat white, with no trace of yellow.   Its nest is built in similar locations and the eggs are like those of the preceding species.

474b.   Prairie Horned Lark (should be Horned Lark).   *Eremophila alpestris.*

Range.—Breeds in the Mississippi Valley from Illinois north to Manitoba and east to the Middle States; winters south to Carolina and Texas.

This sub-species is considerably smaller than the Horned Lark, and the throat is paler yellow, while the line over the eye and the forehead is white.   They are the most abundant and have the most extended range of any of the better known species.   In the Mississippi Valley, where they are of the most common of the nesting birds, they build on the ground in meadows or cultivated fields, and very often in cornfields; the

[Olive buff.]

nests are made of grasses and lined with horse hairs or feathers, and placed in slight hollows generally under a tuft of grass or sods.   They raise two broods a season and sometimes three, laying the first set of eggs in March and another in June or July.   The three or four eggs have an olive buff ground color and are thickly sprinkled with drab and lavender; size .83 x .60.

[1] Introduced on Vancouver Island, British Columbia.

[2] Now House Sparrow.

474c.   Desert Horned Lark (should be Horned Lark).   *Eremophila alpestris.*

Range.—Plains of western United States, east of the Rockies and west of Kansas and Dakota; breeds north to Alberta, and winters south to Mexico, Texas and southern California.

This species is like 474b but paler on the back; nest and eggs the same.

474d.   Texan Horned Lark (should be Horned Lark).   *Eremophila alpestris.*

Range.—Coast of southeastern Texas.

A pale variety like 474c. , but   smaller;   throat   bright   yellow, and breast tinged with yellow.   Nest and eggs like those of the others.

474e.   California Horned Lark (should be Horned Lark).   *Eremophila alpestris.*

Range.—Lower California and southern California.

This bird is similar to the last but the yellow areas are brighter, and the nape and back are ruddy.

474f.   Ruddy Horned Lark (should be Horned Lark).   *Eremophila alpestris.*

Range.—Sacramento Valley, California.
This variety has the yellow areas brighter than in any other and the back and nape are more ruddy.   The eggs cannot be distinguished from those of the others.

[Olive buff.]

474g.   Streaked Horned Lark (should be Horned Lark).   *Eremophila alpestris.*

Range.—Northwestern United States (Washington, Oregon and northern California).
Similar to the last, but with the back broadly streaked with black, the ruddy less intense and the underparts tinged with yellowish.

474h.   Scorched Horned Lark (should be Horned Lark).   *Eremophila alpestris.*

Range.—Western Mexico, north in summer to southern Arizona.
This variety has the back and nape nearly a uniform pinkish ruddy with but little streaking.

474i.   Dusky Horned Lark (should be Horned Lark).   *Eremophila alpestris.*

Range. Northwestern United States and southern British Columbia, wintering south to central California.
Similar to 474b but slightly darker above.

474j. Sonoran Horned Lark (should be Horned Lark).   *Eremophila alpestris.*

Range.—Gulf coast of northern Lower California.
The upperparts of this variety are very pale pinkish brown.

474k. Hoyt's Horned Lark (should be Horned Lark).   *Eremophila alpestris.*

Range.—Interior of British America, west of Hudson Bay and east of Alaska,
south in winter in the interior of the United States to Kansas.
Much larger than the last; equal in size and similar to 474a but with the
throat yellowish and the upperparts darker and brighter.

474l. Montezuma Horned Lark (should be Horned Lark).   *Eremophila alpestris.*

Range.—Western New Mexico and eastern Arizona, south in winter to northern
Mexico.
This variety has the upperparts pale brownish and not streaked; throat and
forehead yellowish.

474m. Island Horned Lark (should be Horned Lark).   *Eremophila alpestris.*

Range.—Santa Barbara Islands, California.
Similar to 474g but darker.   With the exception of the three large varieties
of Horned Larks found north of our borders, neither the eggs nor, in most cases,
the birds can be identified without the precise location where they were taken.

CROWS, JAYS and allies.   Family CORVIDAE.

475. Black-billed Magpie.   *Pica pica.*

Range.—Western North America from the Great Plains to the Pacific and
from Alaska to Arizona and New Mexico.

[Grayish white.]

These large handsome birds have the entire head,
neck and breast velvety black, abruptly defined
against the white underparts.   The back, wings and
tail are greenish or bluish black, and the scapulars,
white; length of bird 20 inches. They are well known
throughout the west, where their bold and thievish
habits always excite comment.   They nest in bushes
and trees at low elevations from the ground, making
a very large nest of sticks, with an opening on the
side, and the interior is made of weeds and mud,
lined with fine grasses; these nests often reach a diameter of three feet and are
made of quite large sticks. During April or May, they lay from four to eight
grayish white eggs, plentifully spotted with brown and drab. Size 1.25 x .90.

476. Yellow-billed Magpie.   *Pica nuttalli.*

Range.—Middle parts of California, west of the
Sierra Nevadas.

This species is slightly smaller than the last and
has a yellow bill and lores, otherwise being precisely like the more common species. Their habits do
not differ from those of the other, the nests are the
same and the eggs are indistinguishable.   Size
1.25 x .88.

[Grayish white.]

Photo by R. B. Rockwell.

NEST OF BLACK-BILLED MAGPIE.

477. Blue Jay. *Cyanocitta cristata.*

Range.—North America, east of the Plains and north to Hudson Bay; resident and very abundant in its United States range.

[Greenish buff.]

These beautiful and bold marauders are too well known to need description, suffice it to say that they are the most beautiful of North American Jays; but beneath their handsome plumage beats a heart as cruel and cunning as that in any bird of prey. In the fall, winter and spring, their food consists largely of acorns, chestnuts, berries, seeds, grain, insects, lizards, etc., but during the summer months they destroy and devour a great many eggs and young of the smaller birds, their taste for which, being so great that they are known to watch a nest until the full complement of eggs is laid before making their theft. They nest in open woods or clumps of trees, indifferently, in pines or young trees, building most often below twenty feet from the ground; the nests are made of twigs and rootlets, lined with finer rootlets. During May they lay from four to six eggs of a greenish or brownish buff color spotted with olive brown. Size 1.10 x .80. Data.—Chester County, Pa., May 23, 1886. Nest in an oak sapling, fifteen feet above ground; made of sticks, rootlets and grass. Collector, Samuel B. Ladd.

477a. Florida Blue Jay (should be Blue Jay). *Cyanocitta cristata.*

Range.—Florida and the Gulf coast.

The nesting habits and eggs of this smaller subspecies are the same as those of the northern Blue Jay. Like our birds, they frequently nest near habitations.

478. Steller's Jay. *Cyanocitta stelleri.*

Range.—Pacific coast from southern California to Alaska; resident and breeding throughout its range.

All the members of this sub-genus are similar in plumage, having a sooty black head, crest and neck, shading insensibly into dark bluish on the back and underparts, and brighter blue on the wings and tail. They usually have a few streaks or spots of pale blue on the forehead. They are just as noisy, bold and thievish as the eastern Jay and are also excellent mimics like the latter. They nest in fir trees at any height from the ground and in April or May deposit their three to six greenish blue eggs which are spotted with various shades of brown. Size 1.25 x .90. Their nests are more bulky than those of the eastern Jay and are usually made of larger sticks and held together with some mud.

[Greenish blue.]

478a. Blue-fronted Jay (should be Steller's Jay). *Cyanocitta stelleri.*

Range.—Coast ranges of California and Oregon.

The nesting habits and eggs of this variety are indistinguishable from those of the preceding. The bird has more blue on the forehead.

478b. Long-crested Jay (should be Steller's Jay). *Cyanocitta stelleri.*

Range.—Southern Rocky Mountains from Arizona to Wyoming.

No general difference can be found between the eggs of this species and the Steller Jay, and the nests of each are constructed similarly and in like situations.

478c. Black-headed Jay (should be Steller's Jay). *Cyanocitta stelleri.*

Range.—Northern Rocky Mountains from northern Colorado to British Columbia.

The eggs of this subspecies cannot be identified from those of the other varieties. Like the others, their nests are made of sticks plastered together with mud and lined with weeds and rootlets.

478d. Queen Charlotte Jay (should be Steller's Jay). *Cyanocitta stelleri.*

Range.—Queen Charlotte Islands, British Columbia.

479. Scrub Jay. *Aphelocoma coerulescens.*

Range.—Locally distributed in Florida.

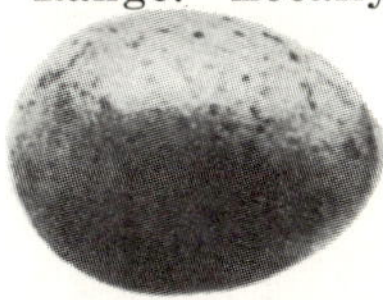
[Greenish blue.]

All the birds of this genus have no crests or decided markings, are white or grayish below, and more or less intense blue above, with the back grayish or brownish blue. This species is 11.5 inches long, has a pale blue crown and a nearly white forehead. It has a very limited distribution, being confined chiefly to the coast districts of middle Florida, and very abundant in some localities and rare in adjoining ones. They build shallow structures of small sticks and weeds lined with fine rootlets and placed at low elevations in bushes or scrubby trees. The three or four eggs, which are laid in April or May are dull greenish blue, marked with olive brown. Size 1.00 x .80. Data.—Titusville, Fla., April 17, 1899. Nest of sticks in a scrub oak, five feet from the ground. Collector, C. H. Jenkins.

480. Woodhouse's Jay (should be Scrub Jay). *Aphelocoma coerulescens.*

Range.—United States west of the Rockies and from Oregon and Wyoming to Mexico.

This species has the crown and forehead bluish, and the underparts gray, streaked with bluish gray on the breast. It is also larger than the last, being 12 inches long. They are very abundant in the Great Basin between the Rockies and the Sierra Nevadas, breeding during April or May in scrubby trees or bushes at low elevations and generally near streams. They lay from three to five eggs of a dull bluish green color, spotted with umber and lilac gray. Size 1.08 x .80. Data.—Iron County, Utah, May 3, 1897. 4 eggs. Nest of sticks and weeds in a small pine tree. Collector, Harry Cooley.

[Bluish green.]

480.1. Blue-eared Jay (should be Scrub Jay). *Aphelocoma coerulescens.*

Range.—Interior of Mexico north to the southern boundary of Texas.
The nesting habits of this species are the same as those of the others of the genus and the eggs are similar but the markings are generally more prominent and larger. Size 1.10 x .80.

480.2. Texan Jay (should be Scrub Jay). *Aphelocoma coerulescens.*

Range.—Southeastern Texas.
It is not likely that the eggs of this species differ essentially from those of many of the others.

481. California Jay (should be Scrub Jay). *Aphelocoma coerulescens.*

Range.—Pacific coast of California and Washington.

[Bright bluish green.]

This is a very abundant species both about habitations and in low woodlands. They are very bold and familiar, stealing everything they may take a fancy to, and frequently robbing smaller birds of their eggs and young. They are said to be more tame and familiar than the eastern Blue Jay, thereby bringing their bad habits much more frequently to the attention of the masses. They nest most often in bushes or low trees in thickets, and sometimes in larger trees, but not as a rule, far above the ground. Their eggs are a bright bluish green color, specked and spotted with brownish and lavender. Size 1.10 x .80.

481a.　Xantus' Jay (should be Scrub Jay).　*Aphelocoma coerulescens.*

Range.—Lower California.
The habits and nests and eggs of this lighter colored variety do not differ from those of the California Jay.

481b.　Belding's Jay (should be Scrub Jay).　*Aphelocoma coerulescens.*

Range.—San Pedro Martir Mts., Lower California.
A darker variety of the California Jay, whose nesting habits will not differ in any essential particular.

481.1.　Santa Cruz Jay (should be Scrub Jay).　*Aphelocoma coerulescens.*

[Greenish blue.]

Range.—Santa Cruz Island, California.
This species is the largest and darkest colored bird of the genus *Aphelocoma*. It is said to be a very abundant species on the island from which it takes its name, and to have the habits and traits common to all the members of the Jay family. The nesting habits are the same as those of the others, but the eggs are slightly larger, averaging 1.15 x .85. The one figured is from a set of three in the collection of John Lewis Childs, taken by R. H. Beck on May 10, 1897.

482.　Mexican Jay.　*Aphelocoma ultramarina.*

Range.—Arizona and southwestern New Mexico south into Mexico.

This species differs from the preceding ones in having the upperparts of a uniform bluish, and in being without streaks on the underparts, and with no dusky ear patches. These birds, while they have the usual Jay traits, are more sociable during the breeding season and often small companies of from two to ten pairs nest in the same clump of trees, placing their nests in crotches at low elevations. The nests are made of small sticks and rootlets and generally lined with finer rootlets or horse hair. The eggs are a bright robin blue color, unmarked and number from three to six. Size 1.20 x .85.

[Robin blue.]

482a.　Couch's Jay (should be Mexican Jay).　*Aphelocoma ultramarina.*

Range.—Eastern Mexico, north to western Texas.

483.　Green Jay.　*Cyanocorax yncas.*

Range.—Northeastern Mexico and the Lower Rio Grande Valley in Texas.

[Grayish buff.]

This handsome species has a bright blue crown and patches under the eyes, the rest of the upper parts being greenish; throat and sides of head black, underparts greenish white. This gaudy and noisy bird has all the habits common to other Jays including that of robbing birds' nests. They build generally in tangled thickets or low bushes, placing their nests at a low elevation and making them of twigs, weeds, moss, etc., lined with fine rootlets. Their four or five eggs, which are laid during April or May, are grayish buff in color, spotted with various shades of brown and lavender gray. Size 1.20 x .85.

484. Canada Jay (should be Gray Jay). *Perisoreus canadensis.*

Range.—Southeastern British Provinces and the adjacent portions of the United States; west to the Rockies.

[Grayish.]

This is the bird that is well known to hunters of "big game" by various names such as "Whiskey Jack," "Moose Bird," "Camp Robber," etc. During the winter months, owing to the scarcity of food, their thieving propensities are greatly enhanced and they remove everything from the camps, which looks as though it might be edible. Birds of this genus are smoky gray on the back and lighter below, shading to white on the throat; the forehead and part of the crown is white and the nape blackish. Their nests are placed at low elevations in bushes or fir trees, and are usually very different from any of the preceding Jays' nests. They are nearly as high as wide, and are made of small twigs, moss, catkins, weeds and feathers making a soft spongy mass which is placed in an upright crotch. The eggs are a yellowish gray color spotted and blotched with brown and grayish. Size 1.15 x .80. Data.—Innisfail, Alberta, March 12, 1903. Nest a beautiful structure of twigs, moss and feathers in a willow bush, 6 feet from the ground. The thermometer registered 32 below zero the day the eggs were taken. Collector, W. Blackwood.

484a. Rocky Mountain Jay (should be Gray Jay). *Perisoreus canadensis.*

Range.—Rocky Mountains from Montana to Arizona.
This variety has the whole crown white and only a small amount of blackish on the nape. Its nesting habits and eggs are precisely like those of the last.

NEST AND EGGS OF GRAY JAY, SHOWING CONSTRUCTION.

484b.   Alaskan Jay (should be Gray Jay).   *Periosoreus canadensis.*

Range.—Alaska.

A very similar bird to the Canada Jay but with the forehead yellowish or duller; the nests and eggs are like those of the others of the genus.

484c.   Labrador Jay (should be Gray Jay).   *Perisoreus canadensis.*

Range.—Labrador.

This is a darker variety of the Canada Jay.   Its eggs cannot be distinguished from those of any of the others of the genus.

485.   Oregon Jay (should be Gray Jay).   *Perisoreus canadensis.*

Range.—Mountain ranges from northern California to British Columbia.

These birds are very similar to 484 but have the whole under parts white.   Like the Canada Jays they appear to be wholly fearless and pay little or no attention to the presence of mankind.   Their nesting habits and eggs are the same as the preceding except that they have generally been found nesting near the tops of tall fir trees.   Size of eggs, 1.05 x .80.

485a.   Gray Jay.   *Perisoreus canadensis.*

Range.—British Columbia to northern California, east of the coast ranges.
This bird is said to be larger and grayer than the preceding.

486.   Common Raven.   *Corvus corax.*

Range.—North America west of the Rockies and from British Columbia southward.

[Pale greenish white.]

The Raven is like a very large Crow, length 24 inches, but has the feathers on the neck lengthened and stiffened. Their habits are similar to those of the Crow, but more dignified, and they remain mated for life. Besides grasshoppers and worms, they feed largely upon animal matter such as lizards, shell fish, frogs, eggs and young of birds, and carrion. They nest on ledges of high inaccessible cliffs or the tops of tall trees, making large nests of sticks lined with smaller ones and hair or wool; the eggs are laid in April or May, number from four to seven, and are light greenish in color, blotched with umber and drab.   Size 1.95 x 1.25.

486a.   Northern Raven (should be Common Raven).   *Corvus corax.*

Range.—Eastern North America chiefly north of the United States and northwest to Alaska; south on some of the higher ranges to Georgia.

This variety is like the last but is larger.   They are not nearly as abundant as the western form and are very rare within the United States.   A few pairs still breed on some of the rocky islands off the coast of Maine; more off New Brunswick and Newfoundland, and they are quite common on the cliffs of Labrador and Alaska.   Their nesting habits and eggs are like those of the last.

487. White-necked Raven. *Corvus cryptoleucus.*

Range.—Mexico and the border of the United States; north to eastern Kansas.

This small Raven is of about the size of the Crow, and has the bases of the neck feathers white. They are very abundant in some localities, especially in southern Arizona. Their food consists chiefly of animal matter, the same as the large Ravens, and they are not nearly as shy, frequently feeding in camps upon refuse which is thrown out to them. They build at low elevations in any tree, but preferably in mesquites, making their nests of sticks and lining them with hair, leaves, bark, wool or anything soft. During June they lay from four to six pale bluish green eggs, generally sparingly spotted or scratched with dark brown and drab. Size 1.75 x 1.20.

[Pale bluish green.]

488. Common Crow. *Corvus brachyrhynchos.*

[Greenish white.]

Range.—Whole of North America south of the Arctic Circle; most abundant in eastern United States; rare in many localities in the west.

These birds, against which the hand of every farmer is uplifted, are very shy and cunning; as is well known, they nearly always post a sentinel in some tree top to keep watch while the rest of the flock is feeding in the field below. In the fall and winter, large numbers of them flock, and at night all roost in one piece of woods; some of the "crow roosts" are of vast extent and

contain thousands of individuals. Crows nest near the tops of large trees, preferably pines, either in woods or single trees in fields. Their nests are made of sticks and lined with rootlets, and the eggs, which are laid in April or May, range from four to seven in number, are a bluish or greenish white, sparingly or very densely specked, spotted and blotched with various shades of brown and lilac. Size 1.60 x 1.15.

488a. Florida Crow (should be Common Crow).
Corvus brachyrhynchos.

Range.—Florida.
This variety has a slightly shorter tail and wings than the last.

[Bluish white.]

[Bluish white.]

489. Northwestern Crow. *Corvus caurinus.*

Range.—Northwest coast from Oregon to Alaska.
This small Crow which is but 16 inches in length, is found only on the coast, where they feed upon shell fish and offal. They nest, as do the Ravens, either on ledges or in tree tops. The eggs resemble those of the Common Crow, but are smaller. Size 1.55 x 1.05.

490. Fish Crow. *Corvus ossifragus.*

Range.—South Atlantic and Gulf coasts, north in summer to Connecticut.

[Bluish green.]

From Virginia southward, this small Crow (length 16 inches) is more abundant on the coast than the Common Crow which is often in company with this species. As a rule they are less shy than are their larger relatives, and, when engaged in searching for food, will frequently approach human beings, apparently with little fear. Their food consists of grain, berries, and animal matter, which they pick up often from the surface of the water. Their nesting habits are like those of the Common Crow and the eggs are similar and have as great variations, but are smaller. Size 1.45 x 1.05.

491. Clarke's Nutcracker. *Nucifraga columbiana.*

Range.—Mountains of western North America from Mexico to Alaska.

[Grayish blue.]

The Clarke Crow, as this bird is often known, is a common resident in most of its range. The adults are grayish with black wings and central tail feathers, the tips of the primaries and outer tail feathers being white. Their tail is short and their flight slow and somewhat undulating like that of some of the Woodpeckers. Their food consists of anything edible from seeds and larvae in the winter to insects, berries, eggs and young birds at other seasons. In the spring they retire to the tops of ranges, nearly to the limit of trees, where they build their large nests of sticks, twigs, weeds, strips of bark, and fibres matted together so as to form a soft round ball with a deeply cupped interior; the nest is located at from ten to forty feet from the ground in pine trees and the eggs are laid early before the snow begins to leave. They are three in number, grayish in color with a greenish tinge and finely spotted over the whole surface with dark brown and lavender. Size 1.30 x .90. Data.—Salt Lake Co., Utah, April 25, 1900. Nest placed in pine 40 feet up on a horizontal branch, and not visible from below. The tree was at the upper edge of a pine forest at an altitude of about 3000 feet above Salt Lake City. The nest was discovered by seeing the parent fly into the tree; the next day a nest was found with three young nearly ready to fly. Collector, W. H. Parker. This set of three eggs is in the oölogical collection of Mr. C. W. Crandall.

492. Piñon Jay. *Gymnorhinus cyanocephalus.*

[Bluish white.]

Range.—Western United States between the Rockies and Sierra Nevadas, and from southern British Columbia to Arizona.

This Crow-like Jay has a nearly uniform bluish plumage, and is found abundantly in the pine belts of its range. Their habits are similar to those of the Clarke Crow and the nests are similarly built at lower elevations in pines or junipers. During April or May they lay from three to five eggs of a bluish white color specked and spotted with brown. Size 1.20 x .85.

STARLINGS.   Family STURNIDAE.

493.   Common Starling.   *Sturnus vulgaris.*

[Bluish Green.]

Range.—A European species which has casually been taken in Greenland.   It was liberated a number of years ago in Central Park, New York City, and has now become abundant there and is spreading slowly in all directions.[1]

They build their nests in all sorts of locations such as are used by the English Sparrow,[2] wherever they can find a sufficiently large crevice or opening; less often they build their nests in trees, making them of straw, twigs and trash.   They lay from four to six pale bluish green eggs; size 1.15 x .85. Two broods are reared in a season.

BLACKBIRDS and allies.   Family ICTERIDAE.

494.   Bobolink.   *Dolichonyx oryzivorus.*

Range.—Eastern North America, breeding from New Jersey north to Nova Scotia and Manitoba, and west to Utah and Nevada; winters in South America.

[Grayish White.]

This black and white bird is well known in the east, where his sweet, wild music, often uttered on the wing, is much admired.   He sings all day long during May and June to his Sparrow-like mate who is sitting on her nest concealed in the meadow grass.   They are quite sociable birds and several pairs often nest in the same field, generally a damp meadow; the nests are hollows in the ground, lined with grass and frequently with the top slightly arched to conceal the eggs, which are grayish white, clouded, spotted and blotched with brownish, gray and lilac; size .84 x .62. They number from four to six and are laid in June.

495.   Brown-headed Cowbird.   *Molothrus ater.*

Range.—North America from the Atlantic to eastern California, and from New Brunswick and Manitoba southward; winters from the southern half of the United States southward.

[White.]

These uncivilized members of the bird world build no nests for themselves, but slyly deposit their egg in the nest of some other bird from the size of a Robin down, probably the greater number being in Warblers and Sparrows nests; the eggs are hatched and the young cared for by the unfortunate birds upon which they are thrust.   The eggs are white, spotted and specked all over, more or less strongly with brown and yellowish brown; size .85 x .64.

495a.   Dwarf Cowbird (should be Brown-headed Cowbird).   *Molothrus ater.*

Range.—Southwestern United States and Mexico, wintering south of our borders.

This variety is like the last, but slightly smaller.   The nesting habits of the two are identical and the eggs are indistinguishable.   It is believed that Cowbirds do more damage to the smaller birds than all other dangers combined, as their young being larger and stronger either crowd or smother the other young or else starve them by getting most of the food brought to the nest.

[1] Now spread over almost all of North America, even into Alaska and Mexico.

[2] Now House Sparrow.

496. Bronzed Cowbird. *Tangavius aeneus.*

Range.—Mexico; north in summer to the Lower Rio Grande in Texas.[1]

This parasite is larger than the Cowbird,[2] being 9 inches long, and is glossy black with brassy reflections on the upper and under parts. They are abundant in southern Texas where they deposit their eggs in the nests of other birds, apparently preferring those of Orioles; their eggs are pale bluish green, unmarked; size .90 x .70.

[Light blue-green.]

497. Yellow-headed Blackbird.   *Xanthocephalus xanthocephalus.*

Range.—North America west of the Mississippi to eastern California, breeding from the southern parts of the United States north to British Columbia and Hudson Bay and wintering from southern United States downward.

This large handsome Blackbird with bright yellow head and breast is very abundant in some parts of the west, where they nest in large colonies in sloughs and marshes, being especially abundant in the Dakotas and Manitoba.   The nests are made of strips of rushes, skillfully woven together and attached to upright cane near the surface of the water. They lay from four to six eggs having a grayish white ground color, finely specked and spotted with shades of brown and gray; size 1.00 x .70. Data.—Harrison, S. D., June 21, 1891.   4 eggs in a nest made of grasses, placed in rushes over the water. Collector, W. C. Colt.

[Grayish white.]

498. Redwinged Blackbird. *Agelaius phoeniceus.*

Range.—North America east of the Rockies and from the southern British Provinces southward to the Gulf; winter in southern United States.

These birds are familiar to every frequenter of the country, in their range; too familiar to many, for the enormous flocks do considerable damage to grain fields in the fall. They also do a great amount of good at other seasons in the destruction of injurious insects and weed seed.   They breed from April in the southern parts of their range to May and June in the northern, making their nests of grasses, woven and twisted together and placing them in bushes in swamps

[Bluish white.]

or over water, and sometimes on the ground in clumps of grass. Their eggs are from three to five in number, bluish white boldly spotted, clouded or lined with blackish brown and purplish. Size 1.00 x .70. The nests and eggs of the numerous subspecies are all precisely the same as those of this bird, so we will but enumerate the varieties and their ranges. To identify these varieties other than by their ranges will require micrometer calipers and the services of the men who separated them.

498a.   Sonoran Red-Wing (should be Redwinged Blackbird). *Agelaius phoeniceus.*

Range.—A slightly larger variety found in southwestern United States.

498b.   Bahaman Red-Wing (should be Redwinged Blackbird). *Agelaius phoeniceus.*

Range.—Bahamas and southern Florida.

This species has a slightly longer bill.

498c.   Florida Red-Wing (should be Redwinged Blackbird). *Agelaius phoeniceus.*

Range.—Florida and Gulf coast.

A smaller species with a longer bill.

[1] Also breeds in Arizona and New Mexico.

[2] Now Brown-headed Cowbird.

Photo by R. B. Rockwell.

NEST AND EGGS OF YELLOW-HEADED BLACKBIRD.

498d.   Thick-billed Red-wing (should be Redwinged Blackbird).   *Agelaius phoeniceus.*

Range.—Breeds in the interior of British America; in winter south through the Plains to southwestern United States.

498e.   San Diego Red-wing (should be Redwinged Blackbird).   *Agelaius phoeniceus.*

Range.—Great Basin between the Rockies and Sierra Nevadas, from British Columbia to Mexico, wintering in the southern parts of its range.

498f.   Northwestern Red-wing (should be Redwinged Blackbird).   *Agelaius phoeniceus.*

Range.—Pacific coast from California to British Columbia.

499.   Bicolored Blackbird (should be Redwinged Blackbird).   *Agelaius phoeniceus.*

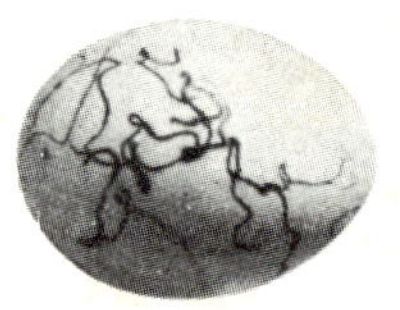

Range.—Pacific coast, west of the Sierra Nevadas, from Washington south to Lower California.

The males of this species are distinguished from those of the Redwings by the absence of light margins to the orange red shoulders. They are fairly abundant in their restricted localities, building their nests in swamps about ponds and streams. The nests are like those of the Redwings, and the eggs are similar and with the same great variations in markings, but average a trifle smaller; size .95 x .67.

[Dull bluish white.]

500.   Tricolored Blackbird.   *Agelaius tricolor.*

Range.—Pacific coast of California and Oregon; rare east of the Sierra Nevadas.

This species differs from the Redwing in having the shoulders a much darker red and the median coverts white instead of buffy. Like the last species they have a limited range and are nowhere as common as are the Redwings in the east. Their nests are like those of the Redwings and the eggs are not distinguishable in their many variations, but they appear to be more often lined than those of the former.

[Dull bluish white.]

501.   Eastern Meadowlark.   *Sturnella magna.*

Range.—North America east of the Plains and north to Nova Scotia and Manitoba; winters from New England southward.

This handsome dweller among our fields and meadows is frequently heard giving his high, pleasing, flute-like whistle with its variations; his beautiful yellow breast with its black crescent is not so frequently seen in life, for they are usually quite shy birds. They artfully conceal their nests on the ground among the tall grass of meadows, arching them over with dead grass. During May or June they lay four to six white eggs, speckled over the whole surface with reddish brown and purplish; size 1.10 x .80.

[White.]

501a.   Texas Meadowlark (should be Eastern Meadowlark).   *Sturnella magna.*

Range.—A brighter and slightly smaller variety found along the Mexican border.

501b. Western Meadowlark. *Sturnella neglecta.*

Range.—North America west of the Mississippi and from Manitoba and British Columbia southward, its range overlapping that of the eastern Meadowlark in the Mississippi Valley, but the two varieties appear not to intermingle. This variety is paler than the eastern, but the greatest point of difference is in the songs, they being wholly unlike, and that of the western bird much louder, sweeter and more varied than the simple whistle of the eastern form. The nesting habits of both varieties are the same and the eggs indistinguishable. [1]

501c. Florida Meadowlark (should be Eastern Meadowlark). *Sturnella magna.*

Range.—Florida and the Gulf coast.
A very similar bird to the northern form but slightly smaller and darker. There are no differences between the eggs of the two varieties.

502. Troupial. *Icterus icterus.*

Range.—Northern South America; claimed by Audubon to have been taken in South Carolina. This large Oriole is frequently kept in captivity. [2]

503. Black-headed Oriole. *Icterus graduacauda.*

Range.—Mexico and the Lower Rio Grande Valley in Texas.
This large Oriole has a wholly black head, neck, fore breast, tail and wings; yellowish underparts and greenish yellow back; it is 9.5 inches in length. They are quite abundant and resident in southern Texas where they build at low elevations in trees, preferably mesquites, making the nests of woven grasses and hanging them from the small outer twigs of the trees; the nests are more like those of the Orchard Oriole and not long and pensile like those of the Baltimore. The three to five eggs are grayish white,

[White.]

blotched, clouded, spotted or streaked with brownish and purple. Size 1.00 x .70. Data.—Brownsville, Texas, April 6, 1897. 5 eggs. Nest of threads from palmetto leaves, hanging from limb of mesquite, 10 feet above ground in the open woods. Collector, Frank B. Armstrong.

504. Scott's Oriole. *Icterus parisorum.*

Range.—Western Mexico north to the adjoining states; north to Nevada.

This handsome black and yellow species does not appear to be abundant in any part of its range. Their nests are swung from the under side of leaves of the yucca palm or from small branches of low trees, and are made of grass and fibres. The eggs are bluish white, specked and blotched chiefly about the large end with blackish brown and lilac gray. Size .95 x .65. Data.—Chiricahua Mts., Arizona,

[Bluish white.]

June 5, 1900. Nest placed on the under side of a yucca palm leaf, being hung from the spines, about 4 feet from the ground. Altitude 7000 feet. Collector, O. W. Howard.

[1] Now breeding as far east as Ohio.

[2] Not recorded from North America.

505. Hooded Oriole. *Icterus cucullatus.*

Range.—Mexico, north in summer to the Lower Rio Grande Valley in Texas.

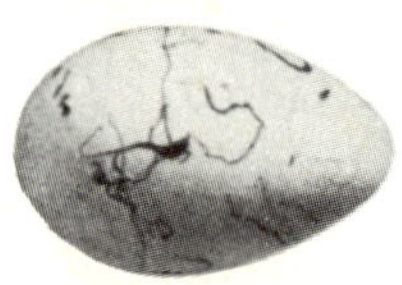
[White.]

This species is orange yellow except for the face, throat, fore back, wings and tail, which are black; the wings are crossed by two white bars. These handsome birds are the most abundant of the Orioles on the Lower Rio Grande, where their pure mellow whistle is heard at frequent intervals throughout the day. They generally build their nests in hanging moss from mesquite trees, turning up at the ends and lining the pocket with moss, or else make a shallow hanging nest of fibres and suspend it from yuccas. During May or June they lay from three to five eggs of a white color, spotted (rarely lined) with purplish brown and gray. Size .85 x .60.

505a. Arizona Hooded Oriole (should be Hooded Oriole). *Icterus cucullatus.*

Range.—Western Mexico; in summer north to southern Arizona, New Mexico and California.

This variety is like the last but more yellowish. Their nests are made of a wiry grass compactly woven together and partially suspended to mistletoe twigs growing from cottonwood trees; nests of this type are perfectly distinct from those of the preceding, but when they are made of fibre and attached to yuccas, they cannot be distinguished from nests of the former variety. Their eggs are similar to those of the Hooded Oriole, but generally more strongly marked and usually with some zigzag lines. Size .85 x .60.

506. Orchard Oriole. *Icterus spurius.*

Range.—United States, east of the Plains, breeding from the Gulf to southern New England, and Canada in the interior. Winters beyond our borders.

[Bluish white.]

The adult male of this species is a rich chocolate brown and black, it requiring three years to attain this plumage. They nest commonly about habitations in their range, usually preferring orchard trees for sites. Their nests are skillfully woven baskets of fresh grasses, about as high as wide; they are generally placed in upright forks and well concealed by drooping leaves. They lay from four to six bluish white eggs, spotted and blotched with brown and lavender. Size .80 x .55. Data.—Avery's Island, La., May 10, 1896. Nest of grass, lined with thistledown; semi-pensile in drooping twigs of a willow. Collector, E. A. McIlhenny.

507. Baltimore Oriole. *Icterus galbula.*

Range.—North America, east of the Rockies, breeding from southern United States north to New Brunswick and Saskatchewan.

[White.]

This beautiful and well-known eastern Oriole can readily be identified by its orange flame color and entirely black head. Even better known than the birds are the pensile nests which retain their positions on the swaying drooping branches all through the winter. Although they build in many other trees, elms seem to be their favorites. Their nests are made of plant fibres and frequently string, and often reach a length of about 10 inches and about half that in diameter; they are usually attached to drooping branches by the rim so that they rock to and fro, but are sometimes held more firmly in position by having their side bound to a branch. Their eggs, which are laid in May and June, are white, streaked and lined with blackish brown and grayish. Size .90 x .60.

508. Bullock's Oriole. *Icterus bullockii.*

Range.—North America, west of the Plains and from British Columbia southward, wintering in Mexico.

This handsome species is as abundant in the west as the Baltimore Oriole is in the east, and breeds throughout its United States range. Their nests are similarly made and in similar locations, and the eggs are hardly distinguishable from those of the preceding, but the ground color is generally of a pale bluish white tint and the markings are usually finer, the lines running around the eggs and often making a very handsome wreath about the large end. Size of eggs, .94 x 62.

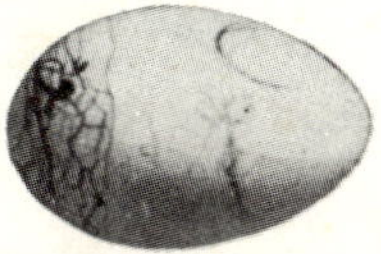

[Bluish white.]

509. Rusty Blackbird. *Euphagus carolinus.*

Range.—North America east of the Plains, breeding from northern New England and the Adirondacks northward; winters in southern United States.

[Bluish green.]

But few of these birds breed within our borders, the majority of them passing on to the interior of Canada. They generally nest in pairs, or at the most three or four pairs in a locality, building their large substantial nests of moss, twigs and grass, lined with fine green grass; this structure is situated in bushes or low trees in swampy places and at from 3 to 20 feet from the ground. The eggs are laid in May or June; they vary from three to five in number, of a pale bluish green color, spotted, blotched and clouded with shades of brown and gray. Size .96 x .71.

510. Brewer's Blackbird. *Euphagus cyanocephalus.*

Range.—North America west of the Plains, and from British Columbia and Saskatchewan southward.

This western representative of the preceding is of about the same size (10 inches long), but differs in having a purplish head and greenish black body. They nest abundantly throughout their range either in bushes or trees at low elevations or upon the ground; the nests are made of sticks, rootlets and grasses, lined with finer grass and moss, and the eggs, which are very variable, are dull whitish, clouded and blotched with brownish and streaked with blackish. Size 1.00 x .75.

[Dull white.]

511. Common Grackle. *Quiscalus quiscula.*

Range.—Eastern United States from the Gulf to Massachusetts; winters along the Gulf.

[Dull greenish white.]

This species, which is commonly known as Crow Blackbird, nests in trees or bushes anywhere in its range, and on the coast frequently constructs its nests among the large sticks of Osprey nests. Large pines appear to be favorite sites for them to locate their large nests of twigs, weeds, grass and trash. They are placed at any elevation from nearly on the ground to 50 feet above it. The eggs range from three to five and are greenish white, splashed, spotted and scrawled with various shades of brown and gray, and with streaks of black. Size 1.10 x .80. The nesting habits and eggs of the subspecies of this Grackle do not differ in any particular. Like those of this variety the eggs show an endless number of patterns of markings.

511a. Florida Grackle (should be Common Grackle).
Quiscalus quiscula.

Range.—South Atlantic and Gulf States.

A smaller variety of the preceding; length about 11 inches. Eggs indistinguishable.

511b. Bronzed Grackle (should be Common Grackle).
Quiscalus quiscula.

[Grayish white.]

Range.—North America east of the Rockies, breeding from the Gulf to Hudson Bay and Labrador. Winters in the southern parts of the United States. This is the most common and widely distributed of the Crow Blackbirds and is distinguished by the brassy color of the upper parts.

513. Boat-tailed Grackle. *Cassidix mexicanus.*

Range.—South Atlantic and Gulf States; north to Virginia.

This handsome bird measures about 16 inches in length, is iridescent with purplish and greenish, and has a very long, graduated and hollowed tail. These Grackles are very abundant residents along the Gulf, breeding in large colonies in swamps, placing their nests of weeds, moss, grasses, etc., in bushes, trees, cane or rushes, but a few inches above the water, while those in trees are sometimes 50 feet above the ground. The eggs are laid in March, April or May, are from three to five in number, and are a dull bluish or grayish white, streaked, lined, clouded and blotched with brown, black and gray; size 1.25 x .95.

[Grayish white.]

513a. Great-tailed Grackle. *Cassidix mexicanus.*

Range.—Mexico to southern and eastern Texas.

This variety is larger than the last (length 18 inches) and the tail is very broad and flat. Like the former, they nest in bushes, rushes or trees at any elevation from the ground. The nests are built of the same materials and the eggs are similar to those of the Boat-tailed Grackle, but larger; size 1.28 x .88.

[Grayish white.]

FINCHES, SPARROWS and allies. Families FRINGILLIDAE and PLOCEIDAE.

514. Evening Grosbeak. *Hesperiphona vespertina.*

Range.—Western United States in the Rocky Mountain region; north to Saskatchewan; south in winter to Mississippi Valley and casually east to New England and the intermediate states.

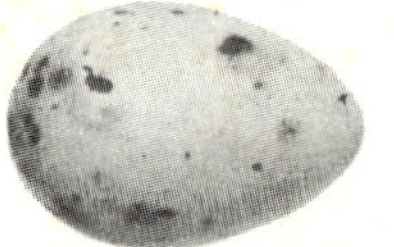

These are dull and yellowish birds, shading to brownish on the head; with a bright yellow forehead and superciliary line, black wings and tail, and white inner secondaries and greater coverts. They breed in the mountainous portions of their range, placing their flat nests of sticks and rootlets in low trees or bushes. The eggs are laid in May or June and are greenish white spotted and blotched with brown; size .90 x .65. Data.—Willis, N. M., June 26, 1901. Nest of twigs lined with rootlets and moss. Collector, F. J. Birtwell.

[Greenish white.]

514a. Western Evening Grosbeak (should be Evening Grosbeak). *Hesperiphona vespertina.*

Range.—Western United States, breeding in the mountains from New Mexico to British Columbia.

The nesting habits and eggs of this variety are the same as those of the preceding, and the birds can rarely be separated.

515.   Pine Grosbeak.   *Pinicola enucleator.*

Range.—Eastern North America, breeding from northern New England northward, and wintering to southern New England and Ohio and casually farther.

With the exceptions of northern Maine and the mountains in Colorado, where a few pairs probably breed every year, these handsome rose-colored birds appear in the United States only during the winter. They build in conifers making their nests of small twigs and rootlets, lined with fine grasses and lichens. During the latter part of May or June they lay three or four eggs, which have a ground color of light greenish blue, spotted and splashed with dark brown, and with fainter markings of lilac. Size 1.00 x .70. Pine Grosbeaks have been separated into the following sub-species, the chief distinctions between them being in their ranges. The nesting habits and eggs of all are alike.

[Greenish blue.]

515a.   Rocky Mountain Pine Grosbeak (should be Pine Grosbeak).   *Pinicola enucleator.*
Range.—Rocky Mountain region from New Mexico to Montana.

515b.   California Pine Grosbeak (should be Pine Grosbeak).   *Pinicola enucleator.*
Range.—Higher parts of the Sierra Nevadas in California.

515c.   Alaskan Pine Grosbeak (should be Pine Grosbeak).   *Pinicola enucleator.*
Range.—Interior of Northwest America from Alaska south to British Columbia.

515d.   Kadiak Pine Grosbeak (should be Pine Grosbeak).   *Pinicola enucleator.*
Range.—Kadiak Island and the southern coast of Alaska.

516.   Bullfinch.   *Pyrrhula pyrrhula.*
Range.—Northern Asia; accidental in Alaska.

517.   Purple Finch.   *Carpodacus purpureus.*

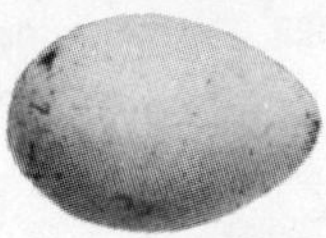
[Greenish blue]

Range.—North America east of the Plains, breeding from the Middle States north to Labrador and Hudson Bay; winters in the United States.

These sweet songsters are quite abundant in New England in the summer, but more so north of our borders. While they breed sometimes in trees in orchards, I have nearly always found their nests in evergreens, usually about three-fourths of the way up. The nests are made of fine weeds and grasses and lined with horse hair. The eggs, which are usually laid in June, are greenish blue, spotted with dark brownish; size .85 x .65.

517a.   California Purple Finch (should be Purple Finch).   *Carpodacus purpureus.*

Range.—Pacific coast, breeding from central California to British Columbia and wintering throughout California.
The nesting habits and eggs of this darker colored variety are just like those of the last.

518.   Cassin's Finch.   *Carpodacus cassinii.*

Range.—North America west of the Rockies, breeding from British Columbia south to New Mexico.

This species is similar to the last but the back, wings and tail are darker and the purplish color of the preceding species is replaced by a more pinkish shade. The nesting habits and eggs are the same as those of those of the eastern Purple Finch; size of eggs .85 x .60. Data.—Willis, New Mexico, June 23, 1901. Nest made of twigs and rootlets and lined with horse hair. Collector, F. J. Birtwell.

[Greenish blue.]

519. House Finch. *Carpodacus mexicanus.*

Range.—United States west of the Plains and from Oregon and Wyoming to Mexico. [1]

This is one of the best known of western birds, and nests commonly in all situations from trees and bushes to vines growing on porches. Their nests are made of rootlets and grasses and are lined with horse hair. Their nesting season includes all the summer months, they raising two and sometimes three broods a season. The three to five eggs are pale greenish blue with a few
[Greenish blue.] sharp blackish brown specks about the large end. Size .80 x .55.

519b. St. Lucas House Finch (should be House Finch). *Carpodacus mexicanus.*

Range.—Southern Lower California. A slightly smaller variety of the preceding.

519c. San Clemente House Finch (should be House Finch). *Carpodacus mexicanus.*

Range.—San Clemente and Santa Barbara Islands. Somewhat darker than the last.

520. Guadalupe House Finch. *Carpodacus amplus.*

Range.—Guadalupe Island, Lower California.
Similar to the House Finch, but deeper red and slightly larger. Their nesting habits and eggs are precisely like those of the House Finch but the eggs average larger; size .85 x .60.

520.1. San Benito House Finch. *Carpodacus mcgregori.*

Range.—San Benito Island, Lower California.
A newly made species, hardly to be distinguished from the last. Eggs probably the same.

521. Red Crossbill. *Loxia curvirostra.*

Range.—Northern North America, breeding in the Alleghanies and from northern New England northward; winters south to the middle portions of the United States and casually farther.

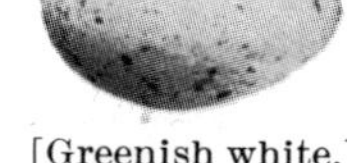

The birds are very curious both in appearance and actions, being very "flighty" and restless, and apt to remain to breed on any of the mountains. They build during March or April, making their nests of twigs, rootlets, moss, feathers, etc., and placing them in forks or on branches of trees (usualfy conifers) at any height from the ground. The eggs are greenish
[Greenish white.]
white, spotted with brown and with lavender shell markings; size .75 x .55.

521a. Mexican Crossbill (should be Red Crossbill). *Loxia curvirostra.*

Range.—Mountain ranges from central Mexico north to Wyoming.
A larger variety of the preceding. The eggs will not differ except perhaps a trifle in size.

522. White-winged Crossbill. *Loxia leucoptera.*

Range.—Northern North America, breeding in the Alleghanies and from northern Maine northward; winters to middle portions of the United States.
This species is rosy red with two white wing bars. Like the last, they are of a roving disposition and are apt to be found in any unexpected locality. Their nesting habits are the same as those of the American Crossbill,[2] but the eggs average larger
[Greenish white.] and the markings are more blotchy; size .80 x .55.

[1] Introduced on L.I., N.Y. and spreading rapidly into southern New England and Pennsylvania.

[2] Now Red Crossbill.

523. Aleutian Leucosticte (should be Gray-crowned Rosy Finch). *Leucosticte tephrocotis.*

[White.]

Range.—Aleutian and Pribilof Islands; south to Kadiak.

This is the largest of the genus, and can be distinguished from the others by its very dark chestnut coloration and the gray hindneck and cheeks. Like the other Leucostictes, they are found in flocks and frequent rocky or mountainous country, where they are nearly always found on the ground. They build in crevices among the rocks or under ledges or embankments. making the nest of weeds and grasses. Their four or five pure white eggs are laid during June. Size .97 x .67. Data.—St. George Islands of the Pribilof group. Nest of coarse grasses and twigs, lined with fine grass and feathers. Taken June 8, 1897 by J. Macoun.

524. Gray-crowned Rosy Finch. *Leucosticte tephrocotis.*

Range.—Rocky Mountain region from Saskatchewan south to northern United States and also breeding in the Sierra Nevadas; winters on the lowlands of north-western United States and east to Manitoba.

[White.]

The habits and breeding habits of this species are like those of the last. The bird is paler colored and the gray is restricted to the hind head. They nest on the ground in June, laying four or five white eggs. Data.—Banff, Canada., June 9, 1902. Nest made of strips of bark and grass, built in a fissure of a rock at the side of a bunch of grass. The parent bird was secured. Collector, W. Raine.

524a. Hepburn's Leucosticte (should be Gray-crowned Rosy Finch). *Leucosticte tephrocotis.*

Range.—Higher ranges from Washington and British Columbia to Alaska.

This variety is like the Aleutian Leucosticte but the brown is a great deal paler. The nesting habits and eggs are, in all probability, like those of the last.

525. Black Rosy Finch. *Leucosticte atrata.*

Range.—Rocky mountain region of northern United States; known to breed in Idaho.

This species is black in place of the brown of the others; the gray is restricted to the hind part of the head and the rosy is rather more extensive on the wings. Their eggs probably cannot be distinguished from those of the Gray-crowned variety.

526. Brown-capped Rosy Finch. *Leucosticte australis.*

Range.—Breeds at high altitudes in the Rockies in Colorado; south to New Mexico in winter.

A similar bird to the Gray-crowned Leucosticte[1] but with no gray on the head. They nest on the ground above timber line on the higher ranges of the Rockies.

527. Greenland Redpoll (should be Hoary Redpoll). *Acanthis hornemanni.*

Range.—Greenland and northern Europe; south in winter to Labrador.

This large Redpoll nests at low elevations in trees and bushes, its habits and eggs being similar to the more common American species.

527a. Hoary Redpoll. *Acanthis hornemanni.*

Range.—Breeds in the Arctic regions and winters south to the northern parts of the United States.

This variety is smaller than the last and is considerably darker but still retains the white rump of the Greenland Redpoll. Its nesting habits are the same as those of the next.

---

[1] Now Gray-crowned Rosy Finch.

NEST AND EGGS OF EASTERN MEADOWLARK.

528. Common Redpoll. *Acanthis flammea.*

Range.—Breeds within the Arctic Circle; winters south to New York, Kansas and northern California and casually farther.

[Bluish green.]

This species is similar to the last but much darker, and the rump is also streaked with blackish. These handsome birds are often met with in winter, feeding on seeds of the weed stems that project above the snow. Their flight and song is similar to that of the Goldfinch or Pine Siskin. They nest at low elevations, either in trees or bushes. The eggs number from three to six and are pale bluish green, sparingly specked with reddish brown. Size .65 x .50. Data.—Mouth of Great Whale River, Hudson Bay, May 16, 1899. Nest in a willow 4 feet from the ground; made of fine rootlets and grass, lined with feathers. Collector, A. P. Lowe.

528a. Holboell's Redpoll (should be Common Redpoll). *Acanthis flammea.*

Range.—Arctic regions; south casually to the border of the United States.

A slightly larger variety of the Common Redpoll. Eggs probably not distinguishable.

528b. Greater Redpoll (should be Common Redpoll). *Acanthis flammea.*

Range.—Breeds in southern Greenland; in winter south through Labrador to the northern border of the United States.

This variety is larger and darker than the Common Redpoll. It has been found breeding abundantly in southern Greenland, where its nesting habits are the same as those of the Common Redpoll and the eggs similar but averaging a trifle larger.

529. American Goldfinch. *Spinus tristis.*

Range.—North America east of the Rockies, and from Labrador and Manitoba southward.

[Bluish white.]

These beautiful birds are among our sweetest songsters from May until September. They are resident throughout their United States range, where they breed in August or early in September, being one of the latest nesting birds that we have. Their nests are located in bushes, at a height of generally below fifteen feet above the ground, being placed in upright forks, and made of plant fibres and thistle down firmly woven together. They lay from three to six plain bluish white eggs. Size .65 x .50. The majority of nests that I have found have been in alders over small streams.

529a. Western Goldfinch (should be American Goldfinch). *Spinus tristis.*

Range.—Rocky Mountains from Mexico to British Columbia.

This variety is slightly larger and (in winter) paler than the last.

529b. California Goldfinch (should be American Goldfinch). *Spinus tristis.*

Range.—Pacific coast from Washington to Lower California.

Similar to the eastern Goldfinch but back said to be slightly greenish yellow.

530. Lesser Goldfinch. *Spinus psaltria.*

Range.—United States, west of the Plains and from Oregon to Mexico.

Bluish white.

This species has greenish upper parts and yellow below; the crown, wings and tail are black, the bases of the lateral tail feathers and primaries being whitish. They are common in portions of their range, nesting in similar locations to those chosen by the common Goldfinch and laying from three to five eggs which are similar but slightly smaller. Size .60 x .45. Data.— Riverside, California, May 20, 1891. 5 eggs. Nest made of fine grasses lined with cotton; 5 feet from the ground in a small tree. Collector, Harvey Hall.

530b. Mexican Goldfinch. *Spinus psaltria mexicanus.*

Range.—Mexico north to the Lower Rio Grande in southern Texas.[1]

A similar bird to the last but with the entire upper parts and cheeks, black.[2] The habits, nests and eggs are identical with those of the Arkansas Goldfinch.

[1] No longer recognized as a valid form.

[2] Now Lesser Goldfinch.

531. Lawrence's Goldfinch.   *Spinus lawrencei.*

Range.—Pacific coast of California, wintering along the Mexican border.

This grayish colored Goldfinch has a black face and yellow breast, rump, wing coverts and edges of the primaries. They are quite common in their restricted range, nesting either in upright crotches or in the forks of horizontal limbs. The four or five eggs which they lay are pure white; size .60 x 45. Data.—Santa Monica Canyon, Cal., April 26, 1903. Nest in a cypress tree 12 feet up; composed of grasses, feathers, etc. Collector, W. Lee Chambers.

532. Black-headed Siskin.   *Spinus notatus.*

Range.—Mountainous regions of Central America and southern Mexico; accidental in the United States. [1]

526.1. European Goldfinch.   *Carduelis carduelis.*

[Greenish white]

Range.—Europe. Introduced into several localities in eastern United States and appears to have gained a strong hold in New York. Has been found nesting in Central Park, New York City, and in Cambridge and Worcester, Mass. Their nests are made of plant fibres, grasses and weeds and the eggs are greenish white, sparsely spotted and lined with blackish brown. [2]

Photo by Norman W. Swayne.

NEST AND EGGS OF AMERICAN GOLDFINCH.

[1] Not recorded from North America.

[2] Probably extirpated except in Bermuda; last reports from Long Island in mid-1950's.

533. Pine Siskin. *Spinus pinus.*

Range.—Breeds from northern United States northward, in the Alleghanies and in the Rockies south to New Mexico. Winters throughout the United States.

Siskins are of the size of the Goldfinch (5 inches long), and their calls, songs and habits are similar to those of this bird. Their plumage is grayish brown, streaked with dusky and the bases of the wing and tail feathers are yellow. Like the Crossbills, they frequently feed along our northern borders, but very sporadically. Their nests are built on horizontal branches of pines or cedars at any elevation from the ground, being made of grasses and rootlets lined with hair or pine needles, and of rather frail and flat construction. Their  [Greenish white] eggs are laid during May or June and are greenish white, specked with reddish brown; size .68 x .48. Data.—Hamilton Inlet, Labrador, June 17, 1898. Nest on branch of a spruce, 10 feet from the ground; made of grass, lined with moss and feathers. Collector, L. Dicks.

534. Snow Bunting. *Plectrophenax nivalis.*

Range.—Breeds in the Artic regions, and winters irregularly in large flocks through the United States to Oregon, Kansas, and Georgia.

These birds are only seen in the United States in large roving flocks, during the winter when they feed on weed seeds on side hills. Their nests are built on the ground, being sunk [Greenish white.] into sphagnum moss, and made of grasses lined with feathers. Their four or five eggs are a light greenish white, spotted and splashed with yellowish brown and lilac. Size .90 x .65.

534a. Pribilof Snowflake (should be Snow Bunting). *Plectrophenax nivalis.*

Range—Pribilof and Aleutian Islands, Alaska.
A slightly larger variety which is resident on the islands in its range. Eggs like those of the preceding; laid from May to July.

535. McKay's Bunting. *Plectrophenax hyperboreus.*

Range.—Western Alaska; known to breed on Hall's Island.
This beautiful species is, in summer, entirely white except for the tips of the primaries and a black spot on end of central tail feathers, thus being very distinct from the preceding, which has the back and the wings to a greater extent black, at this season. Their eggs probably very closely resemble those of the last species.

536. Lapland Longspur. *Calcarius lapponicus.*

Range.—Breeds in northern North America; winters south casually to New York, Ohio and Oregon and occasionally farther.
These sparrow-like birds are 6.5 inches long and have a black crown, cheeks and throat, and chestnut band on nape. Like the Snowflakes they nest on the ground in moss, but the four to six eggs that they lay are grayish, heavily mottled and blotched with chocolate brown; size .80 x .60.

[Grayish.]

536a. Alaskan Longspur (should be Lapland Longspur). *Calcarius lapponicus.*

Range.—Northwest North America, breeding in Alaska; winter south to Oregon. This sub-species is like the last but slightly paler. Eggs indistinguishable.

537. Smith's Longspur. *Calcarius pictus.*

Range.—Breeds in Hudson Bay and Mackenzie River districts and winters south to Texas chiefly on the Plains.

[Grayish.]

This species is of the size of the last but is a rich buff color below, and the other markings are very different. These birds together with the next species are very common on the prairies in central United States in winter. They nest on the ground like the preceding species but the nests are scantily made of grasses and not warmly lined like those of the last. The eggs are similar but paler; size .80 x .60. Data.—Herschell Island, Arctic Ocean, June 10, 1901. Nest built in a tuft of grass; made of fine roots and grass, lined with feathers. Collector, Rev. I. O. Stringer.

538. Chestnut-collared Longspur. *Calcarius ornatus.*

Range.—Plains in the interior of North America, breeding from Kansas north to Saskatchewan; very abundant in the Dakotas and Montana.

[Dull white.]

This handsome species in the breeding plumage has the throat white, breast and belly black, and a chestnut collar on the nape. They are one of the most abundant breeding birds on the prairies, nesting in hollows on the ground either in the open or protected by a tuft of grass. The nests are made of grasses and sometimes moss; three or four eggs laid in June or July; white, blotched. lined and obscurely marked with brown and purplish; size .75 x .55.

539. McCown's Longspur. *Rhynchophanes mccownii.*

Range.—Great Plains, breeding from Kansas to the Saskatchewan.

[Grayish white.]

This Longspur which breeds in company with the preceding, throughout its range, can be distinguished from it by the small black patch on the breast, the black crown, and chestnut wing coverts. Their nesting habits are the same, and at this season all the Longspurs have a sweet song often uttered during flight, like that of the Bobolink. Their eggs are of the same size and similarly marked as the last, but the ground color is more gray or olive.

540. Vesper Sparrow. *Pooecetes gramineus.*

Range.—Eastern United States, breeding from Virginia and Missouri north to Manitoba and New Brunswick; winters in the southern half of the United States.

[Whitish.]

A streaked grayish, buffy and white bird distinguished by its chestnut shoulders and white outer tail feathers. They are abundant birds in eastern fields where their loud piping whistle is known to many frequenters of weedy pastures. They build on the ground, either in grassy or cultivated fields, lining the hollow scantily with grasses. Their four or five eggs are usually laid in May or June; they are dull whitish, blotched and splashed with light brown and lavender tints; size .80x.60.

540a. Western Vesper Sparrow (should be Vesper Sparrow). *Pooecetes gramineus.*

Range.—This paler variety is found in North America west of the Plains and south of Saskatchewan.

Its nesting habits are like those of the preceding and the eggs are indistinguishable.

540b. Oregon Vesper Sparrow (should be Vesper Sparrow). *Pooecetes gramineus.*

A browner variety found on the coast of Oregon and northern California.

Its nesting habits are like those of the eastern bird and the eggs similar but averaging a trifle smaller.

541.   Ipswich Sparrow.   *Passerculus princeps.*

Range.—Breeds on Sable Island, off Nova Scotia; winters on coast of South Atlantic States. This a large and pale colored form of the common Savanna Sparrow. Its nesting habits are similar to those of the latter and the eggs are marked the same but average larger. Size .80 x .60.

542.   Sandwich Sparrow (should be Savannah Sparrow).   *Passerculus sandwichensis.*

Range.—Breeds on the Alaskan coast; winters south to northern California.

A streaked Sparrow like the next but with the yellow superciliary line brighter and more extended. Its nesting habits are precisely like those of the next variety which is common and well known; the eggs are indistinguishable.

[Grayish white]

542a.   Savannah Sparrow.   *Passerculus sandwichensis.*

Range.—North America east of the Plains, breeding from the Middle States north to Labrador and the Hudson Bay region.

Similar to the last but with the superciliary line paler and the yellow reduced to a spot on the lores. Their nests are hollows in the ground, lined with grasses and generally concealed by tufts of grass or weeds. Their three to five eggs vary greatly in markings from finely and evenly dotted all over to very heavily blotched, the ground color being grayish white. Size .75 x .55. They nest most frequently in swampy places on or near the coast.

[Grayish white.]

542b.   Western Savanna Sparrow (should be Savannah Sparrow).   *Passerculus sandwichensis.*

Range.—Western North America from Alaska to Mexico.

A slightly paler form whose nesting habits and eggs do not differ from those of the last.

542c.   Bryant's Marsh Sparrow (should be Savannah Sparrow).   *Passerculus sandwichensis.*

Range.—Salt marshes of California from San Francisco Bay south to Mexico.

Slightly darker and brighter than the eastern Savannah Sparrow and with a more slender bill. The eggs are not different from many specimens of 542a; they are light greenish white heavily blotched with various shades of brown and lavender. Size .75 x .55.

543.   Belding's Marsh Sparrow (should be Savannah Sparrow).   *Passerculus sandwichensis.*

Range.—Pacific coast marshes of southern California and southward.

This species is similar to the last but darker and more heavily streaked below. They breed abundantly in salt marshes, building their nests in the grass or patches of seaweed barely above the water, and making them of grass and weeds, lined with hair; the eggs are dull grayish white, boldly splashed, spotted and clouded with brown and lavender. Size .78 x .55.

[Grayish white.]

544.   Large-billed Sparrow (should be Savannah Sparrow).   *Passerculus sandwichensis.*

Range.—Coast of southern and Lower California.

Similar to the Savannah Sparrows but paler and grayer, without yellow lores and a larger and stouter bill. They are common in salt marshes, often in company with the last species and their nesting habits are similar to and the eggs not distinguished with certainty from those of the latter.

544a.   St. Lucas Sparrow (should be Savannah Sparrow).   *Passerculus sandwichensis.*

Range.—Southern Lower California.

A slightly darker form of the preceding, having identical habits, and probably, eggs.

Photo by A. R. Spaid.

NEST AND EGGS OF VESPER SPARROW.

544b. Lagoon Sparrow (should be Savannah Sparrow). *Passerculus sandwichensis.*

Range.—Salt marshes, Abreojos Point, Lower California.

544c. San Benito Sparrow (should be Savannah Sparrow). *Passerculus sandwichensis.*

Range.—Breeds on San Benito Islands; winters in southern Lower California. The nesting habits and eggs of these very similar subspecies are identical.

545. Baird's Sparrow. *Ammodramus bairdii.*

Range.—Plains, breeding from northern United States to the Saskatchewan; south in winter to the Mexican border.

[White.]

These Sparrows breed abundantly on the plains of Dakota and northward, placing their nest in hollows on the ground in fields and along road sides. During June or July, they lay three to five dull whitish eggs, blotched, splashed and spotted with light shades of brown and gray. Size .80 x .60. Data.— Crescent Lake, N. W. Canada., June 8, 1901. Nest in a tuft of grass, a few inches above the ground; of grass, lined with hair. Collector, Walter Raine.

546. Grasshopper Sparrow. *Ammodramus savannarum.*

Range.—United States east of the Plains, breeding from the Gulf to Canada.

[White.]

A stoutly built Sparrow marked on the upper parts peculiarly, like a quail; nape grayish and chestnut. These birds are common in dry fields and pastures, where their scarcely audible, grasshopper-like song is heard during the heat of the day. Their nests are sunken in the ground and arched over so that they are very difficult to find, especially as the bird will not flush until nearly trod upon. The four or five eggs, laid in June, are white, specked with reddish brown. Size .72 x .55.

546a. Western Grasshopper Sparrow (should be Grasshopper Sparrow). *Ammodramus savannarum.*

Range.—West of the Plains from British Columbia to Mexico.

Slightly paler than the last; has the same nesting habits; eggs indistinguishable.

546b. Florida Grasshopper Sparrow (should be Grasshopper Sparrow). *Ammodramus savannarum.*

Range.—Central Florida.

A local form, darker above and paler below than the common species. Eggs not different in any particular.

547. Henslow's Sparrow. *Passerherbulus henslowii.*

Range.—United States east of the Plains, breeding locally from Maryland and Missouri north to Massachusetts and Minnesota.

[White.]

This species is similar in form and marking to the last, but is olive green on the nape, and the breast and sides are streaked with blackish. Their nesting habits are very similar to those of the Grasshopper Sparrow, the nests being difficult to find. The eggs are greenish white, spotted with reddish brown. Size .75 x .55. Data.—Lancaster, Mass., June 10, 1902. 4 eggs. Nest on the ground in a meadow; made of grasses and lined with fine grass. Collector, John E. Thayer.

547a. Western Henslow's Sparrow (should be Henslow's Sparrow). *Passerherbulus henslowii.*

Range.—A paler and very local form found in the Plains in South Dakota and probably, adjoining states.

Eggs not apt to differ from those of the preceding.

548. Le Conte's Sparrow. *Passerherbulus caudacutus.*

Range.—Great Plains, breeding from northern United States to Assiniboia; winters south to Texas and the Gulf States.

A bird of more slender form than the preceding, and with a long, graduated tail, the feathers of which are very narrow and pointed. They nest on the ground in damp meadows, but the eggs are difficult to find because the bird is flushed from the nest with great difficulty. The eggs are white and are freely specked with brown. Size .70 x .52. Data.—Crescent Lake, N. W. Canada, June 10, 1901. Nest built in a tuft of prairie grass 4 inches above the ground; made of grass, lined with finer and a few hairs. Collector, Walter Raine.

[White.]

549. Sharp-tailed Sparrow. *Ammospiza caudacuta.*

Range.—Breeds in marshes along the Atlantic coast from Maine to South Carolina and winters farther south.

These birds are very common in nearly all the salt marshes of the coast, nesting in the marsh grass. I have nearly always found their nests attached to the coarse marsh grass a few inches above water at high tide, and generally under a piece of drifted seaweed. The nests are made of grasses, and the four or five eggs are whitish, thickly specked with reddish brown. Size .75 x .55. The birds are hard to flush and then fly but a few feet and quickly drop into the grass again.

[White.]

549.1. Nelson's Sparrow (should be Sharp-tailed Sparrow). *Ammospiza caudacuta.*

Range.—Breeds in the fresh water marshes of the Mississippi valley from Illinois to Manitoba.

This species is similar to the Sharp-tailed Finch[1] but more buffy on the breast and generally without streaks. The nesting habits are the same and the eggs indistinguishable.

549a. Acadian Sharp-tailed Sparrow (should be Sharp-tailed Sparrow). *Ammospiza caudacuta.*

Range.—Breeds in the marshes on the coast of New England and New Brunswick; winters south to the South Atlantic States.

This paler variety of Nelson's Sparrow[1] nests like the Sharp-tailed species and the eggs are the same as those of that bird.

550. Seaside Sparrow. *Ammospiza maritima.*

Range.—Atlantic coast, breeding from southern New England to Carolina and wintering farther south.

This sharp-tailed Finch is uniform grayish above and light streaked with dusky, below. They are very abundant in the breeding range, where they nest in marshes in company with *caudacutus.*[2] Their nests are the same as those of that species and the eggs similar but slightly larger. Size .80 x .60. Data.—Smith Island, Va., May 20, 1900. Nest situated in tall grass near shore; made of dried grass and seaweed. Collector, H. W. Bailey.

[White.]

All the members of this genus have a habit of fluttering out over the water, and then gliding back to their perch on the grass, on set wings, meanwhile uttering a strange rasping song. The nesting habits and eggs of all the subspecies are precisely like those of this variety, and they all occasionally arch their nests over, leaving an entrance on the side.

[1] Should be Sharp-tailed Sparrow.

[2] Now *caudacuta.*

550a. Scott's Seaside Sparrow (should be Seaside Sparrow). *Ammospiza maritima.*

Range.—Coasts of Florida and north to South Carolina. Above blackish streaked with brownish gray ; below heavily streaked with black.

550b. Texas Seaside Sparrow (should be Seaside Sparrow). *Ammospiza maritima.*

Range.—Coast of Texas. Similar to 550, but streaked above.

550c. Fisher's Seaside Sparrow (should be Seaside Sparrow). *Ammospiza maritima.*

Range.—Gulf coast. This form is similar to 550a, but darker and more brownish.

550d. Macgillivray's Seaside Sparrow (should be Seaside Sparrow). *Ammospiza maritima.*

Range.—Coast of South Carolina. Like 550c but grayer.

551. Dusky Seaside Sparrow. *Ammospiza nigrescens.*

Range.—Marshes of Indian River near Titusville, Florida.
This species is the darkest of the genus, both above and below, being nearly black on the upperparts. Their habits are like those of the others and the eggs are not likely to differ.

552. Lark Sparrow. *Chondestes grammacus.*

Range.—Mississippi Valley from the Plains to Illinois and casually farther east, and from Manitoba to Texas; winters in Mexico.
This handsome Sparrow has the sides of the crown and ear patches chestnut, and the sides of the throat and a spot on the breast, black. They are sweet singers and very welcome birds in their range, where they are quite abundant. Their nests are generally placed on the ground in the midst of or under a clump of weeds or tuft of grass, but sometimes in bushes or even trees; they are made of grasses and weeds and the eggs, which are usually laid in May, are white marked chiefly 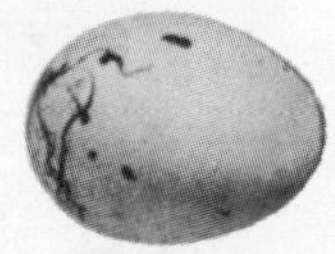
[White.]
about the large end with blackish zigzag lines and spots. Size .80 x .60.

552a. Western Lark Sparrow (should be Lark Sparrow). *Chondestes grammacus.*

Range.—United States west of the Plains; breeds from British Columbia to Mexico.
This paler and duller colored variety is common on the Pacific coast; its habits and nests and eggs are like those of the last.

553. Harris' Sparrow. *Zonotrichia querula.*

Range.—Mississippi Valley, chiefly west, breeding in Manitoba and Saskatchewan, the exact range being unknown.
Although the birds are abundant during migrations, they seem to suddenly and strangely disappear during the breeding season. Supposed nests have been found a few inches above the ground in bushes and on the ground in clumps of grass, the eggs being whitish, thickly spotted with shades of brown. Size .85 x .65.

[Whitish.]

554. White-crowned Sparrow. *Zonotrichia leucophrys.*

Range.—North America breeding abundantly in Labrador and about Hudson Bay, and casually in northern New England and in western United States in the Rockies and Sierras. [1]

Winters along our Mexican border and southward. A handsome species with a broad white crown bordered on either side by black, and with a white superciliary line and black lores ; the underparts are uniform grayish white. These birds appear to be nowhere as common as the White-throated Sparrows with which they associate during migrations and in the breeding grounds. They build on the ground, generally near the edges [Pale greenish blue.] of woods or in clearings, and lay from four to six eggs similar but larger, and with as much variation in markings as those of the Song Sparrow; pale greenish blue, spotted and splashed with reddish brown and grayish. Size .90 x .65. Data.—Nachook, Labrador, June 10, 1897. Nest of fine grasses on the ground in a clump of grass. Collector, G. Ford.

Photo by C. H. Morrill.

NEST AND EGGS OF SAVANNAH SPARROW.

[1] Does not breed south of Newfoundland and central Quebec.

554a. Intermediate Sparrow (should be White-crowned Sparrow). *Zonotrichia leucophrys.*

Range.—Rocky Mountains and westward from Mexico to Alaska, breeding chiefly north of the United States.

This bird is like the last but the lores are white. Its nesting habits and eggs cannot be distinguished from those of the former.

554b. Nuttall's Sparrow (should be White-crowned Sparrow). *Zonotrichia leucophrys.*

Range.—Pacific coast from British Columbia to Lower California.

Similar to the last but smaller and browner above; nests on the ground or in bushes, the eggs not being distinguishable from those of the other White-crowns.

557. Golden-crowned Sparrow. *Zonotrichia coronata.*

Range.—Pacific coast from Mexico to Alaska, breeding chiefly north of our borders.

This species has the crown yellow, bordered by black on the sides. Their habits are like those of the White-crowned Sparrows, they feeding upon the ground among the dead leaves, and usually being found in flocks and often accompanied by many of the last species. They nest upon the ground or in low bushes, and in May or June lay three or four eggs very similar to the last. Size .90 x .65.

[Pale greenish blue.]

558. White-throated Sparrow. *Zonotrichia albicollis.*

Range.—North America east of the Plains and breeding from the northern tier of states northward; winters from the Middle States southward.

To my mind this is the most beautiful of Sparrows, with its bright and softly blended plumage and the pure white throat boldly contrasting with its grayish breast and sides of the head; the lores are adorned with a bright yellow spot. They are one of the most abundant of Sparrows in the east during migrations and their musical piping whistle is heard from hedge and wood. They nest most abundantly north of our borders, laying their three or four eggs in grass lined hollows in the ground, or more rarely in nests in bushes. The eggs are white or bluish white, thickly spotted with several shades of brown. Size .85 x .62.

[White.]

They nest most often in thickets or on the edge of swamps, in just such places as they are met with on their migrations.

559. American Tree Sparrow. *Spizella arborea.*

Range.—North America east of the Plains, breeding north of the United States to the Arctic coast, east of the Rockies; winters within the United States.

A larger bird but somewhat resembling the common Chipping Sparrow, but browner above, with a black spot on the breast and no black on the head. They are quite hardy birds and winter in many of the northern states where they may be found in flocks upon the snow, feeding on seeds of protruding weeds. They breed very abundantly in Labrador and about Hudson Bay, placing their green nests in hollows on the ground or moss; their three or four eggs are greenish white, abundantly speckled all over the surface with reddish brown. Size .80 x .55 Data.—Foothills of Black Mountains, McKenzie River, Arctic America, June 13, 1899. Nest on the ground under a tuft of grass on level plain ; made of grasses and moss and lined with feathers. Collector, I. O. Stringer.

[Greenish white.]

559a. Western Tree Sparrow (should be American Tree Sparrow). *Spizella arborea.*

Range.—North America west of the Plains, breeding in Alaska and wintering to Mexico. A paler form of the last, the nesting habits and eggs of which are the same.

560. Chipping Sparrow. *Spizella passerina.*

Range.—North America east of the Plains, breeding from the Gulf to the interior of Canada and Newfoundland.

Photo from life by C. A. Reed.

GRASSHOPPER SPARROW ON NEST.

As indicated by their name *socialis*,[1]Chipping Sparrows are sociable birds not only with others of the bird tribe, but with man. In all localities that are not overrun with English Sparrows,[2]you will find these confiding birds nesting in trees and shrubs in the yard and in vines from porches, while in orchards, nearly every tree has its tenant. They are smaller birds than the last (5.5 in. long) and have the brown crown bordered by blackish and a black line through the eye. Their nests, which may be found at any height from the ground and in any kind of a tree or shrub, are made of fine grass and weed stems, lined with hair; their three to five eggs are a handsome greenish blue, sparingly specked chiefly about the large end with blackish brown and purplish. Size .70 x .52.

[Bluish white.]

560a. Western Chipping Sparrow (should be Chipping Sparrow). *Spizella passerina.*

Range.—Western North America, chiefly west of the Rockies, from Mexico to Alaska; winters in Mexico.

This variety is much duller colored than the last and has but little brown on the back; its nesting habits are the same and the eggs do not appear to differ in any respect from those of the eastern bird.

561. Clay-colored Sparrow. *Spizella pallida.*

Range.—Interior of United States and Canada, from the Mississippi Valley to the Rockies, breeding from Iowa and Colorado northward; winters in Mexico.

These birds can best be described as like the Chipping Sparrow with the brown largely replaced with blackish. They breed quite abundantly in Manitoba and Minnesota, placing their nests on or near the ground, and making them of fine grasses. The eggs cannot be distinguished with certainty from those of the preceding but average a trifle smaller. Size .65 x .50

[Bluish white] Data.—Barnsley, Manitoba, May 24, 1900. Nest of grass stalks lined with fine grass, one foot above ground in tuft of grass. Collector, Chris P. Forge.

562. Brewer's Sparrow. *Spizella breweri.*

Range.—Western United States from Mexico to British Columbia rarely and chiefly between the Rockies and the Sierras; most abundant in New Mexico and Arizona.

This bird is similar to the last but is paler and more finely streaked. Their nesting habits are like those of *pallida* and the eggs are indistinguishable. [Bluish white.]

563. Field Sparrow. *Spizella pusilla.*

Range.—North America east of the Plains, breeding from the Gulf to southern Manitoba and Quebec; winters in the Gulf States.

These are abundant birds along roadsides, in thickets, or on dry sidehills, where they nest indifferently on the ground or in bushes, making their nests of grass and weed stems. They are the birds whose high piping song is most frequently heard on hot sultry days in summer. Their eggs are laid in May or June;

[Bluish white.]

they are pale bluish white, speckled and blotched with yellowish brown and grayish purple. Size .65 x .50.

563a. Western Field Sparrow (should be Field Sparrow). *Spizella pusilla.*

Range.—Great Plains from Mexico to Montana, breeding in the northern half of its range and wintering in the southern.

A paler form of the last, whose general habits and eggs are the same as those of the eastern bird.

---

[1] Now *Spizella passerina.*

[2] Now House Sparrow.

564. Worthen's Sparrow. *Spizella wortheni.*

Range.—Southern New Mexico southward through central Mexico.
This pale colored species is the size of the Field Sparrow but has no decided markings anywhere. It is a rare bird within our borders and uncommon anywhere. I am not able to find any material in regard to their eggs.

565. Black-chinned Sparrow. *Spizella atrogularis.*

Range.—Mexican border of the United States and southward.
This slim-bodied, long-tailed species is grayish with a dusky streaked, reddish brown patch on the back and a black face, chin and throat. Their habits are similar to those of the Field Sparrow and their nests are made near the ground in bushes, but the eggs are plain bluish green, about like unmarked [Greenish white] Chipping Sparrows' eggs. Size .65 x .50. Data.—Colton, California, May 10, 1885. Nest made of weed stems, lined with fine grasses and horse hair; placed in low bush. Collector, R. B. Herron.

566. White-winged Junco. *Junco aikeni.*

Range.—Breeds in the Black Hills of Dakota and Wyoming; winters in Colorado and casually to Kansas.
This species is like the next but larger and with the wings crossed by two white bars. Its habits are like those of the common Juncos, the nests are placed on the ground, concealed under overhanging rocks or tufts of grass, and the eggs are like those often seen of the Slate-colored Junco; 3 or 4 in number, pinkish white specked and spotted with light reddish brown. Size .75 x .55.

[White.]

567. Slate-colored Junco. *Junco hyemalis.*

Range.—North America east of the Plains, breeding in the northern tier of states and northward; winters in southern United States.
This species is slaty gray on the head, neck, breast, flanks, back, wings and central tail feathers; the rest of the underparts are white, sharply defined against the gray. They migrate through the United States in large flocks, usually accompanied by White-throated or Fox Sparrows. They breed very abundantly in the northern parts of their range, frequently in the immediate vicinity of houses but generally [White] on the edges of clearings etc., placing their nests on the ground and generally partially concealed by rocks, stumps, sods or logs; the nests are made of grasses, lined with hair, and the four or five eggs are white or greenish white, variously speckled with reddish brown either over the entire surface or in a wreath about the large end. Size .80 x .55.

567a. Oregon Junco. *Junco oreganus.*

Range.—Pacific coast from California to Alaska, breeding north of the United States.
This sub-species is entirely unlike the preceding, having a black head, neck, throat, breast, wings and tail, and brown back; the remainder of the underparts are white, washed with pinkish brown on the sides. The habits and nesting habits of this western Junco are the same as those of the eastern, the birds building in similar localities and making the nests of the same material. There appears to be little, if any, difference between the eggs of the two varieties.

567b.   Shufeldt's Junco (should be Oregon Junco).   *Junco oreganus.*

Range.—Pacific coast breeding from Oregon to British Columbia and wintering south to the Mexican boundary.

Said to be slightly larger and duller colored than the Oregon Junco; eggs the same.

567b.   Coues' Junco. (should be Slate-colored Junco).   *Junco hyemalis.*

Range.—Arid regions of interior British Columbia and south through the Rocky Mountain region to Mexico; west to California.[1]

A similar variety to the last but paler. Its habits are not characteristic.

567c.   Thurber's Junco (should be Oregon Junco).   *Junco oreganus.*

Range.—The Sierra Nevadas from Oregon to southern California.

Similar to 567a but paler and back more pinkish ; eggs will not differ.

567d.   Point Pinos Junco (should be Oregon Junco).   *Junco oreganus.*

Range.—A very locally confined variety breeding in pine woods of southwestern California, about Monterey and Santa Cruz.

Similar to 567c but with the head and neck slaty instead of black.

567e.   Carolina Junco (should be Slate-colored Junco).   *Junco hyemalis.*

Range.—Alleghanies in Virginia, the Carolinas and Georgia.

A slightly larger bird than the Slate-colored Junco and with the bill horn color instead of pinkish white.   They have been found to breed very abundantly in the higher ranges of the Carolinas, nesting under banks, in tufts of grass, or occasionally in small bushes, in fact in such locations as are used by 567. Their eggs which are laid during May, June or July (probably two broods being raised) are similar to those of the Slate-colored species but slightly larger.

567.1.   Montana Junco (should be Oregon Junco).   *Junco oreganus.*

Range.—From northern Idaho and Montana north to Alberta; winters south to Mexico.

This variety is like 567g but darker on the head and throat and with less pink on the sides.   Its nesting habits and eggs do not differ from those of the Pink-sided Junco.

567g.   Pink-sided Junco (should be Oregon Junco).   *Junco oreganus.*

Range.—Breeds in mountains of Idaho, Wyoming and Montana and winters south to Mexico.

This species has the head and breast gray, the back brownish and the sides pinkish brown.   They breed at high altitudes in the ranges, placing their nests of grasses under sods or overhanging rocks; their eggs are pinkish white before being blown and are spotted over the whole surface but more heavily at the large end with pale reddish brown and gray.   Size .80 x .60.

[White.]

570b.   Gray-headed Junco.   *Junco caniceps.*

Range.—Rocky Mountain region from Wyoming south to Mexico.

This species is similar to the Slate-colored Junco but has a reddish brown patch on the back.   They nest on the ground in mountainous regions, concealing the nests in tufts of grass or under logs, stones, etc.   The eggs are creamy or bluish white, specked over the whole surface, but most numerously about the larger end with reddish brown.   Size .75 x .60.   Data.—Custer Co., Colo., June 4, 1897.   Slight nest of small rootlets and fine grass placed under a tuft of grass.   Altitude over 8,000 feet. Collector, D. P. Ingraham.   (Crandall collection.)

[White.]

---

[1] No longer recognized as a valid form.

570.　Mexican Junco.　*Junco phaeonotus.*

Range.—Mountains of western Mexico north to southern Arizona.

Similar to the preceding species but upper mandible blackish and the gray on throat shading insensibly into the grayish white underparts.　They are quite abundant in the higher ranges of southern Arizona, where they breed, placing their nests on the ground in similar locations to those chosen by other Juncos; the three or four eggs are greenish white, finely speckled chiefly about the large end with reddish brown.　Size .76 x .60.

570a.　Red-backed Junco (should be Gray-headed Junco).　*Junco caniceps.*

Range.—Breeds in the mountains of New Mexico and Arizona and southward. This variety is like the last but the reddish brown on the back does not extend to the coverts or wings.　The nesting habits are like those of the last but the eggs are only minutely specked about the large end.

571.　Baird's Junco.　*Junco bairdi.*

Range.—Southern Lower California.

This gray headed species with rusty back and sides is locally confined to the southern parts of the California peninsula where it is resident.　Its eggs are not likely to differ from those of the Pink-sided Junco[1]which it most nearly resembles.

571.1.　Townsend's Junco.　*Junco townsendi.*

Range.—Mountains of northern Lower California; resident and breeding. Similar to the Pink-sided Junco but duller colored; eggs probably the same.[2]

571.1.　Guadalupe Junco.　*Junco insularis.*

Range.—Guadalupe Island off Lower California.

Resembles the Pink-sided Junco[1]but is smaller, darker and duller colored. They are common on the island where they nest in the pine groves, laying their first sets in February or March.　The nests are like those of the genus and the eggs are greenish white, finely dotted with reddish brown at the large end.　Size .77 x .60.

573.　Black-throated Sparrow.　*Amphispiza bilineata.*

Range.—Breeds from central Texas to Kansas; winters in southern Texas and Mexico.

This species is grayish brown above, with black throat, white superciliary and line on side of throat.　This is a common species that nests on the ground or at low elevations in bushes, making their nests of weed stems and grasses.　The three to five eggs are bluish white, unmarked and similar to those of the Eastern Bluebird but smaller.　Size .72 x .55.

[Bluish white.]

573a.　Desert Sparrow (should be Black-throated Sparrow).　*Amphispiza bilineata.*

Range.—Southwestern United States from western Texas to southern California, and north to Colorado and Nevada; winters in Mexico.

Like the last but paler above.　An abundant bird among the foothills and on plains throughout its range.　Found generally in sage brush and thickets where it nests in bushes or on the ground laying three or four bluish white eggs like those of the last.

574.　Sage Sparrow.　*Amphispiza belli.*

Range.—Southern half of California and southward.

These grayish, black and white birds are abundant in sage brush and thickets, nesting on the ground or at low elevations in bushes, and during May or June, laying from three to four eggs of a pale greenish white color, spotted and blotched with reddish brown and purplish.　Size .75 x 60.　Data.—Coronado Beach, San Diego, Cal., May 21, 1887.　Nest of grasses in a clump of bushes, one foot from the ground.　Collector, A. M. Ingersoll.

[Greenish white.]

[2] No longer recognized as a valid form.

574.1. Sage Sparrow. *Amphispiza belli.*

Range.—Sage deserts of the Great Basin from Oregon and Montana, south to Mexico.

This sub-species is abundant throughout its range where it nests near or on the ground, in or under bushes and generally concealed from view. The nests are made of grass and sage bark lined with fine grass; the eggs are like those of the last species, greenish white, spotted and blotched with shades of brown and purplish.

574b. Gray Sage Sparrow (should be Sage Sparrow). *Amphispiza belli.*

Range.—A smaller and paler variety found in Lower California.

The nests and eggs of this pale variety probably do not differ in any respect from those of the better known varieties.

575. Pine-woods Sparrow (should be Bachman's Sparrow). *Aimophila aestivalis.*

Range.—Florida and southern Georgia.

These birds are common in restricted localities in their range, nesting on the ground under bushes or shrubs; the nests are made of grasses and the four or five eggs are pure white with a slight gloss. Size .75 x 60. The birds are said to be fine singers and to frequent, almost exclusively, pine barrens.

575a. Bachman's Sparrow. *Aimophila aestivalis.*

Range.—South Atlantic and Gulf States; north to Indiana and Illinois.

This variety is common in most localities in its range, frequenting pine woods and barrens chiefly, and nesting on the ground in May or June. Their nests are made of grasses and lined with very fine grass, and have the tops completely arched over leaving a small entrance on the side. The eggs are pure white with a slight gloss and measure .75 x 60.

[White.]

576. Botteri's Sparrow. *Aimophila botterii.*

Range.—Mexican plateau north to southern Texas, New Mexico and Arizona.

They nest in abundance in tall grass in the lowlands of their range, the nests being difficult to find because the bird flushes with great difficulty. The nests are on the ground, made of grass, and the three to five eggs are pure white, measuring .75 x 60.

578. Cassin's Sparrow. *Aimophila cassinii.*

Range.—Plains and valleys from Texas and Arizona north to Kansas and Nevada.

These birds breed in numbers on the arid plains, placing their grass nests on the ground at the foot of small bushes or concealed in tufts of grass, and during May lay four pure white eggs which are of the same size and indistinguishable from those of others of the genus.

[White.]

579. Rufous-winged Sparrow. *Aimophila carpalis.*

Range.—Plains of western Mexico and north to southern Arizona.

This pale colored bird bears a remote resemblance to the Tree Sparrow.[1] They nest commonly in dry arid regions, placing their nests at low elevations in bushes or cacti, preferably young mesquites, and making them of coarse grass lined with finer. Two broods are raised a season and from May to August sets of four or five plain bluish white eggs may be found. Size .75 x 60.

[Bluish white.]

[1] Now American Tree Sparrow.

580. Rufous-crowned Sparrow. *Aimophila ruficeps.*

Range.—Local in southern half of California and in Lower California.

A brownish colored species both above and below, which is found on mountains and hillsides in restricted localities. They nest on the ground placing their grass structures in hollows, usually at the foot of a small bush or shrub and well concealed. They lay from three to five pale bluish white eggs. Size .80 x .60.

580a. Scott's Sparrow (should be Rufous-crowned Sparrow). *Aimophila ruficeps.*

Range.—Western Texas, New Mexico and Arizona south in Mexico.

A paler species, above, than the last, and whitish below. It is quite a common species on the mountain ranges where it nests on the ground, in clumps of grass or beneath shrubs or overhanging rocks; the nests are made of grasses and weeds scantily put together. The eggs are white, untinted. Size .80 x. 60.

580b. Rock Sparrow (should be Rufous-crowned Sparrow). *Aimophila ruficeps.*

[White.]

Range.—Middle and southern Texas and south in Mexico.

This variety frequents rocky mountain sides where it nests abundantly under rocks or at the foot of shrubs, the nests being made of coarse grasses loosely twisted together and lined with finer grass. The birds are shy and skulk off through the underbrush upon the approach of anyone so that the nests are quite difficult to find. The three to five eggs are pure white and of the same size as those of the last.

580c. Laguna Sparrow (should be Rufous-crowned Sparrow). *Aimophila ruficeps.*

Range.—Mountains of southern Lower California.

The nests and eggs of this very similar variety to *ruficeps* proper are not likely to differ in any particular from those of that species.

581. Song Sparrow. *Melospiza melodia.*

Range.—North America, east of the Plains, breeding from Virginia to Manitoba and New Brunswick, and wintering chiefly in the southern half of the United States.

[White.]

A favorite and one of the most abundant in all sections of the east. They are sweet and persistent songsters and frequent side hills, pastures, roadsides, gardens and dooryards if English Sparrows be not present. They nest indifferently upon the ground or in bushes, generally artfully concealing the nest by drooping leaves; it is made of grass and weed stems, lined with fine grass or, occasionally, horse hair. As is usual in the case of birds that abound about habitations they frequently choose odd nesting sites. They lay two and sometimes three sets of eggs a season, from May to August, the eggs being three to five in number and white or greenish white, marked, spotted, blotched or splashed in endless variety of patterns and intensity, with many shades of brown; some eggs are very heavily blotched so as to wholly obscure the ground color while others are specked very sparingly. They measure .80 x .60 with great variations. The very numerous subspecies into which the genus is divided are similarly marked but vary greatly in color depending chiefly upon the nature of the regions they inhabit, those in humid regions where the rainfall is great being very dark and brownish while those of the dry arid regions are pale and have a "washed out" appearance; between such regions they assume all intermediate stages of plumage. The eggs show all manner of changes in coloration and marking but those of any of the subspecies are not distinguishable from some types of those of the eastern bird.

581a. Desert Song Sparrow (should be Song Sparrow). *Melospiza melodia.*
Range,—Desert regions of southern Nevada, Arizona and southeastern California. The eggs of this very pale form are the same as those of the last.

581b. Mountain Song Sparrow (should be Song Sparrow). *Melospiza melodia.*
Range.—Rockies and the Great Basin from Oregon and Montana southward. This variety is paler than the Song Sparrow but darker than 581a. Eggs the same.

581c. Heermann's Song Sparrow (should be Song Sparrow). *Melospiza melodia.*
Range.—California, west of the Sierra Nevadas.
Similar to 581 but with less brown and the markings blacker and more distinct. The nesting habits are the same and the eggs similar to large dark specimens of the eastern Song Sparrow. Size .85 x .62.

581d. Samuels' Song Sparrow (should be Song Sparrow). *Melospiza melodia.*
Range.—Coast regions of California, chiefly in the marshes.
Similar to the last but smaller. They nest on the ground in marsh grass, usually in sandy districts along the shore. The eggs average smaller than those of 581. Size .78 x .58. .58.

581e. Rusty Song Sparrow (should be Song Sparrow). *Melospiza melodia.*
Range.—Pacific coast of Oregon and British Columbia.
A dark species with the upper parts dark reddish brown and heavily streaked with the same below. The nesting habits and eggs are like those of 581 .

581f. Sooty Song Sparrow (should be Song Sparrow). *Melospiza melodia.*
Range.—Pacific coast from British Columbia to Alaska.
A darker bird, both above and below, even than the last. Eggs like the last but averaging a trifle larger. Size .82 x .62.

581g. Brown Song Sparrow (should be Song Sparrow). *Melospiza melodia.*
Range.—Southern Lower California.
A light colored form like the Desert Song Sparrow; said to build in cattails above water as well as on the ground; eggs not different from others of the genus.

581h. Santa Barbara Song Sparrow (should be Song Sparrow). *Melospiza melodia.*
Range.—Breeds on Santa Barbara Islands; winters on adjacent coast of California.
A variety of the same size but paler than 581d . Nesting or eggs not peculiar.

581i. San Clemente Song Sparrow (should be Song Sparrow). *Melospiza melodia.*
Range.—San Clemente and Santa Rosa Island of the Santa Barbara group.
Slightly larger than the last; habits and eggs the same.

581j. Dakota Song Sparrow (should be Song Sparrow). *Melospiza melodia.*
Range.—North Dakota, breeding in the Turtle Mountains.
Practically indistinguishable from the common Song Sparrow; the eggs will not differ.

581k. Merrill's Song Sparrow (should be Song Sparrow). *Melospiza melodia.*
Range.—Northwestern United States; eastern Oregon and Washington to Idaho.
Very similar to, but lighter than the Rusty Song Sparrow.

581l.. Alameda Song Sparrow (should be Song Sparrow). *Melospiza melodia.*
Range. Salt marshes of San Francisco Bay, California.
Similar to, but still smaller than Samuels' Song Sparrow. Eggs will not differ.

581m. San Diego Song Sparrow (should be Song Sparrow). *Melospiza melodia.*
Range.—Southern coast of California; north to Monterey Bay.
Similar to, but smaller and lighter than 581c .

581n. Yakutat Song Sparrow (should be Song Sparrow). *Melospiza melodia.*
Range.—Coast of Alaska from Cross Sound to Prince Williams Sound.
Similar to the Sooty Song Sparrow but larger and grayer. Eggs probably average larger.

581o. Kenai Song Sparrow (should be Song Sparrow). *Melospiza melodia.*
Range.—Kenai Peninsula on the coasts.
Like the last but still larger; length about 7 inches.

581.1. Kadiak Island Song Sparrow (should be Song Sparrow). *Melospiza melodia.*
Range.—Kadiak Island, Alaska.
Similar to and nearly as large as the next species, but browner.

581r. Aleutian Song Sparrow (should be Song Sparrow). *Melospiza melodia.*
Range.—Found on nearly all the islands of the Aleutian group, excluding Kadiak.

[Bluish white.]

This is the largest of the Song Sparrows being nearly 8 inches in length; it is similar in appearance to the Sooty Song Sparrow but grayer. It nests either on the ground or at low elevations in bushes, the nest usually being concealed in a tuft of grass or often placed under rocks or, sometimes, driftwood along the shores. The nests are made of grasses and weed stems, and the eggs are similar to those of the Song Sparrow but much larger and more elongate. Size .90 x .65.

583. Lincoln's Sparrow. *Melospiza lincolnii.*
Range.—North America, breeding from northern United States north to the Arctic regions; most abundant in the interior and the west; rare in New England.

[Greenish white.]

This bird is shy and retiring and skulks off through the underbrush of thickets and swamps that it frequents upon the approach of anyone; consequently it is often little known in localities where it is quite abundant. They nest on the ground like Song Sparrows, and rarely in bushes. Their eggs are very similar to those of the Song Sparrow, three or four in number, greenish white in color, heavily spotted and blotched with chestnut and gray. Size .80 x 58. Data.—Estes Park, Colorado, June 20, 1890. Nest of grass placed on a slight elevation in swampy marsh. Collector, Wm. G. Smith.

583a. Forbush's Sparrow (should be Lincoln's Sparrow). *Melospiza lincolnii.*
Range. Pacific coast of Oregon and British Columbia.
Similar to the preceding but darker and browner. Eggs probably like those of the last.

584. Swamp Sparrow. *Melospiza georgiana.*

[Greenish white.]

Range.—North America, east of the Plains, breeding from middle United States north to Labrador and Hudson Bay.
This common and dark-colored Sparrow frequents swampy places where it breeds; owing to its sly habits it is not commonly seen during the breeding season. Its nests are made of grasses and located on the ground usually in places where the walking is extremely treacherous. The eggs are similar to those of the Song Sparrow but are generally darker and more clouded and average smaller. Size .75 x .55.

585. Fox Sparrow. *Passerella iliaca.*
Range.—Eastern North America, breeding from southern Canada northward, and northwest to Alaska; winters in southern United States.

[Greenish white.]

This large handsome species, with its mottled grayish and reddish brown plumage and bright rufous tail, is very common in eastern United States during migrations, being found in open woods and hedges in company with Juncos and White-throated Sparrows, with which species their song vies in sweetness. They nest usually on the ground, but sometimes in low bushes; the nests are made of grasses and are concealed beneath the overhanging branches of bushes or evergreens. The three or four eggs are greenish white, spotted and blotched with brown. Size .94 x .68. Data.—Nashvak, Labrador, June 14, 1897. Nest on the ground; made of fine grasses. Collector, G. Ford.

585a.   Shumagin Fox Sparrow (should be Fox Sparrow).   *Passerella iliaca.*

Range.—Shumagin Islands and the Alaska coast to Cook Inlet.

Similar to the last but paler, being one of the several recent unsatisfactory sub-divisions of this genus.   The nesting habits and eggs of all the varieties are like those of the common eastern form.

585f.   Kadiak Fox Sparrow (should be Fox Sparrow).   *Passerella iliaca.*

Range.—Breeding on Kadiak Island; winters south to California.

Like the last but browner above and below.

585e.   Sooty Fox Sparrow (should be Fox Sparrow).   *Passerella iliaca.*

Range.—Coast of Washington and British Columbia; south to California in winter.

Upperparts and tail uniform brownish umber, below heavily spotted.

585g.   Townsend's Fox Sparrow (should be Fox Sparrow).   *Passerella iliaca.*

Range.—Southern coast of Alaska; winters south to California.   Like the last but more rufous above.

585l.   Yakutat Fox Sparrow (should be Fox Sparrow).   *Passerella iliaca.*

Range.—Coast of Alaska about Yakutat Bay.   Very similar to 585e.

585b.   Thick-billed Sparrow (should be Fox Sparrow).   *Passerella iliaca.*

Range.—Mountains of eastern California and western Nevada; locally confined.

Entire upper parts and breast spots gray; wings and tail brown.   It nests in the heaviest underbrush of the mountain sides, building on or close to the ground.

585c.   Slate-colored Sparrow (should be Fox Sparrow).   *Passerella iliaca.*

Range.—Rocky Mountain region, breeding from Colorado to British Columbia.

This variety which is similar to, but smaller than the last, nests in thickets along the mountain streams.   The eggs are like those of 585, but average smaller.

585d.   Stephens' Sparrow (should be Fox Sparrow).   *Passerella iliaca.*

Range.—Breeds in the San Bernadino and San Jacinto Mts. in southern California.

Like the Thick-billed Sparrow, but bill still larger and bird slightly so.

586.   Olive Sparrow.   *Arremonops rufivirgata.*

Range.—Eastern Mexico and southern Texas.

This odd species has a brownish crown, olive greenish upper-parts, wings and tail, and grayish white underparts.   They are common resident birds along the Lower Rio Grande, being found in tangled thickets, where they nest at low elevations, making their quite bulky nests of coarse weeds and grass and sometimes twigs, lined with finer grass and hair; they are often partially domed with an entrance on the side.   Their eggs are plain white, without markings; often several broods are raised in a season and eggs may be found from May until August.

[White.]

688.2.   House Sparrow.   *Passer domesticus.*

These birds, which were imported from Europe, have increased so rapidly that they have overrun the cities and villages of the country and are doing inestimable

damage both by driving out native insect eating birds and by their own destructiveness.   They nest in all sorts of places but preferably behind blinds, where their unsightly masses of straw protrude from between the slats, and their droppings besmirch the buildings below; they breed at all seasons of the year, eggs having often been found in January, with several feet of snow on the ground and the mercury below zero.   The eggs number from four to eight in a

[White.]

set and from four to eight sets a season; the eggs are whitish, spotted and blotched with shapes of gray and black.   Size .88 x .60.

688.3.   European Tree Sparrow.   *Passer montanus.*

Another European species very similar to the last, that has been naturalized chiefly about St. Louis, Mo.   Their eggs are like those of the last but smaller.

587. Rufous-sided Towhee. *Pipilo erythrophthalmus.*

Range.—North America east of the Plains, breeding from the Gulf to Manitoba.

The well-known Towhee, Ground Robin or Chewink[1] is a bird commonly met with in eastern United States; it frequents thickets, swamps and open woods where they nest generally upon the ground and sometimes in bushes near the ground. The nests are well made of grasses, lined with fine grasses and rootlets, and the eggs, which are laid in May or June, are pinkish white, generally finely sprinkled but sometimes with bold markings of light reddish brown, with great variations. Size .90 x .70. Towhees are noisy birds and at frequent intervals, while they are scratching among the leaves for their food they will stop and utter their familiar "tow-hee" or "che-wink" and then again will mount to the summit of a tree or bush and sing their sweet refrain for a long time.

[Purplish white.]

587a. White-eyed Towhee (should be Rufous-sided Towhee). *Pipilo erythrophthalmus.*

Range.—Florida and the Altantic coast to South Carolina.

This variety is like the preceding except that the eyes are white instead of red. There is no difference between their nesting habits and eggs, except that they much more frequently, and in some localities, almost always, nest in trees.

588. Arctic Towhee (should be Rufous-sided Towhee). *Pipilo erythrophthalmus.*

Range.—Great Plains, breeding from northern United States to the Saskatchewan.

This species is similar to the eastern Towhee[1] but has the scapulars and coverts tipped with white. They nest abundantly in suitable localities in Montana and North Dakota and more commonly north of our borders. Like the eastern Towhee, they nest on the ground under the protection of overhanging bushes, the nests being made of strips of bark and grasses and lined with fine rootlets. Their three or four eggs, which are laid during May, June or July, are pinkish white, profusely speckled with reddish brown; very similar to those of the eastern Towhee. Size .92 x .70.

[Pinkish white.]

588a. Spurred Towhee (should be Rufous-sided Towhee). *Pipilo erythrophthalmus.*

Range.—Breeds from Mexico to British Columbia, west of the Rockies.

Similar to the last but with less white on the back. The nesting habits and eggs are like those of the Towhee,[1] but in some localities the nests are most often found in bushes above the ground.

588b. Oregon Towhee (should be Rufous-sided Towhee). *Pipilo erythrophthalmus.*

Range.—Pacific coast from California to British Columbia; winters to Mexico. Similar to the last but with still fewer white markings on the back and the chestnut flanks brighter. The nesting habits and eggs of this variety differ in no essential particular from those of the preceding Towhees.

588c. San Clemente Towhee (should be Rufous-sided Towhee). *Pipilo erythrophthalmus.*

Range.—San Clemente Is. and other of the Santa Barbara group.

Black of male said to be duller. Probably no difference between the eggs and others.

588d. San Diego Towhee (should be Rufous-sided Towhee). *Pipilo erythrophthalmus.*

Range.—Coast of southern California and Lower California. Said to be darker than 588a.

588e. Mountain Towhee (should be Rufous-sided Towhee). *Pipilo erythrophthalmus.*

Range.—Southern Lower California. Similar to 588; bill said to be larger.

---

[1] Now Rufous-sided Towhee.

589.   Guadalupe Towhee (should be Rufous-sided Towhee).   *Pipilo erythrophthalmus.*

Range.—Guadalupe Island, Lower California.

Similar to 588b but smaller and with a relatively shorter tail. The nesting habits and eggs of this species will not likely be found to differ essentially from those of others of the genus.

591.   Brown Towhee.   *Pipilo fuscus.*

Range.—Mexico and north to Arizona and New Mexico and casually farther to Colorado.

[Greenish blue.]

These birds have a brownish crown and under tail coverts, the rest of the plumage being brownish gray, lighter below. A common species in the valleys and on the side hills, nesting in bushes near the ground, and sometimes on the ground; the nests are made of grasses, weeds and twigs lined with rootlets, and the three or four eggs are greenish blue sparingly spotted or scrawled with blackish brown, the markings being similar to those on many Redwinged Blackbirds' eggs.   Size 1.00 x .70.

Photo by C. A. Reed.

NEST AND EGGS OF RUFOUS-SIDED TOWHEE.

591a. St. Lucas Towhee (should be Brown Towhee). *Pipilo fuscus.*

Range.—Southern Lower California.

This variety is like the last but is usually paler below. It is abundant in the region about the cape where they nest in thickets, either in the bushes or on the ground. The eggs cannot be distinguished from those of the Canon Towhee.[1]

591b. California Towhee (should be Brown Towhee). *Pipilo fuscus.*

Range.—Pacific coast of California.

This variety is similar to the Canon Towhee[1] but is browner, both above and below. They are one of the most common of California birds, frequenting scrubby thickets, both on mountain sides and in valleys and cañons, from which their harsh scolding voice always greets intruders. They place their nests in bushes at low elevations from the ground and sometimes on the ground; they are made of twigs, strips of bark, weeds and coarse grasses, lined with fine rootlets. Their three or four eggs are laid in April or May; they are light bluish green marked like the others with purplish or brownish black. Size .95 x 72.

591c. Anthony's Towhee (should be Brown Towhee). *Pipilo fuscus.*

[Greenish blue.]

Range.—Southern California and south through Lower California.

A very similar bird to the last but slightly smaller and lighter below. The habits and nesting habits of these birds are in every way identical with those of the California Towhee and the eggs cannot be distinguished from those of that variety. They are fully as abundant in the southern parts of California as the others are in the northern.

592. Abert's Towhee. *Pipilo aberti.*

Range.—Arizona and New Mexico north to Colorado and Nevada and east to southeastern California.

This bird is wholly brownish gray both above and below shading into reddish brown on the under tail coverts; the face is black. They are abundant in the valleys of Arizona and New Mexico, but unlike the preceding species, they are generally wild and shy. They nest in chaparral thickets along streams, the nests being constructed similarly to those of the California Towhee, and the eggs are not easily distinguishable from those of that species, but they are usually more sparsely specked and the markings more distinct. Size 1.00 x .75.

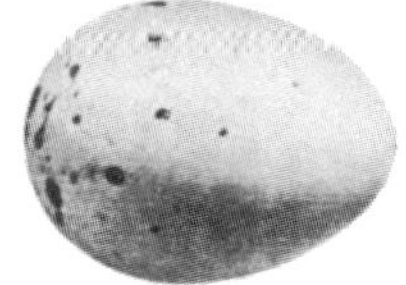

[Greenish blue.]

592.1. Green-tailed Towhee. *Chlorura chlorura.*

Range.—Western United States, chiefly west of the Rockies, from Montana and Washington south to Mexico; wintering in southwestern United States.

[Whitish.]

This handsome and entirely different plumaged species from any of the preceding would, from appearance, be better placed in the group with the White-throated Sparrow than its present position. It has a reddish brown crown, the remainder of the upper parts, wings and tail being greenish yellow; the throat is white, bordered abruptly with gray on the breast and sides of head. They are most frequently met with on rocky hill sides which are overgrown with tangled thickets, in which these birds place their nests on the ground. The nests are built similarly to those of the eastern Towhee,[2] and the eggs, too, are similar, being whitish, finely dotted and specked with reddish brown, the markings being most numerous around the larger end. Size .85 x.65.

[1] Now Brown Towhee.

[2] Now Rufous-sided Towhee.

593. Cardinal. *Richmondena cardinalis.*

Range.—Eastern United States, north to New York and Illinois, west to the Plains and Texas. Resident in most of its range.

These beautiful fiery red and crested songsters are one of the most attractive of our birds, and in their range, nest about habitations as freely as among the thickets and scrubby brush of wood or hillside. Their nests are rarely placed higher than ten feet from the ground in bushes, brambles, vines, brush piles or trees; they are loosely made of twigs, coarse grasses and weeds, shreds of bark, leaves, etc., and lined with fine grass or hair. They frequently lay two or three sets of eggs a season, the first being completed usual-

[Bluish white.]

ly early in May; three or four, and sometimes five, white or pale bluish white eggs are laid; they are very varied in markings but usually profusely spotted, more heavily at the large end, with reddish brown and lavender. Size 1.00 x .70.

593a. Arizona Cardinal (should be Cardinal). *Richmondena cardinalis.*

Range.—Northwestern Mexico and southern Arizona.
A larger and more rosy form of the Cardinal. Its eggs cannot be distinguished from those of the eastern Redbird.

593b. St. Lucas Cardinal (should be Cardinal). *Richmondena cardinalis.*

Range.—Southern Lower California.
Like the last but smaller and with less black on the forehead; eggs the same.

Photo by Paul R. Powell.

NEST OF CARDINAL.

593c.　Gray-tailed Cardinal (should be Cardinal).　*Richmondena cardinalis.*

Range.—Northeastern Mexico and southern Texas.
The male of this species is like the eastern Cardinal but the female is said to be grayer.　The nesting habits are the same and the eggs identical with those of the latter.

593d.　Florida Cardinal (should be Cardinal).　*Richmondena cardinalis.*

Range.—Southern Florida.
Supposed to be a deeper and richer shade of red.　　Eggs like those of 593.

594.　Pyrrhuloxia.　*Pyrrhuloxia sinuata.*

Range.—Northwestern Mexico and the southern border of New Mexico, Arizona and western Texas.

[Bluish white.]

This species is of similar form and crested like a Cardinal, but the bill is very short and hooked like that of a Parrot; the plumage is grayish, with wings and tail dull reddish; face and throat, and middle of belly rosy red.　Their habits are the same as those of the Cardinal, but their nests are said to be slighter; they are placed in similar locations to those of the latter, the two species often nesting together in the same thicket.　Their eggs are like those of the Cardinal but average smaller, although the ranges overlap so that the eggs cannot be distinguished.　Size .90 x .70.　Data.—San Antonio, Texas, May 16, 1889. Nest of fine grasses, lined with rootlets; 4 feet from ground in a mesquite tree. Collector, H. P. Atwater.

594a.　Texas Pyrrhuloxia (should be Pyrrhuloxia).　*Pyrrhuloxia sinuata.*

Range.—Northeastern Mexico and southern Texas.
Said to be grayer and the bill to average larger than that of the last.　There are no differences in the nesting habits or eggs between the two varieties.

594b.　St. Lucas Pyrrhuloxia (should be Pyrrhuloxia).　*Pyrrhuloxia sinuata.*

Range.—Southern Lower California.
Smaller than the Arizona Cardinal but with a larger bill.　The eggs are like those of the others but may average a trifle smaller.

595.　Rose-breasted Grosbeak.　*Pheucticus ludovicianus.*

Range.—United States, east of the Plains, breeding from the Middle States and Ohio north to Manitoba and Nova Scotia.
This beautiful black and white bird with rosy red breast and under wing coverts, is one of the most pleasing of our songsters.　They nest either in bushes or trees, generally between six and twenty feet from the ground and usually in thick clumps of trees or scrubby apple trees.　The three or four eggs, which are laid in June, are greenish blue, spotted, most heavily about the larger end, with reddish brown.　Size 1.00 x .75.　Data.—Worcester, Mass., June 5, 1899.　Nest of twigs and rootlets in small apple tree in woods; nest very frail, eggs showing through the bottom.　Collector A. C. White.

[Greenish blue.]

596. Black-headed Grosbeak.
Pheucticus melanocephalus.

[Pale greenish blue.]

Range.-United States, west of the Plains, breeding from Mexico north to British Columbia; winters south of the United States.

This species is of the size of the last (8 inches long), and is a bright cinnamon brown color with black head, and black and white wings and tail. The habits of this bird are the same as those of the Rose-breasted Grosbeak and its song is very similar but more lengthy. Their nests, like those of the last, are very flimsy structures placed in bushes or trees, usually below twenty feet from the ground; they are open frameworks of twigs, rootlets and weed stalks, through which the eggs can be plainly seen. The eggs are similar to those of the preceding but are usually of a paler color, the markings, therefore showing with greater distinctness. Size 1.00 x .70.

Photo by J. B. Pardoe.
NEST OF ROSE-BREASTED GROSBEAK.

597. Blue Grosbeak. *Guiraca caerulea.*

Range.—Southeastern United States, breeding from the Gulf north to Pennsylvania and Illinois, and casually to New England.

Smaller than the last two species and deep blue, with wings and tail blackish, and the lesser coverts and tips of greater, chestnut. It is a fairly common species in the southerly parts of its range, nesting most frequently in low bushes or vines in thickets; the nest is made of rootlets, weed stalks and grasses and sometimes leaves. The three or four eggs are bluish white, unmarked. Size .85 x .65. Data.—Chatham Co., Ga., June 10, 1898. 3 eggs. Nest of roots, leaves and snake skin, lined with fine rootlets, 3 feet from the ground in a small oak bush. Collector, Troup D. Perry.

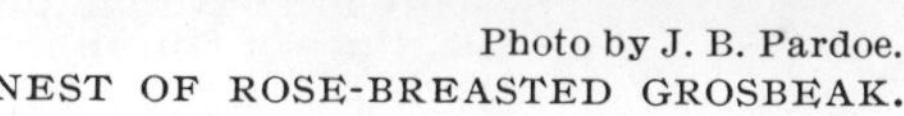

[Bluish white.]

597a. Western Blue Grosbeak (should be Blue Grosbeak). *Guiraca caerulea.*

Range.—Western United States north to Kansas, Colorado and northern California.

Slightly larger than the last and lighter blue; nests the same and eggs not distinctive.

598. Indigo Bunting. *Passerina cyanea.*

Range.—United States, east of the Plains, breeding north to Manitoba and Nova Scotia; winters south of the United States.

[Pale bluish white]

This handsome species is rich indigo on the head and neck, shading into blue or greenish blue on the upper and underparts. They are very abundant in some localities along roadsides, in thickets and open woods, where their song is frequently heard, it being a very sweet refrain resembling, somewhat, certain passages from that of the Goldfinch. They nest at low elevations in thickets or vines, building their home of grass and weeds, lined with fine grass or hair, it being quite a substantial structure. The eggs, which are laid in June or July, are pale bluish white. Size .75 x .52.

599. Lazuli Bunting. *Passerina amoena.*

Range.—Western United States, breeding from Mexico to northern United States and the interior of British Columbia; east to Kansas.

This handsome bird is of the size of *cyanea*, but is azure blue above and on the throat, the breast being brownish and the rest of the underparts, white. It is the western representative of the Indigo Bunting, and its habits and nesting habits are in all respects the same as those of that species, the nests being made of twigs, grasses, strips of bark, weeds, leaves, etc. The eggs are like those of the last, pale bluish white. Size .75 x .55.

[Pale bluish white]

600. Varied Bunting. *Passerina versicolor.*

Range.—Mexico and north to southern Texas.

The general color of this odd bird is purplish, changing to bright blue on the crown and rump, and with a reddish nape. They are quite abundant in some localities along the Lower Rio Grande, where they nest in bushes and tangled under brush, the nests being like those of the last species, and rarely above five feet from the ground. The eggs are pale bluish white, three or four in number, and laid during May or June. [Pale bluish white.] Size .75 x .55.

600a. Beautiful Bunting (should be Varied Bunting). *Passerina versicolor.*

Range.—Southern Lower California.
Slightly smaller but very similar to the last; eggs will not differ.

601. Painted Bunting. *Passerina ciris.*

Range.—South Atlantic and Gulf States; north to Illinois in the interior.

Without exception, this is the most gaudily attired of North American birds, the whole underparts being red, the head and neck deep blue, the back yellowish green, and the rump purple, the line of demarcation between the colors being sharp. They are frequently kept as cage birds but more for their bright colors than any musical ability, their song being of the character of the Indigo Bunting, but weaker and less musical. They are very abundant in the South Atlantic and Gulf States, where they nest usually in bushes or

[White.]

hedges at low elevations, but occasionally on branches of tall trees. Their nests are made of weeds, shreds of bark, grasses, etc., lined with fine grass, very much resembling that of the Indigo. Their eggs are laid in May, June or July, they frequently raising two broods; they are white or pale bluish white, speckled with reddish brown. Size .75 x .55.

602. White-collared Seedeater. *Sporophila torqueola.*

Range.—Eastern Mexico, breeding north to the Lower Rio Grande Valley in Texas.

This peculiar, diminutive Finch is but 4.5 inches in length, and in plumage is black, white and gray. In restricted localities in southern Texas, they are not uncommon during the summer months. They build in bushes or young trees at low elevations making their nests of fine grasses or fibres, firmly woven together and usually placed in an upright crotch. The eggs are pale greenish blue, plentifully speckled with reddish and umber brown, and some markings of lilac. Size .65 x .45. Data.—Brownsville, Texas, May 7, 1892. Nest of fine fibre-like material lined with horse hairs, on limb of small tree in open woods near a lake of fresh water; 6 feet above ground. Collector, Frank B. Armstrong. This set is in the collection of Mr. C. W. Crandall.

[Greenish blue.]

603. Black-faced Grassquit. *Tiaris bicolor.*

Range.—This small Finch is a Cuban species which casually strays to southern Florida.

They are abundant on the island, building large arched nests of grass, with a small entrance on the side. They lay from three to six white eggs, specked with brown. Size .65 x .50.

603.1. Melodious Grassquit. *Tiaris canora.*

Another Cuban Finch which has been taken in the Florida Keys. Eggs like the last.

604. Dickcissel. *Spiza americana.*

Range.—Interior of the United States, breeding from the Gulf to northern United States, west to the Rockies, east to the Alleghanies.

A sparrow-like Bunting with a yellow breast patch, line over eye and on side of throat; throat black, chin white and wing coverts chestnut. These sleek-coated, harmoniously colored birds are very common in dry bush-grown pastures and on the prairies. They are very persistent singers, and their song, while very simple, is welcome on hot days when other birds are quiet. They nest anywhere, as suits their fancy, on the ground, in clumps of grass, in clover fields, bushes, low trees, or in thistles. The nests are made of weeds, grasses, leaves and rootlets, lined with fine grass, and the three to five eggs are bluish white. Size .80 x .60.

[Bluish white.]

605. Lark Bunting. *Calamospiza melanocorys.*

Range.—A bird of the Plains, abundant from western Kansas to eastern Colorado and north to the Canadian border; winters in Mexico.

These black and white birds have a sweet song which they often utter while on the wing after the manner of the Bobolink, all their habits being similar to those of this bird, except that this species likes the broad dry prairies where it nests on the ground under the protection of a tuft of grass or a low bush. Their four or five eggs are like those of the last but slightly larger. Size .85 x .65. Data.—Franklin Co., Kansas. 4 eggs. Nest in cornfield in a hollow on the ground at the base of a stalk; made of straw and weeds. Collector, Victor Smith.

[Bluish white.]

TANAGERS. Family THRAUPIDAE.

606. Blue-headed Euphonia. *Tanagra elegantissima.*

Range.—Mexico, north casually? to southern Texas. [1]

This beautiful little Tanager is admitted to our avifauna on the authority of Giraud as having occurred in Texas.

[1] Not recorded from North America.

607.   Western Tanager.   *Piranga ludoviciana.*

Range.—United States, west of the Plains and north to British Columbia.

[Bluish green.]

This handsome species is black and yellow, with an orange or reddish head. They are common and breed in suitable localities through their range, nesting as do the eastern Tanagers in trees usually at a low elevation, the nests being saddled on the forks of horizontal branches; they are made of rootlets, strips of bark, and weed stalks and are usually frail like those of the Grosbeaks. Their eggs, which are laid in May or June, are bluish green, specked with brown of varying shades. Size .95 x .65.

608.   Scarlet Tanager.   *Piranga olivacea.*

These beautiful scarlet and black birds frequent, chiefly, woodlands although they are very often found breeding in orchards and small pine groves. They are quiet birds, in actions, but their loud warbling song is heard at a great distance, and is readily recognized by its peculiarity. They nest upon horizontal limbs or forks at elevations of four to twenty feet, making frail nests of twigs, rootlets and weeds; they are often found in pine trees, but apparently just as frequently in other kinds. Their eggs are greenish

[Greenish blue.]

blue, specked and spotted with various shades of brown. Size .95 x .65. Data.— Holden, Mass., May 31, 1898. Nest on low limb of an oak, 4 feet above ground; of weeds and rootlets and very frail. Collector, A. C. White.

609.   Hepatic Tanager.   *Piranga flava.*

[Bluish green.]

Range.—Western Mexico, north to New Mexico and Arizona in summer.

This species is similar to the next but is darker red on the upper parts and bright vermilion below. They nest on the lower horizontal branches of trees, usually live oaks, making the nests of rootlets and weeds; the eggs are bluish green, like those of the next, but the markings appear to average more blotchy and brighter. Size .92 x .64.

610.   Summer Tanager.   *Piranga rubra.*

Range.—Eastern United States, breeding from the Gulf to New York and Kansas, and casually farther; west to Texas; winters south of our borders.

This bird is of the size of the Scarlet Tanager, but is of a uniform rosy red color, darker on the back. They are very common in the South Atlantic and Gulf States.   Their nests are located at low elevations on horizontal branches of trees in open woods, edges of clearings, or along the roadside; the nests are made of strips of bark, weed stems, leaves, etc., and are frail like those of the other Tanagers.

[Light bluish green]

Their eggs are light bluish green, specked and spotted with reddish brown, and not distinguishable with certainty from those of the Scarlet Tanager. Size .92 x .64.

610a.   Cooper's Tanager (should be Summer Tanager).   *Piranga rubra.*

Range.– Western United States, breeding from the Mexican border and Texas north to central California and Nevada.

Similar to but slightly larger than the last. There are no differences between the nesting of this form and the last and the eggs are not in any way different.

SWALLOWS. Family HIRUNDINIDAE.

611. Purple Martin. *Progne subis.*

Range.—Breeds throughout the United States and temperate British America; winters in South America.

[White.]

These large, lustrous, steely-blue Swallows readily adapt themselves to civilization and, throughout the east, may be found nesting in bird houses, provided by appreciative land owners or tenants; some of these houses are beautiful structures modelled after modern residences and tenanted by twenty or thirty pairs of Martins; others are plain, unpainted soap boxes or the like, but the birds seem to take to one as kindly as the other, making nests in their compartments of weeds, grass, mud, feathers, etc. They also, and most commonly in the west, nest in cavities of trees making nests of any available material. During June or July, they lay from four to six white eggs; size .95 x .65. Data.—Leicester, Mass., June 16, 1903. 5 eggs in Martin house; nest of grasses. Collector, A. J. Green.

611a. Western Martin (should be Purple Martin). *Progne subis.*

Range.—Pacific coast from Washington south.

The nesting habits, eggs, and birds of this form are identical with those found in the east.

611.1. Cuban Martin. *Progne cryptoleuca.*

Range.—Cuba and southern Florida (in summer).

Slightly smaller than the Purple Martin and the eggs average a trifle smaller.

612. Cliff Swallow. *Petrochelidon pyrrhonota.*

Range.—Whole of North America, breeding north from the south Atlantic and Gulf States.

[White.]

These birds can easily be recognized by their brownish throat and breast, whitish forehead and buffy rump. They build one of the most peculiar of nests, the highest type being a flask shaped structure of mud securely cemented to the face of a cliff or under the eaves of a building, the entrance being drawn out and small, while the outside of the nest proper is large and rounded; they vary from this typical nest down to plain mud platforms, but are all warmly lined with grass and feathers. In some localities, cliffs resemble bee hives, they having thousands of these nests side by side and in tiers. Their eggs are creamy white spotted with reddish brown; size .80 x .55 with great variations. Data.—Rockford, Minn., June 12, 1890. Nest made of mud, lined with feathers; placed under the eaves of a freight house. Collector, M. B. Rich.

612.1. Cuban Cliff Swallow (should be Cave Swallow). *Petrochelidon fulva.*

Range.—West Indies and Central America; accidental on Florida Keys.

612.2. Mexican Cliff Swallow (should be Cave Swallow). *Petrochelidon fulva.*

Range.—Mexico; north in summer to southern Arizona.

A similar but smaller variety of the Cliff Swallow; eggs will not differ.

613. Barn Swallow. *Hirundo rustica.*

Range.—Whole of North America; winters south to South America.

This Swallow is the most beautiful and graceful of the family, and is a familiar sight to everyone, skimming over the meadows and ponds in long graceful sweeps, curves and turns, its lengthened outer tail feathers streaming behind. Throughout their range, they nest in barns, sheds or any building where they will not be often disturbed, making their nests of mud and attaching them to the rafters; they are warmly lined with feathers and the outside is rough, caused by the pellets

[White.]

which they place on the exterior. Before the advent of civilized man, they attached their nests to the sides of caves, in crevices among rocks and in hollow trees, as they do now in some localities. Their eggs cannot be distinguished from those of the Cliff Swallow. Data.—Penikese Is., Mass., July 2, 1900. Nest on beam in sheep shed; made of pellets of mud, lined with feathers. Collector, Chas. E. Doe.

614. Tree Swallow. *Iridoprocne bicolor.*

Range.—Whole of temperate North America, breeding from middle United States northward; winters in the Gulf States and along the Mexican border and southward.

This vivacious and active species is as well known as the last, and nests about habitations on the outskirts of cities and in the country. They naturally nest in holes in trees or stumps, preferably in the vicinity of water, but large numbers now take up their abode in houses provided for them by man, providing that English Sparrows [1] are kept away. They make their nests of straws and grasses, lined with feathers, and lay

[White.]

four to six plain white eggs; size .75 x .50. Data.—Portage, Mich., May 26, 1897. Nest in a gate post; hole about 6 inches deep, lined with feathers. Collector, Chas. Sickles.

615. Violet-green Swallow. *Tachycineta thalassina.*

Range.—United States in the Rocky Mountains and west to the Pacific coast, breeding from Mexico to British Columbia; winters south of our borders.

This very beautiful species is smaller than the last, but, like it, is white below, but the upper parts are blue, green and purple without gloss. They are common in their range and nest, usually in holes in trees, less often in banks and under eaves; the nests are made of grass and feathers, and the eggs are pure white, four or five in number; size .72 x .50.

[White.]

615a. St. Lucas Swallow (should be Violet-green Swallow). *Tachycineta thalassina.*

Range.—Southern Lower California. Practically the same bird as the last but with the wing very slightly shorter. Nesting habits or eggs will not differ.

615.1. Bahama Swallow. *Callichelidon cyaneoviridis.*

Range.—Bahamas; casual at Dry Tortugas, Florida.

This very beautiful species is similar to the western Violet-green Swallow, as are also its eggs.

[1] Now House Sparrow.

616. Bank Swallow. *Riparia riparia.*

Range.—Whole of North America, north to the limit of trees, breeding from the middle portions of the United States northward; winters south of our borders.

This dull-colored Swallow is grayish above and white below, with a gray band across the breast, they breed in holes in embankments, digging small tunnels from one to three feet in length, enlarged and lined at the end with grass and feathers. During May, June or July, according to latitude,they lay from four to six pure white eggs; size .70 x .50.

[White.]

617. Rough-winged Swallow. *Stelgidopteryx ruficollis.*

Range.—United States, breeding from Mexico north to southern New England, Manitoba and British Columbia; winters south of our borders.

This species is slightly larger than the last and similar but with the throat and breast grayish and with the outer web of the outer primary provided with recurved hooks. They nest in holes in embankments, in crevices in cliffs or among stones of bridges or buildings. Their eggs are like those of the Bank Swallow but average a trifle larger; size .75 x .52.

[White.]

WAXWINGS and SILKY FLYCATCHERS. Families BOMBY-CILLIDAE and PTILIGONATIDAE.

618. Bohemian Waxwing. *Bombycilla garrulus*

Range.—Breeds in the Arctic regions except in the Rockies where it nearly reaches the United States; winters south to the northern tier of states.

This handsome crested, grayish brown Waxwing resembles the common Cedar Waxwing but is larger (length 8 inches), has a black throat, much white and yellow on the wing and a yellow tip to tail. Their nests are made of rootlets, grass and moss, and situated in trees usually at a low elevation. The eggs resemble those of the Cedar bird but are larger and the marking more blotchy with Indistinct edges; dull bluish blotched with blackish brown; size .95 x .70. Data.—Great Slave Lake, June 23, 1884. Nest in a willow 8 feet from the ground. Collected for Josiah Hooper. (Crandall collection).

[Dull bluish.]

619. Cedar Waxwing. *Bombycilla cedrorum.*

Range.—Whole of temperate North America, breeding in the northern half of the United States and northward.

These birds are very gregarious and go in large flocks during the greater part of the year, splitting up into smaller companies during the breeding season and nesting in orchards or groves and in any kind of tree either in an upright crotch or on a horizontal bough; the nests are made of grasses, strips of bark, moss, string, etc., and are often quite bulky. Their eggs are of a dull grayish blue color sharply speckled with blackish brown; size .85 x .60. Data.—Old Saybrook,

[Dull bluish.]

Conn., June 22, 1900. Nest composed of cinquefoil vines, grasses, wool and cottony substances; situated on an apple tree branch about 10 feet from the ground. Collector, John N. Clark. This species has a special fondness for cherries, both wild and cultivated, and they are often known as Cherry-birds. They also feed upon various berries, and frequently catch insects in the air after the manner of Flycatchers. Their only notes are a strange lisping sound often barely audible.

Photo by F. R. Miller.

[Section of the bank removed to show nest.]

NEST AND EGGS OF BANK SWALLOW.

620. Phainopepla. *Phainopepla nitens.*

Range.—Southwestern United States and Mexico; north to southern Utah and Colorado.

This peculiar crested species is wholly shining blue black except for a patch of white on the inner webs of the primaries. Their habits are somewhat like those of the Cedar-bird, they being restless, and feeding upon berries or insects, catching the latter in the air. They make loosely constructed nests of twigs, mosses, plant fibres, etc., placed on branches of trees, usually below 20 feet from the ground, in thickets or open woods near water; the eggs are two or three in number, light

[Light gray.]

gray, spotted sharply with black; size .88 x .65. Data.—Pasadena, Cal., July 15, 1894. Nest in an oak 10 feet up; composed of weeds and string. Collector, Horace Gaylord.

SHRIKES. Family LANIIDAE.

621. Northern Shrike. *Lanius borealis.*

Range.—North America, breeding north of our borders; winters in northern half of the United States and casually farther south.

All Shrikes are similar in nature and plumage, being grayish above and white below, with black wings, tail and ear patches, and with white outer tail feathers and bases of primaries; the present species may be known by its larger size (length over 10 inches) and wavy dusky lines on the breast. They are bold and cruel birds, feeding upon insects, small rodents and small birds, in the capture of which they display great cunning and courage; as they

[Grayish white.]

have weak feet, in order to tear their prey to pieces with their hooked bill, they impale it upon thorns. They nest in thickets and tangled underbrush, making their nests of vines, grasses, catkins, etc., matted together into a rude structure. During April or May they lay from four to six grayish white eggs, spotted and blotched with yellowish brown and umber; size 1.05 x .75.

622. Loggerhead Shrike. *Lanius ludovicianus.*

Range.—United States, east of the Plains, breeding north to New England and Illinois; winters in Southern States.

Like the last but smaller (length 9 inches), not marked below and with the ear patches sharply defined. They nest in hedges or thickly tangled brush, showing a predilection for dense thorn bushes, where they place their piles of weeds, grasses, feathers and rubbish; the four or five eggs are laid in April or May; they are like those of the last, but smaller, aver-

[Grayish white.] aging .96 x .72.

622a. White-rumped Shrike (should be Loggerhead Shrike). *Lanius ludovicianus.*

Range.—North America, west of the Plains, breeding north to Manitoba and the Saskatchewan; winters south to Mexico.

Like the last but paler and the rump white. Their nesting habits and eggs are in every respect like those of the Loggerhead Shrike.

622b. California Shrike (should be Loggerhead Shrike). *Lanius ludovicianus.*

Range.—Pacific coast north to British Columbia.

Similar to the eastern form but with the breast washed with brownish and with indistinct wavy bars. The eggs cannot be distinguished from those of the others.

622c. Island Shrike (should be Loggerhead Shrike). *Lanius ludovicianus.*

Range.—Santa Barbara Islands, California.

Like the last but smaller and darker. Eggs not distinguishable.

Photo from life by I. E. Hess.

LOGGERHEAD SHRIKE AND NEST.

VIREOS. Family VIREONIDAE.

623. Black-whiskered Vireo. *Vireo altiloquus.*

Range.—A Central American species, breeding in Cuba, Bahamas and southern Florida.

Like the Red-eyed Vireo but with a dusky streak on either side of the chin. They build pensile nests of strips of bark and fibres, swung from the forks of branches. The eggs cannot be distinguished from those of the next species, being white, more or less specked about the large end with reddish brown and umber. Size .78 x .55.

[White.]

624. Red-eyed Vireo. *Vireo olivaceus.*

Range.—United States, east of the Rockies, breeding north to Labrador, Manitoba and British Columbia.

This is the most common of the Vireos in the greater part of its range and is a most persistent songster, frequenting groves, open woods or roadsides. Their eyes are brown, scarcely if any more red than those of any other species and I have yet to see one with red eyes outside of mounted museum specimens. They swing their nests from the forks of trees at any elevation from the ground but usually below ten feet, and I have found them where the bottom rested on the ground; they are made of strips of bark, fibre, etc., and often have pieces of string or paper woven into the sides; they are one of the most beautiful of bird homes and are woven so strongly that old nests hang to the branches for several seasons. Their three or four eggs, often accompanied by one of the Cowbirds, are laid in May or June; they are white, sparingly specked with blackish brown. Size .85 x .55.

[White.]

625. Yellow-green Vireo. *Vireo flavoviridis.*

Range.—Southern Texas and southward to South America.

Similar to the Red-eye but greener above and more yellowish on the sides. The nesting habits are the same and the eggs indistinguishable from those of that species.

626. Philadelphia Vireo. *Vireo philadelphicus.*

Range.—Eastern United States breeding from northern New England and Manitoba northward.

This rather uncommon species is much smaller than the Red-eye (length 5 in.) and is yellowish below, and without black edges to the gray crown. It nests like the others of the family, in forks of limbs and the eggs do not differ from those of the Red-eyed Vireo except in size, averaging .70 x .50.

[White.]

627. Warbling Vireo. *Vireo gilvus.*

Range.—North America east to the Plains, breeding north to Labrador.

This Vireo is nearly as abundant as the Red-eye but is not generally as well known, probably because it is usually higher in the trees and more concealed from view. Their nests are like those of the Red-eye, but smaller and usually placed higher in the trees. The birds are even more persistent singers than are the latter but the song is more musical and delivered in a more even manner, as they creep about among the foliage, peering under every leaf for lurking insects. The eggs are pure white, spotted with brown or reddish brown. Size .72 x .52.

[White.]

627a. Western Warbling Vireo (should be Warbling Vireo). *Vireo gilvus.*

Range.—Western United States, breeding from Mexico to British Columbia.

This species is like the last but said to be a trifle smaller and paler colored. Its nesting habits and eggs are precisely like those of the eastern form.

628.　Yellow-throated Vireo.　*Vireo flavifrons.*

Range.—United States east of the Plains, breeding from the the Gulf to Manitoba and New Brunswick.

This handsome bird is wholly unlike any others of the Vireos, having a bright yellow throat and breast; the upper parts are greenish and the wings and tail gray, the latter with two white bars.　They are fairly common breeding birds in northern United States, placing their handsome basket-like structures in forks of branches and at any elevation from the ground; the nests are like those of the preceding Vireos but are frequently adorned on the outside with lichens, thereby adding materially to their natural beauty.　The four or five eggs are pinkish or creamy white, speckled about the large end with reddish brown.　Size .80 x .60.

[Creamy white.]

629.　Solitary Vireo.　*Vireo solitarius.*

Range.—Eastern United States, breeding from southern New England and the northern states north to Hudson Bay; winters in the Gulf States and southward.

A beautiful Vireo with a slaty blue crown and nape, greenish back, white wing bars and underparts, the flanks being washed with greenish yellow; a conspicuous mark is the white eye ring and loral spot.　They build firm, pensile, basket-like nests of strips of birch and grapevine bark, lined with fine grasses and hair, suspended from forks, usually at low elevation and often in pine or fir trees (of some twenty nests that I have found in New England all have been in low branches of conifers).　Their three or four white eggs are specked with reddish brown.　Sixe .80 x .60.

[White.]

629a.　Cassin's Vireo (should be Solitary Vireo).　*Vireo solitarius.*

Range.—United States west of the Rockies; north to British Columbia.

Similar to the last but with the back grayish.　The nests and eggs of this form are in all particulars the same as those of the eastern Solitary Vireo.

629b.　Plumbeous Vireo (should be Solitary Vireo).　*Vireo solitarius.*

Range.—Rocky Mountain region, breeding from Mexico to Dakota and Wyoming.

Like the Blue-headed Vireo[1] but with the yellowish wholly replaced by leaden gray.　The nesting habits of this common variety are the same as those of the last and the eggs are indistinguishable in all respects.

629c.　Mountain Solitary Vireo (should be Solitary Vireo).　*Vireo solitarius.*

Range.—Mountains of Carolina and Georgia; winters in Florida.

Said to be larger and darker than *solitarius* proper.　From all accounts, the habits, nests or eggs of this species differ in no wise from many of those of the northern Solitary Vireo, whose nests show great variations in size and material.

629d.　St. Lucas Solitary Vireo (should be Solitary Vireo).　*Vireo solitarius.*

Range.—Southern Lower California.

Similar to 629a but with the flanks more yellow.　Their nesting habits or eggs will not differ from the others.

630.　Black-capped Vireo.　*Vireo atricapilla.*

Range.—Central Texas north to Kansas; winters in Mexico.

This peculiar Vireo has a black crown and sides of head, broken by a white eye ring and loral stripe; upper parts greenish, below white.　They appear to be fairly common in certain localities of their restricted range, and nest at low elevations in mesquites or oaks, placing the nests in forks the same as other Vireos; they are of the ordinary Vireo architecture, lined with grasses.　The three or four eggs are pure white, unmarked.　Size .70 x .50.　Data.—Comal Co., Texas, May 21, 1888. 4 eggs.　Nest located in a scrub Spanish oak, 5 feet from the ground.　Collector, G. B. Benners (Crandall collection).

[White.]

---

[1] Now Solitary Vireo.

Photo from life by C. A. Reed.

RED-EYED VIREO ON NEST.

631.　White-eyed Vireo.　*Vireo griseus.*

Range.—Eastern United States, breeding from the Gulf to northern United States.

[White.]

This Vireo has white eyes, as implied by its name, is yellowish green on the sides and with two prominent bars. They have no song, like the other Vireos, but a strange medley of notes resembling those of the Chat or Shrike. They nest near the ground in tangled thickets, making large nests for the size of the birds and not always suspended; they are made of weeds, leaves, grass, bark or any trash. Their three or four eggs are laid late in May or early in June; they are white, sparingly speckled with brown; size .75 x .55.

631a.　Key West Vireo (should be White-eyed Vireo).　*Vireo griseus.*

Range.—Southern Florida.

This grayer and paler variety nests in the same manner and the eggs are not distinct from those of the last form.

631b.　Bermuda White-eyed Vireo (should be White-eyed Vireo).　*Vireo griseus.*

Range.—Bermudas.

This variety is said to be slightly smaller and to have no yellow on the sides. Its eggs are probably the same as those of the others.

631c.　Small White-eyed Vireo (should be White-eyed Vireo).　*Vireo griseus.*

Range.—Eastern Mexico north to southern Texas.

Said to be slightly smaller and grayer than the common White-eyed Vireo. Its eggs will not differ.

632.　Hutton's Vireo.　*Vireo huttoni.*

Range.—Resident on the California coast; chiefly in the southern parts.

[White.]

A similar species to *noveboracensis*[1] but with the under parts tinged with yellow. These birds are quite common but shy, nesting at any height from the ground in open woods or groves; the nests are made of grasses and moss and swung from forked limbs; the three or four eggs are pure white, finely specked with reddish brown. Size .70 x .50.

632a.　Stephens' Vireo (should be Hutton's Vireo).　*Vireo huttoni.*

Range.—Northwestern Mexico and the boundary of the United States.

This variety, which is more yellowish than the last, appears to be rather uncommon but as far as I can learn its habits and nesting do not differ from those of the other Vireos; the eggs are white, specked with brown. Size .70 x .50.

632c.　Anthony's Vireo (should be Hutton's Vireo).　*Vireo huttoni.*

Range.—Pacific coast from Oregon (and Cal. in winter) to British Columbia.

The nesting habits and eggs of this darker and smaller variety are the same in all respects as those of the Hutton Vireo.

633.　Bell's Vireo.　*Vireo bellii.*

Range.—Interior of the United States, breeding from Texas to Minnesota and Dakota.

[White.]

The nesting habits of this smaller species are just the same as those of the larger varieties, they suspending their small grass-woven baskets in the forks of bushes or trees and usually at a low elevation. Their nests are handsome and compact little structures, being often made almost wholly of strips of bark lined with very fine grasses. The eggs are white, specked with reddish brown. Size .70 x .50. Data.—Austin, Texas, June 16, 1898. Nest of strips of bark, fibres and grasses, neatly woven and swung from the fork of a low bush, 2 feet from the ground. Collector, Harry Kofahl.

633.1.　Least Vireo (should be Bell's Vireo).　*Vireo bellii.*

Range.—Western Mexico, Arizona and southern California.

This Vireo is slightly smaller and grayer than the last; they are quite common in southern Arizona, nesting the same as 633 at low elevations in bushes or small trees. The eggs cannot be distinguished from those of 633.

---

[1] Now *griseus.*

634. Gray Vireo. *Vireo vicinior.*

Range.—Southwestern United States from western Texas, southern California and Nevada southward.

This species is grayish above and grayish white below, with white eye ring, lores and wing bar. They are not uncommon birds in the Huachuca Mts. of southern Arizona, where they nest in bushes at low elevations, making the semi-pensile structures of woven strips of bark and grasses, lined with fine round grasses attached by the rim to a fork and sometimes stayed on the side by convenient twigs. Eggs white, specked with brown. Size .72 x .53.

[White.]

HONEYCREEPERS. Family COEREBIDAE.

635. Bahama Honeycreeper. *Coereba bahamensis.*

Range.—Bahamas, casually to southern Florida and the Keys.

This peculiar curved-billed species is dark brown above, with the underparts, superciliary line and spot at base of primaries, whitish; the rump and a breast patch are yellow. They nest at low elevations in bushes or trees usually in tangled thickets, making a large dome-shaped nest of grasses, leaves and fibres and, during May or June, lay from three to five pale creamy white eggs, speckled sparingly all over the surface and more abundantly at the large end with reddish brown. Size .65 x .50.

WOOD WARBLERS. Family PARULIDAE.

Warblers as a family may be classed as the most beautiful, interesting and useful birds that we have. With few exceptions, they only return from their winter quarters as the trees shoot forth their leaves or flowers, they feed largely among the foliage upon small, and mostly injurious, insects. They are very active and always flitting from branch to branch, showing their handsome plumage to the best advantage. Their songs are simple but effectively delivered and the nests are of a high order of architecture.

636. Black-and-white Warbler. *Mniotilta varia.*

Range.—North America east of the Plains, breeding from the Gulf States north to the Hudson Bay region; winters from our southern borders to South America.

This striped black and white Warbler is usually seen creeping about tree trunks and branches after the manner of a Nuthatch. They are very active gleaners and of inestimable value to man. They nest on the ground in woods or swamps, making their nest of strips of bark and grass, placed among the leaves usually beside stones, stumps or fallen trees. Their three to five eggs are white, finely specked and wreathed with reddish brown. Size .65 x .50. Data.—Worcester, Mass., June 3, 1889. Nest of strips of bark on the ground in an old decayed stump. Collector, C. A. Reed.

[White.]

637. Prothonotary Warbler. *Protonotaria citrea.*

Range.—South Atlantic and Gulf States, north in the interior to Iowa and Illinois.

This species is often known as the Golden Swamp Warbler because of the rich golden yellow of the head and underparts. They frequent and nest in the vicinity of swamps or ponds, nesting in the cavities of trees or stubs at low elevations, filling the cavity with leaves, moss and grasses, neatly cupped to receive the four to seven eggs, which are creamy or pinkish white, profusely spotted with reddish brown and chestnut. Size .72 x .55. Data.—Quincy, Mo., June 1, 1897. 5 eggs. Nest in hole of a dead stub 6 feet up, in timber some distance from water; made of moss and grasses, lined with hair. Collector, Philo W. Smith, Jr.

[Creamy white.]

638. Swainson's Warbler. *Limnothlypis swainsonii.*

Range.—South Atlantic and Gulf States, north to Virginia and Indiana, and west to eastern Texas; winters in Mexico and the West Indies. [1]

This species is brownish above and white below, with a whitish superciliary stripe. It has been found breeding most numer-

[Bluish white.] ously in thickets and tangled underbush about swamps and pools in any locality. Their nests are either in bushes or attached to upright rushes over water after the manner of the Long-billed Marsh Wren, being made of leaves, moss, rootlets, etc, lined with fine grasses or hair, and deeply cupped for the reception of the three or four unmarked white or bluish white eggs which are laid during May or June. Size .75 x .58. Data.— Near Charlestown, S. C., May 12, 1888. 3 eggs. Nest in canes 4 feet from ground, made of strips of rushes, sweet gum and water oak leaves, lined with pine needles. Collector, Arthur T. Wayne.

639. Worm-eating Warbler. *Helmitheros vermivorus.*

Range.—United States east of the Plains, breeding north to southern New England and Illinois; winters south of our borders.

This bird can be identified in all plumages by the three light buff and two black stripes on the crown and narrower black stripes through the eye. Their habits are similar to those of   [White.] the Ovenbird, they feeding largely upon the ground amid dead leaves. They are quite abundant in most localities in their range, nesting in hollows on the ground in open woods or shrubbery on hill sides; the nest is made of leaves, grasses and rootlets, lined with hair or finer grasses, and is usually placed under the shelter of some small bush. They lay (in May, June or July) three to six eggs, white, marked or blotched either sparingly or heavily with chestnut or lavender. Size .70 x .52.

640. Bachman's Warbler. *Vermivora bachmanii.*

Range.—Southeastern United States, along the Gulf coast to Louisiana and north to Virginia and Missouri. [2]

This species is one of the rarest of the Warblers, but is now much more abundant than twenty years ago, when it had apparently disappeared. They are greenish above, and yellow below, and on the forehead and shoulder, and with black patches on the crown and breast. They have been found breeding in Missouri, nesting on the ground like others of this genus; the eggs are white wreathed about the large end and sparingly specked over the whole surface with reddish brown and chestnut. Size .65 x .50,

641. Blue-winged Warbler. *Vermivora pinus.*

Range.—Eastern United States breeding north to southern New England and in the Mississippi Valley to Minnesota; winters south of our borders.

This common species has the crown and underparts yellow, line through the eye black, and white wing bars and spots on outer

[White.]   tail feathers. They breed most abundantly in the northern half of their United States range, placing their nests on the ground in thickets or on the edge of woods; the nests are made of strips of bark, usually grapevine, and leaves, and are usually high and deeply cupped, they are almost always placed among the upright shoots of young bushes. The eggs are white, finely specked with reddish brown with great variations as to markings. Size .65 x .50. Data.—Old Saybrook, Conn., June 1, 1900. 5 eggs. Nest composed chiefly of dry beech leaves and strips of cedar bark, lined with shreds of bark and fine grass; situated on the ground among a bunch of weeds in the woods. Collector, John N. Clark.

---

[1] Breeds north to Maryland.

[2] Extremely rare.

642. Golden-winged Warbler. *Vermivora chrysoptera.*

Range.—Eastern United States, breeding north to the southern parts of the British Provinces, winters south of the United States.

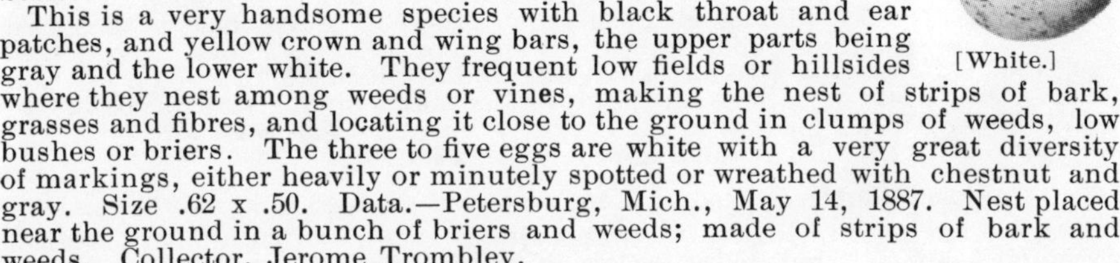

This is a very handsome species with black throat and ear patches, and yellow crown and wing bars, the upper parts being gray and the lower white. They frequent low fields or hillsides [White.] where they nest among weeds or vines, making the nest of strips of bark, grasses and fibres, and locating it close to the ground in clumps of weeds, low bushes or briers. The three to five eggs are white with a very great diversity of markings, either heavily or minutely spotted or wreathed with chestnut and gray. Size .62 x .50. Data.—Petersburg, Mich., May 14, 1887. Nest placed near the ground in a bunch of briers and weeds; made of strips of bark and weeds. Collector, Jerome Trombley.

643. Lucy's Warbler. *Vermivora luciae.*

Range.—Western Mexico, north commonly to Arizona and casually to southern Utah. [1]

This small gray and white Warbler is especially distinguished by a chestnut rump and patch in center of the crown. Besides nesting in forks of low bushes, this species is said to place the domiciles in almost any crevice or nook that suits their fancy, [White.] such as loose bark on tree trunks, holes in trees, or other birds nests. The eggs which are usually laid during May are white, sparingly specked and wreathed with reddish brown. Size .60 x .50.

644. Virginia's Warbler. *Vermivora virginiae.*

Range.—Western Mexico, north to Arizona and New Mexico, and also less commonly to Colorado. [2]

This species is similar to the last but has the rump and a patch on the breast, yellow. They are found quite abundantly in some localities, usually on mountain ranges, nesting in hollows on the ground beside rocks, stumps or in crevices among the rocks; the nests are made of fine strips of bark and grasses, skillfully woven together, and the three to five eggs are pure [White.] white, specked and wreathed with reddish brown. Size .62 x. 50. Data.—Estes Park, Colo., June 20, 1880. Nest sunken in the ground and well hidden under a rocky ledge. Collector, W. G. Smith.

645. Nashville Warbler. *Vermivora ruficapilla.*

Range.—North America east of the Plains, breeding from New York and Illinois north to Hudson Bay and Labrador; winters south of our borders.

This small species is yellow below and greenish above, with an ashy gray head and neck, enclosing a chestnut crown patch. [White.] They breed abundantly in New England, usually on side hills covered with clumps of young pines, the nests being placed flush with the surface of the ground and usually covered with overhanging grass; they are made of grasses and pine needles, the eggs are white, finely specked with bright reddish brown. Size .60 x .45. Data.—Worcester, Mass., June 23, 1895. Nest of pine needles and grasses in hollow in the moss on a scrubby pine hillside. Collector, C. A. Reed.

645a. Calaveras Warbler (should be Nashville Warbler). *Vermivora ruficapilla.*

Range.—Western United States, breeding on ranges from California and Idaho north to British Columbia; winters in Mexico.

A slightly brighter colored form of the last species. Their habits are the same and the eggs cannot be distinguished from those of the eastern bird.

[1] Breeds north to Nevada and Utah.

[2] Breeds north to Idaho and Utah.

646. Orange-crowned Warbler. *Vermivora celata.*

Range.—North America, chiefly in the interior, breeding north of the United States except in the Rockies south to Arizona and New Mexico; winters in the Gulf States and southward.

This plainly clad, greenish colored species has a concealed patch of orange brown on the crown. They have been found [White.] breeding about Hudson Bay and in the Mackenzie River district, placing their nests in hollows on the ground, usually on the side of banks or hills and concealed by small tufts of grass or bushes. The three or four eggs are white, speckled with reddish brown. Size .64 x .45.

646a. Lutescent Warbler (should be Orange-crowned Warbler). *Vermivora celata.*

Range.—Pacific coast, breeding from California to Alaska; winters in Mexico.

Similar to the last but more yellowish below. They make their nests of leaves, rootlets, moss, etc., lined with hair, and placed on the ground, concealed by tufts of grass or by bushes. The eggs are like those of the last. Data.—Danville, Cal. April 21, 1898. Nest on the ground on a side hill; among weeds in the shade of a large oak. Collector, Claude Cummings.

646b. Dusky Warbler (should be Orange-crowned Warbler). *Vermivora celata.*

Range.—Santa Barbara Islands, off California.

Said to be duller colored and darker than the others. The eggs cannot be distinguished.

647. Tennessee Warbler. *Vermivora peregrina.*

Range.—Eastern North America, breeding from the northern tier of states, northward; winters to northern South America.

This species has greenish upper parts, white lower parts and superciliary line, and gray crown and nape. They nest either on the ground or at low elevations in bushes, making the structure [White.] of grasses and fibres, lined with hair; they are found on wild, tangled hillsides and mountain ranges. The eggs are pure white, sparingly specked with reddish brown. Size .62 x .45.

648. Parula Warbler. *Parula americana.*

Range.—Eastern United States, breeding in the southern half.

The upper parts of this handsome species are bluish gray with a greenish patch in the middle of the back; the throat and breast are yellow with a patch of black and chestnut. They are abundant birds in suitable localities, breeding in swamps, especially those [White.] with old or dead trees covered with hanging moss (usnea). The nests may be found at any height from the ground, and are usually made by turning and gathering up the ends of the hanging moss to form a pocket, which is lined with fine grass or hair. The four to six eggs are white or creamy white, wreathed with specks of reddish brown and chestnut. Size .64 x .44.

648a. Northern Parula Warbler (should be Parula Warbler). *Parula americana.*

Range.—Northern half of eastern United States and southern Canada; winters from the Gulf States southward.

The nesting habits of the northern form of the Blue-yellow-backed Warbler[1] are in all respects like those of the last, and like them, where moss grown swamps are not to be found, they have been known to construct nests of moss suspended from branches of trees, or to nest in bunches of dead leaves. Data.—Oxford, Mass., June 7, 1895. Nest in a dead pine swamp; made in end of hanging moss about 6 feet from the ground. Large colony breeding. Collector, C. A. Reed.

---

[1] Now Parula Warbler.

649. Sennett's Warbler (should be Olive-backed Warbler). *Parula pitiayumi.*

Range.—Eastern Mexico, north to the Lower Rio Grande Valley in Texas.
This species is similar to the Parula but is more extensively yellow below, and has black lores and ear coverts. Their habits are the same as those of the last and their nests are generally placed in hanging moss, and are also said to have been found hollowed out in the mistletoe which grows on many trees in southern Texas, New Mexico and Arizona. The eggs cannot be distinguished from those of the last.

650. Cape May Warbler. *Dendroica tigrina.*

Range.—Eastern North America, breeding from northern New England and Manitoba northward; winters south of the United States.

This beautiful Warbler is yellow below and on the rump, streaked on the breast and sides with black; the ear coverts and sometimes the throat are chestnut. They are very local in their distribution both during migrations and in their breeding grounds. They nest in the outer branches of trees, preferably conifers, making the nest of slender twigs, rootlets, grasses, etc.,  [White.] lined with hair; the four or five eggs are white, variously specked with reddish brown and lilac; size .65 x .48.

651. Olive Warbler. *Peucedramus taeniatus.*

Range.—Mountains of New Mexico and Arizona southward.

 This peculiar species may readily be recognized by its saffron or orange-brown colored head and neck, with broad black bar through the eye. They nest at high elevations in coniferous trees on the mountain sides, placing their nests either on the horizontal boughs or forks at the end of them. The nests are very beautiful structures made of moss, lichens, fine rootlets and [Grayish blue.] grasses and setting high on the limb like those of the Blue-gray Gnatcatcher. The eggs are grayish white with a bluish tinge, thickly speckled with blackish; size .64 x .48. Data.—Huachuca Mts., Arizona, June 21, 1901. Nest in a sugar pine near extremity of branch, 25 feet from the ground and 20 feet out from the trunk of the tree; composed of lichens and fine rootlets, lined with plant down. Collector, O. W. Howard.

652. Yellow Warbler. *Dendroica petechia.*

Range.—Breeds in the whole of North America; winters south of our borders.

This well-known and very common species is wholly yellow, being more or less greenish on the back, wings and tail, and the male is streaked on the sides with chestnut. They nest anywhere in trees or bushes, either in woods, pastures, parks or dooryards, and their sprightly song is much in evidence throughout the summer. The nests are usually placed in upright crotches or  forks, and are made of vegetable fibres and fine grasses compactly [Greenish white] woven together and lined with plant down and hair; the eggs, which are laid in May or June, are greenish white, boldly specked in endless patterns with shades of brown and lilac; size .65 x .50.

652a. Sonora Yellow Warbler (should be Yellow Warbler). *Dendroica petechia.*
Range.—Arizona, New Mexico and western Texas, southward.
This form is brighter yellow, especially above, than the last. The nesting habits are the same and the eggs indistinguishable from those of the preceding.

652b. Alaskan Yellow Warbler (should be Yellow Warbler). *Dendroica petechia.*
Range.—Breeds in Alaska and on the coast south to Vancouver; winters south of the United States.
Similar to the common Yellow Warbler but slightly darker above; its eggs and nesting habits are the same.

653. Mangrove Warbler (should be Yellow Warbler). *Dendroica petechia.*

[Greenish white.]

Range.—Southern Lower California and western Mexico and Central America.

This species is very similar to the Yellow Warbler but the entire head and neck of the male are yellowish chestnut. Their nesting habits or eggs do not vary in any essential particular from those of the common Yellowbirds of the United States.

654. Black-throated Blue Warbler. *Dendroica caerulescens.*

Range.—Eastern North America breeding from northern United States northward; winters in the Gulf States and southward.

These black-throated bluish-backed Warblers are abundant in swampy woodland both during migrations and at their breeding grounds; either sex can readily be identified in any plumage, by the presence of a small white spot at the base of the primaries. They nest in underbrush or low bushes only a few inches above the ground, making the nests of bark strips, moss rootlets, etc., lined with fine grasses or hair; the

[Buffy white.]

eggs are pale buffy white more or less dotted with pale brownish; size .65 x .50. Data.—Warren, Pa., June 9, 1891. 3 eggs. Nest one foot from the ground in brush; made of fine pieces of rotten wood, laurel bark and lined with fine grasses. Collector, R. B. Simpson.

654a. Cairns' Warbler (should be Black-throated Blue Warbler). *Dendroica caerulescens.*

Range.—Mountain ranges of North Carolina to Georgia.

A darker form whose habits and eggs are identical with those of the last.

655. Myrtle Warbler. *Dendroica coronata.*

Range.—Eastern North America, breeding from northern United States northward. Winters in the southern half of eastern United States.

This beautiful gray, white and black Warbler can readily be identified by its yellow rump, side patches and crown patch. It is one of our most common species during migrations when it is found west to the Rockies and casually farther. They nest on the lower branches of coniferous trees, making their homes of rootlets, plant fibres and grasses; during June or the latter part

[White.]

of May, three or four eggs are laid; they are white, spotted with several shades of brown and lilac; size .70 x .50. Data.—Lancaster, N. H., June 7, 1888. Nest in a small spruce, about 6 feet up; made of fine twigs, lined with feathers. Collector, F. B. Spaulding.

656. Audubon's Warbler. *Dendroica auduboni.*

Range.—Mountain ranges of western United States from British Columbia to Mexico.

This bird resembles the last in the location of the yellow patches but has a yellow instead of a white throat, and is otherwise differently marked. They are as abundant in suitable localities as are the Myrtle Warblers in the east, nesting on the outer branches of coniferous trees at any height from the ground. The nests are made of bark strips, rootlets, plant fibre, grasses and pine

[Bluish white.]

needles, the three to five eggs are greenish or bluish white marked with brown and lilac; size .68 x .52. The one figured is from a beautiful set of four in Mr. C. W. Crandall's collection, and the ground color is a delicate shade of blue. Data.—Spanaway, Washington, April 23, 1902. Nest on the limb of a large fir in a clump of three in prairie country. Collector, J. H. Bowles.

656a. Black-fronted Warbler (should be Audubon's Warbler). *Dendroica auduboni.*

Range.—Mountains of southern Arizona and Mexico.

Similar to the preceding, but with the forehead and ear coverts black. Their nests and eggs are in no way different from those of Audubon's Warbler.

657.   Magnolia Warbler.
Dendroica magnolia.

Range.—North America east of the Rockies, breeding from northern United States to Hudson Bay region and in the Alleghanies, south to Pennsylvania. Winters south of our borders. This species, which is one of the most beautiful of the Warblers, is entirely yellow below and on the rump, the breast and sides being heavily streaked with

[White.]

black; a large patch on the back and the ear coverts are black. They build in coniferous trees at any elevation from the ground making their nests of rootlets and grass stems, usually lined with hair; the eggs are dull white, specked with pale reddish brown; size .65 x .48. Data.—Worcester, Mass., May 30, 1895. 4 eggs. Nest of fine rootlets and grasses about 30 feet up on the end of a limb of a pine overhanging a brook. Collector, C. A. Reed.

658.   Cerulean Warbler.
Dendroica cerulea.

Range.—United States east of the Plains, breeding chiefly in the northern half of the Mississippi Valley, rare east of the Alleghanies and casual in New Eng-

Photo by J. B. Pardoe.

NEST AND EGGS OF YELLOW WARBLER.

land.   The beautiful Warblers are light blue gray above, streaked with black on back, white below, with a grayish blue band on breast and streaks on the sides; they have two wide white wing bars and spots on the outer tail feathers.   They are found chiefly in the higher trees where they glean on the foliage; they build also usually above twenty feet from the ground in any kind of tree, placing the nests well out on the horizontal limbs, generally in a fork.   The nests are made of fine strips of bark, fibres, rootlets, etc., lined with hair; the eggs are white or pale bluish white, specked with reddish brown; size .62 x .48.   Data.—Fargo, Ontario, June 2, 1901.   Nest in a burr oak, 18 feet from the ground on a horizontal limb.   Collector, H. Gould.

[White.]

NEST AND EGGS OF MAGNOLIA WARBLER.

659. Chestnut-sided Warbler. *Dendroica pensylvanica.*

Range.—United States, east of the Plains, breeding in the Middle States and Illinois, north to Manitoba and New Brunswick. Winters south of our border.

The adults of this handsome species may readily be known by the white underparts and the broad chestnut stripe on the flanks; the crown is yellow. They frequent low brush in open woods or on hillsides and pastures, nesting at low elevations, usually below three feet from the ground, and often concealing their nests beneath the leaves in the tops of low small bushes. The nests are made of grasses, weed stems and some fibres, but they do not

[White.]

have as wooly an appearance as those of the Yellow Warblers which nest in the same localities and similar locations. Their eggs are white or creamy white (never greenish white), specked with brown and gray. Size .65 x .50. Data.— Worcester, Mass., June 6, 1890. Nest in the top of a huckleberry bush, 2 feet from the ground; made of grasses and plant fibres. Bird did not leave nest until touched with the hand. Collector, A. J. White.

660. Bay-breasted Warbler. *Dendroica castanea.*

Range.—North America, east of the Plains, breeding from northern United States north to the Hudson Bay; winters in Central and South America.

This species has the crown, throat and sides a rich chestnut; forehead and face black; underparts white. They nest in coniferous trees in swampy places, making their nests of bark shreds and rootlets and placing them in horizontal forks at elevations of from five to thirty feet from the ground. The three or four eggs are laid late in May or during June; they are white, usually quite heavily spotted and blotched with reddish brown, umber and grayish. Size .70 x .50.

[White.]

661. Black-poll Warbler. *Dendroica striata.*

Range.—North America, east of the Rockies, breeding from northern United States north to Labrador and Alaska; winters in South America.

This black and white Warbler has a solid black cap, and the underparts are white, streaked with black on the sides. In the woods they bear some resemblance to the Black-and- white Warbler, but do not have the creeping habits of that species. During migrations they are found in equal abundance in swamps or orchards. In their breeding range, they nest at low elevations

[White.]

in stunted pines or spruces, making their nests of rootlets and lichens, lined with feathers. The eggs are dull whitish, spotted or blotched with brown and neutral tints. Size .72 x .50. Data.—Grand Manan, N. B., June 12, 1883. Nest and four eggs on branch of a stunted spruce 2 feet from the ground. Collector, S. F. Cheney.

662. Blackburnian Warbler. *Dendroica fusca.*

Range.—North America, east of the Plains, breeding from Massachusetts and Minnesota north to Hudson Bay; south in the Alleghanies to the Carolinas. Winters in Central and South America.

This species is, without exception, the most exquisite of the family; the male can always be known by the bright orange throat, breast and superciliary stripe, the upper parts being largely black. They arrive with us when the apple trees are in bloom and after a week's delay pass on to more northerly dis-

[Greenish white] tricts. Their nests are constructed of rootlets, fine weed stalks and grasses, lined with hair, and are placed on horizontal limbs of coniferous trees. The three or four eggs are greenish white, specked, spotted and blotched with reddish brown and neutral tints. Size .70 x .48. Data.—Lancaster, Mass., June 21, 1901. Nest in a white pine, 38 feet from the ground on a limb 4 feet from the trunk; composed of fine rootlets and hair, resembling the nest of a Chipping Sparrow. Collector, John E. Thayer.

663.   Yellow-throated Warbler.   *Dendroica dominica.*

Range.—South Atlantic and Gulf States, north to Virginia and casually farther; winters in Florida and the West Indies. [1]

This species has gray upper parts with two white wing bars, the throat, breast and superciliary line are yellow, and the lores, cheeks and streaks on the sides are black.   These birds nest abundantly in the South Atlantic States, usually in pines, and either on horizontal limbs or in bunches of Spanish moss.   The [Greenish white.] nests are made of slender pieces of twigs, rootlets and strips of bark, and lined with either hair or feathers, the eggs are three to five in number, pale greenish white, specked about the large end with reddish brown and gray.   Size .70 x .50.   Data.—Raleigh, N. C., May 3, 1890.   Nest 43 feet up on limb of pine; made of grasses and hair.   Collector, C. S. Brimley.

663a.   Sycamore Warbler (should be Yellow-throated Warbler).   *Dendroica dominica.*

Range.—Mississippi Valley, breeding north to Ohio and Illinois, and west to Kansas and Texas; winters south of the United States.

This bird is precisely like the last except that the superciliary stripe is usually white.   Their nesting habits are precisely like those of the last, and the nests are usually on horizontal branches of sycamores; the eggs cannot be distinguished from those of the Yellow-throated Warbler.

664.   Grace's Warbler.   *Dendroica graciae.*

Range.—Southwestern United States, abundant in Arizona and New Mexico.

This Warbler is similar in markings and colors to the Yellow-throated variety except that the cheeks are gray instead of black. The nesting habits of the two species are the same, these birds building high in coniferous trees; the nests are made of rootlets and bark shreds, lined with hair or feathers; the eggs are white, dotted with reddish brown and lilac.   Size .68 x .48.

[White.]

665.   Black-throated Gray Warbler.   *Dendroica nigrescens.*

Range.—United States from the Rockies to the Pacific coast and north to British Columbia; winters south of our borders.

The general color of this species is grayish above and white below as is a superciliary line and stripe down the side of the throat; the crown, cheeks and throat are black and there is a yellow spot in front of the eye.   They inhabit woodland and thickets and are common in such localities from Arizona to Ore- [Greenish white.] gon, nesting usually at low elevations in bushes or shrubs; the nests are made of grasses and fibres, woven together, and lined with hair or fine grasses, resembling, slightly, nests of the Yellow Warbler. The eggs are white or greenish white, specked with reddish brown and umber. Size .65 x .52.   Data.—Waldo, Oregon, June 1, 1901.   Nest 3 feet from the ground in a small oak in valley.   Collector, C. W. Bowles.   (Crandall collection.)

666.   Golden-cheeked Warbler.   *Dendroica chrysoparia.*

Range.—Central and southern Texas south to Central America. [2]

This beautiful and rare species is entirely black above and on the throat, enclosing a large bright yellow patch about the eye and a small one on the crown.   In their very restricted United States range, the birds are met with in cedar timber where they nest at low elevations in the upright forks of young trees of this variety.   Their nests are made of strips of cedar bark, interwoven with plant fibres and spider webs making compact nests, which they line with hair and feathers.   Their three or four eggs are white, dotted and specked with reddish brown and umber.   Size .75 x .55.

[White.]

[1] Breeds regularly north to New Jersey.

[2] Breeds wholly within State of Texas.

Photo by C. A. Reed.

PRAIRIE WARBLER NEST.

667. Black-throated Green Warbler. *Dendroica virens.*

Range.—Eastern United States, breeding from southern New England, South Carolina in the Alleghanies, and Illinois north to Hudson Bay; winters south of the United States.

These common eastern birds are similar to the last but the entire upper parts are olive greenish. They are nearly always found, and always nest, in pines, either groves or hillsides covered with young pines. The nests are usually placed out among the pine needles where they are very difficult to locate, and resemble nests of the Chipping Sparrow. I have found them at heights ranging from six to forty or fifty feet from the ground. The three or four eggs, which they lay in June, are white, wreathed and speckled with brownish and lilac. Size .60 x .50.

[White.]

668. Townsend's Warbler. *Dendroica townsendi.*

Range.—Western United States, from the Rockies to the Pacific and from Alaska southward; winters in Mexico.

This is the common western representative of the last species, and is similar but has black ear patches and the crown is black. They nest in coniferous woods throughout their United States and Canadian range, the nests being placed at any height from the ground and being constructed like those of the Black-throated Green. Their eggs are not distinguishable from those of the latter. Size .60 x .50.

[White.]

669. Hermit Warbler. *Dendroica occidentalis.*

Range.—Western United States and British Columbia chiefly on the higher ranges. Winters south to Central America.

This peculiar species has the entire head bright yellow and the throat black; upperparts grayish, underparts white. They are found nesting in wild rugged country, high up in pine trees, the nests being located among bunches of needles so that they are very difficult to find. The nests are made of rootlets, shreds of bark, pine needles, etc., lined with fine grasses or hair. The three or four eggs are laid during June or the latter part of May; they are white or creamy white, and sometimes with a faint greenish tinge, specked and wreathed with brown and lilac gray. Size .68 x .52.

670. Kirtland's Warbler. *Dendroica kirtlandii.*

Range.—Eastern United States; apt to be found in any of the South Atlantic, Middle or Central States, and in Ontario, Canada. Winters in the Bahamas where by far the greater number of specimens have been found. [1]

This very rare Warbler is bluish gray above, streaked with black, and yellow below with the throat and sides streaked. Until the summer of 1903, the locality where they bred was a mystery. The capture of a specimen, in June, in Oscodo Co., Michigan, led to the search for their nests by N. A. Wood, taxidermist for the Michigan Museum at Ann Arbor. He was successful in his quest and found two nests with young and one egg. The nest in which the egg was found contained two young birds also. It was in a depression in the ground at the foot of a Jack pine tree and only a few feet from a cart road. The nest was made of strips of bark and vegetable fibres, lined with grass and pine needles. The egg is white, sprinkled with brown in a wreath about the large end. Size .72 x .56. It is estimated that there were thirteen pairs of the birds in this colony.

---

[1] Breeds wholly within a small area in the Lower Peninsula of Michigan; winters in Bahamas.

671. Pine Warbler. *Dendroica pinus.*

Range.—Eastern United States, breeding from the Gulf to southern British Provinces; winters in the Gulf States and southward.

This common eastern species is greenish above and dull yellowish below, streaked with dusky on the sides. They are almost exclusively found in pine woods, either light or heavy growth, where they can always be located by their peculiar, musical lisping trill. They nest high in these trees, placing their nests in thick bunches of needles, so that they are very difficult to locate. They nest from March in the south to May

[Dull white.]

in the northern states, laying three or four dull whitish eggs, specked or blotched with shades of brown and lilac; size .68 x .52. Data.—Worcester, Mass., May 28, 1891. Nest 30 feet up in a pine; made of pine needles and rootlets. Collector, C. A. Reed.

672. Palm Warbler. *Dendroica palmarum.*

Range.—Interior of North America, breeding about Hudson Bay and northward and wintering in the lower Mississippi Valley and the West Indies.

This species is brownish yellow above and yellow on the throat and breast, the crown and streaks on the sides are chestnut. They are found during migrations on or near the ground on the edges of woods or thickets and along roadsides; they have a peculiar habit of "teetering" their tail which will readily identify them. They nest on the ground in, or on the edges of swampy places, lining the hollow with grasses and rootlets. In May or June they lay three or four eggs which are creamy white, variously specked with brown and lilac; size .68 x .52.

[Creamy white.]

672a. Yellow Palm Warbler (should be Palm Warbler). *Dendroica palmarum.*

Range.—Eastern North America, breeding from Nova Scotia, northward.

This is the common Yellow Red-poll Warbler of the eastern states, and is very abundant during migrations. Their habits are the same as the very similar, if not identical, interior species. Their nests are also like those of the last, placed on the ground and the eggs are indistinguishable.

673. Prairie Warbler. *Dendroica discolor.*

Range.—Eastern United States, breeding from the Gulf to Massachusetts and Ontario; winters in southern Florida and the West Indies.

A species readily recognized by its bright yellow underparts and the black stripes on the face and sides; several bright chestnut spots are in the middle of the greenish back. These birds will be found on dry scrubby hillsides and valleys, where they nest in low bushes, and the male will be found in the tops of the tallest lookout trees delivering his quaint and very peculiar lisping song. Their nests are handsomely made of vegetable fibres and grasses, closely woven together and lined with hair; this structure is

[Whitish.]

placed in the top of low bushes so that it is well concealed by the upper foliage. Their three to five eggs are whitish, specked and spotted with shades of brown and neutral tints; size .64 x .48. Data.—Worcester, Mass., June 23, 1891. Nest in the top of a young walnut, two feet from ground; made of plant fibres and grasses. Four eggs. Collector, C. A. Reed.

Photo by C. A. Reed.

ARCHED NEST OF OVENBIRD.

Photo by J. B. Canfield.

NEST AND EGGS OF LOUISIANA WATERTHRUSH.

674. Ovenbird. *Seiurus aurocapillus.*

Range.—North America east of the Rockies, breeding from the middle portions of the United States, north to Labrador and Alaska. Winters from the Gulf States southward.

[White.]

This species is fully as often known as the Golden-crowned Thrush, because of its brownish orange crown bordered with black. They are woodland birds exclusively and nest on the ground, arching the top over with rootlets or leaves, the nest proper being made of grasses and leaf skeletons. As they are concealed so effectually, the nests are usually found by flushing the bird. The four to six eggs are white, slightly glossy and spotted, blotched or wreathed with reddish brown and lilac; size .80 x .60. Data.—Old Saybrook, Conn., June 19, 1899. Domed nest with a side entrance on the ground in woods. Collector, J. N. Clark.

675. Northern Waterthrush. *Seiurus noveboracensis.*

Range.—Eastern North America, breeding from northern United States north to Hudson Bay and Newfoundland. Winters from the Gulf to South America.

[White.]

This species is uniform brownish olive above and white below, streaked heavily with blackish; it has a whitish superciliary line. It is known in most of the United States only as a migrant, being found in moist woods or swampy places. They nest in such localities in their breeding range, placing their nests among the cavities of rootlets and stumps, the nest being made of moss, leaves and rootlets. Their eggs are white, profusely specked and blotched with reddish brown and lavender gray. Size .80 x .60. Data.—Listowell, Ontario, May 28, 1895. Nest in a turned-up root over water;made of moss, grass and hair. Collector, Wm. L. Kells. This set of five is in the collection of Mr. C. W. Crandall.

675a. Grinnell's Water-Thrush (should be Northern Waterthrush). *Seiurus noveboracensis.*

Range.—Western North America, migrating between the Mississippi Valley and the Rockies; breeds from northern United States north to Alaska; winters in the south.

This sub-species is said to be very slightly larger, darker on the back, and paler below. Their nesting habits and eggs are identical with those of the last.

676. Louisiana Waterthrush. *Seiurus motacilla.*

Range.—Eastern United States, breeding from the Gulf, north to southern New England, Ontario and Minnesota; winters south of our borders.

[White.]

This species is similar to the last but is larger, grayer and less distinctly streaked on the underparts. They nest in swampy places, concealing their home in nooks among roots of trees or under overhanging banks, the nest being made of leaves, moss, mud, grasses, etc., making a bulky structure. The eggs,which are laid in May and number from four to six, are white, spotted and blotched with chestnut and neutral tints. Size .76 x .62.

677. Kentucky Warbler. *Oporornis formosus.*

Range.—Eastern United States, breeding from the Gulf to New York and Michigan; winters south of the United States to South America.

[White.]

These birds are common in parts of the Mississippi Valley, frequenting underbrush and shrubbery. They nest on the ground in open woods or on shrubby hillsides, making large structures, of leaves and strips of bark, lined with grasses. The eggs are white, sprinkled with dots or spots of reddish brown and gray. Size .70 x .55. Data.— Greene Co., Pa., May 26, 1894. 4 eggs. Nest a mass of leaves, lined with rootlets, placed on the ground at the base of a small elm sprout in underbrush on a hillside. Collector, J. Warren Jacobs.

678.　Connecticut Warbler.　*Oporornis agilis.*

Range.—Eastern United States; known to breed only in Manitoba and Ontario.

These birds have greenish upperparts and sides, yellowish underparts, and an ashy gray head, neck and breast; they have a complete whitish ring about the eye, this distinguishing them in any plumage from the two following species. They are quite abundant in New England in fall migrations being found in swampy thickets. They have been found breeding in Ontario by Wm. L. Kells, the nest being on the ground in the woods among raspberry vines. It was made of leaves, bark fibres, grass, rootlets and hair. The eggs are white, specked with brown and neutral tints. Size .75 x .55.

679.　Mourning Warbler.　*Oporornis philadelphia.*

Range.—Eastern United States, breeding from northern New England, Pennsylvania, (Philadelphia) and Nebraska northward.

Very similar to the last but with no eye ring and a black patch on the breast. The habits and nesting habits of this species are very similar to those of *agilis*, the nest being on or very close to the ground. With the exception of on mountain ranges it breeds chiefly north of our borders. The eggs are white, specked with reddish brown. Size .72 x .55. They cannot be distinguished from those of the last. Data.—Listowell, Ontario, June 5, 1898. Nest in a tuft of swamp grass in low ground; not very neatly made of dry leaves, grasses and hair. Collector, Wm. L. Kells. (Crandall collection.)

[White.]

680.　MacGillivray's Warbler.　*Oporornis tolmiei.*

Range.—Western United States from the Rockies to the Pacific, breeding north to British Columbia; winters in Mexico and Central America.

Similar to the last but with white spots on the upper and lower eyelids, black lores, and the black patch on the breast mixed with gray. These ground inhabiting birds are found in tangled thickets and shrubbery where they nest at low elevations, from one to five feet from the ground. Their nests are made of grasses and shreds of bark, lined with hair and finer grasses, and the eggs are white, specked, spotted and blotched with shades of brown and neutral tints; size .72 x .52. Data.—Sonoma, Cal., May 17, 1897. A small nest, loosely made of grasses (wild oats) lined with finer grasses; placed in blackberry vines 14 inches from the ground in a slough in the valley. Collector, Henry W. Carriger. (Crandall collection.)

[White.]

681.　Maryland Yellow-throat (should be Yellowthroat).　*Geothlypis trichas.*

Range.—Eastern United States; this species has recently been still further sub-divided so that this form is supposed to be restricted to the south Atlantic coast of the United States.

The Maryland Yellow-throat is represented in all parts of the United States by one of its forms. They are ground loving birds, frequenting swamps and thickets where they can be located by their loud, unmistakable song of "Witchery, witchery, witch." They nest on or very near the ground, making their nests of grass, lined with hair; these are either in hollows in the ground at the foot of clumps of grass or weeds, or attached to the weed stalks within a few inches of the ground. They lay from three to five eggs in May or June; these are white, specked about the larger end with reddish brown and umber, and with shell markings of stone gray. Size .70 x .50. All the sub-species of this bird have the same general habits of this one and their eggs cannot be distinguished from examples of the eastern form; the birds, too, owing to the great differences in plumage between individuals from the same place, cannot be distinguished with any degree of satisfaction except by the ones who "discovered" them.

[White.]

681a. Western Yellow-throat (should be Yellowthroat). *Geothlypis trichas.*

Range.—This variety, which is said to be brighter yellow below, is ascribed to the arid regions of western United States; not on the Pacific coast.

681b. Florida Yellow-throat (should be Yellowthroat). *Geothlypis trichas.*

Range.—South Atlantic and Gulf coast to Texas.

681c. Pacific Yellow-throat (should be Yellowthroat). *Geothlypis trichas.*

Range.—Pacific coast from British Columbia southward.

681d. Northern Yellow-throat (should be Yellowthroat). *Geothlypis trichas.*

Range.—Eastern United States from New Jersey to Newfoundland and west to the Mississippi Valley; winters south to the Bahamas and Mexico.

This is the common Yellow-throat which breeds so abundantly in New England and in the Mississippi Valley whose nests so many have tried to find without success, for the birds are very knowing and glide off upon the approach of anyone and are very careful not to betray their treasures; the birds, the nests, and the eggs are like the ones described as 681.

681e. Salt Marsh Yellow-throat (should be Yellowthroat). *Geothlypis trichas.*

Range.—Salt marshes of San Francisco Bay.

682. Belding's Yellowthroat. *Geothlypis beldingi.*

Range.—Lower California.

This peculiar species is like the common Yellow-throat but has the black mask bordered by yellow instead of white, and the black on the forehead extends diagonally across the head from in front of one eye to the rear of the other. Their habits are like those of the other Yellow-throats and the nests are similar to those of the latter, which are frequently placed in cane over the water. Nests found by Mr. Walter E. Bryant were situated in clumps of "cat-tails" between two and three feet above the water; the nests were made of dry strips of these leaves, lined with fibres; the eggs were like those of the common Yellow-throats but larger; size .75 x .56.

682.1. Gray-crowned Yellowthroat. *Chamaethlypis poliocephala.*

Range.—Mexico north to the Lower Rio Grande Valley in Texas.

This Yellow-throat has the crown and ear coverts gray, only the lores and forehead being black. The nests and eggs of these birds, which are fairly common about Brownsville, Texas, do not differ from those of the other Yellow-throats.

683. Yellow-breasted Chat. *Icteria virens.*

Eastern United States, breeding from the Gulf coast north to southern New England and Minnesota.

This strange but handsome species is very common in underbrush and thickets in the south; they are usually shy and endeavor, with success, to keep out of sight, but their strange song and calls, consisting of various whistles and squawks mingled together, are often heard. Their nests are built in bushes or briers at low elevations, being made of grass, strips of bark and leaves, lined with finer grass; their eggs are white, sharply specked and spotted with various shades of brown and lavender; size .90 x .70.

[White.]

683a. Long-tailed Chat (should be Yellow-breasted Chat). *Icteria virens.*

Range.—United States west of the Plains, breeding from Mexico to British Columbia.

This bird is said to be grayer and to have a slightly longer tail than the last. Its nesting habits and eggs are precisely the same.

684.　Hooded Warbler.　*Wilsonia citrina.*

Range.—Eastern United States, breeding north to southern New England and Michigan; winters south of our borders.

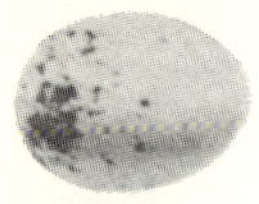

This yellow and greenish species can be identified by its black head, neck and throat, with the large yellow patch about the eye and the forehead. The members of this genus are active flycatchers, darting into the air after passing insects in the manner of the Flycatchers. They frequent tangled thickets where they build their nests within a few inches of the ground, making them of leaves, bark and grass, lined with hair; the four or five eggs are white, specked with reddish brown and neutral tints; size .70 x .50. Data.— Doddridge Co., Mo., May 29, 1897. Nest one foot from the ground in a small bush; made of leaves, strips of bark and fine grasses. Collector, R. B. Simpson.

[White.]

685.　Wilson's Warbler.　*Wilsonia pusilla.*

Range.—Eastern North America, breeding from northern United States northward; south to Central America in winter.

These handsome little black-capped flycatching Warblers are abundant during migrations, especially in the spring, being found on the edges of woods and in orchards. They nest on the ground, usually on the edges of swamps, embedding their nests in the ground under the shelter of low branches or on the edges of banks; the nest is of bark strips, fibres and leaves, and the eggs are white, specked with reddish brown; size .60 x .50.

[White.]

685a.　Pileolated Warbler (should be Wilson's Warbler).　*Wilsonia pusilla.*

Range.—Western United States, breeding in the Rocky Mountain region from Mexico to Alaska; winters south of the United States.

Similar to the eastern form but the yellow underparts and greenish back are brighter. Like the last species, this form nests on the ground or very close to it, in weeds or rank undergrowth, in swamps. Their eggs which are laid in May or June are not distinguishable from those of the last.

685b.　Golden Pileolated Warbler (should be Wilson's Warbler).　*Wilsonia pusilla.*

Range.—Pacific coast of North America, breeding from southern California in mountain ranges north to British Columbia.

686.　Canada Warbler.　*Wilsonia canadensis.*

Range.—Eastern North America, breeding from Mass., New York, and Michigan north to Labrador and Hudson Bay; winters in Central America.

This handsome Warbler is plain gray above and yellow below, with a black stripe down the sides of the neck and across the breast in a broken band. They frequent swamps or open woods with a heavy growth of underbrush, where they build their nests on or very close to the ground. I have always found them in Massachusetts nesting about the roots of laurels, the nests being made of strips of bark, leaves and grass; in June or the latter part of May they lay from three to five white eggs, specked and wreathed with reddish brown and neutral tints; size .68 x .50. Data.—Worcester, Mass., June 10, 1891. Nest on the ground under laurel roots in swampy woods; made entirely of strips of laurel bark lined with fine grass. Collector, C. A. Reed.

[White.]

Photo from life by C. A. Reed.

MALE AMERICAN REDSTART FEEDING YOUNG.

687. American Redstart. *Setophaga ruticilla.*

Range.—North America, chiefly east of the Rockies, breeding in the northern half of the United States and north to Labrador and Alaska; winters south of our borders.

[White.]

The male of this handsome, active and well-known species is black with a white belly, and orange patches on the sides, wings and bases of outer tail feathers. They breed abundantly in swamps, open woods or thickets by the roadside, placing their nests in trees or bushes at elevations of from three to thirty feet above ground and usually in an upright fork. The nests are very compactly made of fibres and grasses, felted together, and lined with hair. Their eggs are white, variously blotched and spotted with brown and gray; size .65 x .50. Data.—Chili, N. Y., June 1, 1894. Nest, a cup-shaped structure of plant fibres lined with fine grasses and hair; 4 feet from the ground in the crotch of a small chestnut. Collector, E. H. Short.

688. Painted Redstart. *Setophaga picta.*

Range.—Southern New Mexico and Arizona, southward.

[White.]

This beautiful Redstart is black with a large white patch on the wings coverts, white outer tail feathers, and with the belly and middle of the breast bright red. These active birds, which have all the habits and mannerisms of the common species, nest on the ground in thickets or shrubbery usually near water, and generally conceal their homes under overhanging stones or stumps; the nests are made of fine shreds of bark and grasses, lined with hair; the eggs are white, dotted with reddish brown; size .65 x .48. Data.—Chiricahua Mts., Arizona, May 31, 1900. Nest of fine bark and grass under a small bush on the ground. Collector, O. W. Howard.

689. Slate-throated Redstart. *Mioborus miniatus.*

Range.—Mexico; admitted to our avifauna on the authority of Giraud as having occurred in Texas. [1]

This species is similar to the last but has a chestnut crown patch, more red on the underparts, and less white on the tail; it is not probable that their nesting habits or eggs differ from those of the last.

690. Red-faced Warbler. *Cardellina rubrifrons.*

Range.—Southern Arizona and New Mexico, southward.

This attractive little Warbler is quite common in mountain ranges of southern Arizona. They nest on the ground on side hills, concealing the slight structure of grasses and rootlets under overhanging shrubs or stones. Their eggs are specked and blotched with light reddish brown and lavender. Size .64 x .48. Data.—Chiricahua Mts., Arizona, May 31, 1902. Nest in a depression under a tuft of grass growing about 8 feet up on the side of a bank. Collector, Virgil W. Owen.

[White.]

691. Red Warbler. *Ergaticus ruber.*

Range.—Highlands of Mexico; north to Texas, according to Giraud. [2]

692. Brasher's Warbler. *Basileuterus culicivorus.*

Range.—Central America and eastern Mexico; Texas (Giraud). [3]

693. Bell's Warbler. *Basileuterus belli.*

Range.—Same as the last; occurring in Texas, according to Giraud. [4]

This yellowish species is similar to the last but has a patch of chestnut on each side of the head. Its eggs have not been described.

[1] Not recorded from North America.
[2] Not recorded from North America.
[3] Not recorded from North America.
[4] Not recorded from North America.

WAGTAILS and PIPITS. Family MOTACILLIDAE.

694. White Wagtail. *Motacilla alba.*

Range.—An Old World species; accidental in Greenland.
These birds are abundant throughout Europe, nesting on
the ground, in stone walls, or in the crevices of old buildings,
etc., the nests being made of grass, rootlets, leaves, etc.; the
eggs are grayish white, finely specked with blackish gray.
Size .75 x .55.

[White.]

695. Swinhoe's Wagtail (should be White Wagtail). *Motacilla alba.*

Range.—Eastern Asia; accidental in Lower California and probably Alaska.

696. Yellow Wagtail. *Motacilla flava.*

Range.—Eastern Asia; abundant on the Bering Sea coast of Alaska in the
summer.

[White.]

These handsome Wagtails are common in summer on the coasts
and islands of Bering Sea, nesting on the ground under tufts of
grass or beside stones, usually in marshy ground. Their eggs
number from four to six and are white, profusely spotted with
various shades of brown and gray. Size .75 x .55. Data.—Kam-
chatka, June 20, 1896. Nest on the ground; made of fine rootlets, grass and moss, lined neatly with animal fur.

697. Water Pipit. *Anthus spinoletta.*

Range.—North America, breeding in the Arctic regions, and in the Rocky
Mountains south to Colorado, winters in southern United States and southward.

The Titlarks[1] are abundant birds in the United States during
migrations, being found in flocks in fields and cultivated
ground. Their nests, which are placed on the ground in
meadows or marshes under tufts of grass, are made of moss
and grasses; the four to six eggs are dark grayish, heavily
spotted and blotched with brown and blackish. Size .75 x .55.

[Gray.]

698. Meadow Pipit. *Anthus pratensis.*

Range.—Whole of Europe; accidental in Greenland.
This species is similar to the American Pipit[1] and like that species nests on
the ground; they are very abundant and are found in meadows, woods or thickets in the vicinity of houses. Their nests are made chiefly of grasses, lined
with hair; the eggs are from four to six in number and are grayish, very heavily spotted and blotched with grayish brown. Size .78 x .58.

699. Red-throated Pipit. *Anthus cervinus.*

Range.—An Old World species; accidental in the Aleutians and Lower California.
The nesting habits of this bird are like those of the others of the genus.

700. Sprague's Pipit. *Anthus spragueii.*

Range.—Interior of North America, breeding from Wyoming north to Saskatchewan. Winters in the plains of Mexico.

[Grayish white.]

These birds are common on the prairies and breed abundantly on the plains of the interior of northern United States
and Manitoba. They have a flight song which is said to be
fully equal to that of the famous European Skylark. They
nest on the ground under tufts of grass or up-turned sods,
lining the hollow with fine grasses; their three or four eggs
are grayish white, finely specked with grayish black or purplish. Size .85 x .60. Data.—Crescent Lake, Canada. Nest of fine dried
grasses, built in the ground at the side of a sod. Collector, Walter Raine.

---

[1] Now Water Pipit.

DIPPERS. Family CINCLIDAE.

701. American Dipper. *Cinclus mexicanus.*

Range.—Mountains of western North America from Alaska to Central America.

These short-tailed, grayish colored birds are among the strangest of feathered creatures; they frequent the sides of mountain streams where they feed upon aquatic insects and small fish. Although they do not have webbed feet, they swim on or under water with the greatest of ease and rapidity, using their wings as paddles. They have a thrush-like bill and the teetering habits of the Sandpiper, and they are said to be one of the sweetest of songsters. They nest among the rocks along the banks of swiftly flowing streams, and sometimes beneath falls; the nests are large round structures of green moss, lined with fine grass and with the entrance on the side. The eggs are pure white, four or five in number, and laid during May or June. Size 1.00 x .70.

WRENS; MIMIC THRUSHES. Families TROGLODYTIDAE and MIMIDAE.

702. Sage Thrasher. *Oreoscoptes montanus.*

Range.—Plains and valleys of western United States, east of the Sierra Nevadas, from Montana to Mexico.

This species is abundant in the sage regions of the west, nesting on the ground or at low elevations in sage or other bushes. Their nests are made of twigs, rootlets and bark strips, lined with fine rootlets; the three or four eggs are a handsome greenish blue, brightly spotted with reddish brown and gray. Size .95 x .70. Data.—Salt Lake Co., Utah, May 11, 1900. Nest placed in a sage bush; made of twigs of the same and lined with bark strips. Collector, W. H. Parker. (Crandall collection.)

[Greenish blue.]

703. Mockingbird. *Mimus polyglottos.*

Range.—South Atlantic and Gulf States, north to New Jersey and Illinois.

These noted birds are very common in the south where they are found, and nest about houses in open woods, fields, and along roadways; their nests are rude, bulky structures of twigs, grasses, leaves, etc., placed in trees or bushes at low elevations; the three to five eggs are usually dull greenish blue, boldly spotted with brownish. Size .95 x .72.

[Dull greenish blue.]

703a. Western Mockingbird (should be Mockingbird). *Mimus polyglottos.*

Range.—Southwestern United States from Texas to California, and southward.

This subspecies is as common in its range, and its habits are the same as those of the eastern bird. The nests and eggs are identical with those of the last, and like that variety they frequently nest in odd places as do all common birds when they become familiar with civilization.

704. Catbird. *Dumetella carolinensis.*

Range.—North America, breeding from the Gulf States to the Saskatchewan; rare on the Pacific coast; winters in the Gulf States and southward.

This well-known mimic is abundant in the temperate portions of its range, frequenting open woods, swamps, hillsides and hedges. Their nests are usually low down in bushes or trees, and are constructed similarly to those of the Mockingbird, of twigs and rootlets; a tangled mass of vines and briers is a favorite place for them to locate their home. Their eggs are laid in the latter part of May or during June, and are from three to five in number and a bright bluish green in color, unmarked. Size .95 x .70.

[Bluish green.]

705. Brown Thrasher. *Toxostoma rufum.*

Range.—Eastern North America, breeding from the Gulf States north to Canada. Winters in the Gulf States and southward.

This large, handsome songster is found breeding in just such localities as are preferred by the Catbird and the two are often found nesting in the same hedge or thicket. The nests, too, are similar but that of the Thrasher is usually more bulky; besides building in bushes, they frequently nest on the ground, lining the hollow under some bush with fine rootlets. Their three to five eggs are laid during May or June; they are whitish or pale greenish white, profusely dotted with reddish brown. Size 1 05 x .80.

[Greenish white.]

706. Long-billed Thrasher. *Toxostoma longirostre.*

Range.—Southern Texas ana northeastern Mexico.

[Greenish white.]

Very similar to the last but darker above and with the spots on the breast blacker and more distinct. This species which is very abundant in the Lower Rio Grande Valley nests the same as the last species in thick hedges and the eggs are very similar to those of the Brown Thrasher, but in a large series, average more sparingly marked over the whole surface and with a more definite wreath about the large end. Data.—Corpus Christi, Texas, May 12, 1899. Nest of twigs and vines in a bush in thicket. Six feet from the ground. Collector, F. B. Armstrong.

707. Curve-billed Thrasher. *Toxostoma curvirostre.*

Range.—Mexico, north to southern Texas and eastern New Mexico.

This species is a uniform ashy gray above and soiled white below; the bill is stout and decurved. These birds are as numerous in the Lower Rio Grande Valley as are the Sennett Thrashers,[1] frequenting thickets where they breed in scrubby bushes and cacti. Their nests are rather larger and more deeply cupped than are those of the last species and the eggs can easily be distinguished. They have a ground color of light bluish green, minutely dotted evenly all over the surface with reddish brown.

[Bluish green.]

Size 1.10 x .80. Data.—Brownsville, Texas, April 6, 1900. 5 eggs. Nest of sticks and thorns on a cactus in a thicket; 6 feet from. the ground. Collector, Frank B. Armstrong.

707a. Palmer's Thrasher (should be Curve-billed Thrasher). *Toxostoma curvirostre.*

Range.—Very abundant in southern Arizona and southward into Mexico.

The nesting habits and eggs of these birds are exactly like those of the last; they show a preference for placing their nests of sticks and thorny twigs upon cacti at elevations below five feet from the ground. Like the last, they generally raise two broods a season.

708. Bendire's Thrasher. *Toxostoma bendirei.*

Range.—Southern Arizona and Mexico; north locally to southern Colorado.

This species is not as abundant in the deserts of southern Arizona as are the last species with which they associate. They nest at low elevations in mesquites or cacti, laying their first sets in March and early April and usually raising two broods a season; their three or four eggs are dull whitish, spotted and blotched with brownish drab and lilac gray. Size 1.00 x .72. Data.—Tucson, Arizona, April 15, 1896. Nest 3 feet up in a cholla cactus; made of large sticks lined with fine grasses. Collector, O. W. Howard.

[Grayish white.]

---

[1] Now Long-billed Thrasher.

709. Gray Thrasher.   *Toxostoma cinereum.*

[Pale greenish white.]

Range.—Southern Lower California.

This species is similar to *curvirostre* but the under-parts are spotted with dusky. Their habits and nests are similar to those of the other Thrashers and the three or four eggs are pale greenish white, spotted with reddish brown. Size 1.08 x .75. Data.—Santa Anita, June 3, 1896. 3 eggs. Nest in a cactus. Collector, Coolidge & Miller.

709a. Mearns' Thrasher (should be Gray Thrasher).   *Toxostoma cinereum.*

Range.—Northern Lower California.

This species is described as darker than the last and with larger, blacker spots on the breast and underparts.

710. California Thrasher.   *Toxostoma redivivum.*

Range.—Southern half of California, west of the Sierra Nevadas.

[Bluish green.]

This species is more brownish than the other curve-billed species and has a much longer and more curved bill. They are common in the underbrush of hillsides and ravines, where they locate their nests at low elevations. Their nests are made of sticks and grass, lined with rootlets, and the three or four eggs are bluish green with spots of russet brown. Size 1.12 x .82. Data.—San Diego, Cal., Feb. 7, 1897. Nest of sticks and rootlets in a grease-wood bush 4 feet from the ground. Collector, Chas. W. Brown.

710a. Pasadena Thrasher (should be California Thrasher).   *Toxostoma redivivum.*

Range.—Southern California.

A paler form of the last, having the same habits, and with the nests and eggs indistinguishable.

711. Le Conte's Thrasher.   *Toxostoma lecontei.*

Range.—Desert regions of southwestern United States, chiefly in the valleys of the Gila and Colorado Rivers.

[Pale greenish blue.]

This species is much paler than the last and has a shorter bill. It is fairly common but locally distributed in its range and nests at low elevations in bushes or cacti. The three or four eggs are pale greenish blue, sparingly dotted with reddish brown. Size 1.10 x .75. Data.—Phoenix, Arizona, April 2, 1897. 3 eggs. Large nest of dry twigs, rootlets, etc., lined with bits of rabbit hair and feathers; 4 feet from the ground in a small shrub. Collector, Geo. F. Breninger.

711a. Desert Thrasher (should be Le Conte's Thrasher).   *Toxostoma lecontei.*

Range.—Northern Lower California.

This form of the last is said to differ in being darker above. It is a very locally confined race, chiefly about Rosalia Bay, Lower California. Its eggs will not be distinctive.

712. Crissal Thrasher.   *Toxostoma dorsale.*

Range.—Southwestern United States from western Texas to eastern California; north to southern Utah and Nevada.

[Pale greenish blue.]

This species may be known from any other of the curve-billed Thrashers by its grayish underparts and bright chestnut under tail coverts. These sweet songsters are abundant in suitable localities, nesting at low elevations in chaparral. Their nests are large, and bulkily made of sticks and rootlets; the eggs range from two to four in number and are pale greenish blue, unmarked. Size 1.10 x .75. Data.—Phoenix, Arizona, April 15, 1897. Nest of thorns lined with hair, in a chaparral bush 2 feet from the ground. Collector, Will M. Fickas.

713. Cactus Wren. *Campylorhynchus brunneicapillus.*

Range.—Southwestern United States from Texas to eastern California; north to southern Nevada and Utah.

[Creamy white.]

This species is the largest of the Wrens, being 8.5 inches in length. They are very common in cactus and chaparral districts, where they nest at low elevations in bushes or cacti, making large purse-shaped structures of grasses and thorny twigs, lined with feathers and with a small entrance at one end. They raise two or three broods a year, the first set of eggs being laid early in April; the eggs are creamy white, dotted, so thickly as to obscure the ground color, with pale reddish brown. Size .95 x .65. Data.—Placentia, Cal., April 15, 1901. Nest in cactus about 6 feet from the ground; made of grasses and lined with feathers and rabbit fur; nest 8 inches in diameter, 18 inches long. Collector, Hartwell Bradford.

713a. Bryant's Cactus Wren (should be Cactus Wren). *Campylorhynchus brunneicapillus.*

Range.—Northern Lower California and coast of southern California.

The nesting habits of this variety differ in no respect from those of the last.

713b. St. Lucas Cactus Wren (should be Cactus Wren). *Campylorhynchus brunneicapillus.*

Range.—Southern Lower California.

Eggs indistinguishable from those of the last.

713c. Desert Cactus Wren (should be Cactus Wren). *Campylorhynchus brunneicapillus.*

Range.—Desert regions of southwestern United States, taking the place of 713 in New Mexico and Arizona, and confining that variety to the Lower Rio Grande Valley in Texas.

715. Rock Wren. *Salpinctes obsoletus.*

Range.—United States, west of the Plains, breeding north to British Columbia, and south to Mexico; winters in southwestern United States and southward.

[White.]

This species appears to be quite abundant on rocky hillsides throughout its range; like most of the Wrens they draw attention to themselves by their loud and varied song. They nest in crevices or beneath overhanging rocks, making the nest out of any trash that may be handy, such as weeds, grass, wool, bark, rootlets, etc.; their eggs range from four to eight in number and are pure white, finely specked with reddish brown. Size .72 x .50.

716. Guadalupe Rock Wren (should be Rock Wren). *Salpinctes obsoletus*

Range.—Guadalupe Island, Lower California.

A similar but darker and browner species than the Rock Wren. It breeds in abundance throughout the island from which it takes its name, placing its nests in crevices among the boulders or cavities of fallen tree trunks and, as is often done by the last species, lining the pathway to the nest with small pebbles. The eggs, which are laid from January to April, resemble, in all respects, those of the common Rock Wren.

717. Cañon Wren. *Catherpes mexicanus.*

Range.—Northeastern Mexico and the Lower Rio Grande Valley in Texas.

The habits of the White-throated Wren[1] are the same as those of the Cañon Wren, which variety is more common and better known; the eggs of this species are not distinguishable from those of the next.

717a. Cañon Wren. *Catherpes mexicanus.*

Range.—Rocky Mountain region and west to the Sierra Nevadas; north to Wyoming and Idaho and south to New Mexico and Arizona.

The Cañon Wrens are uniform rusty brown all over except the large sharply defined white throat patch; the underparts, wings and tail are barred with black, and the back is specked with white. Their name is well chosen for they are found abundantly in rocky canyons, ravines, and side hills. They nest in crevices or caves among the rocks, placing their nests in small niches; they are made of twigs, leaves, grasses and feathers, and the three to six eggs, which are laid from April to June according to locality, are white, sprinkled and blotched with reddish brown and lilac. Size .72 x .52.

[1] Now Cañon Wren.

717b.   Dotted Cañon Wren (should be Cañon Wren).   *Catherpes mexicanus.*

Range.—Pacific coast from Oregon to Lower California.

The habits and eggs of this coast form of the White-throated Wren[1] do not vary in any particular from those of the preceding variety.

718.   Carolina Wren.   *Thryothorus ludovicianus.*

Range.—Eastern United States, breeding from the Gulf to southern New England and Illinois; resident in the greater part of its range.

[White.]

These loud-voiced songsters are well known in the south where they are very abundant, being found along banks of streams, in thickets, along walls, or about brush heaps. They nest in almost any suitable nook or corner, in hollow trees or stumps, bird boxes, about buildings, and in brush or bushes. When in exposed positions, the nest, which is made of all sorts of trash, is arched over; the eggs, which are laid from March to June, and frequently later, as several broods are sometimes reared in a season, are white, profusely specked with light reddish brown and purplish. Size .74 x .60

718a.   Florida Wren (should be Carolina Wren).   *Thryothorus ludovicianus.*

Range.—Southern Florida.

A similar bird to the last but darker above and brighter below. Its eggs are not distinguishable from those of the last.

718b.   Lomita Wren (should be Carolina Wren).   *Thryothorus ludovicianus.*

Range.—Southern Texas.

This sub-species is abundant along the Lower Rio Grande in southern Texas, where its habits are the same as those of the others and the eggs are not distinctive.

719.   Bewick's Wren.   *Thryomanes bewickii.*

Range.—South Atlantic and Gulf States, and the Mississippi Valley north to Minnesota and locally to the Middle States in the east.

[White.]

This species is not common on the Atlantic coast but in the interior it is the most abundant of the Wrens, nesting in holes in trees, stumps, fences, bird boxes, tin cans, etc., filling the cavities with grass and rootlets. Their eggs are laid in the latter part of April or May; they are white, specked and usually wreathed about the large end with reddish brown and purplish. Size .65 x .50.

719a.   Vigors' Wren (should be Bewick's Wren).   *Thryomanes bewickii.*

Range.—Pacific coast of California.

This bird similar to the last has the same general habits and the eggs are not in any way different from those of Bewick's Wren.

719b.   Baird's Wren (should be Bewick's Wren).   *Thryomanes bewickii.*

Range.—Southwestern United States, from western Texas to eastern California and north to Colorado and Nevada.

Like the two preceding Wrens, this one nests in natural or artificial cavities, and the four to seven eggs that they lay are precisely like, in every respect, those of the others.

719c.   Texas Bewick's Wren (should be Bewick's Wren).   *Thryomanes bewickii.*

Range.—Texas, north in summer to western Kansas.

A very abundant bird in Texas. Nesting habits not unusual nor eggs distinctive.

719d.   Southwest Bewick's Wren (should be Bewick's Wren).   *Thryomanes bewickii.*

Range.—Coast of southern California.

---

[1] Now Cañon Wren.

From "Nature and the Camera".   Photo by A. R. Dugmore.

NEST OF LONG-BILLED MARSH WREN.

719e.   Northwest Bewick's Wren (should be Bewick's Wren).   *Thryomanes bewickii.*

Range.—Pacific coast from Oregon to British Columbia.
These last two sub-species have recently been separated from Vigors' Wren, but their habits and eggs remain the same as those of that variety.

719.1.   San Clemente Wren (should be Bewick's Wren).   *Thryomanes bewickii.*

Range.—San Clemente Island, California.
This species is similar to Vigors' Wren but is grayer and paler above. It is not peculiar in its nesting habits and the eggs are like those of 719.

720.   Guadalupe Wren (should be Bewick's Wren).   *Thryomanes bewickii.*

Range.—Guadalupe Island. [1]
A very similar species to the Vigors Wren; nesting habits and the eggs are not apt to differ in any respect.

721.   House Wren.   *Troglodytes aedon.*

Range.—North America east of the Mississippi, breeding from the Gulf north to Manitoba and Ontario; winters in the southern half of the United States.
This familiar and noisy little Wren is the most abundant and widely distributed of the Wrens; they are met with on the edges
[Pinkish white.] of woods, swamps, fields, pastures, orchards and very frequently build about houses, in bird houses or any nook that may suit them; they fill the cavity of the place they may select with twigs, grass, feathers, plant down, etc., and lay from five to nine eggs in a set and frequently three sets a year. The eggs are pinkish white, very profusely and minutely dotted with pale reddish brown so as to make the egg appear to be a nearly uniform salmon color and with a wreath of darker spots about the large end. Size .65 x .52. Data.—Gretna, N. Y., May 29, 1896. Nest three foot from the ground in cavity of an apple tree; made of twigs and grass, and lined with hair and feathers. Collector, L. S. Horton.

721a.   Parkman's Wren (should be House Wren).   *Troglodytes aedon.*

Range.—Pacific coast from British Columbia southward.
The habits and eggs of this variety are the same in every particular as those of the eastern House Wren.

721b.   Western House Wren (should be House Wren).   *Troglodytes aedon.*

Range.—United States, from the Mississippi Valley to eastern California.
This variety is grayer above and below than the eastern form, but its habits and eggs do not differ in any respect.

722.   Winter Wren.   *Troglodytes troglodytes.*

Range.—Eastern North America, breeding from northern United States northward, and south in the Alleghanies to North Carolina; winters in the United States.

These are the smallest of the Wrens, being but four inches in length; they have a very short tail which, like those of the others, is carried erect over the back during excitement or anger. They are very sly birds and creep about through stone walls and under brush like so many mice; they have a sweet song but not as loud as that of the House Wren. Their nests are placed in crevices of
[White.] stumps, walls, old buildings or in brush heaps, being made of twigs and leaves, lined with feathers. Their eggs, which are laid during May or June, are pure white, finely and sparingly dotted with reddish brown; size .60 x .48.

---

[1] Extinct.

722a. Western Winter Wren (should be Winter Wren). *Troglodytes troglodytes.*

Range.—Western North America from the Rockies to the coast, north to Alaska.

This species is much browner both above and below and is more heavily barred than the last; its habits and eggs are like those of 722.

722b. Kadiak Winter Wren (should be Winter Wren). *Troglodytes troglodytes*

Range.—Kadiak Island, Alaska.

Said to be slightly larger and paler than 722a.

723. Alaskan Wren (should be Winter Wren). *Troglodytes troglodytes.*

Range.—Aleutian and Pribilof Islands, Alaska.

Larger and paler than the Western Winter Wren. The habits of this species are similar to those of the eastern Winter Wren; they nest between boulders and in crevices of rocks or stumps, making their nests of moss and rootlets, lined with feathers. The eggs are like those of the Winter Wren but slightly larger; size .65 x .51.

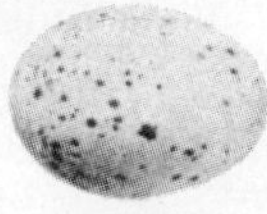
[White.]

724. Short-billed Marsh Wren. *Cistothorus platensis.*

[White.]

Range.—Eastern United States, breeding from the Gulf to Manitoba and Maine.

This species does not appear to be as common anywhere as is the Long-billed variety, whose habits and nests are similar. They nest in or on the borders of marshes, the nests being globular structures of grasses, lined with hair, and with the entrance on the side; they are attached above the ground or water in marsh grass or reeds. Their eggs, which number from six to eight, are pure white; size .64 x .48.

725. Long-billed Marsh Wren. *Telmatodytes palustris.*

Range.—United States east of the Rockies, breeding from the Gulf north to Manitoba and New England; winters in southern United States.

These birds are very abundant in suitable localities throughout their range, breeding in colonies in large marshes and in smaller numbers in small marshy places. Their nests are similar to those of the last, being globular and attached to cattails or reeds; the entrance is a small round hole in the side of the rush-woven structures and the interior is neatly finished with fine grass and hair. They lay from five to eight eggs of a pale chocolate color, dotted and spotted with darker shades of the same; size .64 x .45.

[Pale brown.]

Data.—Delray, Mich., May 27, 1900. Six eggs. Nest a ball of woven flags and grasses, lined with cattail down, and attached to rushes in salt marsh over two feet of water. Collector, Geo. W. Morse.

725a. Tule Wren (should be Long-billed Marsh Wren). *Telmatodytes palustris.*

Range.—Western United States on the Pacific coast; north to British Columbia.

The nesting habits and eggs of these birds are in all respects like those of the last.

725b. Worthington's Marsh Wren (should be Long-billed Marsh Wren). *Telmatodytes palustris.*

Range.—Coast of South Carolina and Georgia.

The habits and eggs of this paler form are identical with those of 725.

725c. Interior Tule Wren (should be Long-billed Marsh Wren). *Telmatodytes palustris.*

Range.—United States west of the Rockies, except the Pacific coast; north to British Columbia. This variety is like the Tule Wren but slightly paler; its nesting habits and eggs are the same..

725.1. Marian's Marsh Wren (should be Long-billed Marsh Wren). *Telmatodytes palustris.*

Range.—West coast of Florida.

This species is similar to the Long-billed variety but is darker and more barred above and below. Its nests and eggs will not be found to differ materially from those of the others of this genus.

CREEPERS. Family CERTHIIDAE.

726. Brown creeper. *Certhia familiaris.*

Range.—Eastern North America, breeding from the northern tier of states northward; winters in the United States.

[White.]

These peculiar, weak-voiced creepers are common in northern United States during the winter, when they may be seen slowly toiling up the tree trunks, searching the crannies of the bark for larvae. They make their nests behind loose hanging bark on old tree stubs, usually at low elevations, building them of twig, bark, moss, etc., held together with cobwebs. The eggs, which are laid in May or June, are pure white, specked and spotted with reddish brown; they average in size .58 x .48. The nests are most often found under the loosened bark on coniferous trees.

726a. Mexican Creeper (should be Brown Creeper). *Certhia familiaris.*

Range.—Western Mexico north to southern Arizona.

The nesting habits of this brighter colored form are the same as those of the others.

726b. Rocky Mountain Creeper (should be Brown Creeper). *Certhia familiaris.*

Range.—Rocky Mountains, breeding from New Mexico to Alaska.

The eggs of this grayer variety cannot be distinguished from those of the eastern birds and the nests are in similar situations.

726c. California Creeper (should be Brown Creeper). *Certhia familiaris.*

Range.—Pacific coast from southern California north to Alaska.

An abundant species, especially on mountain ranges, breeding behind the bark chiefly on pine trees. The eggs are not different from those of the others.

726d. Sierra Creeper (should be Brown Creeper). *Certhia familiaris.*

Range.—Sierra Nevada Mountains in California and the Cascade Range in Oregon.

Very similar to the last and with the same habits; eggs indistinguishable.

NUTHATCHES, TITMICE and WRENTITS. Families SITTIDAE, PARIDAE and CHAMAEIDAE.

727. White-breasted Nuthatch. *Sitta carolinensis.*

Range.—United States east of the Rockies, breeding from the Gulf to southern Canada; resident throughout its range.

These birds are creepers, but unlike the last species, these run about on the trunks, either up or down; their tails are not pointed and stiffened like those of the Brown creepers, and their plumage is gray and black above with a black crown, and white below. They nest in holes in trees, usually deep in the woods and at any elevation from the ground; they nearly always use deserted [White.]   Woodpeckers' holes but are said at times to excavate their own, with great labor as their bills are little adapted for that work. They line the cavities with bark strips and hair or feathers, and, during April or May, lay from four to nine white eggs, profusely specked with reddish brown and lilac. Size .80 x .60. Data.—Lancaster, Mass., May 16, 1902. Nest in hole in an oak tree, 45 feet above ground; made of fine strips of bark fibre and hair. Collector, John E. Thayer.

727a.   Slender-billed Nuthatch (should be White-breasted Nuthatch).   *Sitta carolinensis.*
Range.—North America, west of the Rockies and from Mexico to British Columbia.
This species is as abundant in the west as the last is in the east, and nests in like situations.   The eggs cannot be distinguished from those of the eastern birds.

727b.   Florida White-breasted Nuthatch (should be White-breasted Nuthatch).   *Sitta carolinensis.*
Range.—Florida and the South Atlantic coast to South Carolina.
The habits and eggs of these birds are like those of the northern ones.

727c.   Rocky Mountain Nuthatch (should be White-breasted Nuthatch).   *Sitta carolinensis.*
Range.—Rocky Mountains from Mexico north to British Columbia.
Their nesting habits or eggs are not distinctive in any respect.

727d.   St. Lucas Nuthatch (should be White-breasted Nuthatch).   *Sitta carolinensis.*
Range.   Mountain ranges of Lower California.
Said to be like 727 a but with the wings and tail slightly shorter.

728.   Red-breasted Nuthatch.   *Sitta canadensis.*
Range.—North America, breeding from the northern tier of states northward, and farther south in mountain ranges; winters south to southern United States.

[White.]

This species is smaller than the last and has reddish brown underparts and a black stripe through the eye.   The breeding habits are the same as those of the White-bellied variety, but these birds almost invariably coat the tree below the opening with pitch, for what purpose is unknown.   They lay from four to six white eggs, numerously spotted with reddish brown; size. 60 x. 50.   Data.—Upton, Maine, June 21, 1898.   Nest in hole of dead birch stub, 20 feet from the ground; made of strips of bark and a few feathers. 5 eggs.   Collector, Col. John E. Thayer.

729.   Brown-headed Nuthatch.   *Sitta pusilla.*
Range.—South Atlantic and Gulf States.

[White.]

This species has a yellowish brown crown and whitish underparts. Their habits are like those of the other Nuthatches, they nesting in cavities at varying heights, from two to fifty feet from the ground.   That they sometimes depart from the usual custom is evidenced by the data accompanying this egg.   They lay from four to seven eggs, white with profuse markings of reddish brown; size .60 x .48.   Data.—St. Mary's, Ga.   Nest situated under the bark of an old dead pine stump, 4 feet from the ground; made of fine strips of bark.   Collector, Outram Bangs.

730.   Pigmy Nuthatch.   *Sitta pygmaea.*
Range.—North America west of the Rockies, breeding from Mexico north to British Columbia.   Resident throughout its range.

[White.]

This species has an olive gray crown bordered by dusky, the back is ashy blue and the underparts soiled white or rusty.   They are common in mountains of western United States, nesting in holes in trees the same as the other species of Nuthatches.   They lay from five to nine eggs which are white, speckled thickly with reddish brown; size .60 x .50.   Data.—Huachucha Mts., Arizona, May 25, 1901.   Nest in cavity (10 inches deep) in dead pine stump about 15 feet from the ground; composed of a mass of vegetable down; altitude 9000 feet.   Collector, O. W. Howard.

730a.   White-naped Nuthatch (should be Pigmy Nuthatch).   *Sitta pygmaea.*
Range.—Lower California.
Like the last but grayer above and white below.   Its habits and eggs are the same as those of the Pigmy Nuthatch.

731.   Tufted Titmouse.   *Parus bicolor.*

Range.—Eastern United States, resident and breeding from the Gulf north to New York and Illinois.[1]

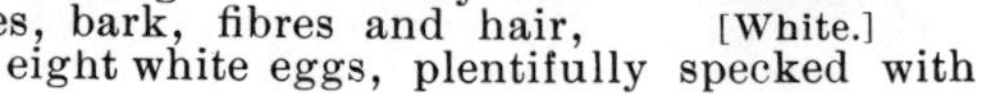

This species has a grayish crest and upper parts, and is white beneath with brownish sides and black forehead.   These common and noisy birds nest in natural cavities in trees or in holes deserted by Woodpeckers; they may be found at any elevation, from two to thirty feet from the ground.   They line the bottom of the cavity with leaves, bark, fibres and hair,   [White.] and during April or May lay five to eight white eggs, plentifully specked with reddish brown.   Size .74 x.54.

731a.   Texan Tufted Titmouse.   *Parus bicolor texensis.*

Range.—Southeastern Texas. [2]

Similar to the last but with the forehead brown instead of black.   The habits and eggs of these birds do not differ from those of the eastern form.

732.   Black-crested Titmouse.   *Parus atricristatus.*

Range.—Lower Rio Grande Valley in Texas and southward.

This Titmouse has a black crest and the forehead is white; otherwise similar to the preceding.   Like the last, these birds nest in deserted Woodpeckers' holes and natural cavities in trees, either in open woods or in the vicinity of habitations.   Their [White.]   eggs are sparsely spotted with reddish brown, and not usually distinguishable from those of the Tufted Titmouse.   Size .70 x .54.   Data.— Brownsville, Texas, May 11, 1892. Nest of moss, hair, down and wool in cavity in tree in open woods near town; 4 feet from the ground.   Collector, Frank B. Armstrong.

733.   Plain Titmouse.   *Parus inornatus.*

Range.—California and Oregon west of the Sierra Nevadas.

This common, slightly crested Titmouse is grayish brown above and grayish white below.   They nest anywhere in cavities that meet with their approval, about old buildings, in fence posts, etc., as well as holes in trees.   Their eggs range from five to eight in number and are white, usually spotted with pale brownish.   Size .72 x .52.   Data.—Tulare Co., California, April   [White.] 3, 1895.   Nest in an oak tree, 32 feet from the ground, in a natural cavity of a horizontal limb; composed of grasses, feathers and fur.   Collector, Virgil W. Owen.

733a.   Gray Titmouse (should be Plain Titmouse).   *Parus inornatus.*

Range.—Southeastern United States, from Colorado and Nevada southward.

The nesting habits of this gray Titmouse are just the same as those of the other.

733b.   Ashy Titmouse (should be Plain Titmouse).   *Parus inornatus.*

Range.—Southern Lower California.

The habits of this varity are the same as those of the Plain Titmouse and doubtless the eggs are also.

734.   Bridled Titmouse.   *Parus wollweberi.*

Range.—Mexico north to southern Arizona, New Mexico and western Texas.

This handsome species is quite abundant in the mountains of southern Arizona and nests in woods or about ranches, lining the cavities of trees with moss, down, leaves, etc.   The three to seven eggs that they lay are pure white, unmarked.   Size .65 x .52. Data.—Huachuca Mountains, Arizona, April 5, 1901.   Nest in the [White.]   natural cavity of a live oak, 12 feet from the ground; cavity lined with bark and feathers.   Collector, O. W. Howard.

---

[1] Breeds north to New England.

[2] No longer recognized as a valid form.

From "The Condor".

NEST OF TOWNSEND'S SOLITAIRE.

735.   Black-capped Chickadee. *Parus atricapillus*.

Range.—Eastern North America, breeding from the Middle and Central States northward to Labrador; only migratory to a slight extent.

The Chickadee is too well known to need any description; suffice it to say that they are the favorites, with everybody, among all the North American birds. They breed in holes in trees in orchards or woods, and also in bird boxes. I have found by far the greater number in decayed birch stubs. They line the cavities with fine grasses and feathers, and during May or June lay from five to eight white eggs, dotted with reddish brown; size .55 x .45.

[White.]

735a.   Long-tailed Chickadee (should be Black-capped Chickadee). *Parus atricapillus*.

Range.—Rocky Mountain region, north to British Columbia.

This variety is very similar to the last but has a slightly longer tail and the colors are purer. Its nesting habits are the same and the eggs are indistinguishable from those of the eastern Chickadee. [1]

735b.   Oregon Chickadee (should be Black-capped Chickadee). *Parus atricapillus*.

Range.—Pacific coast from California to Alaska.

The habits and eggs of this slightly darker variety are just the same as those of the common Chickadee of the east. [1]

736.   Carolina Chickadee. *Parus carolinensis*.

Range.—Southern United States from the Gulf to New Jersey and Illinois.

The southern Chickadee is smaller than the northern and the wing coverts and feathers have little or no white edgings. Their nesting habits are in every particular the same as those of *atricapillus* and the eggs cannot be distinguished with certainty, but average smaller; size .53 x .40.

[White.]

736a.   Plumbeous Chickadee (should be Carolina Chickadee). *Parus carolinensis*.

Range.—Eastern and central Texas.

This variety is said to be more plumbeous above and much whiter below than the preceding. No differences can be found in the eggs of the two varieties and the nesting habits are the same.

737.   Mexican Chickadee. *Parus sclateri*.

Range.—Mountains of western Mexico north to southern Arizona.

This species has the black more extended on the throat and the under parts are grayish of a lighter shade than the upper, the cheeks, however, remaining white. Their nests are in hollow stubs and the eggs are indistinguishable from those of the foregoing Chickadees.

738.   Mountain Chickadee. *Parus gambeli*.

Range.—Rocky Mountain region and west to the Pacific; north to British Columbia chiefly in higher ranges.

This handsome little Titmouse has a white superciliary line, leaving a black stripe through the eye. Their habits are like those of the other Chickadees and they are equally confiding and inquisitive. Their eggs range from five to eight in number and are either pure white or faintly marked with reddish brown; size .60 x .45. Data.—Estes Park, Colorado, June 8, 1803. Nest in an old Sapsucker's hole in a live aspen tree,28 feet from the ground; cavity lined with hair and fur. Collector, E. B. Andrews.

[White.]

---

[1] Now Black-capped Chickadee.

739. Gray-headed Chickadee. *Parus cinctus.*

Range.—Northern Alaska and eastern Siberia.
This bird, which is most like the Hudsonian Chickadee,[1] nests in the usual manner and its eggs are like those of the common Chickadee of the east.[2]

740. Boreal Chickadee. *Parus hudsonicus*

Range.—Western half of British America.

[White.]

These brown-capped Chickadees are very abundant throughout the northwest and are even tamer than our United States varieties. They usually make their nests at low elevations in dead and decayed stumps and line the bottom of the cavity, which varies from three to eight inches in depth, with moss and fur. Their eggs, which they lay in May, June or July, are white, specked with reddish brown and cannot with any certainty be distinguished from those of the Black-capped Chickadees, the eggs of all the species showing considerable variations; size .60 x .45.

740a. Kowak Chickadee (should be Boreal Chickadee). *Parus hudsonicus.*

Range.—Kowak River, northwest Alaska.

A larger and grayer form of the last species; nesting habits and eggs not differing.

740b. Columbian Chickadee (should be Boreal Chickadee). *Parus hudsonicus.*

Range.—Rocky Mountains from northern United States to Alaska.

Like 740 but with the crown slaty instead of brownish. No difference can be distinguished either in their habits or eggs.

740c. Canadian Chickadee (should be Boreal Chickadee). *Parus hudsonicus.*

Range. Eastern half of Canada and northern New England and New York.

These birds were formerly 740 in company with the western ones, but they are now supposed to be a trifle smaller and with the crown duller; this division does not affect the similarity of their habits and eggs.

741. Chestnut-backed Chickadee. *Parus rufescens.*

Range.—Pacific coast from Oregon to Alaska.

Range.—This species is similar to the Hudsonian[1] in having a brown crown and black throat, but has in addition, a chestnut colored back and sides. They breed locally in Oregon, more commonly in Washington and are abundant in British Columbia, making the nests of animal fur in holes in dead stubs. Their eggs vary in number from five to eight and are creamy white, dotted with reddish; size .60 x .45. Data.—Dayton, Oregon, May 28, 1806. Nest of hair and fur in willow stub, 10 feet up. Collector, Ellis F. Hadley.

[White.]

741a. California Chickadee (should be Chestnut-backed Chickadee). *Parus rufescens.*

Range.—Coast regions of California.

This variety is not as rufous on the sides as the more northern one. Its habits and eggs are the same.

741b. Barlow's Chickadee (should be Chestnut-backed Chickadee). *Parus rufescens.*

Range.—About Monterey Bay, California.

This variety is said to have no rust on the flanks. Its habits and eggs are like those of the others.

[1] Now Boreal Chickadee.

[2] Now Black-capped Chickadee.

742. Wrentit. *Chamaea fasciata.*

Range.—Pacific coast from southern California north to Oregon.

These peculiar brownish gray colored birds frequent the tangled underbrush of ravines and mountain sides where they lead the life of a recluse. They nest at low elevations in the densest thickets, making them of twigs, strips of bark, grasses and feathers, compactly woven together and located in bushes from one to four feet from the ground. They lay from three to five plain, unmarked, greenish-blue eggs; size .74 x .54.

[White.]

Data.—Wrights, Cal. Nest in a tangle of vines in a deep ravine; composed of strips of bark, moss and grasses, lined with cattle hair; a bulky nest. Collector, H. N. Werner.

742a. Pallid Wren-Tit (should be Wrentit). *Chamaea fasciata.*

Range.—Interior of California from Lower California to the Sacramento Valley.

This duller colored variety has the same nesting habits and similar eggs to those of the Pallid Wren-tit.

743. Common Bushtit. *Psaltriparus minimus.*

Range.—Pacific coast of northern California, Oregon and Washington.

These diminutive little birds build nests that are marvels of architecture, making long purse-like structures, suspended from twigs usually at low elevations from the ground. The nests are made of moss, lichens, fibres, ferns and grasses and lined with feathers or wool; the opening is on one side near the top, and a typical nest averages 12 inches in length, by 4.5 inches in diameter [White.] at the bottom and 3 at the top. Their eggs number from four to nine and are pure white; size .54 x .40. The birds are very active and have the same habits as the Chickadees, being seen often suspended, head downward, from the ends of twigs, in their search for insects.

743a. California Bush-Tit (should be Common Bushtit). *Psaltriparus minimus.*

Range.—California with the exception of the northern part.

This sub-species, which is like the last but with a lighter brown head, has the same habits, nests in the same manner and its eggs are not distinguishable from those of the others.

743b. Grinda's Bush-Tit (should be Common Bushtit). *Psaltriparus minimus.*

Range.—Southern Lower California.

The nesting habits of this variety, which is very similar to the last, do not vary in any respect; eggs indistinguishable.

744. Lead-colored Bush-Tit (should be Common Bushtit). *Psaltriparus minimus.*

Range.—Rocky Mountain region from Wyoming south to Arizona.

This species suspends its semi-pensile nests in bushes or trees, and sometimes from the mistletoe, which grows on numerous trees in southern Arizona. The nests are composed like those of the Cal. Bush-Tit and range from 6 to 10 inches in length. The eggs are white, five or six in number and measure .55 x .42.

744.1. Santa Rita Bush-Tit (should be Common Bushtit). *Psaltriparus minimus.*

Range.—Santa Rita Mts., southern Arizona.

In all probability the nests and eggs of this species will not vary in any respect from those of the last which are very similar.

Photo from life by E. L. Bickford.
COMMON BUSHTIT AND NEST.

745. Black-eared Bushtit. *Psaltriparus melanotis.*

Range.—Northern Mexico north into western Texas and New Mexico.

This species is similar to the Lead-colored Bush-Tit but has the ear coverts glossy black. Like the others, it builds a long pensile nest of similar material and suspended from the extremities of limbs near the ground. The five to seven eggs are pure white. Size .58 x .42.

746. Verdin. *Auriparus flaviceps.*

Range—Mexican border of the United States, north to Colorado and Nevada.

This Bush-tit has a bright yellow head and throat, the upper parts being gray and the belly, white. They are abundant in chaparral brush, locally throughout their range.  [Greenish blue] Their large globular nests are situated in bushes at low elevations from the ground, and are made of twigs and weeds, softly lined with fur and feathers. Their three to six eggs are pale greenish blue, specked and dotted with reddish brown. Size. 58 x .44. Data.—Brownsville, Texas, May 8, 1894. Large nest of sticks and thorns, lined with hair and feathers, and located in a bush in brush thicket, 8 feet from the ground. Collector, F. B. Armstrong. (Crandall collection.)

746a. Baird's Verdin (should be Verdin). *Auriparus flaviceps.*

Range.—Lower California.

This new sub-species is said to have shorter wings and tail, and also to be brighter yellow on the head. Its habits and eggs will not differ from those of the common Verdin or Yellow-headed Bush-Tit.

OLD WORLD WARBLERS.   Family SYLVIIDAE.

747. Arctic Warbler. *Phylloscopus borealis.*

Range.—Asia, casually found in Alaska. [1]

This species breeds in the extreme northern parts of Asia, and I believe its eggs have never been found on this continent. They build their nests of moss and grasses, on the ground in open woods, concealing them under tufts of grass or tussocks of earth. The three to five eggs are white, spotted with pale reddish brown. Size .70 x .50.

[White.]

[1] Breeds in western Alaska.

748. Golden-crowned Kinglet. *Regulus satrapa.*

Range.—North America, breeding from northern United States northward, and south in the Rockies to Mexico, and in the Alleghanies to the Carolinas; winters throughout the United States.

This rugged little fellow appears to be perfectly content in our northern states even during the most severe winters and leaves us early in the spring for his breeding grounds farther north. They are usually found in company with Chickadees and, like them, may be seen hanging to twigs in all sort of positions as they search for their meagre fare. Their nests are large, round structures of green moss, bark strips and fine rootlets, very thickly lined with soft feathers; these are placed in forks or partially suspended among the branches of spruce trees, usually high above the ground. During June they lay from five to ten eggs of a dull whitish or grayish color, spotted heavily with pale brown and lilac. Size .55 x .42.

[Gray.]

748a. Western Golden-crowned Kinglet (should be Golden-crowned Kinglet). *Regulus satrapa.*

Range.—Pacific coast from southern California to Alaska.

This variety is said to be brighter colored than the last; its habits and eggs are the same in all particulars.

Photo by C. A. Smith.

NEST AND EGGS OF BLUE-GRAY GNATCATCHER.

749. Ruby-crowned Kinglet. *Regulus calendula*.

Range.—North America, breeding from the northern border of the United States northward, and farther south in mountain ranges; winters in southern United States.

This little bird is of the size of the Golden-crowned Kinglet (4.25 inches long) and has a partially concealed patch of red on the crown, not bordered by black and yellow as is the last species. Their nests are similar in construction to those of the last species and are situated in coniferous trees at any altitude from the ground. Their four to nine eggs are creamy white, finely specked with reddish brown. Size .56 x .44.

[White.]

749a. Sitkan Kinglet (should be Ruby-crowned Kinglet). *Regulus calendula*.

Range.—Pacific coast, breeding in Alaska.
Said to be brighter than the preceding variety.

749b. Dusky Kinglet (should be Ruby-crowned Kinglet). *Regulus calendula*.

Range.—Guadalupe Island, Lower California.
This species nests during March in the large cypress and pine groves at high elevations above the ground. The nests are similar in construction to those of the common Ruby-crown, and the eggs are scarcely different from some specimens of that species; white, dotted and wreathed with reddish brown. Size .56 x .43.

751. Blue-gray Gnatcatcher. *Polioptila caerulea*.

Range.—United States, east of the Rockies, breeding from the Gulf to the Middle and Central States; casually north to Massachusetts and Minnesota.

These graceful birds are bluish gray above with a black forehead and central tail feathers, and white underparts. They are common in wooded districts in the south, where they saddle their beautiful nests upon horizontal branches or in crotches usually at quite an elevation from the ground; they resemble large Ruby-throated Hummers' nests but the walls are much higher and thicker; they are made of plant fibres and down, lined with cottony substances and hair, and covered on the outside with lichens to match the limb upon which it is placed. Their eggs are bluish white, specked with reddish chestnut. Size .58 x .45. Data.—Chattanooga, Tenn., April 30, 1900. Nest of moss, covered with lichens and lined with hair and feathers; 20 feet from the ground in a small tree. Collector, Harry R. Caldwell.

[Bluish white.]

751a. Western Gnatcatcher (should be Blue-gray Gnatcatcher). *Polioptila caerulea*.

Range.—Western United States and Lower California.
The habits and eggs of this sub-species are the same as those of the eastern bird, and the nests do not differ except, perhaps, in less ornamentation of the exterior.

752. Plumbeous Gnatcatcher (should be Blue-gray Gnatcatcher). *Polioptila caerulea*.

Range.—Mexican boundary from western Texas to southern California.

This species has a bright shining black crown and more black on the tail than the eastern Gnatcatcher. They saddle their nests upon the branches of trees or in upright forks, usually at an elevation of ten feet or more from the ground; the nests are made of plant fibres and fine bark strips, compactly felted together, and with little, if any, ornamental lichens on the exterior.

[Greenish blue]

Their eggs are pale greenish blue, spotted with reddish brown, and vary from three to five in number. Size .54 x .44.

753. Black-tailed Gnatcatcher. *Polioptila melanura.*

Range.—Pacific coast of southern California and northern Lower California.

This bird is very similar to the last but has still less white on the outer tail feathers. Like the last, the nests of this species usually lack the exterior covering of lichens, being made of vegetable fibres and plant down, firmly quilted together and saddled on horizontal limbs or placed in forks of trees at any [Greenish white.] height from the ground. Their eggs are greenish white, specked with bright reddish brown. Size .55 x .44. Data.—Escondido, Cal., May 17, 1903. 5 eggs. Nest on a large limb of a sycamore, 30 feet above ground; made of weed fibres, etc., lined with hair and fine fibres. Collector, J. B. Dixon.

THRUSHES and allies. Family TURDIDAE.

754. Townsend's Solitaire. *Myadestes townsendi.*

Range.—Western United States, breeding from Arizona, New Mexico and southern California north to British Columbia.

This unique species is of a uniform brownish gray color, with a white eye ring, narrow bar on wing, and outer tail feathers, and with the bases of the primaries rusty colored. It is a ground inhabiting bird, feeding upon insects and berries in shrubbery and thickets. Their song is said to be liquid, melodious and often long continued, equalling that of any other bird. They nest on the ground in hollows under banks or crevices about roots of trees or fallen stumps, making a large, loosely constructed pile of weeds [Grayish white.] and trash, hollowed and lined with rootlets. The three or four eggs, which are laid in June, are grayish white, spotted with pale brown, chiefly or most abundantly about the large end. Size .96 x .70. (Plate of nest, p. 320).

755. Wood Thrush. *Hylocichla mustelina.*

Range.—Eastern United States, breeding from North Carolina and Kansas north to northern United States; winters south of our borders.

This Thrush with his brightly spotted breast is the most handsome of this group of musical birds. They are common in damp woods and thickets, in which places they breed, placing their nests of straw, leaves and grasses in [Greenish blue.] low trees usually between four and ten feet from the ground; their nests are often very rustic, being ornamented by pieces of paper and twigs with dead leaves attached hanging from the sides of the quite bulky structures. During May or June they lay three or four greenish blue eggs of about the shade of a Robin's. Size 1.05 x .70.

756. Veery. *Hylocichla fuscescens.*

Range.—Eastern North America, breeding in the northern half of its United States range and in the southern British Provinces.

The Veery is very abundantly distributed in woodland, either moist or dry, and nests on the ground or within a very few inches of it, usually placing its structures of woven bark strips and grasses, in the midst of a clump of sprouts or ferns. The three or four eggs which they lay in May or June are bluish green, much darker than those of the Wood Thrush, [Bluish green.] and nearly the color of those of the Catbird. Size .90 x .65.

From "Nature and the Camera".   Photo from life by A. R. Dugmore.

WOOD THRUSH ON NEST.

756a. Willow Thrush (should be Veery). *Hylocichla fuscescens.*

Range.—Rocky Mountain region, north to British Columbia.
The nests and eggs of this similar bird do not differ from those of the last.

757. Gray-cheeked Thrush. *Hylocichla minima.*

Range.—Breeds from Labrador to Alaska; winters south to Central America.
The nesting habits and eggs of this species are very similar to those of the
following sub-species and the same description will answer for both.

757a. Bicknell's Thrush (should be Gray-cheeked Thrush). *Hylocichla minima.*

Range.—Breeds in the Catskills, White Mountains and
Nova Scotia.
These birds, which are practically identical with the
preceding, build their nests at low elevations in trees, usually
evergreens when present, making them of twigs, moss and
rootlets, lined with fine grasses. The eggs, which are laid
during May or June, are pale greenish blue, spotted and
[Greenish blue.] blotched with pale brown or russet. Size .88 x .64. Data.—
Seal Island, Nova Scotia, June 3, 1901. Nest of green moss and rootlets, in a
spruce, 5 feet from the ground. Collector, H. E. Myers.

758. Swainson's Thrush. *Hylocichla ustulata.*

Range.—Pacific coast, breeding from Oregon and Alaska;
winters in Central America.
This species is very abundant in moist thickets throughout
its range, nesting in bushes and low trees, and making them
of weed stalks, bark strips, grasses and moss, lined with fine
black rootlets. They are found at elevations of from two to
ten feet above the ground. Like the Wood Thrush the birds
are tame while sitting on the nest and will allow a very close [Greenish blue.]
approach, without taking alarm; nests are frequently found which are made
almost entirely out of green moss and are very handsome structures. Their
three to five eggs are laid in May or June; they are greenish blue, spotted with
brown of varying shades. Size .92 x .65. Data.—Eureka, California, July 6,
1899. Nest in a fir tree, 5 feet from the ground; made of moss and strips of
redwood bark. 4 eggs. Collector, F. J. Smith.

758a. Olive-backed Thrush (should be Swainson's Thrush). *Hylocichla ustulata.*

Range.—Eastern North America, breeding chiefly north of the United States,
but locally in the northern parts, and abundantly in mountain ranges.
The nesting habits and eggs of this eastern representative of the last species
are like those of that bird in all respects and the eggs cannot be distinguished
from those of 758.

**758b. California Olive-backed Thrush (should be Swainson's Thrush). *Hylocichla
ustulata.***

Range.—California and southern Oregon.
Nesting habits and eggs identical with those of 758.

758c. Alma's Thrush (should be Swainson's Thrush). *Hylocichla ustulata.*

Range.—Alaska and northern Rocky Mountains.
Its habits are the same and the eggs indistinguishable from those of the last.

759. Alaskan Hermit Thrush (should be Hermit Thrush). *Hylocichla guttata.*

Range.—Pacific coast from British Columbia to Alaska. Winters in Mexico.
The Hermit Thrushes can readily be identified from any other by the reddish
brown tail which is in marked contrast to the color of the back. The nesting
habits and eggs of this species are precisely like those of the eastern Hermit
Thrush, which is a sub-species of this.

759a.   Audubon's Hermit Thrush (should be Hermit Thrush).   *Hylocichla guttata.*

Range.—Rocky Mountain region of the United States.   Winters in Central America.

The nesting habits of this bird are like those of the next except that it more frequently nests in bushes above the ground.   The eggs are not distinctive.

759b.   Hermit Thrush.   *Hylocichla guttata.*

Range.—Eastern North America, breeding in northern United States and north to Labrador; winters in southern United States.

This species, which is noted for its sweet and musical song, frequents damp swamps and thickets where it builds its nest either on the ground or near it, like that of the Wilson Thrush;[1] it is made of shreds of bark, grasses, leaves and root- [Bluish green.] lets, lined with fine rootlets; the three or four eggs, which are deposited in May or June, are bluish green and cannot, with certainty, be distinguished from those of the Veery; size .85 x .65.

759c.   Dwarf Hermit Thrush (should be Hermit Thrush).   *Hylocichla guttata.*

Range.—Pacific coast of United States, from Washington, southward.

The nesting habits and eggs of this slightly smaller and duller colored variety are like those of the other Hermit Thrushes.

760.   Red-winged Thrush.   *Turdus musicus.*

Range.—An Old World species, accidentally straying to Greenland.

This common European bird nests at low elevations in bushes or trees, laying four or five bluish green eggs, spotted with reddish brown; size 1.05 x .75.

761.   American Robin.   *Turdus migratorius.*

Range.- North America east of the Rockies, breeding from the middle portions of the United States, north to the Arctic Ocean.

These common birds nest in trees about houses, in orchards, open woods, in corners of fences, on blinds on houses, and in fact almost every conceivable position. Their nests are made of grasses, firmly cemented together with mud and lined with finer grasses; when placed in trees they are generally firmly saddled in crotches and may be found at any height, from on the ground to sixty feet above it.   Their eggs are greenish blue; size [Greenish blue.]   1.15 x .80.   Eggs may be found at any time from May until July or August as they raise several broods a season.

761a.   Western Robin (should be American Robin).   *Turdus migratorius.*

Range.—United States west of the Rockies and north to British Columbia.

The habits of this species, which differs from the last only in the absence of white tips to the tail feathers, are just the same as those of the eastern bird and the eggs are not distinguishable.

761b.   Southern Robin (should be American Robin).   *Turdus migratorius.*

Range.—The Carolinas and Georgia.

The eggs of this bird, which is said to be smaller and duller colored than the northern variety, show no differences in any respect.

762.   St. Lucas Robin.   *Turdus confinis.*

Range.—Southern Lower California.

This is a very much paler form of the American Robin; its eggs probably will not differ from those of the others.

---

[1] Now Veery.

763.   Varied Thrush.   *Ixoreus naevius.*

Range.—Pacific coast from northern California to Alaska; south to Mexico in winter.

[Greenish blue.]

These handsome birds breed abundantly in Alaska and locally in mountain ranges south to northern California.   They nest at low elevations in trees, making them of moss, twigs, weeds and grasses, forming a flat shallow structure.   Their eggs are greenish blue sharply but sparingly spotted with dark brown; size 1.12 x .80.   Data.—Delta of Kowak River, Alaska, June 11, 1899.   Four eggs.   Nest 12 feet from the ground, against the trunk of a slender spruce and supported by a clump of stiff twigs.   Collector, Joseph Grinnell.

763a.   Pale Varied Thrush (should be Varied Thrush).   *Ixoreus naevius.*

Range.—Interior of western North America, breeding from British Columbia to Alaska.   Its habits and eggs do not differ from those of the last.

Photo by J. B. Pardoe.

NEST AND EGGS OF AMERICAN ROBIN.

764. Bluethroat. *Luscinia svecica.*
Range.—Northern Asia; casually to Alaska.[1]
This beautiful foreigner nests on the ground and lays four to six greenish blue eggs, spotted with reddish brown; size .75 x .50.

765. Wheatear. *Oenanthe oenanthe.*
Range.—Asia; casual in Alaska in summer; nesting habits and eggs like the next.

765a. Greenland Wheatear (should be Wheatear). *Oenanthe oenanthe.*
Range.—Europe and Greenland; casual on the Atlantic coast of North America.
This very abundant Old World species is a common breeding bird in Greenland and probably also in Labrador. They nest in crevices of quarries, holes in the ground, or stone walls, making a rude nest of weeds, moss or grasses, lined with hair or feathers, and during May lay from four to six pale [Pale greenish blue.] greenish blue eggs; size .90 x .60.

766. Eastern Bluebird. *Sialia sialis.*
Range.—Eastern United States, breeding from the Gulf to southern Canada. Winters in the southern half of the United States.

These familiar birds build in cavities in trees, usually below 20 feet from the ground, crevices among ledges, bird boxes and in any suitable nook they may discover about buildings, providing that English Sparrows[2] do not molest them. They raise several broods a year, commencing in April when they lay from three to six pale bluish white eggs (rarely pure white); size .80 x .60. The cavities of their nesting sites are [Bluish white.] lined with grasses and feathers usually, although I have found the eggs on the unlined bottom of cavities in trees.

766a. Azure Bluebird (should be Eastern Bluebird). *Sialia sialis.*
Range.—This pale variety is found in southern Arizona and southward.
Its nesting habits are the same and the eggs are indistinguishable from the last.

767. Western Bluebird. *Sialia mexicana.*
Range.—Pacific coast from Lower California to British Columbia.
The Western Bluebird is as common and familar in its range as the common Bluebird is in the east. It nests in similar locations and its eggs are scarcely distinguishable, although averaging a trifle darker in shade; size .80 x .60.

767a. Chestnut-backed Bluebird (should be Western Bluebird). *Sialia mexicana.*
Range.—Rocky Mountain region from Mexico to Wyoming.
The nesting habits or eggs of this brighter colored bird do not differ from those of the last species.

767b. San Pedro Bluebird (should be Western Bluebird). *Sialia mexicana.*
Range.—San Pedro Martir Mountains in Lower California.
The eggs of this variety will not in all probability be any different from those of the preceding Bluebirds.

768. Mountain Bluebird. *Sialia currucoides.*
Range.—Rocky Mountain region, breeding from New Mexico north to Great Slave Lake; winters in southwestern United States and Mexico.
This azure blue species is common in the greater part of its range and is found west to the Sierra Nevadas in California. Like the Eastern Bluebird they nest in holes in trees or anywhere that they can find a suitable cavity or crevice. Their eggs are slightly larger than those of the other Bluebirds and have a slight greenish tint; size .85 x .64.

---

[1] Breeds in Alaska.

[2] Now House Sparrow.

INDEX